Fog Computing for Intelligent Cloud IoT Systems

Scrivener Publishing
100 Cummings Center, Suite 541J
Beverly, MA 01915-6106

Advances in Learning Analytics for Intelligent Cloud-IoT Systems

Series Editor: Dr. Souvik Pal and Dr. Dac-Nhuong Le

The role of adaptation, learning analytics, computational Intelligence, and data analytics in the field of Cloud-IoT Systems is now intertwined. The capability of an intelligent system depends on various self-decision making algorithms in IoT Devices. IoT based smart systems generate a large amount of data (big data) that cannot be processed by traditional data processing algorithms and applications. Hence, this book series involves different computational methods incorporated within the system with the help of analytics reasoning and sense-making in big data, which is centered in the cloud and IoT-enabled environments.

The series seeks volumes that are empirical studies, theoretical and numerical analysis, and novel research findings. The series encourages cross-fertilization of highlighting research and knowledge of data analytics, machine learning, data science, and IoT sustainable developments.

Publishers at Scrivener
Martin Scrivener (martin@scrivenerpublishing.com)
Phillip Carmical (pcarmical@scrivenerpublishing.com)

Fog Computing for Intelligent Cloud IoT Systems

Edited by

Chandan Banerjee
Netaji Subhash Engineering College, India

Anupam Ghosh
Netaji Subhash Engineering College, India

Rajdeep Chakraborty
Chandigarh University, India

and

Ahmed A. Elngar
Beni Suef University, Egypt

Scrivener
Publishing

This edition first published 2024 by John Wiley & Sons, Inc., 111 River Street, Hoboken, NJ 07030, USA and Scrivener Publishing LLC, 100 Cummings Center, Suite 541J, Beverly, MA 01915, USA
© 2024 Scrivener Publishing LLC
For more information about Scrivener publications please visit www.scrivenerpublishing.com.

Wiley Global Headquarters
111 River Street, Hoboken, NJ 07030, USA

For details of our global editorial offices, customer services, and more information about Wiley products visit us at www.wiley.com.

Limit of Liability/Disclaimer of Warranty
While the publisher and authors have used their best efforts in preparing this work, they make no representations or warranties with respect to the accuracy or completeness of the contents of this work and specifically disclaim all warranties, including without limitation any implied warranties of merchantability or fitness for a particular purpose. No warranty may be created or extended by sales representatives, written sales materials, or promotional statements for this work. The fact that an organization, website, or product is referred to in this work as a citation and/or potential source of further information does not mean that the publisher and authors endorse the information or services the organization, website, or product may provide or recommendations it may make. This work is sold with the understanding that the publisher is not engaged in rendering professional services. The advice and strategies contained herein may not be suitable for your situation. You should consult with a specialist where appropriate. Neither the publisher nor authors shall be liable for any loss of profit or any other commercial damages, including but not limited to special, incidental, consequential, or other damages. Further, readers should be aware that websites listed in this work may have changed or disappeared between when this work was written and when it is read.

Library of Congress Cataloging-in-Publication Data

ISBN 978-1-3941761-4

Cover image: Pixabay.Com
Cover design by Russell Richardson

Set in size of 11pt and Minion Pro by Manila Typesetting Company, Makati, Philippines

Printed in the USA

10 9 8 7 6 5 4 3 2 1

Contents

Preface   xvii

Part I: Study of Fog Computing and Machine Learning   1

1   **Fog Computing: Architecture and Application**   3
Soumen Swarnakar
1.1   Introduction   4
1.2   Fog Computing: An Overview   5
1.3   Fog Computing for Intelligent Cloud-IoT System   10
1.4   Fog Computing Architecture   12
1.5   Basic Modules of Fog Computing   15
1.6   Cloud Computing vs. Fog Computing   17
1.7   Fog Computing vs. IoT   19
1.8   Applications of Fog Computing   21
1.9   Will the Fog Be Taken Over by the Cloud?   23
1.10 Challenges in Fog Computing   24
1.11 Future of Fog Computing   26
1.12 Conclusion   28
      References   29

2   **A Comparative Review on Different Techniques of Computation Offloading in Mobile Cloud Computing**   33
Priyajit Sen, Tamanna Islam, Rajat Pandit
and Debabrata Sarddar
2.1   Introduction   34
2.2   Related Works   35
2.3   Computation Offloading Techniques   37
     2.3.1 MAUI Architecture   37
     2.3.2 Clone-Cloud Based Model   37
     2.3.3 Cuckoo Design   38
     2.3.4 MACS Architecture   39

| | | 2.3.5 | AHP and TOPSIS Design Technique | 39 |

2.3.5   AHP and TOPSIS Design Technique   39
2.3.6   Energy Aware Design for Workflows   39
2.3.7   MCSOS Architecture   39
2.3.8   Cloudlet   40
2.3.9   Jade   40
2.3.10 Phone2Cloud   40
2.4 Conclusion   42
2.5 Future Scope   42
2.6 Acknowledgement   42
     References   42

**3 Fog Computing for Intelligent Cloud–IoT System:
    Optimization of Fog Computing in Industry 4.0   45**
    Mayank Patel, Monika Bhatt and Ankush Patel
3.1 Introduction   46
     3.1.1   Industry 4.0   46
     3.1.2   Fog Computing   49
     3.1.3   Fog Nodes   50
3.2 How Fog Computing with IIoT Brings Revolution   52
     3.2.1   Hierarchical Fog Computing Architecture   59
     3.2.2   Layered Fog Computing Architecture   60
3.3 Applications of Fog Computing on Which Industries Rely 62
     3.3.1   In the Field of Agriculture   62
     3.3.2   In Healthcare Industry   63
     3.3.3   In Smart Cities   63
     3.3.4   In Education   64
     3.3.5   In Entertainment   64
3.4 Data Analysis   64
3.5 Illustration of Fog Computing and Application   65
     3.5.1   Figures   65
3.6 Conclusion   66
3.7 Future Scope/Acknowledgement   66
     References   69

**4 Machine Learning Integration in Agriculture Domain:
    Concepts and Applications   71**
    Ankur Biswas and Rita Banik
4.1 Introduction   72
4.2 Fog Computing in Agriculture   75
     4.2.1   Smart Farming   78
4.3 Methodology   78
     4.3.1   Data Source   80

	4.3.2	Data Analysis and Pre-Processing	80
	4.3.3	Feature Extraction	82
	4.3.4	Model Selection	84
	4.3.5	Hyper-Parameter Tuning	86
	4.3.6	Train-Test Split	87
4.4	Results and Discussion		88
	4.4.1	Modeling Algorithms	89
4.5	Conclusion		92
4.6	Future Scope		94
	References		94

5 Role of Intelligent IoT Applications in Fog Computing 99
Pawan Whig, Dhaya Sindhu Battina, Srinivas Venkata,
Ashima Bhatnagar Bhatia and Yusuf Jibrin Alkali

5.1	Introduction		100
	5.1.1	PaaS/SaaS Platforms Have Various Benefits That are Crucial to the Success of Many Small IoT Startup Businesses	102
5.2	Cloud Service Model's Drawbacks		102
5.3	Fog Computation		103
	5.3.1	Standardization	103
	5.3.2	Growing Use Cases for Fog Computing	104
	5.3.3	IoT Applications with Intelligence	104
	5.3.4	Graphics Processing Units	104
5.4	Recompenses of FoG		105
5.5	Limitation of Fog Computing		106
5.6	Fog Computing with IoT		107
	5.6.1	Benefits of Fog Computing with IoT	108
	5.6.2	Challenges of Fog Computing with IoT	108
5.7	Edge AI Embedded		109
	5.7.1	Key Software Characteristics in Fog Computing	110
	5.7.2	Fog Cluster Management	111
	5.7.3	Technology for Computing in the Fog	111
	5.7.4	Concentrating Intelligence	111
	5.7.5	Device-Driven Intelligence	112
5.8	Network Intelligence Objectives		112
5.9	Farming with Fog Computation (Case Study)		112
5.10	Conclusion		115
	References		116

6 SaaS-Based Data Visualization Platform—A Study in COVID-19 Perspective 119
S. Majumder, A. Shaw, R. Keshri and A. Chakraborty
6.1 Introduction 120
    6.1.1 Motivation and the Problem of Interest 120
6.2 Summary of Objectives 121
6.3 What is a Pandemic? 121
6.4 COVID-19 and Information Gap 121
6.5 Data Visualization and its Importance 122
6.6 Data Management with Data Visualization 123
6.7 What is Power BI? 123
    6.7.1 Data Collection & Wrangling 123
    6.7.2 Data Description & Source 123
    6.7.3 Data Transformation 124
6.8 Output Data 124
6.9 Design & Implementation 124
    6.9.1 Integration Design 124
    6.9.2 High-Level Process Flow 124
    6.9.3 Solution Flow 125
6.10 Dashboard Development 126
    6.10.1 Landing Page 126
    6.10.2 Approach and Design 127
    6.10.3 Helpline Information 127
        6.10.3.1 Approach and Design 127
    6.10.4 Symptom Detection 128
        6.10.4.1 Approach and Design 128
    6.10.5 Testing Lab Information 128
        6.10.5.1 Approach and Design 129
    6.10.6 Hospital Information 129
        6.10.6.1 Approach and Design 129
    6.10.7 Oxygen Suppliers Information 130
        6.10.7.1 Approach and Design 131
    6.10.8 COVID Cases Information 131
        6.10.8.1 Approach and Design 131
    6.10.9 Vaccination Information 132
        6.10.9.1 Approach and Design 132
    6.10.10 Patients' Information 133
        6.10.10.1 Approach and Design 133
6.11 Advantages and its Impact 133
6.12 Conclusion and Future Scope 134
    References 135

7   **A Complete Study on Machine Learning Algorithms
for Medical Data Analysis**   **137**
Inderdeep Kaur and Aleem Ali
  7.1   Introduction   138
         7.1.1   Importance of Machine Learning Algorithms
                  in Medical Data Analysis   138
  7.2   Pre-Processing Medical Data for Machine Learning   141
  7.3   Supervised Learning Algorithms for Medical Data Analysis   143
         7.3.1   Linear Regression Algorithm   143
         7.3.2   Logistic Regression Algorithm   144
         7.3.3   Decision Trees Algorithm   146
                  7.3.3.1   Advantages of Decision Tree Algorithm   147
                  7.3.3.2   Limitations of Decision Tree Algorithm   148
         7.3.4   Random Forest Algorithm   148
                  7.3.4.1   Advantages of Random Forest Algorithm   149
                  7.3.4.2   Limitations of Random Forest Algorithm   149
                  7.3.4.3   Applications of Random Forest Algorithm
                             in Medical Data Analysis   150
         7.3.5   Support Vector Machine Algorithm   150
                  7.3.5.1   Advantages of SVM Algorithm   151
                  7.3.5.2   Limitations of SVM Algorithm   152
                  7.3.5.3   Applications of SVM Algorithm
                             in Medical Data Analysis   152
         7.3.6   Naive Bayes Algorithm   152
         7.3.7   KNN (K-Nearest Neighbor Algorithm)   153
                  7.3.7.1   Applications of K-NN Algorithm   154
         7.3.8   Deep Learning Algorithm   155
         7.3.9   Deep Learning Application   155
  7.4   Unsupervised Learning Algorithms for Medical
         Data Analysis   156
         7.4.1   Clustering Algorithm   157
         7.4.2   Principal Component Analysis Algorithm   159
         7.4.3   Independent Component Analysis Algorithm   160
         7.4.4   Association Rule Mining Algorithm   162
  7.5   Applications of Machine-Learning Algorithms
         in Medical Data Analysis   163
  7.6   Limitations and Challenges of Machine Learning
         Algorithms in Medical Data Analysis   165
  7.7   Future Research Directions and Machine Learning
         Developments in the Realm of Medical Data Analysis   167

7.8   Conclusion   168
      References   169

Part II: Applications and Analytics   173

8   Fog Computing in Healthcare: Application Taxonomy, Challenges and Opportunities   175
Subrata Datta and Priyanka Datta
8.1   Introduction   176
8.2   Research Methodology   179
8.3   Application Taxonomy in FC-Based Healthcare   181
      8.3.1   Diagnosis   181
      8.3.2   Monitoring   181
      8.3.3   Notification   183
      8.3.4   Zest of Applications of FC in Healthcare   187
8.4   Challenges in FC-Based Healthcare   189
      8.4.1   QoS Optimization   189
      8.4.2   Patient Authentication and Access Control   190
      8.4.3   Data Processing   190
      8.4.4   Data Privacy Preservation   191
      8.4.5   Energy Efficiency   191
8.5   Research Opportunities   192
      8.5.1   Research Opportunity in Computing   193
      8.5.2   Research Opportunity in Security   193
      8.5.3   Research Opportunity in Services   194
      8.5.4   Research Opportunity in Implementation   194
8.6   Conclusion   194
      References   195

9   IoT-Driven Predictive Maintenance Approach in Industry 4.0: A Fiber Bragg Grating (FBG) Sensor Application   203
Dipak Ranjan Nayak, Pramod Sharma,
Ambarish G. Mohapatra, Narayan Nayak, Bright Keswani
and Ashish Khanna
9.1   Introduction   204
9.2   Review of Related Research Articles   208
      9.2.1   Studies on FBG Sensors and Their Role
              in Industry 4.0   213
              9.2.1.1   Magnetostrictive Material   213
              9.2.1.2   Magneto-Optical (MO) Materials   214
              9.2.1.3   Magnetic Fluid (MF) Materials   215

9.2.1.4   Magnetically Sensitive Materials
and Their Application   215
9.2.1.5   Optical Fiber Current Sensors   215
9.3   Research Gaps   220
9.4   Emerging Research Directions   221
9.5   The Broad Concept of FBG Sensor Applications
in Industry 4.0   222
9.6   Conclusion   223
References   223

10 Fog Computing-Enabled Cancer Cell Detection System Using
Convolution Neural Network in Internet of Medical Things   229
Soumen Santra, Dipankar Majumdar and Surajit Mandal
10.1   Introduction   230
10.2   Fog Computing: Approach of IoMT   232
10.3   Relationship Between IoMT and Deep Neural Network   235
10.4   Fog Computing Enabled CNN for Medical Imaging   236
10.5   Algorithm Approach of Proposed Model   237
10.6   Result and Analysis   240
10.7   Conclusion   241
References   241

11 Application of IoT in Smart Farming and Precision Farming:
A Review   245
Suparna Biswas and Soumik Podder
11.1   Introduction   246
11.2   Methodologies Used in Precision Agriculture   248
11.3   Contribution of IoT in Agriculture   250
11.4   IoT Enabled Smart Farming   253
11.5   IoT Enabled Precision Farming   255
11.6   Machine Learning Enable Precision Farming   258
11.7   Application of Operational Research Method
in Farming System   264
11.8   Conclusion   270
11.9   Future Scope   272
References   272

12 Big IoT Data Analytics in Fog Computing   279
Manash Kumar Mondal, Riman Mandal and Utpal Biswas
12.1   Introduction   279
12.2   Literature Review   282
12.3   Motivation   283

12.4		Fog Computing	285
	12.4.1	Fog Node	287
	12.4.2	Characteristics of Fog Computing	288
	12.4.3	Attributes of Fog Node	290
	12.4.4	Fog Computing Service Model	291
	12.4.5	Fog Computing Architecture	293
	12.4.6	Data Flow and Control Flow in Fog Architecture	294
	12.4.7	Fog Deployment Models	296
12.5		Big Data	296
	12.5.1	What is Big Data?	297
	12.5.2	Source of Big Data	298
	12.5.3	Characteristic of Big Data	299
12.6		Big Data Analytics Using Fog Computing	300
12.7		Conclusion	303
		References	304

13 IOT-Based Patient Monitoring System in Real Time   **309**
Suparna Biswas, Tirtha Chakraborty, Souvik Mitra,
Shubham Banerjee, Tuhin Sarkar and Sourav Paul

13.1		Introduction	310
13.2		Components Used	312
	13.2.1	Node MCU	313
	13.2.2	Heart Rate/Pulse Sensor	315
	13.2.3	Temperature Sensor (LM35)	319
13.3		IoT Platform	320
	13.3.1	ThingSpeak—IoT Platform Used in This Work	321
13.4		Proposed Method	322
13.5		Experimental Setup and Result	323
13.6		Conclusion	327
		References	328

14 Fog Computing and Its Emergence with Reference
to Applications and Potentialities in Traditional
and Digital Educational Systems: A Scientific Review   **331**
P. K. Paul

14.1		Background	332
14.2		Objectives	333
14.3		Methods	334
14.4		Fog Computing: Basics and Advantages	334
	14.4.1	Existing Major Works	337
	14.4.2	Fog Computing Advantages	338
	14.4.3	Fog Computing: Applications	340

14.4.3.1   In Smart Homes and Residences   340
14.4.3.2   In Smart Cities and Township Projects   341
14.4.3.3   In Monitoring Video Surveillance   341
14.4.3.4   In Intelligent Healthcare and Medical
            Systems   341
14.5   Growing Fog Computing Applications Emphasizing
        Education   342
14.6   Impact of Fog Computing in Education   343
        14.6.1   Cases of Fog in Education   343
                  14.6.1.1   In Collaborative Teaching–Learning
                              Process   343
                  14.6.1.2   In the Promotion of On-Campus
                              Education   344
                  14.6.1.3   In Developing and Managing Online
                              Education   344
                  14.6.1.4   In Continuing Workshop and Training   344
                  14.6.1.5   In Promoting Blended and Hybrid
                              Modes of Education   345
                  14.6.1.6   In Uses of Cloud Computing
                              for the Library and for Archival   345
                  14.6.1.7   In Developing Examination and Allied
                              Evaluation Processes   345
14.7   Education Industry and Fog: Future Context   345
14.8   Fog Computing and Its Role in IOT Security:
        The Context of Campus   347
        14.8.1   Issues and Disadvantages of Fog in General
                  and in Educational Systems   348
14.9   Concluding Remarks   349
        References   349

Part III: Security in Fog Computing   **355**

15 **Blockchain Security for Fog Computing**   357
    Saiyam Varshney and Gur Mauj Saran Srivastava
    15.1   Introduction   358
    15.2   State of the Art   360
    15.3   Security Issues in the Fog Computing Environments   361
            15.3.1   Trust and Authentications in Fog Computing   362
            15.3.2   Data Protection, Privacy, and Access Controls
                      in Fog Computing   362
    15.4   Blockchain Technology   370

15.4.1 Features of Blockchain to Increase
the Transparency 370
15.4.1.1 Peer-to-Peer (P2P) Networks 371
15.4.1.2 Decentralized 371
15.4.1.3 Immutable and Incorruptible 371
15.5 Blockchain Security for Fog Computing Environment 373
15.6 Summary and Conclusion 374
References 375

16 Blockchain Security for Fog Computing
and Internet of Things 379
Awais Khan Jumani, Waqas Ahmed Siddique,
Muhammad Farhan Siddiqui and Kanwal
16.1 Introduction 380
16.1.1 Simply Vital Health 381
16.1.2 Blockchain-Based Frameworks for IoT Security
and Privacy 382
16.1.3 Permissioned Blockchain in IoT 382
16.1.4 Multi-Layer Security Framework 383
16.1.5 Blockchain-Based Supply Chain 385
16.1.5.1 Decentralized 387
16.1.5.2 Transparent 387
16.1.5.3 Open Source 387
16.1.5.4 Autonomy 388
16.1.5.5 Immutable 388
16.1.5.6 Secrecy 388
16.2 Pros and Cons of Blockchain 388
16.3 The Properties of Blockchain 389
16.3.1 Proof of Work (PoW) 389
16.3.2 Proof of Stake (PoS) 390
16.3.3 Smart Contracts 390
16.4 The Attacks on Blockchain 391
16.4.1 Attack of 51% 391
16.4.2 Double-Spending 391
16.4.3 Sybil's Attack 391
16.4.4 DDos's Attack 391
16.4.5 Cracking of the Cryptographic 391
16.4.6 Blockchain 1.0 – Digital Currency 392
16.4.7 Blockchain 2.0 – Digital Economy 392
16.4.8 Blockchain 3.0 – Digital Society 393

16.5   Application of Blockchain Technology
in Healthcare   393
   16.5.1   Electronic Health Records   394
   16.5.2   Public Health   394
   16.5.3   Education   395
16.6   Fog Computing   395
16.7   Confidentiality Concerns in Fog Computing   395
   16.7.1   Security   396
   16.7.2   Confidentiality in Fog Computing   396
   16.7.3   Concerns Regarding Identification and Reliability   396
16.8   Cloud Computing Security   396
16.9   Fog Computing Security Breaches   397
16.10 Optimized Fog Computing   398
16.11 Open Research Issues in Blockchain and Fog
Computing Security   399
16.12 Conclusion   399
   References   400

**17 Fine-Grained Access Through Attribute-Based Encryption
for Fog Computing   405**
Malabika Das
17.1   Introduction   406
17.2   Attribute-Based Encryption   409
17.3   Fine-Grained Access Through ABE   411
17.4   ABE Model for Fine-Grained Access   413
17.5   Application of ABE on Fog Computing   414
17.6   A Comparison of ABE Scheme   417
17.7   Conclusion   421
   References   421

Index   425

Preface

Fog computing is a decentralized computing structure that connects data, devices, and the cloud. It is an extension of cloud computing and is also known as edge *fog networking*, or *fog networking*, or *fogging*. Fog computing is an essential concept in IoT (Internet of Things), as it reduces the burden of processing in cloud computing. It brings intelligence and processing closer to where the data is created and transmitted to other sources.

Fog computing has many benefits, such as reduced latency in processing data, better response time that helps the user's experience, and security and privacy compliance that assures protecting the vital data in the cloud. It also reduces the cost of bandwidth, because the processing is achieved in the cloud, which reduces network bandwidth usage and increases efficiency as user devices share data in the local processing infrastructure rather than the cloud service.

Fog computing has various applications across industries, such as agriculture and farming, healthcare industry, smart cities, education, and entertainment. For example, in agriculture industry, a very prominent example is the SWAMP project, which stands for Smart Water Management Platform. With fog computing's help, SWAMP develops a precision-based smart irrigation system concept used in agriculture, minimizing water wastage.

This book is divided in to three parts. The first part studies fog computing and machine learning, covering fog computing architecture, application perspective, computational offloading in mobile cloud computing, intelligent cloud-IoT system, machine learning fundamentals, and data visualisation. The second part focuses on applications and analytics, spanning various applications of fog computing, such as in healthcare, Industry 4.0, cancer cell detection systems, smart farming, and precision farming. This part also covers analytics in fog computing using big data and patient monitoring system, and the emergence of fog computing with reference to applications and potentialities in traditional and digital educational systems. Last but not least, the third part covers security aspects in fog computing through blockchain and IoT, and fine-grained access though attribute-based encryption for fog computing.

Part I: Study of Fog Computing and Machine Learning

Chapter 1 starts with an overview and introduction to fog computing characteristics followed by a brief description of fog computing's application in intelligent Cloud-IoT systems. Then a detailed fog computing architecture is given, with descriptions of basic modules in this architecture. Following that, a relative comparison of cloud computing and fog computing is drawn by examining the applications of fog computing. The chapter ends with a summary of challenges faced by, and the future scope of fog computing.

Chapter 2 discusses how computation offloading is a critical technology in the rapidly developing field of Mobile Cloud Computing (MCC). MCC can improve application speeds, reduce latency, and extend battery life. Among other things, the effect of computation offloading is influenced greatly by a variety of parameters. After a short introduction and summary of related work, this chapter leads with different computation offloading techniques. The chapter ends with related studies and comparisons of these offloading techniques, along with the future scope of research in mobile offloading.

Chapter 3 explores the optimized and green uses of fog computing in Industry 4.0. After an introduction to Industry 4.0 and fog computing, this chapter focuses on how IoT integration with fog computing will have wide application in Industry 4.0. This chapter also provides two fog computing architectures, hierarchical and layered. This chapter ends with descriptions of various applications for fog computing, plus data analysis with related figures and tables.

Chapter 4 elaborates upon machine learning and its integration in agriculture. This chapter starts by demonstrating the importance of integrating machine learning solutions into agriculture. Then it proceeds to demonstrate fog computing as a backbone for collecting and filtering agricultural data. Afterward, a proposed model is given as methodology, followed by a discussion of the results and various modelling algorithms, such as Decision Trees, Random Forest, XGBoost, CatBoost and LightGBM.

Chapter 5 discuss how smart buildings utilize Internet of Things (IoT) devices, sensors, software, and internet connectivity to monitor various aspects of the building, analyse data, and extract insights to enhance the building's environment and operations, i.e., the role of intelligent IoT applications in fog computing. Following that is a detailed discussion of fog and cloud computing, and fog computing with IoT, Edge, AI, and other network intelligence objectives. The chapter concludes with case studies.

Chapter 6 gives a SaaS-based data visualization platform in Covid-19 perspective. The chapter starts by defining the pandemic in terms of data visualization and Power BI, followed by a summary of data collection and wrangling. A proposal for design and implementation are given, followed by dashboard development. The chapter ends by addressing advantages, impact, and future scope.

Chapter 7 is a complete study of machine learning algorithms for medical data analysis, particularly COVID–19. After an introduction, this chapter explains pre-processing of medical data for machine learning, followed by supervised learning and Support Vector Machine (SVM). Next, Naive Bayes Algorithm and KNN are covered. Thereafter, the chapter covers deep learning algorithms with illustrations of unsupervised learning, and applications of ML algorithms in medical data analysis. All are illustrated with medical data analysis. The chapter ends by addressing future research scope and challenges.

Part II: Applications and Analytics

Chapter 8 illustrates an application of fog computing in healthcare industry. The chapter starts by presenting a layered architecture of fog computing in detail, followed by research methodologies. Then this chapter gives an application taxonomy of fog computing-based healthcare system with disease diagnosis, monitoring, and notification. The chapter ends by considering the challenges and research opportunities of a fog computing-based healthcare system.

Chapter 9 gives an IoT-driven predictive maintenance approach to industry 4.0 with a Fiber Bragg Grating (FBG) sensor application. After a detailed introduction, different ML algorithms are reviewed, such as LDA, DT, kNN, SVM, and RF. Thereafter, research gaps are highlighted with emergent research directions. The chapter ends by covering the broad concept of FBG sensor applications in Industry 4.0.

Chapter 10 proposes a fog computing enabled cancer cell detection system using Convolution Neural Network in Internet of Medical Things (IoMT). After an introduction to fog computing in IoMT, the chapter discusses the relationship between IoMT and Deep Neural Network. The chapter then proposes a model of fog computing enabled CNN for Medical Imaging, followed by an algorithmic approach to proposed models. The chapter concludes with results and analysis.

Chapter 11 gives a detailed, application-based review of smart and precision farming. After the introduction, the chapter starts with methodologies used in precision agriculture, mainly map-based and sensor-based techniques and the contribution of IoT. Then a detailed study of IoT-enabled smart farming and precision farming is provided. Following that is an explanation of machine learning-based precision farming, illustrated with a case study of OR methods in farming systems. The chapter ends with conclusive remarks and a future scope.

Chapter 12 provides analytics of big data obtained from fog computing, with an introduction, literature review, and a summary of motivation. The chapter details fog computing architecture, followed by a thorough discussion on big data, then examines the big data analytics, and ends with concluding remarks.

Chapter 13 reviews the application of a IoT-based patient monitoring system in real time. After an introduction, the components used for this model are discussed, such as Node MCU, Heart Rate/Pulse Sensors, and Temperature Sensors (LM35), followed by a discussion of IoT platforms, such as ThingSpeak. A method is proposed, followed by instructions for experimental setup and results. The chapter concludes with the outcomes of this model and an explanation of how to use IoT-based patient monitoring system effectively in real time.

Chapter 14 is a scientific review of fog computing and its emergence, with reference to applications and potentialities in traditional and digital educational systems. The chapter starts with a background study, followed by a summary of the methods used for this research and the basics and advantages of fog computing. Following that is a report on the increase of fog computing applications and its impact on education and IoT security.

Part III: Security in Fog Computing

Chapter 15 illustrates the use of blockchain security for fog computing. This chapter gives thorough examples and outlines detailed security issues that present in fog computing environments. Following that is a detailed explanation of blockchain architecture, further discussion of the topic, and summary conclusions.

Chapter 16 covers an extension of blockchain security in IoT with fog computing. This chapter starts with a detailed discussion about the types of blockchain, and its pros and cons. Then the chapter discusses the properties of blockchain like PoW, PoS, smart contracts, and blockchain attacks, such as the 51% attack, double spending, Sybil's attack, and DDoS attack.

After that, some major application areas of blockchain are discussed. The chapter then addresses confidentiality concerns in fog computing, and how it can be solved using blockchain. Security breaches in cloud computing and fog computing is are also described, as well as how it can be solved using blockchain. The chapter ends with open research issues in blockchain and fog computing security, such as scalability, privacy and anonymity, consensus mechanisms, fog computing security, smart contract security, and interoperability.

Chapter 17 is about Attribute-Based-Cryptography (ABE), and its application for fine-grained access in fog computing. After an introduction to the basics of public key cryptography, this chapter discusses ABE in detail, followed by how fine-grained access through ABE can be done on fog computing. Then an example of how an ABE model for fine-grained access can be used in fog computing is given, followed by a demonstration of how ABE can be applied to fog computing. The chapter ends with comparisons of few existing ABE schemes, such as KP-ABE, CP-ABE, H-ABE, and MA-ABE.

We are deeply grateful to everyone who helped with this book and greatly appreciate the dedicated support and valuable assistance rendered by Martin Scrivener and the Scrivener Publishing team during publication.

The Editors
March 2024

Part I

STUDY OF FOG COMPUTING AND MACHINE LEARNING

Part 1

1

Fog Computing: Architecture and Application

Soumen Swarnakar

Department of Information Technology, Netaji Subhash Engineering College, Kolkata, India

Abstract

Nowadays, owing to the advancement of electronics and telecommunications and the increasing usage of the Internet, various powerful devices with networking capabilities are attracting industries to accept this technology for the development of their daily business to increase their productivity. Not only the industrial sector but also other sectors, such as public services and assisted living amenities have a huge demand for Information and Communication Technology growth. Therefore, there is a demand for a new model that enables objects to connect to global network. This model is known as the IoT. The use of the IoT has grown according to the demands of the current era. IoT combinations with clouds have brought different benefits to devices that operate on various platforms. Applications based on the IoT generate enormous amounts of data from different sensors. These data were used to make different decisions.

It is true that cloud computing has some issues in data transmission owing to the limitations of networks and infrastructure, which immensely decrease the performance of cloud computing. Therefore, the fog computing model was introduced to act in the middle between cloud computing and IoT. Fog is an extended version of cloud computing that can provide computing facilities at the edge of the network, and it allows this technology to deal with several data locally. As devices connected to the Internet and the use of the Internet of Things (IoT) continue to grow, the need for efficient and scalable computing solutions has become paramount. Fog computing has emerged as a model that extends the features of cloud computing to the network edge, bringing storage, computation, and networking closer to end users and devices.

Email: soumen_swarnakar@yahoo.co.in; soumen.swarnakar@nsec.ac.in

Chandan Banerjee, Anupam Ghosh, Rajdeep Chakraborty and Ahmed A. Elngar (eds.) Fog Computing for Intelligent Cloud IoT Systems, (3–32) © 2024 Scrivener Publishing LLC

This article presents an in-depth analysis of the architecture, applications, and challenges of fog computing. It also discusses the fundamental concepts of fog computing, including its architectural components. Fog computing has been compared with IoT and cloud computing. Furthermore, it explores the different uses of fog computing in different domains, such as healthcare, smart cities, transportation, manufacturing, and agriculture. This paper also examines the different challenging features and future study guidelines in the field of fog computing.

Keywords: IoT, cloud computing, edge computing, fog computing, smart city, sensor, edge nodes

1.1   Introduction

This fog computing can be considered as the computation of the next generation which is an extended version of cloud computing towards the edge of the network. Therefore it is also known as edge computing [16]. Issues faced by cloud computing can be addressed using fog computing.

Currently, the volume of data generation is exploding owing to the vast quantity of data generated daily by sensors, IoT devices, wide volume of internet usage, and so on. Fog computing can report the impractical features of a cloud that cannot fulfill the demands of users in real time. IoT applications, the Industrial Internet of Things, and the Internet of Everything, etc. are different reasons for the motivation or interest in the application of fog computing. Currently, data are one of the most important and essential factors for fulfilling and maintaining existence in today's era, and the usage of fog computing is spreading rapidly across organizations. Fog computing has gained significant attention as a promising paradigm for extending cloud-computing capabilities to network edges. While fog computing offers numerous benefits, such as reduced latency, improved scalability, and enhanced data privacy, it also presents several challenges that need to be addressed. Resource allocation is becoming an issue with respect to IoT application in fog computing [1, 2]. Several features of the different methods for allocating resources are used in fog computing. The objective of this article is to study the latest research on the allocation of resources in the fog area and to conduct a comparative study with cloud and IoT with different applications of fog computing. The justification of this study is to understand the architecture and application of fog computing and to provide a clear idea of the future applications of fog computing. From this article, researchers will benefit from a better understanding and utilization of this technology. Soon, different IoT devices will occupy the world because of the significant increase in the usage of different objects connected by different sensors connected by the Internet [3].

In this study, the remainder is divided into different sections. Section 1.2 presents an overview of Fog Computing, Section 1.3 describes fog computing for intelligent cloud IoT systems, Section 1.4 discusses the architecture of fog computing, Section 1.5 presents the basic module of fog computing, Section 1.6 presents the differences between cloud computing and fog computing, Section 1.7 discusses the differences between fog computing and IoT systems, Section 1.8 presents fog computing applications, Section 1.9 discusses whether fog computing can be taken over by cloud computing, Section 1.10 presents the challenges in fog computing, Section 1.11 discusses the future of fog computing, and finally, the conclusion is drawn in Section 1.12.

1.2   Fog Computing: An Overview

Cloud and fog computing are interrelated. In 2014, CISCO created the word fog computing, so obviously it is a new term for common human beings. As we know, fog exists closer to Earth than clouds, and the same is applicable in technical terms. Cloud capabilities are easier to use using fog computing.

Therefore, fog is an extension technology of cloud computing, which consists of several *edge nodes* connected with physical devices.

These nodes are much closer to devices if related to centralized data centers, which is why they can provide prompt connections. The computation power of edge nodes permits them to execute the processing of an enormous amount of data generated without transferring it to servers at a distance. Fog computing, also known as fog networks or edge computing, is an emerging paradigm that extends cloud-computing capabilities to the edge of a network. It brings computing resources, including storage, processing power, and networking capabilities closer to the data source or end-user devices. Fog computing offers several significant benefits, which contribute to its increasing importance in various domains.

Fog computing [8] can be considered as a decentralized computing arrangement. Here, decentralized indicates that computing resources are not fixed. Computing resources in fog computing will be moved and fixed closer to the IoT devices that generates records. Thus, this idea reduces the latency and network bandwidth usage, which can result in faster computation. Different large organizations have recently utilized fog computing to compute faster.

One of the important factors is the fog node. These are the virtual instances existing in the fog layer, which are used to provide extra benefits to the process of cloud computing. A fog node is a group of computing resources related to a specific sector. A small storage component acts similarly to a fog node. The fog layer is linked with a big cloud that may be a private or public cloud from which the fog nodes fetch records and push the record to it. Fog nodes can be used to provide transient storage ability. If the data are not transient, then it is relocated to the cloud to store the data.

Fog nodes rapidly agree whether to compute a record or send the record to the cloud for computation.

Each fog node has a comprehensive fog node and can be deployed over the entire network. Examples: routers, switches, etc.

The fog consists of *cloudlets*, which are small-scale datacenters situated at the edge of the network. Their main objective is to support resource-intensive Internet of Things applications that require low latency.

Fog computing services are very close to end devices. Because it is closer to end devices, the proposed computing model has important benefits over other conventional computing models. The important features of this study are as follows:

- Geographical distribution
  Fog nodes are widely distributed geographically [4]. These were positioned at different locations. For example, they are located on different positions of roads and highways, on the museum floor, and so on.
- Decentralization
  Fog computing has a decentralized architecture. No central server is available for managing different computing resources and facilities. Therefore, fog nodes are self-organizing and work together to provide a facility for real-time IoT applications to end users.
- Location awareness
  The ability to determine the geographical location of a device is called location awareness. The fog node is linked to the nearby fog node, and it knows the location of the fog client. Location awareness can be used in emergency conditions or targeted advertising.
- Real-time interaction
  The fog application supports real-time interaction instead of batch processing. Real-time stream handling and gaming are used in fog computing. Because fog is very close to the

edge, it offers healthy network information on the local network, traffic information, and status information.

- Save storage space
  Fog computing reduces latency and storage space [21, 22] consumption by avoiding inopportune data from moving across the entire network.
- Low latency
  The time taken for data to move from the source device to the server device is called the latency. By placing computing resources near the edge, the network latency of fog computing can be significantly reduced. This is crucial for applications that require real-time or near-real-time responsiveness, such as Internet of Things (IoT) devices, autonomous vehicles, industrial automation, and healthcare systems. In fog computing, latency is lower because the data do not have to move far away from the device. In the IoT and Cloud model, data generated by sensors are moved to the data center of the cloud, which is situated far from the IoT devices. Therefore, end-to-end delay occurs, such as deferral of data sent from IoT devices to data centers situated remotely, the delay of investigating the data, and the response coming back is delayed by the cloud to the end user. Therefore, cloud computing has a high latency. The nodes of fog computing are much closer to IoT devices [5], which provide different computing facilities, and decisions are made based on local data without the use of the cloud. Therefore latency in response is comparatively much lower [4] than that of cloud computing. With fog computing, data processing and decision making can occur locally, enhancing the overall user experience and enabling faster response times.
- Heterogeneity support
  The fog computing model has various types of nodes, such as set-top boxes, edge routers, high-end servers, and access factors, and even end nodes. Examples include cellular phones, automobiles, and sensors. They have received high-speed servers, edge routers, etc., operated via an operating device with special storage capabilities and computational electricity. It also provides virtual network platform. As different computing nodes and nodes of a virtual network can be used as fog nodes, fog nodes are heterogeneous in nature.

- Mobility support
  Using different protocols, mobility support is an important characteristic for different fog computing applications to communicate directly with movable devices. We know the ID separation protocol developed by CISCO, which can use a directory system that separates the identity of the host from identity of the site.
- Close to the end user
  To remove delays [24] in data communication, fog permits data to be closer to users than in data centers kept in remote locations.
- Bandwidth optimization
  Fog computing optimizes the network bandwidth [20] by processing data at the edge rather than transmitting it to centralized cloud servers. This is particularly valuable in scenarios in which IoT devices or sensors generate massive amounts of data. By locally performing data filtering, preprocessing, and aggregation, fog computing reduces the amount of data transmitted to the cloud. This alleviates network congestion and minimizes bandwidth costs.
- Enhanced privacy and security
  Sensitive data can be processed and stored locally in fog computing, whereas data can be sent to a remote cloud server in cloud computing. This distributed approach to computing enhances privacy and security [9, 14, 27] because data can be kept closer to its source and subject to localized security measures. It reduces the risk of data breaches and unauthorized access and ensures compliance with privacy regulations.
- Improved reliability
  Fog computing increases the reliability and resilience of networked systems. Distributing computing resources across a network mitigates a single point of failure. If a connection to the cloud is lost, fog nodes can continue to function independently and maintain critical operations. This is particularly critical for applications in which uninterrupted connectivity is crucial, such as autonomous, industrial control, and emergency response systems.
- Scalability and agility
  Fog computing enables scalability and agility in the deployment and management of distributed applications. As the

number of edge computing nodes and IoT devices increases, fog computing allows for easy resource scaling by adding more edge devices. It also enables the dynamic provisioning of computing resources based on demand, allowing applications to adapt and respond efficiently to changing workload requirements.

- Cost optimization
  By offloading computational tasks to edge devices, fog computing reduces the need for high-end servers and an expensive cloud infrastructure. It can leverage existing computing resources at the edge, such as routers, gateways, and IoT devices, thereby optimizing resource utilization and reducing operational costs. Fog computing enables cost-effective solutions for deploying and managing distributed applications, particularly in scenarios in which large-scale cloud infrastructure is not feasible or cost prohibitive.

Fog computing plays an important role in enabling effective and reliable computations at the network edge. This has important advantages with respect to reduced latency, optimized bandwidth, enhanced privacy and security, improved reliability, scalability, agility, and cost optimization. As the demand for real-time and edge-centric applications grows, fog computing is becoming increasingly relevant in various domains, including IoT, industrial automation, smart cities, healthcare, and transportation. The characteristics of fog computing are summarized in Figure 1.1.

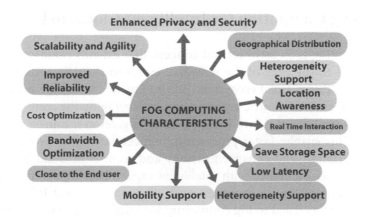

Figure 1.1 Fog computing characteristics.

Fog computing can be considered situated between remote servers and hardware. Therefore, it is easier to decide and control the sending of data to a server or executed locally. A fog serves as a smart gateway that offloads cloud computing, allowing for more effective data processing, storage, and analysis [22].

Decentralization of computing infrastructure is the main factor in fog computation. Here, a flexible computing infrastructure consisting of data, storage, and applications is situated somewhere between the cloud and data source, which is a data generator. Similar to edge computing [16], fog computing reduces the distance between the data source and the location where it is executed. Edge computing and fog computing concepts are nearly the same, as both technologies bring computation and processing closer to the data generation location. Sometimes, it is done to increase efficiency, as well as for compliance and security reasons.

Currently, low-cost sensors are helping to increase the usage of IoT devices. IoT can be implemented successfully when the following requirements are met:

- Reliability of data.
- High data security
- Reduction in latency of data
- Based on the data type, the execution of data at the appropriate location.
- To monitor data through large geographical area

Fog computing meets all the above requirements for IoT networks.

1.3   Fog Computing for Intelligent Cloud-IoT System

Fog computing is an architectural concept that extends cloud computing capabilities to the edge of the network, closer to the data sources in an Internet of Things (IoT) ecosystem [9]. It aims to address the limitations of traditional cloud-centric architectures by leveraging the computational resources available at network edges, such as gateways, routers, and IoT devices. This enables faster processing, reduced latency, improved bandwidth utilization, and enhanced privacy and security in cloud-based IoT systems. When combined with intelligent capabilities, fog computing can further enhance the performance and efficiency of cloud-IoT systems. Some concepts related to fog computing for intelligent cloud-IoT systems are as follows:

- Edge Intelligence: Fog computing enables intelligent processing and decision-making at the edge of the network. By deploying machine learning algorithms and artificial intelligence models on edge devices, data can be analyzed and acted upon in real time without the need to send it to the cloud. This reduces the latency and enables quicker response times for time-sensitive applications.
- Distributed Data Analytics: Fog computing allows data analytics tasks to be distributed across clouds and edge devices. By partitioning data processing and analysis between the cloud and edge, it is possible to strike a balance between computational capabilities and network-bandwidth usage. This approach optimizes overall system performance and reduces the need for extensive data transfer to the cloud.
- Dynamic Resource Allocation: Fog computing enables intelligent resource allocation and management in cloud-IoT systems. By leveraging edge devices' computational capabilities, tasks can be dynamically assigned to the most suitable resources based on factors like proximity, network conditions, and resource availability. This adaptive resource allocation ensures efficient utilization of computing resources and improved system scalability.
- Context-Awareness: Fog computing enhances the context-awareness of cloud-IoT systems by leveraging data from sensors and devices at the edge. Contextual information such as location, environmental conditions, and user preferences can be processed locally to provide personalized services, real-time monitoring, and better decision-making. This localized processing minimizes the need for constant communication with the cloud, thereby reducing latency and conserving the network bandwidth.
- Security and Privacy: Fog computing improves security [17, 27] and privacy in cloud-IoT systems by keeping sensitive data closer to its source. Instead of transmitting all the data to the cloud for processing, fog nodes can perform data filtering, aggregation, and anonymization at the edge. This approach reduces the attack surface and risk of data breaches, making the system more resilient to cyber threats.
- Hybrid Cloud–Fog Collaboration: Fog computing can be seamlessly integrated with cloud computing to create a hybrid cloud–fog architecture. This collaboration allows for

the offloading of resource-intensive tasks to the cloud, while maintaining time-sensitive and critical operations at the edge. The hybrid model provides the benefits of both cloud and fog computing, optimizing the trade-off between scalability, agility, and latency in cloud IoT systems.

These concepts demonstrate how fog computing can enhance cloud-IoT systems by providing intelligence, real-time processing, and efficient resource management to the network edge. By leveraging the strengths of both cloud and fog computing, organizations can build scalable, responsive, and secure IoT ecosystems that can fulfill the demands of a large variety of applications.

1.4   Fog Computing Architecture

Fog computing architecture is generally composed of three different working layers. There are three working layers in the fog computing architecture [6, 8, 25]: the edge layer, fog layer, and cloud layer. The three-layer architecture of fog computing is described below and presented in Figure 1.2.

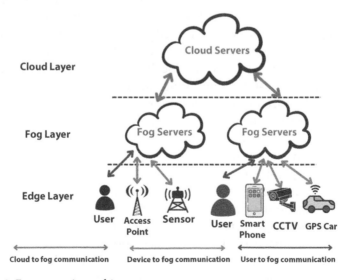

Figure 1.2 Fog computing architecture.

a. Cloud Layer:
   - Cloud layer represents the centralized cloud infrastructure at the top of the architecture. It provides storage, computing power, and advanced analytics capabilities for fog computing deployment.
   - The cloud layer is responsible for handling resource-intensive tasks, storing large datasets, and supporting long-term data analyses.
b. Fog Layer:
   - The fog layer is located closer to the network edge and comprises a distributed network of fog nodes.
   - Fog nodes are interconnected devices that include edge servers, routers, gateways, and IoT devices.
   - These nodes are responsible for processing, analyzing, and storing data locally, thereby reducing latency and network congestion.
   - Fog nodes can be deployed at various levels of the network hierarchy, such as near end-devices, within access points, or at aggregation points.
c. Edge Layer:
   - The edge layer consists of edge devices representing sensors, actuators, and IoT devices that generate data and interact directly with the physical world.
   - These devices are responsible for collecting and transmitting data to fog nodes for local processing and analysis.
d. Communication Infrastructure:
   - Communication infrastructure connects fog nodes and edge devices, facilitating data exchange and communication.
   - It can include wired and wireless networks such as Ethernet, Wi-Fi, cellular networks, and other IoT-specific protocols.
e. Data Processing and Analytics:
   - The fog nodes within the fog layer perform data processing, analytics, and decision-making tasks.
   - This layer can utilize various techniques, including machine learning algorithms, stream processing, and real-time analytics, to extract insights from data.

    f.   Resource Management and Orchestration:
- Resource management and orchestration mechanisms optimize the allocation and utilization of computing, storage, and networking resources within the fog layer.
- This involves tasks such as load balancing, task scheduling, and dynamic resource provisioning to ensure efficient resource utilization.

    g. Security and Privacy:
- The security and privacy layers focus on ensuring the confidentiality, integrity, and availability of data within the fog computing environment.
- This includes encryption mechanisms, access control, authentication, and intrusion detection systems to protect data and preserve user privacy.

    h. Cloud–Fog Integration:
- Cloud–fog integration enables seamless communication and collaboration between cloud and fog layers.
- It allows fog nodes to offload certain tasks to the cloud, access additional resources when needed, and enable the long-term storage and analysis of data.

It is important to note that fog computing architectures can vary depending on specific use cases and deployment scenarios. The described architecture provides a general overview of the components and their relationships within a fog-computing environment.

Different types of fog computing exist, such as client-based, server-based, and hybrid fog computing.

- **Client-Based Fog:** It is based on the computing power of edge devices to execute and analyze data. Client-based fog computation is best for applications that require real-time processing, such as industrial IoT and autonomous vehicles.
- **Server-Based Fog:** It is based on the computing power of servers located in the fog layer to execute and analyze data. Server-based fog computation is best for applications that require extra computing power compared with edge devices.
- **Hybrid Fog:** This fog computation is a mixture of client-based and server-based fog computations. Hybrid fog computing is perfect for applications that require a combination of high computing power and real-time processing.

1.5   Basic Modules of Fog Computing

There are several ways of creating a fog computing system. The well-known parts across these architectures are explained below and are summarized in Figure 1.3.

a.   Physical and Virtual Nodes/End Devices
    In the real world, end devices function as points of inter-action. They may be end devices, such as smart watches, module phone sensors, edge routers, application servers, and edge routers. These devices are record producers and can span a large band of technology. This means that they may have variable processing and storage capacities, and many hardware and software applications.

b.   Fog Nodes
    Fog nodes are independent devices that collect the information produced. Fog nodes fall into three categories: gateways, fog servers, and fog devices. These devices can store the necessary data, whereas fog servers can compute their data to take the course of action. Fog devices are generally connected to servers. The fog gateways redirect information between several fog devices and servers. This layer is responsible for the speed handling and flow of information.

c.   Monitoring Services
    Monitoring services usually include application programming interfaces or APIs that keep track of how the system

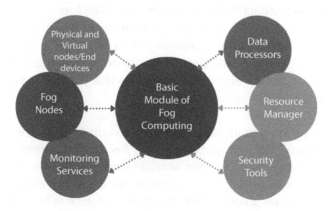

Figure 1.3 Basic modules of fog computing.

will perform and the availability of resources. This guarantees that all fog nodes and end devices are active and communication is not delayed [24]. It is observed that if we wait for a node to be free, then it may be comparatively more costly than to hit the cloud server. The monitor manages such situations. Monitors can be used to assess the present system and predict future resource necessities based on their overall usage.

d. Data Processors

Data processors play an important role in fog computing. The function is to operate on fog nodes. They trim, filter and occasionally rebuild damaged data that flow from end devices. Data processors can decide whether the data should be kept locally on a fog server or sent for long-term storage in the cloud. Data from different sources were homogenized for easy communication and transportation by these processors.

This can be achieved by revealing a programmable and uniform interface with other modules in the system. If one or more sensors do not work, some data processors are so intelligent that they can fill the information based on old historical data. This can prevent any type of application failure.

e. Resource Manager

Fog computing contains different independent nodes that can operate synchronously. The resource manager assigns and frees the resources to several nodes and schedules data transmission between the nodes and the cloud. It also considers the data backup to ensure zero data loss.

As fog modules take up some of the SLA [20] promises of the cloud, great availability is necessary. The resource manager works with the monitor to decide where and when the demand is higher. This confirms that there is no redundancy in the fog servers or data.

f. Security Tools

Fog components can directly interconnect with raw data sources. Encryption is necessary because all communication tends to occur over wireless networks. In some cases, end users directly ask fog nodes for data. Therefore, user and access management are part of safety efforts in fog computing.

1.6   Cloud Computing vs. Fog Computing

Fog computing and cloud computing are two distinct paradigms [10, 14] that serve different purposes in the realm of distributed computing. The key differences between fog computing and cloud computing are as follows:

a. Proximity to End Users and Devices:
    - Fog Computing: Fog computing brings computing resources closer to the network edge, end users, and IoT devices. It extends cloud-computing capabilities to the edge of the network, reduces latency, and improves real-time responsiveness.
    - Cloud Computing: Cloud computing, on the other hand, centralizes computing resources in data centers located at a distance from end users. Users access these resources on the internet.

b. Data Processing and Storage:
    - Fog Computing: In fog computing, data processing and storage occur at the network edge, close to where data are generated. This enables faster processing, reduced bandwidth usage, and localized decision making.
    - Cloud Computing: In cloud computing, data processing and storage occur in centralized datacenters. Users send data to the cloud for processing and the results are sent back to the user.

c. Scalability and Resource Allocation:
    - Fog Computing: Fog computing allows for horizontal scalability because fog nodes can be deployed in a distributed manner to handle increasing workloads. Resources can be dynamically allocated and managed at an edge.
    - Cloud Computing: Cloud computing enables vertical scalability, as additional resources are added to centralized data centers to handle increased demand. Resource allocation [4] and management are performed centrally.

d. Network Bandwidth and Latency:
    - Fog Computing: Fog computing reduces network bandwidth [20] requirements by processing and analyzing data locally at the edge and sending only relevant information to the cloud. This minimizes the latency and congestion.

- Cloud Computing: Cloud computing relies on network connectivity for data transfer between the end user and the cloud, potentially leading to higher latency owing to data transmission over longer distances.

e. Use Case Focus:
- Fog Computing: Fog computing is particularly suitable for latency-sensitive and real-time applications such as IoT, edge analytics, and time-critical systems. It is well suited for scenarios in which immediate decision-making and local data processing are crucial.
- Cloud Computing: Cloud computing is commonly used in applications that require extensive computing

Table 1.1 Difference between cloud computing and fog computing.

Feature requirements	Cloud computing	Fog computing
Architecture	Centralized	Distributed
Proximity to End Users and Devices	Centralizes computing resources in Data Centers located at a distance from end user	Closer to the network edge, closer to end users and IoT devices
Data Processing and Storage	Far from the Data Source, Computing Capability and Storage Powerful	Close to the Data Source, Computing Capability and Storage less Powerful
Scalability and Resource Allocation	High, easy to scale	Scalable with in Network
Network Bandwidth and Latency	High	Medium
Use Case Focus	Suitable for complex modeling and big data analytics	Suitable for latency-sensitive and real-time applications, such as IoT, edge analytics, and time-critical systems
Data Privacy and Security	Less Secure	High Secure

resources, storage, and long-term data analysis. It is suitable for applications with less stringent latency requirements, where data processing can be offloaded to a centralized infrastructure.

f. Data Privacy and Security:
  - Fog Computing: Fog computing enhances data privacy and security by keeping sensitive data localized at the edge. Data can be processed and analyzed within a local network to reduce exposure to potential threats during data transmission.
  - Cloud Computing: Cloud computing involves transmitting data over the Internet to centralized data centers, raising concerns about data privacy and security during transmission and storage.

It is important to note that fog computing and cloud computing are not mutually exclusive or complementary. In certain scenarios, a hybrid approach that combines fog computing at the edge and cloud computing in centralized datacenters may be the most effective solution, leveraging the strengths of both paradigms. The differences between the above two are summarized in Table 1.1.

1.7 Fog Computing vs. IoT

Fog computing and the Internet of Things (IoT) [12, 13, 19] are related concepts, but have distinct differences. There are some key differences between fog computing and IoT:

- Scope and Scale: IoT refers to a network of interconnected devices, sensors, and objects that collect and exchange data. It encompasses a wide range of devices from everyday objects to industrial machinery and infrastructure. On the other hand, fog computing is an architectural paradigm that extends cloud computing capabilities to the edge of the network. It focuses on computation, storage, and processing capabilities at the network edge to enable real-time data processing and analysis.
- Location of Data Processing: In IoT, data are generated by various devices and sensors, which are typically transmitted to a centralized cloud infrastructure for processing and

analysis. However, fog computing emphasizes localized processing at the edge of the network closer to the data sources. It aims to reduce latency, minimize data transfer, and enable real-time decision making by processing data closer to where it is generated.

- Latency and Real-Time Capabilities: IoT systems often rely on cloud computing for data processing, which can introduce latency owing to the time it takes to transmit data to the cloud and receive a response. Fog computing addresses this issue by enabling real-time processing and decision-making at the network edge. By processing data locally, fog computing reduces latency and allows for faster responses, making it wee suited for time-sensitive applications.
- Scalability: IoT systems can involve a large number of devices and generate a vast amount of data. Cloud computing provides scalability for handling such large-scale deployments. Fog computing complements cloud computing by distributing computational resources and enabling localized processing at the edge. This enhances scalability by offloading processing tasks from the cloud to the edge, thereby reducing the overall system load.
- Security and Privacy: Security and privacy [27] are critical concerns in IoT systems. Cloud-based IoT solutions often involve transmitting sensitive data to the cloud, thereby increasing the privacy and security risks. Fog computing mitigates these risks by keeping the data processing and storage closer to the edge, thereby reducing the need to transmit sensitive data to the cloud. This localized approach improves security and privacy because data can be processed and filtered locally before being sent to the cloud, thereby minimizing the attack surface.
- Network Bandwidth Usage: IoT systems generate vast amounts of data and transmit all data to the cloud for processing, which can strain network bandwidth [20]. Fog computing reduces the amount of data sent to the cloud by performing an initial processing and filtering at the edge. It only sends relevant and actionable data to the cloud, optimizing network bandwidth usage and reducing the costs associated with data transfer.

Table 1.2 Difference between fog computing and IoT.

Feature requirements	Fog computing	IoT
Scope and Scale	Distributed	Centralized
Location of Data Processing	Localized processing at the edge of the network, closer to the data sources	Data is generated by various devices and sensors, which is typically transmitted to a centralized cloud infrastructure for processing and analysis
Latency and Real-Time Capabilities	Low Latency	High Latency
Scalability	High scalable	Less Scalable
Security and Privacy	High	Medium
Network Bandwidth Usage	Needs less Bandwidth	Needs more Bandwidth

The fog computing and IoT differences are summarized in Table 1.2.

Overall, while IoT focuses on the network of interconnected devices and data generation, fog computing complements IoT by extending cloud-computing capabilities to the edge of the network. Fog computing enhances IoT systems by providing localized processing, reducing latency, improving scalability, and addressing security and privacy concerns, thereby making it an integral part of a robust and efficient IoT architecture. The combination of fog computing with IoT will bring various benefits to many IoT applications.

1.8   Applications of Fog Computing

There are various applications of fog computing [7, 25] in different areas. These are described as follows, and the summarized presentation is shown in Figure 1.4:

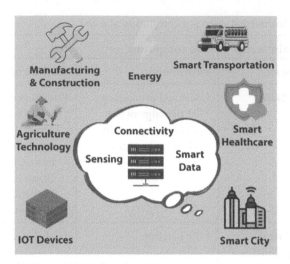

Figure 1.4 Applications of fog computing.

a. Smart Utility Service

   Saving energy is the primary challenge of modern life. Using smart utility facilities, we can achieve this. IoT-related applications create huge amounts of data transmission; this problem can be addressed using fog computing, which can analyze data from different applications for updating continuously.

b. Smart Cities

   Traffic regulation in smart city is another popular example of use of fog computing [15, 23]. Sensor-based road barriers and traffic signals are installed to collect vehicle movement data on busy roads. As real-time data analysis can be performed by fog computing, it helps traffic signals to function properly and accurately.

c. Health Care

   Evolution in healthcare has been introduced by the involvement of IoT with wearable sensors, which has brought about a remarkable change in healthcare systems [30]. A simple watch that tells us time and date, but a smart watch can do the same thing with some extra features by providing different health conditions for users. Currently, wearable sensors are used in smart hospitals to obtain continuous information on different parameters related to health. Fog computing has low latency, which is why it is helpful to these wearable IoT devices, as it guarantees the delivery of data without delay at the time of emergency.

d. Video Surveillance
In different crowds, such as shopping malls, cinema halls, and railway stations, the installation of surveillance cameras is very important to track different movements of public behaviors. Surveillance cameras can gather large amounts of video data. To stop the delay of data transmission from these devices, fog computing is important for helping to identify the anomalies in those places and to alert specific authorities to act against such an event.

e. Fog Computing in Agriculture and Farming
Agricultural production is now being advanced with the benefit of Fog Computing. An example is a Smart Water Management Platform. The agricultural production industry has benefitted and transformed with the help of fog computing. The Smart Water Management Platform (SWAMP) project is a beautiful example, where IoT, autonomous devices, and data analytics [18], etc. have been used. Fog computing allows the platform to collect sensor analysis data from the fields and, subsequently, to improve the allocation of water.

Another application was developed using iFogSim, which is an application of fog computing for smart or precision agriculture. This is an IoT-based farm management systems called Agrifog.

1.9   Will the Fog Be Taken Over by the Cloud?

There are many problems with fog computing, and its adoption by industry is very low. Different industries are contesting to acquire fog technology quickly and perform rapid research to grow and capture the market; however, some companies are taking policies such as waiting and watching the market scenario on fog computing. Denny Strigl who is a former CEO of Verizon Wireless and a lecturer at electrical engineering department in the Princeton, said that it would took nearly twenty years for proper implementation of wireless system which is maneuvered. Fog computation and proper implementation are difficult tasks. Safety and security are the main issues in proper implementation. The final difficulty is confusion, as a human phenomenon. Adding another level of complication in some cases creates a certain fear that individuals and industries will not be ready to control and maintain it. However, industries may be cautious about accepting this challenge. Fog computing is one of the solutions that can create problems in the form of technology to entertain things to marketing and retail. Fog computing will not fully replace cloud computing because, until now, clouds have been preferred for processing high-end batch jobs, which are important for the business world. Thus, it can be said that cloud and fog would be existing technologies and both have usages in different applications, and these are complementary to each other where required.

1.10 Challenges in Fog Computing

This section discusses the key challenges [11, 17, 21] faced by fog computing and explores potential research directions for overcoming these challenges.

a. Scalability and Heterogeneity: Among the different challenges, the scalability and management of many heterogeneous devices and resources are one of them in fog computing [26]. As the number of IoT devices continues to grow, fog nodes must efficiently handle the increasing volume of data and computational demands. Future research should focus on developing scalable architectures, resource-allocation algorithms, and load-balancing mechanisms to handle diverse workloads and ensure the optimal resource utilization.

b. Resource Management and Optimization: Efficient resource management is crucial in fog computing environments to ensure optimal utilization of computing, storage, and networking resources. However, resource management in a highly distributed and dynamic environment is complex. Future research should explore intelligent resource management techniques, including task scheduling, resource allocation, and dynamic provisioning, to optimize resource usage, reduce energy consumption, and improve the overall system performance.

c. Security and Privacy Concerns: As fog computing involves processing and storing sensitive data at the network edge, ensuring security and privacy becomes a critical challenge. Fog nodes are vulnerable to various security threats including unauthorized access, data breaches, and malicious attacks. Future research should focus on developing robust security mechanisms, including authentication, encryption, access control, and intrusion detection systems to protect data and preserve user privacy in fog computing environments.

d. Data Processing and Analytics: Fog computing generates vast quantities of data for execution and analysis in real time. However, processing and analyzing data at the network edge poses challenges owing to the limited computational capabilities and bandwidth constraints. Future research should explore lightweight and efficient data processing techniques, including edge analytics, machine learning, and stream processing algorithms, to enable real-time insights and decision making in the fog layer.

e. Energy Efficiency and Sustainability: Fog computing deployments often consist of resource-constrained devices with limited power resources. Efficient energy management is essential for prolonging the battery life of edge devices and minimizing their environmental impacts. Future research should focus on developing energy-efficient algorithms, power management strategies, and energy-aware protocols to optimize the energy consumption and improve the sustainability of fog computing systems.

f. Interoperability and Standardization: The heterogeneity of devices, protocols, and platforms in fog computing ecosystems presents interoperability challenges. The lack of standardized interfaces and protocols hinders seamless integration and communication between fog nodes and cloud resources. Future research should address interoperability issues by developing standardized protocols, middleware, and APIs to enable seamless communication and collaboration between heterogeneous fog computing devices and cloud platforms.

g. Edge Intelligence and Autonomy: To achieve real-time decision-making and autonomy at the network edge, fog nodes must possess intelligence and self-learning capabilities. Future research should focus on developing intelligent algorithms, machine learning techniques, and edge intelligence frameworks to enable autonomous decision making, context awareness, and adaptive behavior in fog computing systems.

h. Quality of Service (QoS) and Service Level Agreements (SLAs): Fog computing involves the provisioning of various services to end-users and meeting the QoS requirements specified in SLAs is crucial. However, ensuring the QoS in a dynamic and distributed fog environment is challenging. Future research should explore QoS-aware resource management, service placement, and SLA negotiation mechanisms to guarantee reliable service delivery and meet user expectations in fog computing deployments

1.11 Future of Fog Computing

Fog computing can solve difficulties related to internet traffic, space, and congestion. Fog computing provides smart techniques to achieve real-time and distributed features for developing IoT setups [12, 13]. Emerging these types of facilities with the use of fog computation can lead to different business models as well as new openings for network providers and operators. Current research predicts that the fog-computing-related market will be increased to USD 934 million by 2026. We know that in 2017, the global market size for fog computing was expected to be USD 12.87 million and most probably, it will get a fast progress rapidly with a CAGR of 62.6% or more between 2017 and 2026. Therefore, fog computing applications have great scope in the global world.

The future of fog computing appears promising, as it evolves and gains traction in various industries. Some key aspects that highlight potential future developments and trends in fog computing are as follows:

- Edge Intelligence: Fog computing will increasingly incorporate advanced analytics and artificial intelligence capabilities at the edge. This will enable real-time data processing, analysis, and decision making at the network edge, empowering autonomous systems, smart devices, and IoT applications. Edge intelligence will facilitate faster insights, predictive maintenance, and proactive decision making, leading to improved efficiency and performance across industries.
- 5G and Fog Computing Integration: 5G networks synergize with fog computing, unlocking new opportunities and capabilities. 5G's high-speed, low-latency, and high-bandwidth

characteristics align well with the fog computing requirements. The combination of 5G and fog computing will
enable more real-time applications, such as augmented
reality, virtual reality, connected vehicles, smart cities, and
industrial automation, with enhanced performance and user
experience.

- Decentralized Data Governance: Fog computing promotes
a decentralized approach to data processing and storage. In
the future, there will likely be increased emphasis on decentralized data governance frameworks to ensure data privacy,
security, and compliance. Distributed ledger technologies,
such as blockchain may enable secure and transparent data
management and establishing trust [28] among fog nodes
and stakeholders. Trust is very important for assisting in
decision creation and allows independent connections to
be made between resource-constrained IoT devices and fog
nodes, which are called fog clients. The requirements of trust
in fog computing are very important.

- Industry-Specific Fog Solutions: Different industries will
continue to adopt fog computing to address specific challenges. For example, fog computing can facilitate remote
patient monitoring, real-time medical data analysis, and
personalized treatment. In manufacturing, fog computing
can optimize production processes, enable predictive maintenance, and improve supply chain visibility. As fog computing matures, industry-specific solutions [29] will emerge to
cater to the unique requirements of different sectors.

- Edge-to-Cloud Orchestration: Fog computing and cloud
computing will increasingly work together in a coordinated
manner, enabling seamless orchestration of resources and
workload distribution. Applications and services dynamically balance processing between the edge and cloud based
on factors such as latency, resource availability, and energy
efficiency. This hybrid approach maximizes the benefits of
both fog computing and cloud computing, offering a scalable and efficient infrastructure for diverse workloads.

- Energy Efficiency and Sustainability: Energy efficiency is a
significant consideration in fog computing. As the number
of edge devices and sensors increases, more energy-efficient
computing solutions are required. Fog computing can leverage low-power processors, energy-harvesting techniques,

and intelligent resource management to optimize energy consumption and promote sustainability in networked ecosystems.

- Standardization and Interoperability: Standardization and interoperability are essential to realize the full potential of fog computing. Industry consortiums and standardization bodies play a crucial role in establishing common frameworks, protocols, and interfaces to ensure seamless integration and compatibility between different fog-computing platforms and devices. Interoperability enables a vibrant ecosystem of applications, services, and devices that seamlessly work together, fostering innovation and collaboration.

In conclusion, fog computing holds great promise. As technological advancements continue and industries embrace edge-centric solutions, fog computing will evolve to achieve real-time processing, intelligent decision-making, and distributed data management. It will be a key enabler of various transformative technologies, such as IoT, AI, 5G, and decentralized computing, driving innovation and efficiency across industries.

1.12   Conclusion

Fog computing has tremendous potential for addressing the challenges posed by the increasing number of IoT devices and the requirement for real-time data processing. However, several challenges must be overcome to fully realize the benefits of fog computing. By focusing on scalability, resource management, security, data processing, energy efficiency, interoperability, intelligence, and QoS, researchers can pave the way for future advancements in fog computing, enabling its widespread adoption and facilitating innovative applications in various domains. Fog computation is a distributed architecture in which software, computing parts, and storage are kept someplace between the cloud and the data source. Fog computing provides different cloud-computing services to the end users. Explanation of different modules, architectures, and characteristics of fog computing is performed with different diagrams. Fog computing and cloud computing differences, as well as fog computing and IoT differences, are discussed to provide a complete view of their applications and usage. In this article, different security and privacy issues are discussed. Fog computing is an extension of cloud computing for the end users. Fog computing with IoT holds significant promise for the near future. With advancements in technology and industries embracing edge-centric solutions, fog computing will evolve to satisfy real-time processing, intelligent decision-making, and distributed data management. It will be a key enabler of various transformative technologies, such as IoT, AI, 5G, and decentralized computing, driving innovation and efficiency across industries. Research on fog computing is ongoing in a rapid manner, and although this technology is in the beginning stage, but in near future fog computing will play an important role in the development of IT solutions.

References

1. Rahul, S. and Aron, R., Fog computing architecture, application and resource allocation: A review. *2021 Fog Computing Architecture, WCNC- 2021: Workshop on Computer Networks & Communications*, 31–42, May 01, 2021.

2. Jr.,Bachiega, J., Costa, B.G.S., de Carvalho, L.R., Rosa, M.J.F., Araujo, A.P.F., Computational resource allocation in fog computing: A comprehensive survey. *ACM Comput. Surv.*, 55, 14, 336, 1–31, 2023, doi: 10.1145/3586181.

3. Naas, M., II, Parvedy, P.R., Boukhobza, J., Lemarchand, L., iFogStor: An IoT data placement strategy for fog infrastructure. *Fog and Edge Computing (ICFEC), IEEE 1st International Conference on IEEE*, pp. 97–104, 2017, doi: 10.1109/ICFEC.2017.15.

4. Da Costa Bezerra, S.F., Filho, A.S.M., Delicato, F.C., da Rocha, A.R., Processing complex events in fog-based internet of things systems for smart agriculture. *Sensors*, 21, 21, 7226, 2021 Oct 30, doi: 10.3390/ s21217226. PMID: 34770533; PMCID: PMC8587757.

5. Shahzad, M., Panneerselvam, J., Liu, L., Zhai, X., Data aggregation challenges in fog computing. *2019 IEEE Smart World, Ubiquitous Intelligence & Computing, Advanced & Trusted Computing, Scalable Computing & Communications, Cloud & Big Data Computing, Internet of People and Smart City Innovation*, (SmartWorld/SCALCOM/UIC/ATC/CBDCom/IOP/SCI), Leicester, UK, pp. 1717-1721, 2019, DOI: 10.1109/ SmartWorld-UIC-ATC-SCALCOM-IOP-SCI.2019.00306.

6. Habibi, P., Farhoudi, M., Kazemian, S., Khorsandi, S., Leon-Garcia, A., Fog computing: A comprehensive architectural survey. *IEEE Access*, 8, 69105–69133, 2020, doi: 10.1109/ACCESS.2020.2983253.

7. Delfin, S., Sivasanker., N.P., Raj, N., Anand, A., Fog computing: A new era of cloud computing. *3rd International Conference on Computing Methodologies and Communication (ICCMC)*, Erode, India, pp. 1106–1111, 2019, doi: 10.1109/ICCMC.2019.8819633.

8. Abdali, T.-A.N., Hassan, R., Aman, A.H.M., Nguyen, Q.N., Fog computing advancement: Concept, architecture, applications, advantages, and open issues. *IEEE Access*, 9, 75961–75980, 2021, doi: 10.1109/ ACCESS.2021.3081770.

9. Muniswamaiah, M., Agerwala, T., Tappert, C.C., Fog computing and the internet of things (IoT): A review. *2021 8th IEEE International Conference on Cyber Security and Cloud Computing (CSCloud)/2021 7th IEEE International Conference on Edge Computing and Scalable Cloud (EdgeCom)*, Washington, DC, USA, pp. 10–12, 2021, doi: 10.1109/ CSCloud-EdgeCom52276.2021.00012.

10. Elmoghrapi, A.N., Bleblo, A., Younis, Y.A., Fog computing or cloud computing: A study. *International Conference on Engineering & MIS (ICEMIS)*, Istanbul, Turkey, pp. 1–6, 2022, doi: 10.1109/ ICEMIS56295.2022.9914131.

11. Haouari, F., Faraj, R., AlJa'am, J.M., Fog computing potentials, applications, and challenges. *International Conference on Computer and Applications (ICCA)*, Beirut, Lebanon, pp. 399–406, 2018, doi: 10.1109/ COMAPP.2018.8460182.

12. Javed, W. *et al.*, A review on fog computing for the internet of things. *2021 International Conference on Innovative Computing (ICIC)*, Lahore, Pakistan, pp. 1–7, 2021, doi: 10.1109/ICIC53490.2021.9692966.

13. Sadique, K.M., Rahmani, R., Johannesson, P., Fog computing for trust in the internet of things (IoT): A systematic literature review. *2020 International Conference on Computer Science, Engineering and Applications (ICCSEA)*, Gunupur, India, pp. 1–6, 2020, doi: 10.1109/ ICCSEA49143.2020.9132861.

14. Raza, M.R., Varol, A., Varol, N., Cloud and fog computing: A survey to the concept and challenges. *2020 8th International Symposium on Digital Forensics and Security (ISDFS)*, Beirut, Lebanon, pp. 1–6, 2020, doi: 10.1109/ ISDFS49300.2020.9116360.

15. Kanaka Sri Shalini, C.M., Roopa, Y.M., Devi, J.S., Fog computing for smart cities. *2019 International Conference on Communication and Electronics Systems (ICCES)*, Coimbatore, India, pp. 912–916, 2019, doi: 10.1109/ ICCES45898.2019.9002050.

16. PunithaIlayarani, P. and Maria Dominic, M., Anatomization of fog computing and edge computing. *2019 IEEE International Conference on Electrical, Computer and Communication Technologies (ICECCT)*, Coimbatore, India, pp. 1–6, 2019, doi: 10.1109/ICECCT.2019.8869125.

17. Singh, S.K. and Kumar Dhurandher, S., Architecture of fog computing, issues and challenges: A review. *2020 IEEE 17th India Council International Conference (INDICON)*, New Delhi, India, pp. 1–6, 2020, doi: 10.1109/ INDICON49873.2020.9342074.

18. Li, G., Zhao, P., Lu, X., Liu, J., Shen, Y., Data analytics for fog computing by distributed online learning with asynchronous update. *ICC 2019 – 2019 IEEE International Conference on Communications (ICC)*, Shanghai, China, pp. 1–6, 2019, doi: 10.1109/ICC.2019.8761303.

19. Yu, R., Xue, G., Zhang, X., Application provisioning in fog computing-enabled internet-of-things: A network perspective. *IEEE INFOCOM 2018 - IEEE Conference on Computer Communications*, Honolulu, HI, USA, pp. 783–791, 2018, doi: 10.1109/INFOCOM.2018.8486269.

20. Husain, B.H. and Askar, S., Smart resource scheduling model in fog computing. *2022 8th International Engineering Conference on Sustainable Technology and Development (IEC)*, Erbil, Iraq, pp. 96–101, 2022, doi: 10.1109/IEC54822.2022.9807469.

21. Arivazhagan, C. and Natarajan, V., A survey on fog computing paradigms, challenges and opportunities in IoT. *2020 International Conference on Communication and Signal Processing (ICCSP)*, Chennai, India, pp. 0385–0389, 2020, doi: 10.1109/ICCSP48568.2020.9182229.

22. Wang, T., Zhou, J., Chen, X., Wang, G., Liu, A., Liu, Y., A three layer privacy preserving cloud storage scheme based on computational intelligence in fog computing. *IEEE Trans. Emerging Topics Comput. Intell.*, 2, 1, 3–12, 2018, doi: 10.1109/TETCI.2017.2764109.

23. Perera, C., Qin, Y., Estrella, J.C., Reiff-Marganiec, S., Vasilakos, A.V., Fog computing for sustainable smart cities: A survey. *ACM Computing Surveys (CSUR)*, 50, 3, 32, 2017, doi: 10.1145/3057266.

24. Yousefpour, A., Ishigaki, G., Jue, J.P., Fog computing: Towards minimizing delay in the internet of things, in: *Edge Computing (EDGE), 2017 IEEE International Conference on IEEE*, pp. 17–24, 2017, doi: 10.1109/IEEE.EDGE.2017.12.

25. Hu, P., Dhelim, S., Ning, H., Qiu, T., Survey on fog computing: architecture, key technologies, applications and open issues. *J. Network Comput. Appl.*, 98, 27–42, 2017, doi: 10.1016/j.jnca.2017.09.002.

26. Silva, R., Silva, J.S., Boavida, F., Opportunistic fog computing: Feasibility assessment and architectural proposal, in: *Integrated Network and Service Management (IM), 2017 IFIP/IEEE Symposium on IEEE*, pp. 510–516, 2017, doi: 10.23919/INM.2017.7987320.

27. Mukherjee, M., Matam, R., Shu, L., Maglaras, L., Ferrag, M.A., Choudhury, N., Kumar, V., Security and privacy in fog computing: Challenges. *IEEE Access*, 5, 19 293–19 304, 2017, doi: 10.1109/ACCESS.2017.2749422.

28. Dybedokken, T.S., Trust management in fog computing, Master's thesis, NTNU, Trondheim, Norway, 2017.

29. Ashjaei, S.M.H. and Bengtsson, M., Enhancing smart maintenance management using fog computing technology, in: *2017 International Conference on Industrial Engineering and Engineering Management IEEM*, Singapore, 10 Dec 2017, doi: 10.1109/IEEM.2017.829015.

30. Kraemer, F.A., Braten, A.E., Tamkittikhun, N., Palma, D., Fog computing in healthcare-a review and discussion. *IEEE Access*, 5, 9206–9222, 2017, doi: 10.1109/ACCESS.2017.2704100.

A Comparative Review on Different Techniques of Computation Offloading in Mobile Cloud Computing

Priyajit Sen[1]*, Tamanna Islam[2], Rajat Pandit[1] and Debabrata Sarddar[3]

[1]Department of Computer Science, West Bengal State University, Barasat, West Bengal, India
[2]Department of Computer Applications, Maulana Abul Kamal Azad University of Technology, Haringhata, West Bengal, India
[3]Department of Computer Science and Engineering, University of Kalyani, Kalyani, West Bengal, India

Abstract

Computation offloading is a critical technology for rapidly developing mobile cloud computing (MCC). It can improve the application speed, reduce the latency, and extend the battery life; among other things the effect of computation offloading is influenced by a variety of parameters. Offloading tasks to servers or other devices is seen to deal with limited computing resources such as data, hardware, software, and equipment and systems that are used to or connected to a file control block (FCB) network. Many computation tasks, such as games, face recognition, and artificial intelligence can be offloaded using computational devices (mobile, tablet, etc.). After the task is executed on the cloud server, the result is returned to the user device. It explores the concept of offloading data in big data locations, considers application offloading decisions, provides a comparison of different computational offloading frameworks, and assesses the available research in this domain. The survey offers a study of strategies for computational loading based on profiling and decision engine components.

Keywords: Mobile cloud computing, offloading strategies, computation offloading framework, data offloading, cloudlets

*Corresponding author: priyajit91@gmail.com

Chandan Banerjee, Anupam Ghosh, Rajdeep Chakraborty and Ahmed A. Elngar (eds.) Fog Computing for Intelligent Cloud IoT Systems, (33–44) © 2024 Scrivener Publishing LLC

2.1   Introduction

According to the Ericsson Mobility Report 2019, there will be approximately 8.8 billion smartphone subscriptions by 2024, up from the present 7.9 billion subscriptions. In growing nations, such as China and India, the demand for smartphones is increasing daily. Smartphones with operating systems such as Android, iPhone, Symbian, and Windows hold a position in the market. These smartphones have several built-in features and capabilities, including cameras, GPS, Wi-Fi, near-field communication (NFC), and adequate data storage space. In recent years, the hardware and software of smart mobile devices (SMDs) has changed with the introduction of new internal resources. However, computation-intensive mobile phone applications (such as natural language translators, and image processors) require high-speed computation power, fast memory, and high battery back; SMD generally has a low potential capacity for computer-intensive applications. The mobile cloud computing (MCC) environment provides software-level solutions to ease resource constraints in CMS. MCC is a distributed computing model used to solve resource shortages by providing users with powerful computing resources on a remote centralized cloud server. This increases the utility computing vision of the computational cloud for the SMD. However, millions of IoT devices require cloud services for the rapid popularization and development of the IoT. At the same time, we find many drawbacks such as data privacy protection, transmission delay, bandwidth limitations, and many other issues that can be solved with edge computing.

Based on a variety of performance parameters, the suggested offloading technique selects the optimal computing server for each real-time application. The proposed approach ignores other Quality of Service (QoS) criteria while reducing the latency time of each application. Offloading performance can be improved by partitioning and parallel processing. Offloading is classified into two types: full and partial offloading. When an application runs entirely in the cloud on the remote server side, it is called a full offload. Otherwise, if the application runs partially in the cloud, it is called a partial offload. Computational offloading is used if the internal architecture of the operating system distinguishes between user interface and internal computing services. For example, "Cuckoo" is an Android offloading framework. The reason for this type of name is that the cuckoo bird lays eggs to another bird's nest [20]. According to the latest COF research, there are four main characteristics: offloading strategy, multiple points, granularity, privacy, and security. This paper discusses different techniques of cloud computation, their pros and cons, and their solutions.

2.2 Related Works

Offload computing is an essential technology for edge calculation that can extend battery life, reduce latency, and improve the performance of applications. In fact, the effect of offloading calculations is affected by many factors, among which many offloadings do not achieve the target, as expected. In this article, we present a comprehensive survey of offload computing methods for edge computing. We describe the computation of the process and discuss the key to its questions, such as where, if, and what to unload. Around these questions, we explain the application scenarios, influencing factors, and offloading strategies [1]. Existing research on calculus loading and offloading provides a simple comparison of the calculations unframed in the MCC. Problems and challenges regarding calculation offloads in MCC are presented for future research [2]. Selection of best destination to offload (SOBDO), optimally selects a place to offload a computation-intensive job among different locations in the MCC environment. SOBDO basically works with the fixed partition of resource-hungry programs by smaller-sized tasks and applies the logic of auction theory to decide the fittest location to offload a specific task. The SOBDO benchmark differentiates the requirements of communication media, i.e., third-generation mobile connections, Wi-Fi, and Wi-Fi Direct. In addition, the effects of task size and complexity on the unloading process were estimated. SOBDO maps jobs across different devices, clouds, and cloudlets [3]. This survey provides a study on computational offloading. Compare research on work related to load reduction presented is classified based on energy and device performance, and the profile type. The decision considered in this study is also deliberate for comparison [4]. Mobile devices are evolving into powerful computing tools that are being used rapidly. However, users of these devices often face many problems when running rich resource-requiring applications on the device itself. Remote clouds have connectivity issues. Sometimes, user environments contain critical computing resources. In [5], the author claimed that the nearest mobile device can effectively be used as cloud power. In recent times, emerging mobile applications such as health, AR, virtual reality, vehicle recognition, ITS, UAV, and offloading have become the adopted methods to remove some inherent limitations of mobile devices. Using this advanced mechanism, specialized algorithms that decide to offload tasks remotely observe objective indicators [6].

In [7], a new Mobile Edge Computing (MEC) network equipped with unmanned aerial vehicles (UAV) was introduced, which is a novel approach. This considers both power consumption and latency minimization. A heuristic algorithm is proposed, which consists of an assigned task, DE-assisted process, and non-dominant quick-sort technique. In [8], a fairness-sensitive task offload and resource allocation problem was investigated for a wireless metropolitan area network (WMAN) equipped with mobile edge computing (MEC) servers. In [9], the problem of service offload decisions in a vehicle edge computing environment was discussed, and the possibility was given for the same. In [10], single-cell multiuser computing was considered in a multichannel interference wireless environment. In [11], the optimization of power consumption, latency, and financial costs is discussed in terms of overall operating costs. In [12], a wireless communication network, transmitter (PT), and multiple fog servers (FS) were used. The objective is to maximize the computation speed of the system by optimizing the energy beamforming, time allocation, and other computational factors [12]. In [13], it was discussed that there are many offloading techniques for edge networks. Two of the largest offloading types are, (i) static and (ii) dynamic offloading. These two techniques can be classified into three categories: (i) optimization of edge task reduction latency, (ii) optimization of maximization to save UE energy by offloading tasks to the periphery, and (iii) a combination of power consumption optimization and task execution time. In [14], a summary of high-performance, energy-saving, and safety aspects was introduced. Many studies related to mobile computation offloading (MCO) have been conducted in recent years, but there is still a lot to do that consider some performance parameters, exploring elements of fault tolerance from execution time alone at the end of mobile and cloud, task execution patterns, and development orchestration a safer solution [14]. Mobile cloud computing is mobile device performance and efficiency because applications are outsourced reduce complexity and execution time by sending to a remote server for execution. This has also proven to be a suitable solution for smart devices with a limited storage capacity. Discharge technology was analyzed collectively in [15]. In [16], an adaptive offloading model was proposed for mobile data-stream applications. The proposed algorithm was introduced to improve the data stream application performance and energy consumption of the parameters. This study introduces optimal computational relaxation. The application is split into multiple tasks and discharged based on the type and execution pattern. An outsourcing model has been proposed as the principle of mobile cloud computing. Unloading the intended models considers them for communication and execution cost tasks on the cloud. Tasks that run locally on the cloud or phone. Devices are fully synchronized with each other and exchange information that can serve as input for one device and output for the other [17]. In [18], outsourcing decision-making in distributed systems, aims to improve the offload success rate and reduce the energy consumption of mobile devices and other related factors. In [19], the task was formulated as an integer linear problem (ILP) and the authors proposed a two-stage time-driven strategy for solving the problem with minimal response. In [20], different types of algorithms were used for partitioning and offloading programs to improve the performance and save energy.

2.3   Computation Offloading Techniques

2.3.1   MAUI Architecture

The MAUI architecture saves energy on smart devices as the primary working procedure for offloading. In this framework, the entire application runs on our mobile device owing to its continuous profiling process. This avoids the complexity of execution at a distant location. Data were collected using a profiler. It is necessary to acquire information about the part of the code that is running locally and the part that should be running in the cloud, and to select the part of the code by partitioning methods that can maximize the power saving of mobile devices. It handles any errors that may occur, such as network or equipment failure. The detection is based on a timeout mechanism. In connection failures, the MAUI returns control to the local server. The local server either regenerates the process locally or finds another MAUI server to restart the process. This mechanism can save energy in smart devices [15, 20].

2.3.2   Clone-Cloud Based Model

The clone-cloud-based model is a mechanism that fills the gap between the truth and consistency between mobile devices and cloud computing. Various technologies have been developed to address issues related to efficient ejection. Function partitioning by adopting run-time parameters was calculated based on the device storage capacity performance and provided by clone and network code migration costs. A clone cloud is a challenge in delivering basic advanced execution mobile applications using cloud resources. The virtualization of methods that depend on local hardware

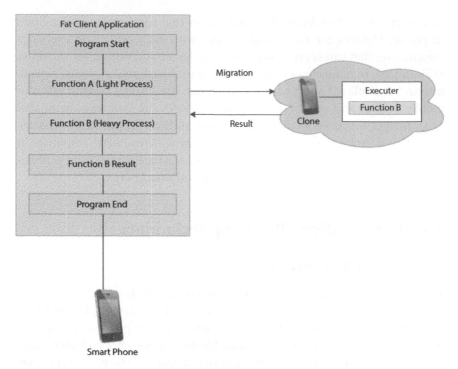

Figure 2.1 Clone-cloud-based framework.

can be run efficiently both in the cloud and by fostering RPC-based local cellular mechanism device components [20]. The clone-cloud-based framework is illustrated in Figure 2.1.

2.3.3   Cuckoo Design

Cuckoo is a renowned open-source framework used for the development of Android and Eclipse. This provides a simple programming model. The developers enable a single interface for the local and distant location implementation of the framework. The Cuckoo determines the location where computations are performed at runtime. In addition, the Cuckoo framework contains a generic remote server. It includes a smartphone application for collecting remote server addresses [20]. A remote server address is required to offload the task from a local device.

2.3.4 MACS Architecture

The MACS architecture is similar to Cuckoo Design; however, in this architecture, dynamic code partitioning is involved at runtime, whereas in cuckoo design, it involves static code partitioning. This is the basic difference between Cuckoo design and MACS architecture. First, Rewriter writes an AIDL stub interface for everyone. At compilation time, this execution should be performed locally or on a cloud server. The second is remote service. The driver forms a dummy remote-control implementation run by the programmer. Cuckoo Resource Manager monitors the accessibility of both local and remote servers. Allocate resources and make them available whenever possible. Systems using the Cuckoo model can use Java VM to outsource it to a remote server [15].

2.3.5 AHP and TOPSIS Design Technique

The application of the TOPSIS and AHP techniques is to integrate the Geographical Information System into dams. TOPSIS was used to select dam sites. Therefore, after the implementation of both methods, the suitability for dam site selection in new regional contexts was compared, assessed, and investigated. It can be said that TOPSIS method is more suitable for dam site selection problems. MCDM can potentially provide a birds-eye view of initial computations to reduce costs and accomplish studies on dam site selection [15, 20].

2.3.6 Energy Aware Design for Workflows

To save energy and improve work performance, an approach was proposed for the nearest cloudlet. First, we must decide which cloudlet should be selected on the smartphone side. The best swap node is selected based on various real-time attributes. We should then observe every task in turn and decide whether outsourcing is necessary. The workflow engine prepares a cluster hierarchy when outsourcing is required. The task is then considered a root node. Task clustering can reduce the energy required for communication [15].

2.3.7 MCSOS Architecture

MCSOS stands for a Mobile Cloud with Smart Offloading System. IT was also proposed for offloading to the nearest cloudlet, as in the previous study. The MCSOS framework leverages and optimizes the MapReduce programming model to optimize power consumption. Depending on the resources, slave nodes can either run tasks locally or offload them to the Computing Associated cloud (CA cloud) [15].

2.3.8   Cloudlet

Cloudlets are small data centers or computer clusters designed to rapidly deliver cloud-computing services to mobile devices. The goal of cloudlets is to enable applications running on mobile devices by using low-latency, high-bandwidth, and reduced-latency wireless connectivity, and by physically hosting cloud computing resources, such as virtual machines, close to the accessing mobile device. To improve the response time, this is intended to eliminate latency delays in wide area networks (WANs) that can occur in traditional cloud computing models [15].

2.3.9   Jade

Jade maximized the benefit of energy aware offloading. The Jade framework automatically switches apps running on mobile devices in remote runtime optimized for wireless connectivity, power consumption, and server capacity. To check how much energy Ngoc saves on mobile devices, the authors ran the facial recognition app on the user device. The application performs facial recognition for over 50 images, where each image is less than 200 KB in size. The Jade framework reduces power consumption for face recognition applications [15].

2.3.10   Phone2Cloud

Phone2Cloud is a semiautomated offload framework. To run our application in the cloud and obtain results, it must be changed manually during preparation. Outsourcing decisions are made by static analysis, which considers the user's delay-tolerance threshold. For delay-tolerant applications, this framework uses a simple model that assumes a Wi-Fi connection. Thresholds are defined based on expected delay transfers to offload data to Wi-Fi [15]. The Phone2Cloud architecture is illustrated in Figure 2.2.

Table 2.1 shows a comparative discussion of different available offloading techniques related to mobile cloud computing. Different techniques are available for offloading, and among them, many have some advantages and disadvantages, which are listed in the above table.

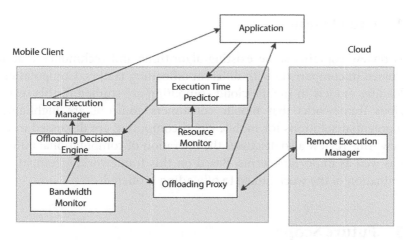

Figure 2.2 Phone2Cloud architecture.

Table 2.1 Comparative discussion among different computation offloading techniques.

Offloading model	Dynamic annotations	Task level granularity	Energy saving	Performance improvement	Security aspect	Adaptive offloading
MAUI	√	-	√	–	–	√
Clone-Cloud Based Model	√					
Cuckoo	–					
MACS	√					
AHP and TOPSIS						
Energy Aware Design	√	√	√	√	–	√
MCSOS			√			
Cloudlet						
Jade	√		√			
Phone2cloud						

2.4 Conclusion

This review contains some existing algorithms and techniques that are discussed in comparison with different offloading factors. Computational offloading models in mobile cloud computing are studied in this review. Various frameworks that mobile consumers confront are highlighted, and potential solutions for mobile cloud computing are discussed in this review. This review also discusses the operation of computational offloading as well as important terms. Based on this framework, a comparative examination of the work linked to offloading is offered.

2.5 Future Scope

In future work, the existing algorithms and techniques may be used to find new energy-saving and delay-reducing work related to computation offloading of mobile devices. As new applications are coming with huge computational load and they are required to be served in a very short time as well as with very low energy consumption of the mobile device, efficient techniques can be adopted to reduce latency and energy consumption.

2.6 Acknowledgement

We extend our sincere acknowledgement to Prof. Debabshis De, Maulana Abul Kalam Azad University of Technology, West Bengal, India and Dr. Anwesha Mukherkee, Mahishadal Raj College, West Bengal, India for their guidance and endeavor support to carry out research work in the field of mobile cloud computing.

References

1. Zheng, T., Wan, J., Zhang, J., Jiang, C., Jia, G., A survey of computation off-loading in edge computing. *2020 International Conference on Computer, Information and Telecommunication Systems (CITS)*, Hangzhou, China, IEEE, 2020.
2. Zhang, Z. and Li, S., A survey of computational offloading in mobile cloud computing. *4th IEEE International Conference on Mobile Cloud Computing, Services, and Engineering*, Oxford, UK, 2016.

3. Misra, S., Wolfinger, B.E., Achuthananda, M.P., Chakraborty, T., Sankar, N., Das, S., Auction-based optimal task offloading in mobile cloud computing. *IEEE Syst. J.*, 13, 3, 2978–2985, 2019.

4. Mathur, R.P. and Sharma, M., A survey on computational offloading in mobile cloud computing. *2019 Fifth International Conference on Image Information Processing (ICIIP)*, Shimla, India, IEEE, 2019.

5. Fernando, N., Loke, S.W., Rahayu, W., Computing with nearby mobile devices: A work sharing algorithm for mobile edge-clouds. *IEEE Transaction Cloud Computing*, 7, 2, 329–343, 2019.

6. Shakarami, A. and Ghobaei-Arani, M., A survey on the computation offloading approaches in mobile computing: A machine learning-based perspective. *Sci. Direct*, 182, 1–24, 2020, https://doi.org/10.1016/j.comnet.2020.107496.

7. Cheng, Y., Liao, Y., Zhai, X., Energy-efficient resource allocation for UAV-empowered mobile edge computing system. *2020 IEEE/ACM 13th International Conference on Utility and Cloud Computing (UCC)*, Leicester, UK, IEEE, 2020.

8. Zhou, J. and Zhang, X., Fairness-aware task offloading and resource allocation in cooperative mobile-edge computing. *IEEE Internet Things J.*, 9, 5, 3812–3824, 2022.

9. Qi, Q., Wang, J., Ma, Z., Sun, H., Zhang, L., Liao, J., Knowledge-driven service offloading decision for vehicular edge computing: A deep reinforcement learning approach. *IEEE Trans. Vehicular Technol.*, 68, 5, 4192–4203, 2019.

10. Liang, S., Wan, H., Qin, T., Li, J., Chen, W., Multi-user computation offloading for mobile edge computing: a deep reinforcement learning and game theory approach. *IEEE 20th International Conference on Communication Technology*, Nanning, China, IEEE, 2020.

11. Chen, W., Yaguchi, Y., Naruse, K., Watanobe, Y., Nakamura, K., QoS-aware robotic streaming workflow allocation in cloud robotics systems. *IEEE Trans. On Serv. Computing*, 14, 2, 544–558, 2021.

12. Zheng, H., Xiong, K., Fan, P., Zhong, Z., Wireless powered communication networks assisted by multiple fog servers. *2019 IEEE International Conference on Communications Workshops (ICC Workshops)*, Shanghai, China, IEEE, 2019.

13. Maray, M. and Shuja, J., Computation offloading in mobile cloud computing and mobile edge computing: Survey, taxonomy, and open issues. *Hindawi Mobile Inf. Syst.*, 1–17, 2022, https://doi.org/10.1155/2022/1121822.

14. Kumar, S., Khanna, A., Tyagi, M., Fore, V., A survey of mobile computation offloading: applications, approaches and challenges. *2018 International Conference on Advances in Computing and Communication Engineering (ICACCE-2018)*, Paris, France, 2018, doi: 10.1109/ICACCE.2018.8441740.

15. Bajpai, A. and Nigam, S., A study on the techniques of computational offloading from mobile devices to cloud. *Adv. Comput. Sci. Technol.*, 10, 7, 2037–2060, 2017.

16. Khanna, A., Kero, A., Kumar, D., Agarwal, A., Adaptive mobile computation offloading for data stream applications. *2017 3rd International Conference on Advances in Computing, Communication & Automation (ICACCA) (Fall)*, Dehradun, India, IEEE, 2017, doi: 10.1109/ICACCAF.2017.8344682.

17. Khanna, A., Kero, A., Kumar, D., Mobile cloud computing architecture for computation offloading. *2016 2nd International Conference on Next Generation Computing Technologies (NGCT)*, Dehradun, India, IEEE, 2016, doi: 10.1109/ NGCT.2016.7877490.

18. Shi, Y., Chen, S., Xu, X., MAGA: A mobility-aware computation offloading decision for distributed mobile cloud computing. *IEEE Internet Things*, 5, 1, 164–174, February, 2018, doi: 10.1109/JIOT.2017.2776252.

19. Yao, D., Gui, L., Hou, F., Sun, F., Mo, D., Shan, H., Load Balancing Oriented Computation Offloading in Mobile Cloudlet. *2017 IEEE 86th Vehicular Technology Conference (VTC-Fall), IEEE,* Toronto, Canada, IEEE, 2017, doi: 10.1109/ VTCFall.2017.8288336.

20. Kumar, K., Liu, J., Lu, Y.-H., Bhargava, B., A survey of computation offloading for mobile systems. *Mobile Networks Appl.*, 18, 129–140, 2013.

3

Fog Computing for Intelligent Cloud–IoT System: Optimization of Fog Computing in Industry 4.0

Mayank Patel*, Monika Bhatt and Ankush Patel

Department of Computer Science and Engineering, Geetanjali Institute of Technical Studies, Udaipur, Rajasthan, India

Abstract

In this study, we discuss the optimized and green use of Fog Computing in Industry 4.0. The idea of Industry 4.0, which uses sensor networks, automated commercial techniques, robots, wise devices and machines, and actuators, and a massive number of various records, is initialized for evaluation and processing.

In industry, the most important technology is actual time. To avoid name delays and ensure factual safety, maximum methods are completed in-house, and the most effective essential data are transmitted to the cloud garage through the community. There is a strong demand for middleware between industrial strategies/tools and the cloud to serve this purpose. The fog is the maximum logical answer for one-of-a-kind industrial scenarios. In production industries, this enables neighborhood processing and tolerable communication delays with robots and actuators. Information gathered from one type of industry technique is often unorganized and needs to be preprocessed locally using a GIS to be refined before being transferred to the cloud. Fog computing performs a critical role in exclusive Industry 4.0 packages by solving distinctive issues. However, the deployment of fog computers in Industry 4.0 also faces exclusive types of very traumatic situations related to programmability, security, heterogeneity, and interoperability. This could save a variety of times and assets desired for big record transfers.

Keywords: Industrial internet of things, industry 4.0, latency, layers, revolution, RFID, server, smart cities

Corresponding author: mayank999_udaipur@yahoo.com

Chandan Banerjee, Anupam Ghosh, Rajdeep Chakraborty and Ahmed A. Elngar (eds.) Fog Computing for Intelligent Cloud IoT Systems, (45–70) © 2024 Scrivener Publishing LLC

3.1   Introduction

3.1.1   Industry 4.0

Industry 4.0 is changing the way companies deliver, create, and offer items. Producers are coordinating unused advances in their manufacturing plants and operations, counting the Web of Things (IoT), cloud computing and analytics, fake insights, and machine learning [1]. These keen manufacturing plants are prepared with advanced sensors, inserted computer programs, and robots that collect and analyze information to form better choices. Commerce insights incorporate information from ERP, supply chains, customers, and other trade forms to form and move forward with modern chronicled perceivability and understanding levels to stow away higher costs.

This technology provides maximum performance, predictive maintenance, improvements in personal development, and unprecedented efficiency and customer responsiveness. The development of a smart factory gives manufacturing companies exclusive access to the fourth revolution [2]. Examination of enormous amounts of information collected by portable sensors gives real-time perception into generation highlights and gives instruments to actualize prescient support once time is diminished. The use of cutting-edge IoT devices in smart factories can increase efficiency and improve operations. Real-time AI-driven insights help retailers transform their analytics, reduce productivity, and save time and money.

With limited resources, well-managed employees can set up cloud-connected cell phones and monitor the production process from anywhere. Search algorithms allow companies to identify errors immediately rather than later, but they are particularly expensive to fix [3]. The principles and technologies of Industry 4.0 can be applied to any type of business, including production and manufacturing as well as oil and gas extraction, mining, and other industries. Augmented reality, virtual reality, and artificial intelligence are also components of Industry 4.0.

The Industrial Revolution means a great change in production and business life with the use of new and innovative technologies. Industry 4.0 began in 1784 with the introduction of water machinery and electricity for large-scale steel production. At one time, we were flooded with the invention of airplanes and cars.

The third mechanical insurgency began in 1969 with the presentation of electronic mechanized computers. In Industry 3.0, machines are currently being utilized.

We are now in the era of Industry 4.0, which has started with cyber and physical systems.

The foremost imperative of the virtual advanced world, Industry 4.0, connects both frameworks and machines within the manufacturing plant [4]. For example, on the off chance that one machine is not working appropriately at that point the machine, I can inform the moment machine, and the moment machine will begin up so that the comparison work can be completed without human impact. Machines can do things and work together without a human-machine interface.

In Industry 4.0, the factories depend on other factories. Suppose there are two factories; the factory is overloaded with production, the factory can be asked to start production, and the factory will automatically transfer the work to the 2nd factory without any interference. In Industry 4.0, machines and systems are controlled in remote locations using various devices and mobile applications.

Let us say your factory is in Delhi and you are in Maharashtra, and you want to control machines and systems to control machines and systems with mobile phones and other devices. Manufacturers can access their equipment for maintenance and software updates, and each system can be tracked on the internet using a unique identifier [5]. Admin messages and other remote actions are easily accessible in remote locations. In general, it can be said that the revolution is defined with the help of information and communication technology, which puts intelligent machine and process networks into operation. The key technologies of Industry 4.0 focuses on the following:

1. The Web of Things is the establishment of Industry 4.0; therefore, these two terms are frequently utilized together. Most bodies of Industry 4.0 (materials, robots, machines, production lines, and items) utilize RFID sensors and labels to supply real-time data regarding their status, trade, or area. Innovation permits workers to better oversee the supply chain, make, and alter items faster, dodge item deficiencies, track client inclinations, select items and item deals, and so on.

2. Advanced Robotics—Industry 4.0 brings more control to the following era of independent robots. Independent robots are modified to perform assignments with negligible human mediation and a shift in length and capability from rambles for stock following independent cellular robots for picking and overhauling [6]. Prepared with the most recent

computer program, manufactured insights, sensors, and computer vision, these robots can perform complex and delicate errands, such as hearing, perusing, and reacting to data obtained from the environment.

3. Artificial Intelligence—Machine learning and AI-based analytics have also been utilized over time. This information is utilized to progress choice making and computerization across all ranges of supply chain administration. Trade administration, fabrication, R&D and building, commerce administration (EAM), and acquisition.

4. Cloud Computing—Cloud Computing could be a "zero-sum virtual commerce change apparatus." From manufactured insights and machine learning to the Web of Things, it supports innovation and empowers businesses to innovate [7]. Data-driven Industry 4.0 advancements dwell within the cloud, whereas cyber and physical frameworks shape the center of Industry 4.0, communication and collaboration on the cloud.

5. Cyber Defense—With the greater use of connectivity and the key realities of Industry 4.0, strong cybersecurity has become a necessity. Businesses can reduce data risk-document breaches and service delays by improving issue detection, prevention, and response using zero-trust execution architectures and technologies, including machine learning and blockchain productivity of the entire network.

6. Additive Manufacturing—Additive manufacturing, or 3D printing, is another important technology at the forefront of Industry 4.0. Originally used as a rapid prototyping tool, 3D printing is now used in applications ranging from mass customization to distribution. For example, 3D printing reduces logistics and costs by allowing products and warehousing to create location information in a digital inventory and display the needs.

Advantages of Industry 4.0

1. Smart products
2. Smart factories
3. Smart assets
4. Empowered people

How Industry 4.0 is used in the Internet of Things. We explain the Internet of Things as communication and data exchange using the Internet from one device to another. For example, you have a smart watch that uses a sensor to alert the user based on body temperature. Suppose your body temperature is high, then the smart watch will remind you to visit the doctor once to check, then the smart watch will send you a message that "do you want to see a doctor" yes or no, and if you click yes, the smart watch will automatically they will send a message to the hospital app to book an appointment for you, in short IoT is a network of physical objects capable of collecting data using sensors and exchanging it with each other or over the internet.

We will now discuss how the concept of Industry 4.0 is used in advanced robotics that are commonly used today in manufacturing units, the medical industry, and space research programs. Robots are programmable machines that can perform a series of actions automatically or semi-autonomously [8]. Advanced robots are trained and taught by humans. Robots communicate work alongside each other and learn from humans. Robots reduce the human workload.

Now, the term AI is introduced in Industry 4.0, and we know that Google on Android phones, if we say "Hey Google, please call XYZ," then Google can recognize your voice and track your intersection and immediately call XYZ. In short, we can define artificial intelligence is a computer program that allows machines to simulate human behavior such as learning, planning, and cognitive reasoning. Machine learning is one of the most common applications in part manufacturing and problem-solving. Machine learning allows machines to learn from past data and to predict the future. This helps to improve productivity and business.

However, if we look around, we will find that fog computing in Industry 4.0 is not so famous; it is a kind of hidden gem. We need to bring it out, study more about it, implement it in many fields, and then we will see how it revolutionizes data storage, data transfer, and access to stored data.

3.1.2 Fog Computing

Managing the data generated by Internet of Things (IoT) sensors and actuators is one of the most challenging aspects of implementing an IoT system. Traditional IoT cloud systems face large, volatile, and high latency issues in cloud ecosystems. One solution is to use a government-distributed model to determine the application, management, and data analysis of the network itself [9]. This method is called the fog calculation.

Fog computing may be a layered demonstration that provides all shared computing resources.

This bolsters the dispersion of conveyed and inactivity-delicate administrations, counting physical issues (physical or virtual) between shrewd gadgets and surrounding (discuss) administrations. Blunder hubs set delicate and back information administration and communication. They can be installed vertically (to support separation), horizontally (to support consolidation), or in groups based on the distance from nodes to failed smart devices. Fog computing reduces response times to requests from/to support applications and provides network connectivity for local services for endpoints and central services, as needed. Fog is not considered a mandatory layer in these ecosystems, and the fog layer is not required to have centralized services (weather) to support the intelligent functions of edge devices.

Depending on what is best for supporting the functionality of the end device, different use cases may have different models. The choice of this representation was based on the goal of capturing complex architectures, including cloud services. The devices that constitute fog infrastructure are called fog nodes [10]. In fog computing, all storage capacity, computing power, data, and applications are located between the cloud and physical host. All these functions are located on the mainframe.

This makes the processing faster, as it is performed almost where the data are created. It increases the efficiency of the system and is used to provide greater security.

3.1.3   Fog Nodes

Fog nodes are the building blocks of the cloud computing architecture. A failed node is either a physical component (port, switch, router, server, etc.) or a virtual component (virtualized switch, virtual machine, cloud, etc.). Associated with smart terminals or access networks to provide computing services to these devices. Failure to know its geographical distribution and ideological position in the context of the group. In addition, the cloud provides a type of data management and communication between the layers of the network where the edge devices are located and cloud services, or, if necessary, central devices (the cloud). To deliver the fog job, the fog operates in a centralized or decentralized manner and can be set up to allow the fog to communicate with each other to provide services or aggregated interaction to ensure horizontal reliability in the field-place scalability [11]. Authentication through mirroring or scaling mechanisms.

Fog computing can be used in the following scenarios.

- It is used when only selected data are sent to the cloud. These selected data were selected for long-term storage and less frequent access to the host.
- It is used when data need to be analyzed in fractions of a second, i.e., low latency.
- It is used when there is a need to provide many services over a large area, in different geographical locations.
- A strictly calculated and processed device must use calculation error.

Concrete examples of the use of fog computing are IoT devices (e.g., Vehicle-to-Car Alliance in Europe), devices with sensors, and cameras (IIoT—Industrial Internet of Things), etc.

Characteristics of fog computing:
The following five features are important for distinguishing weather from other forms of visualization. However, smart devices or IoT users may not be able to use all functions when using cloud services.

Context Location and Low Latency—Mistake calculation gives the least conceivable idleness, as the blunder hubs know their position in setting as an entire and the idleness of communication with other hubs. The roots of cloud computing can be followed back to early plans to bolster wealthy administrations at the edge of the arrangement, counting low-latency applications. Because these hubs are frequently related to savvy gadgets, the examination and reaction of information created by these gadgets is faster than normal cloud administrations or information centers.

Geographical distribution—Not at all like centralized clouds, cloud centers on administrations and applications that require huge but geologically characterized dispersion. For example, cloud computing will play a vital part in providing quality gushing administrations for specialists moving vehicles and getting to substance on thruways and streets.

Heterogeneity—Haze computing underpins the collection and handling of heterogeneous information obtained from distinctive communication systems.

Coordination and Collaboration—Different support of some services (live services are a good example) requires collaboration among different providers. For this reason, cloud products must be able to work together and services must be integrated across the country.

Combined Failed Node Clusters—Failover computing is flexible across clusters or clusters and can be used for flexible computing, integration, data transfer, state change, etc.

3.2   How Fog Computing with IIoT Brings Revolution

This section discusses how sequentially supporting IIoT's existing capabilities and bugs can drive IIoT to realize its true potential. Middleware such as fog can unlock the full potential of IIoT. Drain oversees the assets and communication between the fundamental hubs and can provide nearby forms [12]. IIoT arrangements can contain distinctive sorts of "objects" such as sensors, actuators, gadgets, and administrators. Many gadgets and sensors have limited resources.

For illustration, a weight sensor on item transport or an entryway sensor is mounted on an entryway. Owing to their small size measure, these instruments cannot be scaled to perform critical assignments such as information investigation and substance acknowledgment. Moreover, the small estimate of the sensor permits battery control, which poses another vitality saving issue. Centers such as haze can assist in providing vital information and extending administration errands. From a common point of view, the cloud can be cloud, edge, micro data center, or nano information center (NaDa/nDC), depending on the wants of the business.

This introduces climate sensors and makes them more difficult to operate. Moreover, mist can screen the control utilization of each sensor and appropaitely alter the information era recurrence. Moreover, clouds can be utilized for sun-oriented vitality, warm vitality, and so on. Moreover, it can find and oversee other vitality sources, such as diverse IoT benefit suppliers that have their own frameworks and require ways to collaborate with strides. Sis can address issues with appropriate interoperability, multiprocess elucidation, and application programming interfaces (APIs).

Short-term communication is another imperative error that cloud computer programs can perform in IIoT environments. In this case, a sensor running on Bluetooth or Zigbee requires an arrangement to communicate with the inaccessible IIoT. The publish/subscribe strategy is valuable in the IIoT environment [13]. Within the publish/subscribe show, the person who creates the document is called the publisher and the recipient of the document is called the subscriber. Publisher/subscriber (Pub/Sub) is a great way to share information anonymously between producers and consumers.

In a business environment, middleware plays an important role in mediating and delivering feed/sub services, creating opportunities to improve business processes. With the Internet of Things, robots will have a significant impact on the performance of complex processes and operations. Subsequently, the central robot must be adaptable and capable of controlling to control the robot, particularly in multi-collaborative situations, such as the Mechanical Web of Things. The Robot Working Framework (ROS) is an illustration of middleware. Haze computing can play a critical role in nearly any commerce environment [14].

This study was divided into three parts: Mining, Manufacturing and Automobiles.

Diverse businesses have diverse openings as a part of the IoT or IIoT vision. There are a few curious trade zones where IoT can be utilized with the cloud to attain keen commercial objectives in the future.

1. Mining—Mining is one of the most important industries requiring data analytics. As population increases, the mining industry also increases. Mining involves many risks and is expensive. According to the IBM1, everyone uses it for approximately 3 days.

It uses millions of pounds of mineral and metal resources in life. The use of electronic products and related electronic equipment leads to efficiency and eliminates unnecessary costs and wastage. The machine downtime and operating costs are also more predictable. Gather information before you start drilling to save time and money. Similarly, the use of self-drilling or well-drilling machines and autonomous vehicles is an example of modernizing the mining industry through the use of IoT business models. Mining is also one of the most adventurous industries with some risks. For example, coal or stone mining often involves hazards, such as rockfalls and inhalation. Some of the degradation processes involve the release of pollutants and chemicals. Therefore, using sensor networks to gather information and warn workers in advance is of great help. Additionally, common area fog data can be processed on a large scale to improve the accuracy of sensor networks, especially for weather applications. Maintenance and energy use also major concerns in the mining industry, as they require large machinery and considerable time to complete all mining and harvesting. With the Internet of Things, the mining industry can improve machine control and energy efficiency.

2. Smart Grid and Energy—Shrewd lattice could be an unused sort of network that has been affirmed in later a long time. Keen lattices incorporate renewable vitality, tall productivity vitality, keen meters, and shrewd gadgets. In conventional dispersions, power is conveyed to clients in a month-to-month charge. In any case, with the increment in computerization and individual well-being and the accessibility of different electronic gadgets and machines, the request has become exceptionally solid. Subsequently, two-way communication between clients and e-commerce companies is imperative. Usually, this is the genuine concept of the shrewd

framework. In a savvy framework, control is dispersed to neighborhood dissemination companies (MOLs) that work as microgrids to supply conclusion clients.

Telecom operators are also involved in the construction of smart grids because the entire smart grid concept is not limited to electricity companies. Telecommunications companies have contracted with local service providers to provide two-way communication between service providers and smart meters through an Advanced Metering Infrastructure (AMI). The AMI provides real-time updates to utility service providers. In return, service providers will provide feedback and instructions to the home network (HAN), business networks (IANs), and home networks (BANs) for a certain period, according to the usage needs of the people and the costs of household goods and electricity, smart homes, and smart offices. AMI consists of advanced sensors, smart meters, communication networks (possibly provided by third parties), IT infrastructure, and application and data management. The problem is not only data management, but the integration of smart grids and advanced technology will create large amounts of huge data. This information should be processed in terms of maintenance and pricing. Therefore, it is important for service providers to clearly define their communication and infrastructure requirements. Good communication between energy suppliers and customers can reduce or even prevent failures and make them more predictable. This is important because many businesses face huge losses in unexpected situations. Different types of web applications contain different types of information. A smart home requires less communication than a smart home does, whereas a smart home requires more communication. Therefore, advanced data communication and data-flow control systems must be developed and implemented. Different topology configurations require different procedures, particularly in business environments. Transportation is moving from sensors, equipment, and systems to smart meters. Another flow is between the smart meter and the usage data. Additionally, the number of flows for all types of smart meters (gas, electricity, water, etc.) is increasing. A common approach to traffic management is software-defined networking (SDN) and network function virtualization (NFV). As today's electronic systems become more and more distributed and distributed in the computing role, middleware such as the fog micro data center with SDN and NFV capabilities will play an important role in information management. Thus, the data center can manage microgrids.

3. Transport—Transport is an imperative trade and is the establishment of each nation. Buses, metros and trams, trucks, buses, and private cars constitute a portion of the transportation industry. Transportation frameworks

(ITSs) are a subset of transportation-related web of things. Roadside units (RSUs) can be prepared using sprayers to enact ITS. For example, the cloud can realize Web of Vehicles (IoV), back in-car amusement, provide location-based administrations, and provide savvy stopping and lighting to unravel activity issues and crises. Give great lighting. Providing real-time data on activity and open transport to people on foot and drivers is a case of cloud-based IoT shrewdly transportation.

4. Waste Management—The mechanization of squander administration forms is one of the points of squander administration. Rapid devastation can lead to the development of numerous illnesses. Moreover, this makes squander items recyclable. The collection and preparation of squander can be related to the reuse industry, so that the fundamental assets are apportioned in an opportune way, agreeing to the sort and volume of certain sorts of squander (glass, paper, metal, natural squander, etc.). Other benefits include vitality (WtE) and mechanical squander administration.

5. Food Industry—Nourishment review of nourishment bundling, solidified nourishment, and natural squander is a portion of the nourishment industry. The combination of IoT-enabled nourishment promotion and information analytics has created an urban nourishment industry that jams nourishment quality and diminishes squander.

6. Agriculture—It ought to come as no astonish that sensor systems play a vital role in farming. More critically, VS gets to be imperative in a few circumstances where numerous sensors are required for diverse circumstances and circumstances. Fertilizer rambles can be used for planting, checking, and showering crops.

7. Marketing Strategy—Many countries have different advertising and marketing laws, so advertising can be wise. Larger logos were allowed in certain areas. These posters are large digital screens that can be adjusted from a central location. Similarly, shopping malls and supermarket ads can be customized for each customer. For example, clients who habitually shop at an expansive store like Walmart can make accounts to get advancements and upgrades. When the client enters the store, in the case of an area disappointment within the store/hypermarket, the customer's store begins with communication by means of the customer's account through Wi-Fi. Based on this data, Mist screens client fulfillment by analyzing the nourishment items purchased by clients [15]. Additionally, cloud-based shared publicizing frameworks utilize area-following to decide the time a client spends on a specific walkway. Advanced screens can be set in significant places, permitting clients to see advertisements and offers based on their past buying history and current patterns.

8. Third Best Delivery—In addition to smartphone taxi services such as Uber and Careem, many delivery services are available. UberEATS, Talabat, Food Panda, and Couch Potato are examples of food delivery services from around the country. Similarly, TCS Hazir and TCS HazirSubKuch are popular courier services in Pakistan. For example, TCS HazirSubKuch is always at your service in Pakistan to deliver urgent goods to friends and family, buy groceries, or buy medicines from pharmacies. Different services may require more detailed information and context. Examples include changing essential medications if they are not available, allergy information when purchasing medications, and tracking the location where the product has been delivered (for example, someone in the car). In this case, special fog is important for local operations. In addition to the applications mentioned above, the IIoT can be used to receive data packets when the receiver is not in the field. For example, if the customer is far away and the courier arrives at the door, the door will be opened on a mobile phone. When the delivery person rang, the user's phone rang. Press the phone button to open the door, and the delivery person lets the button in. A door-mounted camera displays the status of the user's phone in real-time. When the door lock is closed, it automatically closes and sends a confirmation message to the user's mobile phone. This service is convenient if your family works and has trouble receiving packages or mail, as delivery can occur during business hours.

9. Smart Parking—In some countries, municipalities provide parking is provided to external entities that act as industries. In addition to smart parking recommendations, parking can be improved by notifying vehicles of the available parking spaces in real time. Recommendations can be made based on healthy trends in parks, which can vary depending on the season, weather, and local events, for example, more contextual recognition, such as sales in a specific store.

We have discussed how fog computing combined with the Industrial Internet of Things (IIoT) can lead to progress in many areas related to Industry 4.0. The main question is how to apply fog computing on a large scale in Industry 4.0.

Cloud computing must be replaced by fog computing. In many cases, uploading and retrieving data from the cloud has high latency, which slows down the process; thus, fog is suitable for this situation.

Reason for use:
Fog computing—Fog models have advantages in applications such as advertising, computing, and entertainment and are suitable for data analysis and data collection sites. Terminal services such as junction boxes and access

points can be easily implemented through atomization. This improves the quality of service and reduces the latency [16]. The main goal of atomization is to provide user-oriented information at the edge of the network.

The benefits of innovation are as follows:

1. It will significantly reduce information traffic in the network, reduce congestion, costs, and delays, remove bottlenecks in the centralized computer system, and improve the security of encrypted data. Virtualization and virtualization systems reduce the exposure to adversaries and increase scalability.
2. Removing the core computing environment reduces the number of large blocks and points of failure.
3. Security is improved by encrypting the data in transit to the edge of the network.
4. Edge computing provides end-users with not only a second-level solution but also a high level of scalability, reliability, and fault tolerance.
5. This consumes less bandwidth.

Fog from the clouds:

Cloud computing uses remote servers, rather than local servers or computers, to store, manage, and process data. It has many advantages. This not only allows businesses to reduce storage resources to free up physical space in the office, but is also safer than storing data locally. Therefore, if local storage fails, the backups are stored in the cloud. Instead of emailing the file, one can free up the bandwidth (but increase the size) by emailing the link to the recipient.

Employees can work anywhere and access information from any network device. According to Gartner, the cloud service market grew by 18% in 2017. However, cloud computing also has disadvantages, the biggest of which is security. Employee and customer information can be exposed if the server where all computer systems are located fails. Depending on the size of the case, this could compromise the data of thousands of users.

It may be an encryption frame of encryption so that no one can take your information on the off chance that your server is compromised. Rosario Culmone and Maria Concetta De Vivo (two computer researchers from the College of Camerino in Italy) recently distributed a paper on cloud computing. "We report a method that employments the organize in an offbeat way to render information undetectable," he composed within the Universal Diary of Electronic Security and Advanced Forensics. "Intangible implies never found." Records are shared on open or private systems and are accessible to downloaders and uploaders. Stay away from your favorite eye.

Increased performance:
Cloud computing is more effective than cloud computing alone This may be because a few applications or administrations are run by the inserted savvy devices.

It was not as it included usefulness and memory to gadgets, such as shrewd lights and other Web of Things (IoT) gadgets, but also powers the framework. The edge exchanges collected information and sends the collected information to the cloud. Currently, one-third of all the information collected by IoT sensors is analyzed *in situ*. In any case, this share is expected to extend as IoT develops. Subsequently, cloud computing will become an enormous commercial tool.

The advantage of 5G:
Fog computing is now just an idea, and it is not clear how it will work. Ideally, IT can move seamlessly from the cloud to the edge (or cloud), based on operational needs. However, this depends on the availability of dynamically allocated data at the runtime. In addition to the benefits mentioned above, cloud computing means that less data need to be sent to the cloud and saves on data transfer costs. 5G data rates are expected to reach Europe in the next few years, with download speeds up to 10 Gbps.

This will allow more devices to connect to the IoT and provide it with more data for processing and analysis.

Fog computing can help achieve this and realize many benefits of 5G. As the Internet of Things continues to grow, cloud computing plays an important role in making businesses more efficient and effective. We believe that optimization is necessary and innovative in Business 4.0; however, to fully understand this, we first need to understand how the cloud works.

Let us take a closer look at the cloud computing architecture.

Fog Computing Architecture
The fog computing architecture consists of a body and elements in hardware and software for the use of IoT (Internet of Things) networks. IoT devices include cloud nodes, cloud aggregation nodes that use cloud data services, remote cloud storage, and local server/cloud for data storage. Let us now understand the details of the fog computing architecture.

1. IoT devices: These devices connect to IoT networks by using different types of radio and wireless devices. This device generates a large amount of data at times. Zigbee, Zwave, RFID, 6LoWPAN, HART, NFC, Bluetooth,

BLE, NFC, ISA-100.11A, etc in IoT. Various wireless technologies are used, such as the IoT protocols IPv4, IPv6, MQTT, CoAP, XMPP, and AMQP.

2. Faulty Node: Any device used for computing, storage, or connectivity in a network is called a faulty node. More failover nodes are deployed over a wider area to support end devices. The bad nodes are associated with different topologies. Artificial nodes are widely used in factories, power plants, railway edges, cars, and oil platforms. It is installed in many places according to different uses, such as examples of fake nodes, such as keyboards, embedded servers, controllers, routers, cameras, etc. In this delicate situation, success results from failure.

3. Fog collecting nodes: Each fog has its own fog collecting node. It can analyze data in seconds and minutes. Collecting IoT data on nodes can take hours or days to complete. It has a larger area. Weather data are required for the node aggregation. These are used to process sensitive information.

4. Remote cloud: All nodes fail to connect to the cloud. Non-urgent or scarce information is processed, analyzed, and stored in the cloud.

5. Local Servers and Cloud: Fog-computing architectures often use dedicated servers/clouds to store private data. Local storage is useful for data security and privacy.

3.2.1   Hierarchical Fog Computing Architecture

1. Terminal layer
   - The terminal layer is used for mobile phones, sensors, smart cars, card readers, smart cards, and so on. It is the main layer of non-functional systems that contain equipment.
   - In this layer, there are devices that can capture data. These devices are distributed in many places that are far from each other.
   - This process focuses on monitoring and data entry. Vehicles with different platforms and models are important in this process.
   - The device operates in a heterogeneous environment and uses different technologies and communication methods.

2. Fog layer
   - The cloud layer includes devices such as routers, gateways, access points, base stations, and fog servers, called fog nodes.
   - An incorrect node is at the end of the network. The edge may be one step away from the end-device. The fault node is located between the end device and the data cloud.

- A crime can be mobile, such as looking at a stationary or moving car, or at a bus stop or cafe.
- An incorrect node provides terminal services. Faulty nodes can temporarily compute, transmit, and store data.
- Core IP networking supports failover and data cloud connectivity and provides cloud interoperability and collaboration to increase processing and storage capabilities.

3. Cloud layer
- This layer comprises equipment that can provide large storage and high-performance machines (servers).
- This layer performs statistical analysis and data expansion for user backup and continuity.
- This tier has large storage capacity and high computing power.
- Big data with powerful cloud computing. The data center provides users with all basic functions of cloud computing. Data centers are scalable and provide on-demand computing services.
- Cloud layer is the end of all cloud architectures. It acts as a backup and provides regular data storage in the cloud. Data that users do not need is usually stored on the cloud.

3.2.2   Layered Fog Computing Architecture

1. Physical and virtualization layer
- This layer consists of nodes (physical and virtual). Nodes play the main role in data collection and are located at different places. Nodes often use technology to sense their surroundings.
- The sensors used in the node collect data from the environment, save the data, and then send it to the gateway to the upper layer for processing.
- The node can be a standalone device, such as a mobile phone, or part of a larger device, such as a car thermometer.

2. Analysis layer
- In this layer, we examine the nodes related to various activities.
- You can check the operating times of the nodes, their temperature, and other physical resources, the maximum battery of the device, etc.

- You can check its ability to monitor the application performance and current status.
- You can check the power consumption of the failed nodes, i.e., how much battery they use during the operation.

3. Preprocessing layer
- This layer performs various operations on the data, which are mostly analysis related.
- This layer cleans files, finds unwanted files, eliminates information clutter, and collects only useful information.
- This level of data analysis involves extracting important and relevant data from big data collected from endpoints.
- Data analysis is an important task to consider before using data for specific purposes.

4. Temporary storage
- This tier is associated with regularly distributed and refreshed data.
- This layer uses storage virtualization such as a VSAN.
- When data are moved from the middle tier to the cloud, they are data deleted from the middle tier.

5. Security operations
- These operations include data confidentiality, integrity, encryption, and decryption.
- Sis computing can include data, usage-based, data-based, and location-based privacy.
- A security layer ensures the security and privacy of the data sent to the failover.

6. Transport layer
- The main function of this layer is to send detailed security data to the cloud for permanent storage. Writing and uploading documents increases productivity.
- Data are sent through a smart gateway before being sent to the cloud. A communication protocol was chosen because of the limited resources of cloud computers.

The fog architecture is a multi-layered architecture. This is a good model for creating fog. The architecture defines the different tasks performed by different processes. The processes used by different systems, the specific devices used by different systems, and their functions and features are defined by the error architecture.

3.3   Applications of Fog Computing on Which Industries Rely

3.3.1   In the Field of Agriculture

Agriculture is an industry that benefits and transforms from climate change. The SWAMP project, which is an Intelligent Water Management Platform, is a very good example. Water is an important factor in agriculture, which uses 70% of fresh water, making it the largest consumer. Resources are often wasted owing to leaks in the distribution and use of water and in the field application process. Traditional methods, such as soil irrigation, waste a large amount of water by moisturizing areas where plants cannot benefit.

The drainage area can use water more efficiently and avoid excess water. Serious problems arise when farmers use more water to avoid bottom water. This not only reduces productivity but also leads to significant material wastage. Therefore, farmers urgently need a solution to this problem and provide appropriate solutions. That is, when the SWAMP project identified and solved these problems through IoT, data analytics, autonomous devices, etc.

With the help of fog, SWAMP developed a clear strategy for agricultural smart irrigation systems to reduce water waste. Fog computing also allows the platform to collect measurements that can be studied to improve water distribution in the field. The SWAMP project released a document on a smart farm, where real data will be collected and stored for analysis. This process discusses the use of two different methods for using fog to filter data: filtering techniques and real-time data. including temperature and humidity sensors.

Haze employs the k-nearest neighbors (kNN) calculation to filter the information and then isolate the information into different groups based on the number of values. Overwhelm is additionally working on the advancement of soil estimations from different profundity sensors for shrewd IoT-based water system. Another application of climate in agribusiness is Agrifog, an IoT-enabled cultivation framework for keen or exactness cultivation. The app was created using iFogSim. It is planned to diminish the time it takes to recognize an item in an opportune way by providing data on item information.

The IoT-fog-based arrangement is cost-effective and provides a comparison of information from cloud-based and cloud-based frameworks. Haze computing as a stage has revolutionized agribusiness; its app permits ranchers to diminish squander, obtain and handle information, and discover ways to use it.

3.3.2   In Healthcare Industry

The healthcare industry frequently depends on unused advances to make strides in its administration and arrangements. Compared to other mechanical advancements, the well-being segment benefits from computer innovation. E-health is one of the foremost imperative angles of cloud utilize in healthcare. eHealth is a web and print stage valuable for healthcare suppliers who frequently alter significantly due to technological disturbance and other changes model.

They use organizing to associate therapeutic gadgets with cloud stages. The application oversees, sends, stores, and collects the fundamental data for handling and installation. With the assistance of the cloud, the symptomatic and assessment handle will be simpler, as pros have come to electronic medical records (EMR) containing data such as X-rays, ultrasound, CT looks, or heart reports. It also protects the information within the private cloud.

With the cloud, applications can store secret information and screen it over diverse systems, rather than removing physical duplicates. The database permits specialists to obtain and analyze a patient's condition and rapidly obtain their restorative records.

3.3.3   In Smart Cities

A smart city is part of a city that uses electronic devices and collects information about citizens living or not living there. This knowledge helps improve the quality of life in cities. With better working and living conditions, people are willing to live in these smart cities. Fog computing creates a valuable, latency-sensitive, and real-time monitoring system that protects the privacy of citizens and visitors. Fog computers have already worked well in many cities, reducing traffic problems. People can share as many posts as they want, and the GPS technology can predict traffic and provide alternative routes and arrival times. Self-driving cars are another important cloud computing application that require extensive data processing. Fog computing plays an important role in bridging the low-cost metrics while executing high-bandwidth real-time tasks. Smart cities that are safe and that understand the needs of their citizens must offer smart solutions. The city council implements an intelligent waste management system that uses sensor data to improve disposal strategies. Smart cities are developing rapidly every day as new solutions emerge. Fog-computing platforms can avoid the cost of data collection.

3.3.4   In Education

Advances in technology have changed the education profession, especially in light of COVID 19. The industry already relies on a variety of electronic devices, and many professionals seeking advancement in the profession receive training through online courses. Fog-computing platforms facilitate communication and monitoring of data storage and network management. This provides system scalability, resilience, and redundancy to ensure privacy, agility, and security. Information systems in education can be structured or unstructured, and their storage is important. Fog computing, edge computing, cloud computing, enormous information analytics, and machine learning move forward with information collection and prepare and utilize it to progress execution. The utilization of cloud computing in instruction is expanding, in agreement with the prerequisites of age. It moves forward with information capacity and upgrades learning by disentangling innovation within the bequest endeavor.

3.3.5   In Entertainment

The entertainment industry has gone a long way over the last few years. Consumers and producers are in demand. ESPN, NBA TV, NBC Sports Network, ThinkSport, and other networks that have live matches, all covering large areas, such as sports fans, want quality and original content every minute of every game. Haze computing oversees video administrations and forms and conveys video administrations from cameras to the cloud and imaging gadgets. Another great case is ARQuake, an expanded reality form of celebrated Shake amusement. Mist computing moves forward with application execution by decreasing inactivity, progressing transmission capacity utilization, and securing client security.

3.4   Data Analysis

Fog Computing in all Sectors (Market Cap)

The value of the global cloud computing market is projected to be US$151.7 million by 2021. Looking ahead, the IMARC Group expects the market to grow with a CAGR of 12.7% from 2022 to 2027, reaching US$322.7 million by 2027.

Given the uncertainty surrounding COVID-19, we are monitoring and assessing its direct and indirect effects. This information is included in the report as important business support.

3.5   Illustration of Fog Computing and Application

3.5.1   Figures

A block diagram of fog computing is shown in Figure 3.1, and its applications are shown in Figure 3.2.

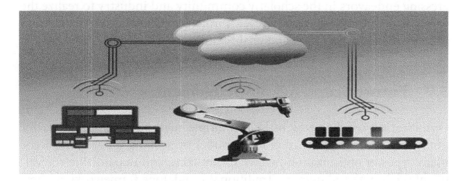

Figure 3.1 Fog computing in Industry 4.0.

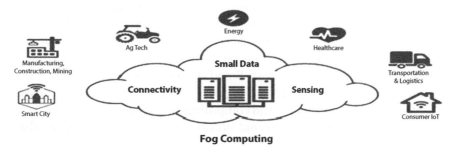

Figure 3.2 Application areas of fog computing.

3.6   Conclusion

Fog computing has emerged as an attractive solution to the IoT computing challenges. Applications experience lower latency because they rely on edge devices that have more computing power than endpoints and are closer to them than more powerful cloud resources. Fog-computing platforms have significantly improved in all areas. The significant increase in the use of IoT devices is related to an increase in fog computing. Fog-computing platforms benefit retailers by offering advanced techniques to process queries and issues in real-time. Retailers can also give their representatives devices to check item data and stock, or self-pay to make strides for client involvement. As of late, individuals from Cisco, Dell, Intel, Microsoft, ARM, and Princeton College shaped the Open Haze Consortium in 2015. This chapter presents a reference design for the Web of Things and portrays the progressing endeavors in the scholarly community and industry to realize the vision of haze computing. However, numerous challenges remain, from security to decreasing asset and vitality utilization.

3.7   Future Scope/Acknowledgement

Optimization mechanisms include multiple methods and strategies for improving the performance of each model by seeking different answers. Many types of optimization involve minimizing and maximizing the values of the inputs and outputs. Traditional standalone frameworks are limited in their simplicity, flexibility, and scalability. Fog-computing platforms are a promising technology that can aid and improve structures in normal use. Dealing with costs is often a necessary issue for system deployment, as cloud services move to the edge of the network.

This phase shows how to optimize science in the age of human capital, the differences between various technologies, and the advantages and disadvantages of various technologies. Many studies have shown that virtualization management must understand the complexity of each virtualized environment in this context. Based on observations by Zheng *et al.*, we propose a well-designed solution to the power consumption problem that clearly defines all latency and computing operations involving a device with critical computing power and nonworking nodes. This implies that the peripheral device is limited.

This study simulates the successful process of cellular equipment and the failure of two types of queues. Equal performance and latency reduce the power consumption. Hence, the theory proposed by Liu *et al.* This release considers and applies queuing principles to assess the effort, execution latency, and cost of downloads in cloud computing accurately. The main objective of the multi-objective optimization problem is to find the best value and electricity distribution for all devices, minimizing energy consumption, execution time, and cost.

Similarly, we performed an in-depth analysis of the energy consumption, execution time, and switching cost in the BZ system based on the queue policy. There are three aircraft models: mobile, FC, and cloud information centers. This specifically includes data usage and Wi-Fi connectivity. All other analyses explored the load factor in the cloud to reduce the power consumption and energy efficiency (QoE).

It checks for changes made by an algorithm called the Fair Association Rule (FCA) to ensure basic cooperation between nebula nodes. The ELBS (Electricity Aware Load Balancing and Scheduling) model is entirely based on cloud computing and uses two levels. First, we modeled the use of composite materials with unfinished business tasks and created tasks that improve balance. Subsequently, techniques called particle swarm optimization (PSO) algorithms have emerged to achieve the best possible response.

Latency Optimization—Latency is a computing community metric that shows how long it takes for data to travel from destination to destination.

The delay was as close to 0 as possible. Community delays can be calculated by specifying the round-trip time (RTT) of a package to its destination. Because cloud computing is a new technology with barriers, latency is one of the most difficult tasks for cloud computing. The working model downloaded from a mobile phone was designed to use an outdoor unit (RSU) to examine the delay. It comes with computers and station equipment that act as a gateway to the surrounding airspace as well as a logging system that prepares the vehicle for duty.

Similarly, the master heuristic planning ideas and algorithms. Another study proposed a delay-sensitive fogger module control strategy to accommodate the difference between the transmission delay of the service provider and the data signal processed by the project. The goal of this strategy is to ensure that the application QoS satisfies the service provider's time constraints and maximizes the capacity in the cloud environment.

People's latency fallback suggests how to reduce latency in cloud computing by intelligently hiding both human- and human-oriented actions based on both situations. First, the authors used machine learning to program media access control (MAC) switches on test equipment to measure customer behavior and manage connections.

Second, the problem of unloading work is solved and several nearby nebula nodes are chosen to reduce power consumption and delay the selection of the discharge power. This is about creating algorithms to stop users.

Cost Optimization—Cost optimization, also known as optimization/cost optimization, is an efficiency that describes the degree to which parallel operations solve problems simultaneously. That is, the asymptotic runtime is the same as that of the avoidance synchronization algorithm while optimizing the device operation involved in device management. Network Time Protocol (NTP), Precision Time Protocol (PTP), Pay Per Point (PPS), Global Positioning System (GPS), and time synchronization infrastructure built using the latest technologies, such as real-time world and Linux expansion, and Beagle Bone Target hardware on black devices.

Fog computing is widely used in homes, especially in the community, and is easy to use. One document recommends using the Gateway Deployment Edition to limit the overall installation costs by limiting the laptop's maximum size, length, scope, and capacity. In addition, meta-heuristic algorithms have been proposed for solving NP-hard problems, such as separation control rules for solving conflicts and genetic algorithms for improving the Count's performance. These collaborations were achieved by taking advantage of a combination algorithm called the Discrete Monkey Genetic Algorithm (DMGA), which works well in small business environments. Medical Cyber-Physical Systems (MCPS), a generation that enables the interaction and intelligence of computing concepts and research tools, are a well-known field, as observed by Gu et al.

Fog computing aims to connect the FC with MCPF mileage proof to provide real-time, low-cost access to these devices. They solved a nonlinear mixed-integer problem, linearized it using linear mixed-integer programming (LP), and proposed a heuristic step. On these boards, we implemented a minimization algorithm called mixed-integer nonlinear programming (MINLP) to achieve satisfactory QoS at low cost. Fog computing aims to shorten the cloud change time and reduce the computational cost; therefore, time and cost should be studied. The implementation of recommendations is a set of rules called group-billing scheduling heuristics to balance the cost and execution of the implementation.

Effective recovery at the expense of the team is paramount to ensure the overall performance of the client.

Reliability Optimization—Measures cloud computing and cloud computing to provide reliability, maintenance services, and improve operational efficiency. Some changes can negatively affect social structure. Good examples include crashes, malfunctions, software errors, intrusions, user errors, and other unforeseen events. Thus, with proper planning and foresight, difficult problems can be solved and serious problems can be avoided.

Much research has been conducted on trust and its function. To solve the complexity of the problem with the optimization strategy, a new method for developing a customer trust system and the following questions are discussed. Estimation of turbidity layer complexity and distribution. The proposed model considers latency and reliability in harsh environments and the short battery life of drones. In this study, we attempted to reduce energy consumption by developing a mathematical model called the proximal Jacobian alternative direction factor method (ADMM).

Another search term is the schema version of the FC. The recommended environment is the VANET, which supports applications such as the detection of urban traffic and the arrival time of smart buses. The new hybrid environment includes cloud computing and VANET to ensure that the bus is real.

New technologies are limited by the time, cost, and space required for their implementation. In this model, different methods of creating and simulating a virtual environment are used to examine each problem and find solutions.

Thus, these solutions will help prevent errors or problems in real space with less time and cost. In general, it is a well-known optimization method that considers a problem in a real object in a virtual form to maximize or minimize solution problems based on the formulation of the problem, such as minimizing power consumption and maximizing the number of packets sent. In practice, there are many ways to solve this problem, depending on the number of problems.

References

1. Buhalis, D. and Amaranggana, A., Smart tourism destinations, in: *Information and Communication Technologies in Tourism*, Springer, pp. 553–564, 2015.
2. Xiang, Z., Du, Q., Ma, Y., Fan, W., A comparative analysis of major online review platforms: Implications for social media analytics in hospitality and tourism. *Tourism Manage.*, 58, 51–65, 2017.
3. Sigala, M., Christou, E., Gretzel, U., *Social media in travel, tourism and hospitality: Theory, practice and cases*, Ashgate Publishing, Ltd, Australia, 2012, https://espace.library.uq.edu.au/view/UQ:334941.
4. Law, R., Buhalis, D., Cobanoglu, C., Progress on information and communication technologies in hospitality and tourism. *Int. J. Contemp. Hospitality Manage.*, 26, 5, 727–750, 2014.

5. Guttentag, D., The past, present and future of augmented reality in tourism. *Tourism Manage. Perspect.*, 31, 292–311, 2019.
6. Neidhardt, J. and Rieder, K., Smart tourism destinations: The interplay between technology adoption, activities and stakeholder collaboration. *J. Destination Marketing & Manage.*, 6, 3, 192–203, 2017.
7. Xiang, Z. and Gretzel, U., Role of social media in online travel information search. *Tourism Manage.*, 31, 2, 179–188, 2010.
8. Gretzel, U. and Wang, D., *Tourism in the age of technology*, Springer, 2016.
9. Buhalis, D., *Tourism in the digital age: Innovations, challenges and opportunities*, Springer, 2018.
10. Egger, R. and Buhalis, D., *ETourism case studies: Management and marketing issues*. Netherlands: Butterworth-Heinemann, United States of America, 2008, https://www.google.co.in/books/edition/ETourism_Case_Studies/ELzaFF9cWLcC?hl=en&gbpv=0.
11. Rashid, M. and Wani, U., II, Role of fog computing platform in analytics of internet of things – Issues, challenges and opportunities, in: *Fog, Edge, and Pervasive Computing in Intelligent IoT Driven Applications*, pp. 209–220, IEEE, United States of America, 2021, https://www.google.co.in/books/edition/Fog_Edge_and_Pervasive_Computing_in_Inte/itsLEAAAQBAJ?hl=en&gbpv=1&dq=Role+of+fog+computing+platform+in+analytics+of+internet+of+things+-+Issues,+challenges+and+opportunities&printsec=frontcover.
12. Callon, M. and Muniesa, F., Economic markets as calculative collective devices. *Organ. Stud.*, 26, 8, 1229–1250, 2005.
13. Dahlander, L. and Gann, D.M., How open is innovation? *Res. Policy*, 39, 6, 699–709, 2010.
14. Lopez de Avila, A., Smart Destinations: XXI Century Tourism, in: *ENTER2015 Conference on Information and Communication Technologies in Tourism*, Lugano, Switzerland, February 4-6, 2015.
15. Fesenmaier, D., Werthner, H., Wöber, K., CAB International, *Destination Recommendation Systems: Behavioral Foundations and Applications*, Cambridge, United States of America, 2006, https://www.google.co.in/books/edition/Destination_Recommendation_Systems/b295Illddi8C?hl=en&gbpv=1&dq=Destination+Recommendation+Systems:+Behavioral+Foundations+and+Applications&printsec=frontcover.
16. Law, R., Buhalis, D., Cobanoglu, C., Progress on information and communication technologies in hospitality and tourism. *Int. J. Contemp. Hospitality Manage.*, 26, 5, 727–750, 2014.

Machine Learning Integration in Agriculture Domain: Concepts and Applications

Ankur Biswas[1]* and Rita Banik[2]

¹Tripura Institute of Technology, Narsingarh, Tripura, India
²ICFAI University Tripura, Tripura, India

Abstract

Agriculture is a crucial factor in the economic development of a nation such as India because it serves as the primary source of food and money for rural people. Increasing agricultural production is necessary, given the realities of a growing world population and climate change, and choosing which crops to cultivate is a crucial part of agricultural planning.

A subset of artificial intelligence known as "machine learning" uses statistical methods to give computers the ability to learn from data and develop forecasts or choices without having to be formally compiled for this purpose. Machine learning has recently been used in many industries, including agriculture, to boost crop productivity, reliability, and the effectiveness of asset usage. Machine learning methods have been applied in agriculture to assess enormous datasets produced by several sensors, including satellite imaging, weather stations, soil sensors, and drone photography. These data are used to create models that, among other things, may estimate agricultural production, identify crop illnesses, and maximize resource utilization. Crop health can be categorized using machine learning algorithms, weed species can be identified, and their densities quantified and meteorological variables that impact crop development can be predicted. Farmers who use this knowledge may decide when to water, fertilize, and use pesticides with confidence. Additionally, soil properties, such as organic matter content and soil fertility, can be predicted using machine learning, which can assist farmers in selecting the best crop management techniques. Moreover, machine learning can be used to estimate agricultural output based on environmental data, such as temperature,

*Corresponding author: abiswas.tit@gmail.com

Chandan Banerjee, Anupam Ghosh, Rajdeep Chakraborty and Ahmed A. Elngar (eds.) Fog Computing for Intelligent Cloud IoT Systems, (71–98) © 2024 Scrivener Publishing LLC

humidity, and rainfall. Ultimately, machine learning is poised to transform agriculture by assisting farmers in making data-driven choices, which may result in higher agricultural yields, better crop quality, and more resource-efficient resource utilization.

This study offers a comparison of several machine learning methods, including a few gradient boosting techniques that achieved an accuracy of above 99%, decision trees, random forest, etc., to forecast the best crop suitable for a particular condition, as well as crop health on the use of pesticides. Finally, recommenders are presented that can forecast crop type and suggest pesticide usage both in general and crop-specific.

Keywords: Smart agriculture, machine learning, lightGBM, prediction, recommender

4.1   Introduction

With over 50% of the population employed and a GDP contribution of more than 17%, agriculture is a key component of the Indian economy. It plays a significant role in maintaining food production and preserving the nation's economic well-being. A wide variety of agricultural products are grown in India, including rice, wheat, sugarcane, cotton, legumes, and oilseeds. The nation has a massive irrigation network that aids in sustaining agricultural production in the face of unpredictable monsoon rains. Nonetheless, the industry still faces several difficulties, including poor productivity, a lack of water, dispersed land ownership, and climate change. The Indian government has launched several programs to address these issues, including the Pradhan Mantri Fasal Bima Yojana (PMFBY), which extends farmers' crop insurance; the Pradhan Mantri Krishi Sinchai Yojana (PMKSY), which encourages water conservation and irrigation efficiency; and the Soil Health Card program, which encourages sustainable soil management. The government has also introduced a number of online platforms, including the National Agricultural Market (e-NAM), which allows farmers to sell their goods online and obtain higher rates, and the Kisan Credit Card program, which makes it simple for farmers to acquire finance. Notwithstanding these difficulties, India's agricultural industry has seen tremendous expansion over the years, and with the adoption of new ideas and technologies, the sector is expected to continue to expand and support the nation's economic development and food security. However, agriculture can be affected by several factors [1, 2]:

1. Climate and weather: These two aspects have a significant impact on agriculture. Crop growth and yield are influenced

by temperature, rainfall quantity, timing, and other weather factors.

2. Soil fertility and quality: These factors are important for agriculture. Crop growth and yield can be influenced by the soil structure, pH, and nutrient availability.

3. Management of pests and diseases: Pests and diseases have a significant effect on crop production. Effective pest and disease management techniques are crucial to prevent crop damage and ensure maximum yield.

4. Water availability: As water is necessary for crop growth, it has a significant impact on agriculture. Irrigation is frequently required to supplement rainfall and ensure crop growth and yield.

5. Agriculture can be impacted by the availability and fragmentation of land, especially in nations with small and dispersed landholdings. This could restrict the application of cutting-edge agricultural techniques and equipment, resulting in decreased output and earnings.

6. Market demand and prices: Market demand and agricultural product prices have a significant impact on farmers' incomes. Production and income may increase in response to high demand and prices, whereas they may decrease in response to low demand and prices.

7. Government policies and support: Government policies and support, such as subsidies, R&D funding, and credit availability can have a significant impact on agriculture. They can assist farmers and promote agricultural investment, thereby increasing output and income.

Recently, numerous sectors, including agriculture, have employed machine learning, a subset of artificial intelligence, to increase agricultural output, dependability, and asset utilization effectiveness. In agriculture, machine learning techniques are used to analyze large datasets generated by several sensors, including satellite imagery, weather stations, soil sensors, and drone photography. Models have been developed using this information, among other things. Through various applications, machine learning can address numerous factors that affect agriculture [3–5]. Here, there are a few examples:

1. Climate and weather: To assist farmers in making knowledgeable choices regarding when to plant, irrigate, or harvest

their crops, machine learning can analyze historical weather data and forecast future weather patterns.

2. Machine learning can be used to analyze soil samples and forecast soil quality and fertility. Farmers who use this information can make well-informed choices regarding crop rotation and nutrient application among other soil management techniques.

3. Management of crop pests and diseases: Crop diseases and pests can be identified and diagnosed using machine learning. This can assist farmers in acting quickly to limit crop damage and prevent the spread of diseases and pests.

4. Water availability: Water demand predictions and irrigation scheduling optimization can be performed using machine learning. This can assist farmers in using water more effectively and guarantee the highest crop yield with the lowest amount of water.

5. Land availability and fragmentation: Land use and cover can be mapped using machine learning to analyze satellite imagery. Based on the size and characteristics of their landholdings, this information can assist farmers in making well-informed decisions about crop rotation and management techniques.

6. Prices and market demand: Machine learning can be used to analyze market data and forecast agricultural product demand and prices. Farmers can make informed decisions about crop selection, production, and marketing tactics.

7. Government support: Machine learning can be used to analyze government support initiatives and determine how they affect agriculture. These data can assist decision makers in developing and implementing policies and programs that support sustainable agriculture and rural development.

In this study, we focused on the management of pesticides to maintain crop health without compromising the overall crop yield. We used data related to pesticide usage obtained from Analytics Vidya, and data related to soil constituents, such as nitrogen, phosphorus, and potassium, as well as rainfall, temperature, and humidity. We forecast the values of 'Crop_health', and 'Crop_type' based on pesticides and soil constituents, respectively. The system consists of two main modules:

i. Crop Recommender—The proposed module will assist the farmers in determining if a specific period is appropriate for planting a specific crop.

ii. Pesticide Recommender—This module will guide the farmers to determine the appropriate quantities of pesticides to be used for a specific crop and achieve maximum and healthy yield.

The remainder of the chapter is organized as follows: *Section 4.2* describes the literature on fog computing and machine learning applications in agriculture. *Section 4.3* presents the methodology adopted for developing the two modules of the proposed work while *Section 4.4* reports the results obtained. *Section 4.5* concludes the chapter with the scope of future work presented in *Section 4.6*.

4.2   Fog Computing in Agriculture

A distributed computing paradigm called fog computing attempts to move the processing power closer to the edge of the network, where data are produced and consumed. Fog computing has a significant impact on agriculture, allowing precision farming and increasing agricultural yield. Farmers can obtain real-time data from sensors and IoT devices, such as soil moisture sensors, temperature sensors, and humidity sensors, by placing fog computing nodes close to the fields. As these data can be handled locally, there is no need to transfer them to the cloud for analysis, allowing for rapid and prompt decision-making. Farmers may also receive real-time input from fog computing, enabling them to quickly modify their irrigation, fertilization, and other agricultural techniques. Fog computing may also be employed to improve the communication between various agricultural systems and equipment, including tractors, drones, and irrigation systems. Farmers may enhance their processes and increase productivity by allowing them to connect with one another in real-time. Fog computing has the potential to transform the agricultural sector by empowering stakeholders to make data-driven choices, streamline their processes, and enhance crop yields. In several ways, fog computing can enable precision agriculture and increase crop yields:

1. Real-time data collection and analysis was made possible using fog computing. Examples of IoT devices that can collect data in real time include soil moisture, temperature, and

humidity sensors. Local analysis of these data enables farmers to quickly decide on irrigation, fertilization, and other farming techniques.

2. Localized processing: Farmers can avoid delays caused by sending data to the cloud for analysis by processing data close to where it is being used. As a result, decisions can be made more quickly, and resources can be used more effectively.

3. Real-time feedback: Farmers may make rapid changes to their agricultural techniques using real-time data from fog computing on crop conditions. For instance, farmers may modify their irrigation systems to minimize crop damage if a sensor detects low soil moisture levels.

4. Communication between devices: Tractors, drones, and irrigation systems are a few examples of agricultural equipment and systems that can communicate through fog computing. As a result, agricultural operations may be better coordinated, lowering the possibility of over- or under-irrigation, and increasing the overall effectiveness.

5. Predictive analytics: Fog computing can shed light on long-term patterns and forecast agricultural yields by examining the data over time. Farmers who use this information may make informed choices regarding crop rotation, planting, and harvesting.

Therefore, real-time data, localized processing, and real-time feedback are all ways that fog computing can support precision agriculture. Fog computing may eventually result in increased crop yields and more sustainable agriculture by enhancing the effectiveness and precision of the agricultural techniques.

Gangwar *et al.* [6] provided a thorough overview of machine learning applications in agriculture, such as crop categorization, yield prediction, disease detection, and precision agriculture. To analyze crops and identify plant diseases, Zhang *et al.* [7] focused on deep learning methods in agriculture such as object identification, picture recognition, and semantic segmentation. The present status of machine learning applications in agriculture, including crop yield prediction, pest and disease control, soil management, and precision agriculture, has been summarized in a comprehensive literature review by Shadkam *et al.* [8]. Mohammad *et al.* [9] provided a general overview of the machine learning methods used in agriculture, including crop categorization, yield prediction, and disease detection, as well as the difficulties and restrictions associated with doing so. Demilie *et al.* [10] focused on the application of image analysis, feature extraction, and classification methods, together with machine learning and deep learning approaches for agricultural disease detection and classification. A general overview of the use of machine learning and artificial intelligence in agriculture, including topics such as yield prediction, crop monitoring, pest and disease detection, and precision farming, was provided by Balamurali *et al.* [11]. Hameed *et al.* [12] focuses on the difficulties and restrictions associated with using machine learning in agriculture, including crop categorization, yield prediction, and pest and disease control. Singh *et al.* [13] utilizes regression, decision trees, and neural networks to illustrate how machine learning is used in precision agriculture to forecast crop output and estimate nitrogen status. In [14], a general overview of the use of artificial intelligence in agriculture was presented, including crop monitoring, yield prediction, pest and disease detection, and precision farming. These include machine learning, computer vision, and robots. Ogunshile *et al.* [15] addressed the benefits and difficulties of using machine learning in agriculture, including crop categorization, yield prediction, pest and disease control, and precision agriculture. These studies demonstrate how machine learning in agriculture is becoming increasingly popular and useful.

Some studies that discuss the application of fog computing in agriculture include a study by Wang *et al.* [16] which provides an overview of the potential advantages and drawbacks of fog computing in agriculture and discusses several case studies of fog computing in practice. Khan *et al.* [17] provides an in-depth review of the role of fog computing in enabling smart agriculture and discusses the various applications of fog computing in agriculture, including precision farming, livestock management, and smart irrigation. The potential benefits of fog computing in agriculture, including improved resource management, higher crop yields, and reduced environmental impacts, are presented in [18]. This study also identifies some issues that must be resolved for the widespread adoption of fog computing in agriculture. In [19], an overview of the current applications of fog computing in precision agriculture was presented, including real-time monitoring of soil moisture, temperature, and other environmental variables. Xiao *et al.* [20] presents a case study of the application of fog computing in precision agriculture, focusing on the use of fog computing to enable real-time monitoring of crop conditions and irrigation management.

Overall, these analyses show that machine learning has enormous promise for improved sustainability, agricultural output, and resource management in agriculture. The availability of high-quality data, requirement for precise and reliable sensors and devices, and requirement for user-friendly and reasonably priced tools for farmers are all issues that must still be resolved. *Section 4.2.1* describes the details of the smart farming adopted in agriculture.

4.2.1   Smart Farming

Smart farming with fog computing entails placing fog computing nodes near areas to gather data from sensors and IoT devices, analyze it locally, and provide producers with authentic responses [21]. This method has several advantages for smart farming:

Data collection in real time: fog computing facilitates real-time data collection from sensors and IoT-enabled devices, such as soil moisture sensors, temperature sensors, and humidity sensors. Local analysis of these data allows farmers to make timely decisions about irrigation, fertilization, and other farming practices.

Farmers can prevent constraints imposed by transmitting data to the cloud for analysis by locally processing the data. This enables a speedier selection and more effective asset utilization.

Real-time feedback: Fog computing can provide farmers with real-time feedback on crop conditions, allowing them to adjust farming practices. For example, farmers can adjust their irrigation systems to avoid crop damage if a sensor detects low soil moisture levels.

Device communication: Fog computing provides communication between various agricultural systems and equipment such as tractors, drones, and irrigation systems. This enables improved agricultural activity synchronization, lowering the danger of over- or under-irrigation and boosting overall efficiency.

Fog computing can provide insights into long-term patterns and estimate future agricultural yields by studying data over time. These data could assist farmers in making strategic planting, harvesting, and crop rotation choices.

Hence, smart farming with fog computing can improve agricultural efficiency, accuracy, and sustainability. Fog computing may help farmers improve their operations and eventually boost crop yields by delivering real-time data, localized processing, and real-time feedback.

4.3   Methodology

The key objective of this study is to create an effective approach for the overall growth of the agricultural sector by building an efficient framework that can provide better ideas to farmers to grow the proper crops and use the right proportion of pesticides with better yields, even during seasons and off seasons. Optimizing the use of pesticides is an important goal for sustainable agriculture, and machine learning is a powerful tool for achieving this goal. In this study, we attempted to optimize the use of pesticides to improve the quality of crops (i.e., whether the crop is healthy, damaged by pesticides, or damaged by other causes) while maintaining yields. We attempted to identify the optimal timing and dosage for pesticide application. The data were obtained from Analytics Vidya and consisted of Season, Crop_Type, Soil_Type, Insects_Count, Pesticide_Used, Number of Doses, Duration_Doses, Crop_quality, etc. These data were first analyzed using machine learning algorithms to identify patterns and optimize the schedule of pesticide use. Crop_quality is assessed based on pesticide data, and appropriate pesticide use is recommended. Based on the analysis of the data, informed decisions will be made about when and how much pesticide is used. Their use is adjusted automatically based on the recommendations of machine learning algorithms. The system is continuously monitored to ensure that it works correctly and produces the desired outcomes. Adjustments will be made as necessary to the improve performance. The effectiveness of the proposed methodology is evaluated by comparing the quality of crops and the usage of pesticides before and after implementing the technology. Agricultural systems must deal with a large amount of data, mostly weather-related characteristics. The levels of nitrogen, phosphorus, and potassium present in the soil are some of the other pertinent variables. Our second attempt was to assess the crop type suitable for a particular soil type and season. Several preprocessing methods were used to prepare the data for the analysis to create the framework. Exploratory data analysis has also been used to comprehend the data, obtain dataset correlations, and uncover and display hidden patterns among the various dataset modules. Subsequently, several machine learning algorithms were used to accurately anticipate the type of crop and its state by applying them to pertinent data. Finally, recommenders are created using a variety of factors. For the system to forecast the ideal crop and its health, certain parameters must be entered into the model. Figure 4.1 shows the overall flow diagram of the system. *Section 4.3.1* describes the source of the dataset used in this study. *Section 4.3.2* details the data analysis and pre-processing applied to the data while *Section 4.3.3* discusses feature extraction. In *Section 4.3.4*, the model selection is presented with hyperparameter tuning, as discussed in *Section 4.3.5*. The final data splitting is presented in *Section 4.3.6*.

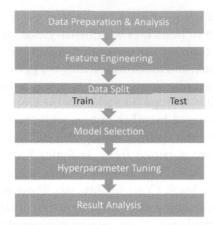

Figure 4.1 The flow diagram of the proposed framework.

4.3.1   Data Source

Two distinct datasets are used in this study. The first dataset offered the level of crop damage linked to pesticide usage. The second dataset includes weather data, such as rainfall, temperature, humidity, and pressure, with information on the soil elements: N (nitrogen), P (phosphorus), and K (potassium). The details of the dataset are shown in Figure 4.2.

4.3.2   Data Analysis and Pre-Processing

Data is crucial for comprehending the data and identifying patterns that may be utilized to create machine learning models. In machine learning, the major objective of data analysis is to draw conclusions from data that may be utilized to produce precise predictions. The following data analysis methods were employed in this study:

1. Exploratory data analysis (EDA), is the process of examining and enumerating key features of the data. This might involve

Dataset 1

Insects_attack	Crop	Soil	Pesticide_usage	Doses_no	Duration	Season	Crop_health

Dataset 2

Nitrogen	Phosphorus	Potassium	Temp	Humidity	Rainfall	Crop_type

Figure 4.2 Dataset parameters.

determining how the data are distributed, spotting outliers, and displaying the information.

2. Statistical analysis is the process of applying statistical techniques to data to identify patterns, connections, and trends. This can assist in choosing suitable machine learning models and improving their performance.

3. Correlation analysis identifies the degree and direction of the association between variables in the data. Choosing the most pertinent characteristics of machine learning models can be aided by this method.

Data derived from the dataset frequently include outliers, noisy data, and missing values. These inaccurate data decrease the prediction accuracy. Therefore, in a typical forecasting system, data preparation comes first, because it may provide a good first interpretation of the dataset. To ensure the quality of the dataset for efficient training and subsequent prediction, some pre-processing was necessary because the collected data also contained some "NaN" or NULL values of Crop_quality, crop type, etc. All null values were removed from the data set. Moreover, in the second dataset, only 12 crops were considered. All other crops were removed. Figure 4.3 shows the

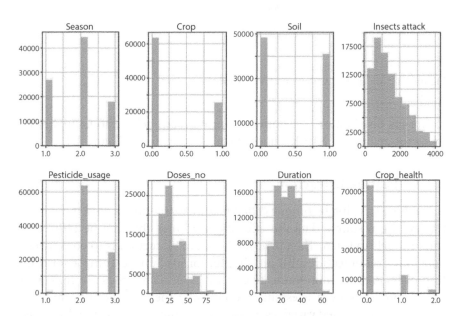

Figure 4.3 Univariate distribution of parameters on the data set 1.

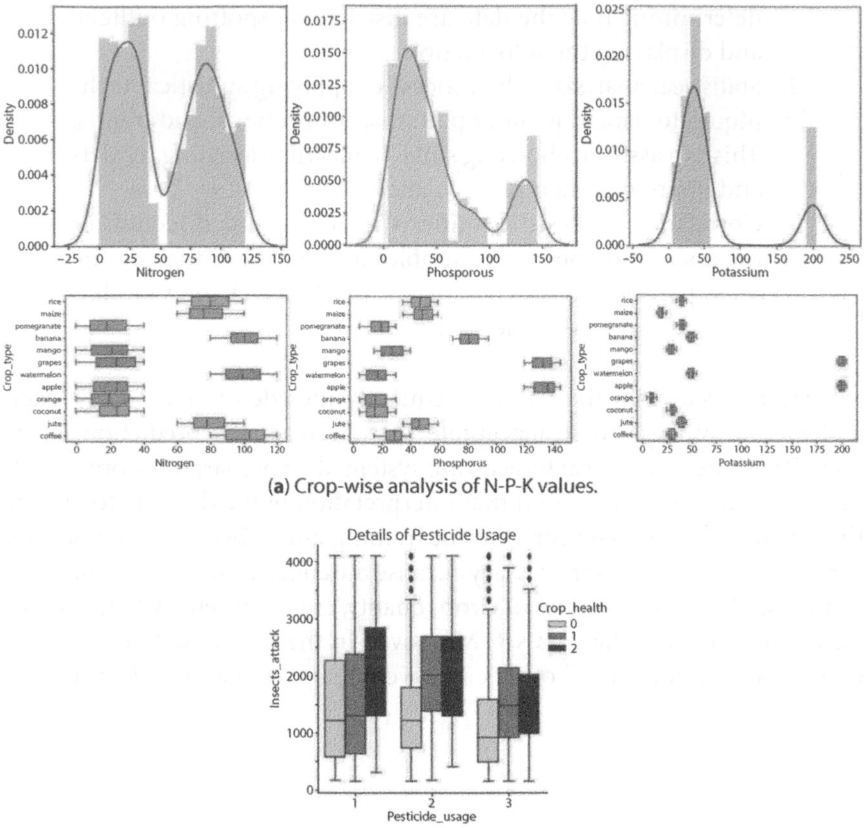

(a) Crop-wise analysis of N-P-K values.

(b)

Figure 4.4 Univariate distribution of N-P-K values.

univariate distribution of parameters for dataset 1 related to Crop_health, while the analysis of N-P-K values of soil is presented in Figure 4.4.

4.3.3   Feature Extraction

A machine learning technique called feature extraction is used to find and retrieve from source data the effective attributes that can be utilized to train models to learn. The purpose of feature extraction is to convert raw data into a set of features that are simpler for machine learning algorithms to process and are more indicative of inherent data trends. To maximize prediction accuracy, it is essential to consider the influence of numerous parameters. Unrelated variables or features should not be included, because they increase the complexity of the model and interact with several other elements. Hence, the feature selection must be completed prior to building a suitable model. For this, a heatmap of the Pearson correlation was used, as presented in Figure 4.5.

It is clear from data analysis that "crop health" are strongly correlated to "insects_attack," "pesticide_usage" and "duration." Although there is less clarity on the relationships of 'doses_no' and other parameters. The second dataset consists of pesticide and weather data related to the quality of crop yield. Similarly, in Figure 4.6, a heatmap of Pearson correlation is given to illustrate and determine the effective attributes of dataset 2. The data from the datasets used were 70% for training and 30% for testing. The effectiveness of the feature selection techniques was evaluated using multiple linear regressions. The RMSE, MAE, and R2 values were obtained using feature selection techniques.

In this dataset, 12 different crops (1—rice, 2—maize, 3—pomegranate, 4—banana, 5—mango, 6—grapes, 7—watermelon, 8—apple, 9—orange, and 10—coffee) were analyzed, and a comparison of feature visualization for most correlated features (temperature, humidity, rainfall, and phosphorus) for each crop is shown. Figure 4.7 represents a graph type called a line plot, sometimes called a line chart or a time-series plot, to show the data

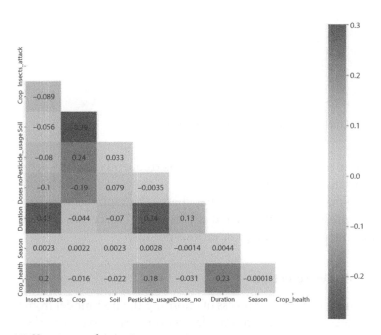

Figure 4.5 Heatmap on dataset 1 parameters.

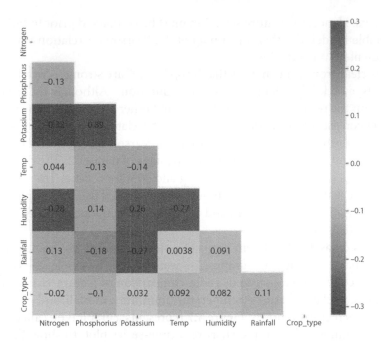

Figure 4.6 Heatmap on dataset 2.

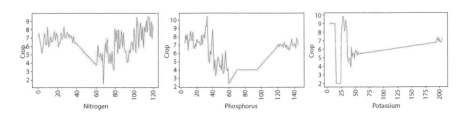

Figure 4.7 Line plot for N_P_K feature visualization.

points connected by straight lines. This is frequently used to demonstrate how a variable changes over time.

A bar plot, sometimes called a bar chart, is a graph that uses rectangular bars to represent data points and is plotted in Figure 4.8. It is frequently used to contrast the rankings of various groups.

4.3.4 Model Selection

In machine learning, the process of choosing the best model from a group of candidates trained on a certain dataset is referred to as model selection. The accuracy and generalizability of the final model were directly affected

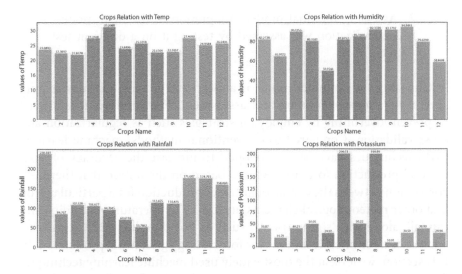

Figure 4.8 Crop-wise feature visualization.

by this process stage in the machine-learning pipeline. There are various phases in the model selection process, including:

1. Identifying the issue and locating pertinent data: It is critical to clearly characterize the issues that need to be resolved and locate the pertinent data that will be used to train and test the models to choose the optimal model.

2. Selecting a collection of candidate models: A set of candidate models can be selected based on the problem and type of data.

3. Creating training and validation sets from the data: Two sets of data were created, one for training the models and the other for assessing their efficacy. Thus, the models were prevented from overfitting the training dataset.

4. Training the candidate models: Training data were used to train each candidate model.

5. Model performance assessment: The performance of each model was assessed using the validation data with an appropriate evaluation metric, such as accuracy, precision, recall, or F1-score.

6. Choosing the best model: The final model was chosen based on its performance on model on the validation set.

7. Assessing the final model: Adaptation of the final model's generalization was assessed by testing it on a different test set.

Choosing the optimum model is an iterative process that may require several iterations of training and assessment. Furthermore, it is crucial to prevent overfitting by employing strategies such as regularization and cross-validation. Compared to conventional methods, machine learning (ML) techniques have been developed to increase the accuracy of agricultural production forecasts. As it is based on the notion that there is a correlation between the overall quantity of production for a particular crop and other meteorological elements, including temperature, humidity, and rainfall, along with soil nutrients, such as N-P-K values [22], regression analysis is a common technique for forecasting agricultural production. In this section, we look at the most widely used machine learning techniques for forecasting agricultural yields, such as Decision Tree, Random Forest, XGBoost, Catboost, and LightGBM [23].

4.3.5   Hyper-Parameter Tuning

The process of selecting ideal hyperparameters for a machine learning model is known as hyperparameter tuning [24]. These variables must be established before the model is trained because they cannot be determined from the data. The learning rate, regularization intensity, number of hidden layers in a neural network, and number of trees in a random forest are examples of hyperparameters. The aim of hyperparameter tuning is to find the ideal collection of hyperparameters that gives the greatest model performance on a validation set. This is crucial because selecting the right hyperparameters may have a significant influence on how well the model works, and sometimes using default settings is not the best option. There are several methods for hyperparameter adjustment, such as:

1. Grid Search: Using a predetermined grid of hyperparameter values, the model was trained and assessed for each set of hyperparameters. The best performance-producing combination was selected.
2. Random Search: Hyperparameters are selected at random from a given range or distribution in this method, and the model is trained and assessed for each set of hyperparameters. The best performance-producing combination is then chosen.

3. Bayesian optimization: This method chooses hyperparameters that are likely to lead to higher performance and employs a probabilistic model to approximate the goal function (such as model performance). A grid or random search is less effective than this approach, particularly when the number of hyperparameters exceeds.

4. By using evolutionary concepts (such as mutation and crossover) to create new candidates, evolutionary algorithms define a population of candidate hyperparameter settings. From among the populations, the optimal hyperparameter set was chosen.

It is vital to note that hyperparameter tuning may be time- and resource-intensive, particularly for complicated models and large datasets. As a result, early halting and parallelization are frequently used to reduce the time and computing resources required for hyperparameter adjustment. Using methods such as stacked cross-validation can help prevent hyperparameters from being overfitted to validation data.

4.3.6 Train-Test Split

A typical machine learning method for assessing a model's performance is the train-test split. The dataset was divided into a training set and a test set using this approach [25]. The model was trained using the training set and its performance was assessed using a test set. To evaluate the model's capacity for generalization, it is crucial to simulate its performance on new, untested data. The steps of the train-test split technique are as follows:

1. The data was divided into a training set and a test set at random, often in a ratio of 70:30 or 80:20, respectively.

2. The model was trained on the training set. This entails providing the model with the training set and utilizing the selected model.

3. The model was evaluated using a test set. This entails feeding the test set to the trained model and evaluating its performance using a measure (such as accuracy or mean squared error, for example).

4. The model can be modified, as required. The model can be modified by altering its hyperparameters or retraining on the complete dataset, depending on how well it performs on the test set.

5. The model was then run on the the the test set. Although this step is optional, it might be helpful to confirm whether the model's performance has been enhanced because of the changes made.

The train-test split approach has drawbacks, and as a result, the accuracy of the findings may not always be guaranteed. This is because performance of the model might be extremely dependent on the exact random split of the data, especially when the dataset is limited. Therefore, other approaches, such as cross-validation and bootstrapping, may be employed to obtain more credible estimations of the model's performance.

4.4   Results and Discussion

Machine learning is a strong decision-making tool for anticipating agricultural production, allowing farmers to choose which crops to produce and what to do throughout the planting season. Machine learning is ubiquitous throughout the planting, growing, and harvesting cycles. It begins with a crop forecast based on soil preparation, seed breeding, and water feed evaluation and concludes with robots picking up the harvest and assessing its ripeness using computer vision. In contrast to statistical models, ML algorithms can be complicated, and the effect of a single independent variable may not be clear. Coefficient metrics, on the other hand, can help with the comprehension and visualization of essential and perhaps linked aspects in ML algorithms. Temperature, humidity, rainfall, and potassium are all indicatively relevant factors for determining suitable crops. This section presents the outcomes of the recommender. Crop forecasting is a hypercritical job for stakeholders at both the regional and national levels to make rapid decisions. Farmers may use an accurate crop cultivation predictor to determine what to transplant and when to sow it.

Two databases were used to achieve the results: the first dataset provides crop quality based on various data on pesticide usage, as discussed earlier. The second dataset provides crop types based on soil nutrients and weather information for 12 crops. The data were acquired from publicly available performance trials, which were finally prepared for this study, as discussed. Stratified sampling was used to divide the final databases into training (70%) and testing (30%) datasets. A variety of ML algorithms were created for the crops to estimate the most suitable crop and crop quality based on soil nutrients, weather conditions, and historical data of pesticides used. While calculating crop type and quality in independent datasets (test datasets not utilized for model calibration), the proposed methods demonstrated a high degree of accuracy, as shown in Table 4.1. The estimated crop type and quality displayed a good degree of correlation with the actual type and quality of the methods in the separate datasets. These findings indicate that the proposed algorithms can reliably predict crop type and quality using database-generated information on N-P-K, pesticides, and weather factors. Section 4.4.1 present the modeling algorithms used in this study.

4.4.1   Modeling Algorithms

In this section, we investigate six classification techniques for the recommenders. Each algorithm displayed accuracy and assessment metrics. The accuracies of all crop and pesticide recommenders are displayed in Table 4.1, and graphically shown in Figure 4.9. The following algorithms were tested in this study:

1. Decision Trees: Decision trees are a modeling method that aids decision-making by building a tree-like representation of options and their potential repercussions.
2. Random Forest: It is an ensemble modeling approach that mixes numerous decision trees to increase forecast accuracy.
3. XGBoost: The widely employed machine learning technique known as eXtreme Gradient Boosting (XGBoost) is utilized for regression and classification applications. It is a specific type of gradient boosting algorithm that outperforms the functionality of conventional gradient boosting models by

Table 4.1 Assessment of multiple ML algorithms' accuracy.

Algorithms	Crop recommender	Pesticide recommender
Decision Tree	97.9	82.2
Random Forest	98.7	82.4
Support Vector	97.1	81.7
XGBoost	98.7	84.4
CatBoost	98.7	80.4
LightGBM	99.1	93.3

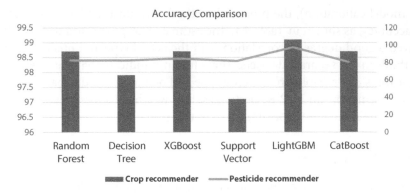

Figure 4.9 Comparison of model's performance.

combining several methods. The capacity of XGBoost to handle large datasets and intricate models is one of its key features. To enable quick and scalable model training, parallel processing and optimal memory use are advantageous. Moreover, XGBoost is renowned for its regularization methods, which deter overfitting by punishing the model complexity. It combines L1 and L2 regularization with the "tree pruning" method, which eliminates branches that do not make a major contribution to the model's efficiency.

The capacity of XGBoost to manage the missing values in a dataset is another feature. The most effective interpolation approach during the training phase includes an internal method for addressing missing data. Many tasks, such as classification, regression, ranking, and recommendation systems, can be completed using XGBoost. The financial, medical, and retail sectors, among many others, have all utilized it. Overall, XGBoost is a strong and flexible algorithm that has gained popularity among machine learning academics and practitioners. It is an effective tool for addressing a variety of data science issues owing to its speed, precision, and adaptability.

4. CatBoost: A well-known gradient boosting method called CatBoost was used to handle the categorized variables in the sample. It has a distinguishing characteristic that sets it apart from XGBoost and LightGBM and can handle categorical values without the requirement for one-hot encoding or label encoding. CatBoost's capability to handle categorical

data organically is one of its primary features. It integrates the category data right into the training process using a method known as "ordered boosting." This implies that categorical variables need not be converted into numerical values as part of data preprocessing.

The capacity of CatBoost's to manage missing data in a dataset is an additional benefit. This provides a built-in method for dealing with missing values, which reduces the chance of data leakage during training.

A variety of other features were also included in CatBoost, such as cross-validation, early halting, and regularization methods. Users can modify the training procedure and fine-tune the model hyperparameters owing to their adaptable API. CatBoost is useful for many different tasks including ranking, regression, and classification. It has been used in several sectors, including e-commerce, healthcare, and banking. CatBoost is a strong and effective algorithm that works especially well with categorical data. It is a useful tool for machine learning practitioners and academics because of its handling of missing data, versatile API, and variety of characteristics.

5. LightGBM: A well-liked gradient-boosting technique created to deal with sizable and high-dimensional datasets is called a light gradient boosting machine (LightGBM). It is comparable to XGBoost and CatBoost, but places more emphasis on speed and effectiveness. The quickness of the LightGBM is one of its key benefits. Instead of using "level-wise" growth, it employs a method called "leaf-wise" growth, which decreases the number of tree levels and increases the training efficiency. Moreover, it bins numerical characteristics using a histogram-based method, which helps save memory and boosts productivity.

Several other features are also included in LightGBM, such as regularized learning, early halting, and cross-validation. Users can modify the training procedure and fine-tune the model hyperparameters owing to their adaptable API. The handling of categorical data using LightGBM is another benefit. To address the imbalance between categorical characteristics with many categories and those with few categories, it employs a method known as "Gradient-based One-Side Sampling" (GOSS). Using this strategy, the model's accuracy is increased whereas the number of categories is decreased. Classification, regression, and ranking are just a few of the many tasks for which LightGBM is useful. It has been used in several sectors, including e-commerce, healthcare, and banking. Overall, LightGBM is a strong and effective method that works well with high-dimensional large-scale datasets. It is an important tool for machine learning practitioners and academics owing to its speed, accuracy, and versatility.

The first dataset included in this study comprises N-P-K values used for crop recommenders whose accuracy ranges from 97.1% to 99.1%. All the other models were outperformed by the LightGBM algorithm. The performance of the other algorithms was satisfactory. The second dataset exclusively contained pesticide usage factors used for pesticide recommenders. The accuracy ranged between 81.7% and 93.3%. LightGBM fared better than any other technique on the second dataset. Here, the performance of CatBoost's is slightly below the best possible range. LightGBM yielded the highest accuracy for both datasets. Because more accuracy leads to greater user profit [26, 27], the hyperparameter tuning for the best model in this study, LightGBM, is shown below:

1. Learning rate: The gradient descent step size was governed by the learning rate. Slower convergence is the outcome of a lower learning rate; however, the performance of the model may be enhanced. In general, the starting points should be in the range of 0.01 and 0.1. Hence, our value was 0.04.
2. Maximum depth: The amount of interactivity among variables is governed by the maximum depth of the tree. Overfitting can occur when the maximum depth is larger, whereas underfitting can occur when the maximum depth is smaller. Setting the maximum depth to 5 is a decent place to start, which may be changed later in response to the model's performance. Hence, the selected value was 18.
3. Other hyper-parameters chosen are: 'n_estimators': 1,392, 'objective': 'multiclass,' 'boosting_type': 'gbdt,' 'subsample': 0.7, 'random_state': 42, 'colsample_bytree': 0.7].

4.5   Conclusion

Information technology is causing significant changes in every area of the world's economy as it becomes more digital, but the agriculture industry has not yet been effectively addressed. Every year, agricultural research reproduced in several locations throughout the world provides many crop production and management databases, and these figures are useful for making broad generalizations (average effect of a management practice across a range of environments). As these datasets have, until now, been kept apart from one another, it is challenging to combine, standardize, and properly analyze them. One of the most crucial and challenging issues is contemporary agriculture is the identification of an appropriate crop. Given that India is a crop-producing nation, the major goal of growing crops is to increase agricultural output to the advantage of both farmers and the nation as a whole. An effective framework may help farm owners make wise management choices on what to plant to align the harvest with the demands of the present market. ML techniques can advance agricultural research and reveal previously hidden potential for every farm in the globe. This study provides an overview by developing a framework for predicting suitable crop_type based on meteorological variables and N-P-K levels found in the soil, and then constructing a recommendation system with an emphasis on utilizing ML techniques to predict crops_quality and estimate the required proportion of pesticide productivity. Crop and Pesticide Recommendation systems assist farmers in choosing which crops to grow and provide quality estimates for specific crops. To determine the accuracy, a variety of machine-learning algorithms were applied. Individual datasets were considered in this investigation (weather data and N-P-K data). The accuracy range for the N-P-K dataset was between 97.1% and 99.1%. All the other models were outperformed by the LightGBM method. The performance of the other algorithms was also satisfactory. The accuracy range for the second dataset in this study was between 81.7% and 93.3%, and contained pesticide data (without N-P-K values). In the second dataset, LightGBM performed better than the other method. By utilizing historical data, this study developed a powerful method for determining the crop quality. Datasets were analyzed using ML, and a pattern-matching approach is utilized to obtain the crop, depending on historical patterns of pesticides and soil. The proposed approach helps farmers decide what crops to use and the quantity of pesticides to use in their area. The goal of this study was to obtain more knowledge about crops that may be utilized to efficiently and effectively harvest various items. A solid crop forecast spanning numerous districts would be beneficial to farmers. This approach aids farmers in choosing the best crop for the season and planting area. This will benefit farmers by lowering their losses and increasing their net crop production. Consequently, the crop's production rate is maximized, which helps the Indian economy. Our research shows that the machine learning process is superior to the conventional experimental procedures. Researchers should create their own dataset and make it available to others through a variety of venues to test and evaluate the chosen models. An in-depth examination of several ML methods employed in different phases of agricultural practice may provide additional support for further research in this field.

4.6   Future Scope

With the ultimate objective of increasing production, conventional agricultural systems are evolving into fully artificial intelligence systems by applying machine learning to analyze sensor data and provide improved ideas and observations for ensuing actions and decisions. The use of ML models in this application field is expected to increase dramatically in the future, paving the way for more comprehensive and practical solutions. All present methodologies, as seen in other application sectors, concentrate on certain techniques and strategies and do not properly integrate with the decision-making process. This combination of computerized data collection, analysis, and choice or help will provide beneficial advantages associated with knowledge-based agriculture for increasing output levels and enhancing the quality of bioproducts. Using machine learning algorithms and the Internet of Things (IoT), a completely automated agricultural system that can anticipate crop production, regardless of location or season, may be created. The examination of the entire collection of data will also be a goal of future work, and techniques to increase the effectiveness of the suggested method will be committed to. As this module predicts the N-P-K of the soil and the weather of the soil, the major goal of this study was to apply the recommendation system of crop_type and crop_health in agriculture. Future applications of the IoT, or the integration of sensors into the soil of a farming area, can expand this idea by updating the data at regular intervals. Technologies such as deep learning can be useful in creating simulated data from scratch. Using ML algorithms and IoT, a completely automated agricultural system that can anticipate crop production regardless of location or season may be created. The examination of the entire collection of data will also be a goal of future work, and techniques to increase the effectiveness of the suggested method will be dedicated to.

References

1. Dias, K.O.G., Piepho, H.P., Guimarães, L.J.M. *et al.*, Novel strategies for genomic prediction of untested single-cross maize hybrids using unbalanced

historical data. *Theor. Appl. Genet.*, 133, 443–455, 2020, doi: 10.1007/s00122-019-03475-1.

2. Dahane, A., Benameur, R., Kechar, B., Benyamina, A., An IoT based smart farming system using machine learning. *Int. Symposium Networks, Comput. Commun. (ISNCC)*, pp. 1–6, 2020, doi: 10.1109/ISNCC49221.2020.9297341.

3. Doowon, J., Artificial intelligence security threat, crime, and forensics: Taxonomy and open issues. *IEEE Access*, 8, 184560–184574, 2020, 10.1109/ACCESS.2020.3029280.

4. Meshram, V.V., Patil, K., Meshram, V.A., Shu, F.C., An astute assistive device for mobility and object recognition for visually impaired people. *IEEE Trans. Hum. Mach. Syst.*, 49, 5, 449–60, 2019, 10.1109/THMS.2019.2931745.

5. Patil, K., Jawadwala, Q., Shu, F.C., Design and construction of electronic aid for visually impaired people. *IEEE Trans. Hum. Mach. Syst.*, 48, 2, 172–82, 2018, 10.1109/THMS.2018.2799588.

6. Liakos, K.G., Busato, P., Moshou, D., Pearson, S., Bochtis, D., Machine learning in agriculture: A review. *Sensors*, 18, 8, 2674, 2018, https://doi.org/10.3390/s18082674.

7. Bouguettaya, A., Zarzour, H., Kechida, A. *et al.*, Deep learning techniques to classify agricultural crops through UAV imagery: A review. *Neural Comput. Applic.*, 34, 9511–9536, 2022, https://doi.org/10.1007/ s00521-022-07104-9.

8. Mishra, S., Mishra, D., Santra, G.H., Applications of machine learning techniques in agricultural crop production: A review paper. *Indian J. Sci. Technol.*, 9, 38, 1–14, 2016, doi: 10.17485/ ijst/2016/v9i38/95032.

9. Sharma, A., Jain, A., Gupta, P., Chowdary, V., Machine learning applications for precision agriculture: A comprehensive review. *IEEE Access*, 9, 4843–4873, 2021, doi: 10.1109/ACCESS.2020.3048415.

10. Demilie, W.B., Plant disease detection and classification techniques: a comparative study of the performances. *J. Big Data*, 11, 5, 2024, https://doi.org/10.1186/s40537-023-00863-9

11. Benos, L., Tagarakis, A.C., Dolias, G., Berruto, R., Kateris, D., Bochtis, D., Machine learning in agriculture: A comprehensive updated review. *Sensors*, 21, 3758, 2021, https://doi.org/10.3390/s21113758.

12. Tian, H., Wang, T., Liu, Y., Qiao, X., Li, Y., Computer vision technology in agricultural automation—A review. *Inf. Process. Agric.*, 7, 1, 1–19, 2020, https://doi.org/10.1016/j.inpa.2019.09.006.

13. Senapaty, M.K., Ray, A., Padhy, N., IoT-enabled soil nutrient analysis and Crop recommendation model for precision agriculture. *Computers*, 12, 61, 2023, https://doi.org/10.3390/computers12030061.

14. Talaviya, T., Shah, D., Patel, N., Yagnik, H., Shah, M., Implementation of artificial intelligence in agriculture for optimisation of irrigation and application of pesticides and herbicides. *Artif. Intell. Agric.*, 4, 58–73, 2020, https://doi.org/10.1016/j.aiia.2020.04.002.

15. Domingues, T., Brandão, T., Ferreira, J.C., Machine learning for detection and prediction of crop diseases and pests: A comprehensive survey. *Agriculture*, 12, 1350, 2022, https://doi.org/10.3390/agriculture12091350.

16. Singh, G. and Singh, J., A fog computing based agriculture-IoT framework for detection of alert conditions and effective crop protection. *2023 5th International Conference on Smart Systems and Inventive Technology (ICSSIT)*, Tirunelveli, India, pp. 537–543, 2023, doi: 10.1109/ICSSIT55814.2023.10060995.

17. Baghrous, M., Ezzouhairi, A., Benamar, N., Smart Farming System Based on Fog Computing and LoRa Technology, in: *Embedded Systems and Artificial IntelligenceAdvances in Intelligent Systems and Computing*, vol. 1076, V. Bhateja, S. Satapathy, H. Satori, (Eds.), Springer, Singapore, 2020, https://doi.org/10.1007/978-981-15-0947-6_21.

18. Whig, P. *et al.*, Fog-IoT-assisted-based smart agriculture application, in: *Demystifying Federated Learning for Blockchain and Industrial Internet of Things*, S. Kautish and G. Dhiman (Eds.), pp. 74–93, IGI Global, Hershey, PA, 2022, https://doi.org/10.4018/978-1-6684-3733-9.ch005.

19. Alharbi, H.A. and Aldossary, M., Energy-efficient edge-fog-cloud architecture for IoT-based smart agriculture environment. *IEEE Access*, 9, 110480–110492, 2021, doi: 10.1109/ACCESS.2021.3101397.

20. Sucharitha, V., Prakash, P., Iyer, G., Agrifog-a fog computing based IoT for smart agriculture. *Int. J. Recent Technol. Eng.*, 7, 210–217, 2019.

21. R, V.S., J, S., P, S.C., K, N., M, S.H., K, M.S., Smart farming: The IoT based future agriculture. *2022 4th International Conference on Smart Systems and Inventive Technology (ICSSIT)*, Tirunelveli, India, pp. 150–155, 2022, 10.1109/ICSSIT53264.2022.9716331.

22. Nath, S., Debnath, D., Sarkar, P., Biswas, A., An efficient implementation of data mining techniques in agriculture. *J. Comput. Theor. Nanoscience*, 17, 1, 154–161, 2020.

23. Wenli, G., Liang, Z., Shengquan, L., Ying, G., Hui, G., Bin, H., Machine learning prediction of lignin content in poplar with Raman spectroscopy. *Bioresource Technol.*, 348, 126812, 2022, https://doi.org/10.1016/j.biortech.2022.126812.

24. Ippolito, P.P., Hyperparameter tuning, in: *Applied Data Science in Tourism. Tourism on the Verge*, R. Egger, (Ed.), Springer, Cham, Springer Nature Switzerland AG, 2022, https://doi.org/10.1007/978-3-030-88389-8_12.

25. Borislava, V., The proportion for splitting data into training and test set for the bootstrap in classification problems. *Business Syst. Res. J.*, 12, 1, 228–242, 2021.

26. Karuppusamy, P., Perikos, I., Shi, F., Nguyen, T.N., Sustainable communication networks and application, in: *Lecture Notes Data Eng. Commun. Technol*, pp. 65–72, 2020.

27. Le, N.T., Wang, J.W., Wang, C.C., Nguyen, T.N., Automatic defect inspection for coated eyeglass based on symmetrized energy analysis of color channels. *Symmetry*, 11, 12, 15–18, 2019.

5

Role of Intelligent IoT Applications in Fog Computing

Pawan Whig[1]*, Dhaya Sindhu Battina[2], Srinivas Venkata[3], Ashima Bhatnagar Bhatia[1] and Yusuf Jibrin Alkali[4]

[1]Vivekananda Institute of Professional Studies-TC, New Delhi, India
[2]Campbellsville University, Campbellsville, KY, United States
[3]Teradata, San Diego, CA, USA
[4]Federal Inland Revenue Service, Abuja, Nigeria

Abstract

Smart buildings utilize Internet of Things (IoT) devices, sensors, software, and Internet connectivity to monitor various aspects of the building, analyze data, and extract insights to enhance the building's environment and operations. Although smart technology provides increased control over a building, it goes beyond simple "command and control" methods. The term "smart building" has likely been mentioned to you as a building owner or facility manager. Smart buildings, like other smart advancements, aim to offer greater control, specifically, control over the building's environment and operations. Imagine the ability to relocate occupants if particle levels become hazardous or the potential to save significant amounts of money on energy bills by strategically operating an HVAC system. These actions lead to tangible benefits that greatly assist the inhabitants, the bottom line, and the environment. Unsurprisingly, 70% of businesses plan to increase their investments in smart-building technologies in the future. The book chapter delves into the IoT in smart buildings and concludes with a case study, providing valuable insights for researchers working in this field.

Keywords: IoT, HVAC, smart building, software, internet, intelligent IoT, fog computing, edge computing, internet of thing, big data analytics, security and privacy

*Corresponding author: pawanwhig@gmail.com

Chandan Banerjee, Anupam Ghosh, Rajdeep Chakraborty and Ahmed A. Elngar (eds.) Fog Computing for Intelligent Cloud IoT Systems, (99–118) © 2024 Scrivener Publishing LLC

5.1   Introduction

The architecture of the Internet of Things (IoT) depends heavily on cloud computing. A cloud platform receives data collected by sensors and devices. It is then combined, normalized, processed using predetermined standards, and utilized [1]. However, real-time and mission-critical applications are not best served by the cloud architecture. Consider a manufacturing process that continuously produces goods at a high rate. If the system does not correct immediately once the sensors detect an abnormality, the flaw spreads. It takes seconds to move from detection to correction [2]. The response time of a self-driving automobile must be measured in milliseconds. The journey from the device through the gateway to the cloud and back is too long for many applications. PaaS- and SaaS-founded cloud technologies are increasingly being used to power the Internet of Things (IoT) because enterprise applications have been slowly moving away from corporate data centers. PaaS and SaaS have emerged in recent years as two key-enabling models for the IoT industry across a variety of use cases. Services are available from PaaS providers and ready for use [3]. Application-level services including billing, software administration, and visualization tools are provided by the SaaS providers. PaaS/SaaS systems include Microsoft Azure, AWS IoT, and Google IoT Core, as shown in Figure 5.1.

With the rise of the Internet of Things (IoT), devices and sensors are now more connected than ever before, leading to a vast amount of data that requires processing and analysis. This surge in data poses a challenge in terms of efficient data transmission and processing. Fog computing has emerged as a promising solution to overcome this challenge.

Fog computing involves bringing data processing and analysis closer to the edge of the network where the data are generated. Instead of sending all the data to a centralized cloud server for processing, fog computing allows localized processing at the network edge. This approach reduces latency and bandwidth usage by enabling real-time analytics and decision-making in close proximity to the data source.

By leveraging fog computing, organizations can benefit from faster response times, improved reliability, and reduced data-transmission costs. It is particularly advantageous in scenarios where low latency is crucial, such as industrial applications, smart cities, and autonomous vehicles.

Furthermore, fog computing enhances the privacy and security of data. Because data are processed locally, sensitive information can be maintained

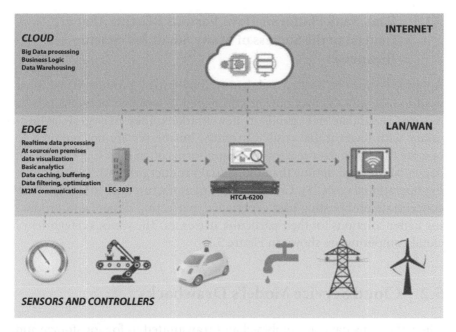

Figure 5.1 Procedure movement of sensor to cloud.

within the local network, reducing the risks associated with transmitting sensitive data over long distances.

This chapter explores the role of intelligent IoT applications in fog computing and the transformation of various industries. The first section provides an overview of fog computing and its benefits, followed by a discussion on intelligent IoT applications and their impact on different industries, including healthcare, transportation, and manufacturing. The next section delves into the technical aspects of implementing intelligent IoT applications in fog computing environments, such as data management, security, and privacy. We explore different approaches to address these challenges and highlight the latest research in this field. The third section focuses on the emerging trends and future of intelligent IoT applications in fog computing, including the integration of machine learning and artificial intelligence, the use of blockchain for secure data management, and the potential for autonomous decision making at the edge of the network. Finally, we conclude with a summary of the key takeaways from this chapter and discuss the potential implications of intelligent IoT applications in fog computing for businesses and society as a whole.

5.1.1   PaaS/SaaS Platforms Have Various Benefits That are Crucial to the Success of Many Small IoT Startup Businesses

Applications can be created and deployed by fast-by-product firms. What used to take months may now be completed in a matter of weeks [4]. As businesses validate new goods in new markets, they may grow as necessary with lower initial costs. Currently, businesses are not required to operate their own data centers. These platforms often offer higher levels of dependability and uptime than individual product firms while also lowering operational costs [5]. Consequently, manufacturers of IoT goods may concentrate on boosting user experience, perfecting design, and producing better solutions for their particular use cases. The various categories of cloud computing are shown in Figure 5.2.

5.2   Cloud Service Model's Drawbacks

Altogether, raw data are combined and transmitted to fog for storage and dispensation in a purely cloud-centric architecture [6]. Despite its benefits, this approach has several significant flaws:

- Unpredictable endpoint response times from the cloud server.
- Unreliable cloud connectivity may cause the service to stop operating.

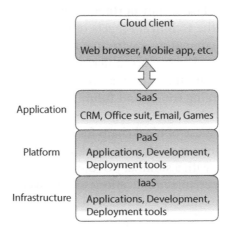

Figure 5.2 Various categories of cloud computing.

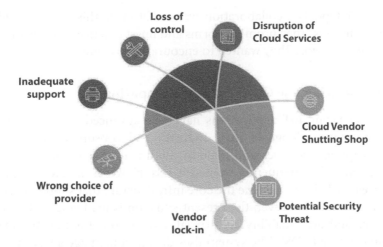

Figure 5.3 Flaws of fog computing.

- Infrastructure may be overloaded with too much data.
- Scaling challenges with an ever-growing number of sensors and actuators Privacy concerns when sensitive customer data is kept in the cloud.

Owing to its flaws, cloud-centric architecture is not ideal for industrial, healthcare, or military applications that are more mission-critical. The flaws in fog computing are illustrated in Figure 5.3.

5.3   Fog Computation

Applications of IIoT benefit greatly from fog computing. Instead of utilizing a distant cloud data center, the design collects, stores, and processes data using local computing nodes situated between the endpoints and cloud datacenters [7]. Connected devices communicate with a nearby node that is often located on the premises by sending and receiving data and commands. The node may be a gateway device with additional processing and storage capabilities, such as a switch or router. It can take in, process, and respond to incoming data in real-time [8].

5.3.1   Standardization

Data and interface compatibility has become a problem as fog computing applications and providers expand. The industry's incompatibility will prevent the technology from being widely used.

In 2015, OpenFog collaboration was established. This is supported by many businesses. They promote norms and finest practices for creating fog computing systems. They wanted to encourage cross-industry [9].

5.3.2   Growing Use Cases for Fog Computing

Consumer-facing IoT applications have also advanced in sophistication and importance alongside IIoT. Industry and consumers have examined intriguing use cases and hype in the initial wave of consumer IoT applications. They frequently wanted it less. However, as the IoT industry develops, IoT will become the core infrastructure that supports crucial daily operations. However, the present situation is inadequate. Real-time reactions and dependability are crucial. Among these is the Automated Driving System (ADS). The system uses data fusion, image analysis, mapping, and forecasts to determine the optimal course of action and controls for the drivetrain. All of this must be completed reliably and without delays in milliseconds. A strong processing node in an automobile with built-in redundancy is required because of data bandwidth and latency requirements [10].

5.3.3   IoT Applications with Intelligence

In addition to ADS, computer vision and artificial intelligence (AI) applications will enhance the demand for fog computing. An intelligent Internet of Things system does not merely gather and analyze data for human use. It must react to circumstances devoid of human help. It uses data from several sensors and real-time AI inference. Subsequently, it directs actuators in machines, drones, and robots to perform certain activities [11]. The AI engine also gathered real-time outcomes in an unsupervised scenario to assess the appropriate course of action. A mixed fog/cloud architecture is required, with edge dispensation bulges handling time-subtle process dreams and AI meddling errands. Fog bulges also perform non-actual operations such as package updates, background data collection, and lasting big information processing.

5.3.4   Graphics Processing Units

Deep Neural Network (DNN) technology is used in cutting-edge AI systems. To attain improved accuracy, DNNs use deep network architectures. However, implementation often requires considerable data flow and a large number of computing units. To address the increasing demands, mechanism knowledge and AI investigators are turning to GPU [12]. GPUs have been ubiquitous in high-performance gaming systems for many years.

Since 2007, Nvidia has been developing Compute Unified Device Architecture (CUDA) technology to use the capability of its graphics hardware for computing tasks other than 3D. The CUDA programming API has enabled researchers in various fields.

5.4   Recompenses of FoG

Some fog recompenses were labeled underneath, as shown in Figure 5.3. It extends the concept of cloud computing by introducing a distributed architecture that includes nodes closer to devices that generate, allowing for more efficient processing and utilization of resources.

1. Reduced Latency
2. Improved Data Processing
3. Improved Safety
4. Improved Scalability
5. Reduced Bandwidth Costs
6. Increased Reliability
7. Improved User Experience.

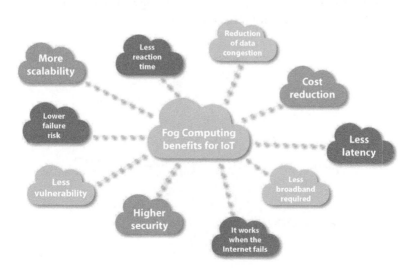

Figure 5.4 Advantages of fog computation.

With the continuous expansion of the Internet of Things (IoT), fog computing is becoming increasingly crucial for organizations aiming to harness the advantages offered by the IoT, as depicted in Figure 5.4.

5.5   Limitation of Fog Computing

This approach has several advantages, such as reducing latency, improving data privacy and security, and enabling real-time decision making. However, there are limitations to fog computing that must be considered, as shown in Figure 5.5.

1. Limited Computing Resources
Fog computing relies on edge devices, such as routers, switches, and gateways, to provide computing resources. These devices have limited processing power, memory, and storage capacity compared with cloud data centers. Therefore, fog computing applications may be limited by the processing power of edge devices, particularly for complex applications such as machine learning and artificial intelligence.

2. Scalability
Fog computing may face scaling challenges when handling large amounts of data and devices. As more devices are added to the network, the computational load on edge devices may increase, leading to performance issues. In addition, the limited storage capacity of edge devices may become a bottleneck when dealing with large datasets.

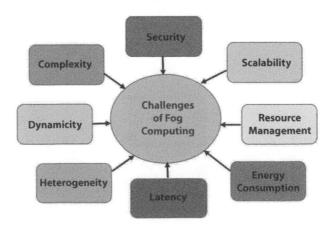

Figure 5.5 Limitations of fog computing.

3. Network Connectivity

Fog computing relies on network connectivity to transmit data and information between edge devices and the cloud. Any disruptions in a network can cause delays in data transmission, which can affect the real-time decision-making capabilities of the system. In addition, the availability and reliability of network connectivity may be limited in remote or rural areas, which may limit the effectiveness of fog computing in such regions.

4. Maintenance and Management

Fog computing requires proper maintenance and management to ensure smooth operation of the system. Edge devices must be monitored and maintained to prevent hardware failures and ensure that they operate at optimal performance levels.

5. Compatibility

Fog computing requires compatibility between devices and systems. Edge devices and cloud services must be able to communicate with each other using common protocols and interfaces. If devices are incompatible, it may be difficult to integrate them into the fog computing architecture.

6. Cost

Fog computing can be more expensive than traditional cloud computing, because it requires more hardware and software infrastructure at the edge of the network. Additionally, the cost of maintaining and managing edge devices can be higher than that for cloud data centers, as the devices are distributed across different locations and may require on-site maintenance.

In conclusion, although fog computing has several advantages over traditional cloud computing, it has several limitations that must be considered. These limitations include limited computing resources, scalability, security, privacy, network connectivity, maintenance and management, compatibility, and cost.

5.6   Fog Computing with IoT

Together, fog computing and the IoT offer many benefits, including improved performance, reduced latency, and enhanced data security and privacy. In this article, we explore the relationship between fog computing and IoT and discuss their benefits and challenges.

5.6.1   Benefits of Fog Computing with IoT

1. Better Performance: Fog computing with IoT offers improved performance by reducing latency and enabling real-time decision making.
2. Reduced Bandwidth: Fog computing with IoT reduces the amount of data that must be transmitted to the cloud for processing and analysis, which can help reduce network congestion and bandwidth requirements.
3. Scalability: Fog computing with IoT is highly scalable because it allows for the addition of new edge devices as the network grows. This approach can help organizations scale their IoT deployment more efficiently and effectively.
4. Cost-Effective: Fog computing with IoT can be more cost-effective than traditional cloud computing.

5.6.2   Challenges of Fog Computing with IoT

1. Limited Computing Resources: Fog computing with IoT relies on edge devices, such as routers, switches, and gateways, to provide computing resources. These devices have limited processing power, memory, and storage capacity compared with cloud data centers. Therefore, fog computing applications may be limited by the processing power of edge devices, particularly for complex applications such as machine learning and artificial intelligence.
2. Compatibility: Fog computing with the IoT requires compatibility between different devices and systems. Edge devices and cloud services must be able to communicate with each other using common protocols and interfaces.
3. Network Connectivity: Fog computing with IoT relies on network connectivity to transmit data and information between edge devices and cloud. Any disruptions in a network can cause delays in data transmission, which can affect the real-time decision-making capabilities of the system. Additionally, the availability and reliability of network connectivity may be limited in remote or rural areas, which may limit the effectiveness of fog computing with the IoT in such regions.
4. Maintenance and Management: Fog computing with IoT requires proper maintenance and management to ensure

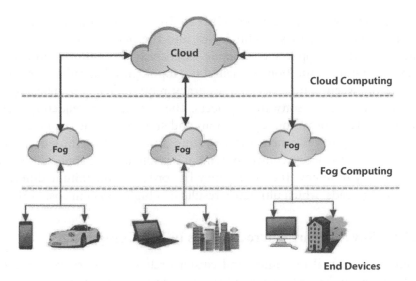

Figure 5.6 Fog calculation with IoT.

smooth operation of the system. Edge devices and cloud services must be updated and patched regularly to prevent security vulnerabilities and ensure compatibility.

5. Data Management: Fog computing with IoT generates vast amounts of data that must be managed effectively. Organizations must implement effective data management policies and tools to ensure that data are stored securely and accessed appropriately.

The relationship between fog computing and IoT Internet and end users is strengthening. Figure 5.6 depicts IoT devices that use fog computing [13].

5.7   Edge AI Embedded

Typical GPUs are far too expensive and power demanding for many embedded or mobile applications. The Nvidia Jetson podium is frequently utilized in ADS and smart drones. Similar embedded AI technologies are being actively developed by Intel, as evidenced by their recent acquisition of the Movidius computer vision semiconductor business. In addition to start-ups, Qualcomm, Mediatek, Huawei, AMD, and other IT companies continue to watch the industry. They added neural network functionality to their next system-on-chip (SOC) [14]. The next several years will see the introduction of these technologies into the market. Software developers and chip suppliers collaborate extensively to optimize processor implementations. Additionally, neural net topologies that satisfy the ideal balance between complexity and accuracy requirements are being optimized by embedded software engineers. The supplies are frequently drastically different for various applications and situations. One such instance is facial recognition, where the real-time and out-of-the-box accuracy requirements for access control systems and photo tagging applications are significantly different. The discrepancy has orders of magnitude different processing needs, which ultimately results in a higher system cost [15].

5.7.1   Key Software Characteristics in Fog Computing

Containers, virtual machines, and cluster orchestration are examples of software technologies that have advanced in terms of offering services and applications for every user. Although separated environments for running user-requested programs are referred to by both the terms "containers" and "VMs," there are significant distinctions between them [16]. Some key software characteristics in fog computing are shown in Figure 5.7.

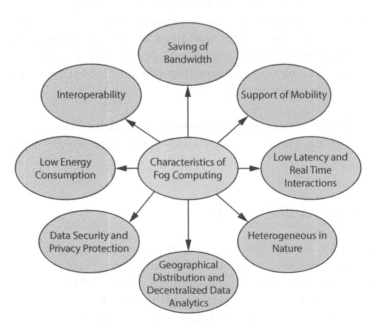

Figure 5.7 Software characteristics in fog computing.

Containers: Small, standalone, executable package of software that includes everything needed to run it, including code, runtime, system tools, system libraries, and settings. The application software dependencies are all included in the container images, making the cross-platform deployment simple [17–22].

Virtual Machines

In contrast to containerization, a Virtual Machine (VM) wraps the entire operating system, including the services and applications inside, as a single virtual machine. VMs are naturally considerably larger and utilize more resources than containers do. Consequently, a system may support considerably fewer virtual machines (VMs) than containers, and VM fetching and initialization can consume far more resources (memory, CPU, and disc space) than container fetching and initialization. Containers outperform virtual machines (VMs) for the two virtualization technologies in a fog-computing environment [23–25].

5.7.2   Fog Cluster Management

The fog cluster management method is essential for cluster management. Container and cluster orchestration technologies benefit intelligence in fog computing by bringing intelligence closer to consumers.

5.7.3   Technology for Computing in the Fog

As previously indicated, current improvements have improved the intellectual capacity of fog and IoT networks. Although there has been much discussion about the use of intelligence in services and applications, such as patient monitoring and video surveillance, its potential to improve system performance and network efficiency has not yet been extensively explored. This essay concentrates on the latter, and in what follows, we'll outline the main thrust, the network goals, and some intelligence analysis techniques.

5.7.4   Concentrating Intelligence

The network edge, where devices and users are prominent, is receiving increasing attention. As a result, we should emphasize the importance of implementing intelligence in fog [26–28].

5.7.5   Device-Driven Intelligence

The importance of human users, who have integrated themselves seamlessly into the IoT environment, should not be overlooked even though gadgets are at the front of the fog and IoT ladder. Humans serve as the network's data sources because their behavioral patterns may be used to teach the network to become smarter, even though technical advancements aid in meeting human requirements. The provision of human requirements has so far been the focus of a sizable number of pertinent studies, such as scheduling home appliances and enhancing living standards in IoT-based smart home systems. In an ideal world, we can imagine a system that learns to carry out more of its network-specific duties while still serving individuals [29–31].

5.8   Network Intelligence Objectives

Although energy and latency reductions are our primary concerns in fog computing, a much wider variety of performance metrics may be as follows:

a) Energy Consumption
Offloading work to adjacent fog nodes can help solve this problem by lowering computational complexity. It is difficult to meet the requirements for when and what to offload. It is anticipated that intelligent algorithms will help with the creation of such methods.

b) Network Bandwidth
As the Internet of Things has developed, the volume of data produced by EUs has increased. Sending all data back to the cloud for processing is difficult because of the limited system bandwidth.

5.9   Farming with Fog Computation (Case Study)

Farming with fog computation is a novel approach in agriculture that leverages the power of fog computing to improve farming practices. In this case study, we explored how a group of farmers in a rural area implemented this approach to improve their yields and reduce costs [32–35].

The farmers in this case study were based in a remote area, where access to technology and resources was limited. They face several challenges, including limited access to water, poor soil quality, and unpredictable weather patterns. These challenges make it difficult for them to grow crops and generate reliable incomes.

Farmers began by installing a network of sensors and IoT devices on their farms. These devices collect data on soil moisture levels, temperature, humidity, and other environmental factors. The data were then transmitted to a nearby fog node, where they were processed and analyzed.

The fog node is equipped with a range of software tools and algorithms that can interpret the data and provide real-time insights into the condition of crops. For example, farmers can use the data to determine when to irrigate their crops, how much fertilizer to use, and when to harvest their crops. One of the key benefits of fog computing is that it can be used to automate many tasks involved in farming. For example, farmers in this case study used fog computing to automate their irrigation systems. The sensors and IoT devices detected when the soil moisture levels were low and automatically activated the irrigation system [36].

Another benefit of fog computing is that it can be used to optimize resource use. For example, the farmers in this case study used the data collected by the sensors to determine the optimal amount of fertilizer to use for their crops. The fog computing solution also enabled farmers to monitor the condition of their crops in real-time. This allowed them to identify potential issues before they became a major problem. For example, if the sensors detected that the temperature in a particular area was too high, farmers could take action to mitigate the risk of crop damage.

In addition to improving the yield and quality of their crops, the fog computing solution also had a positive impact on farmers' bottom line. By reducing the amount of water and fertilizer used, they were able to cut costs and increase their profits. They also experienced fewer crop losses and were able to sell their crops at higher prices. In conclusion, the farmers in this case study were able to leverage the power of fog computing to improve their farming practices and generate reliable income. By using sensors and IoT devices to collect data on their crops and process the data in real time using fog computing, they were able to optimize their use of resources, automate many of their farming tasks, and improve the yield and quality of their crops. This approach has the potential to revolutionize agriculture in remote areas and enable farmers to overcome some of the challenges they face. Figure 5.8 depicts the smart farming model.

There are significant barriers to IoT-cloud computing. Figure 5.9 depicts the clever and smart agriculture.

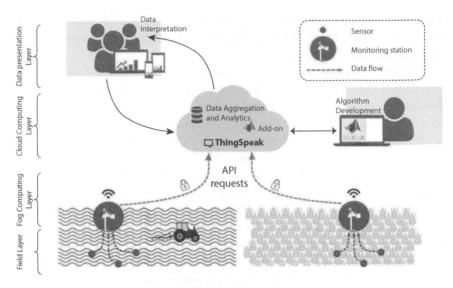

Figure 5.8 Model of clever agriculture.

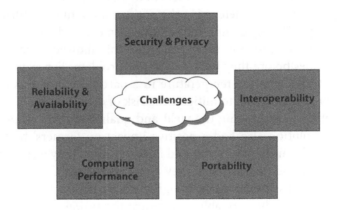

Figure 5.9 Some key obstacles to IoT cloud computing.

Case 1

To address security issues, continuous computing can be employed to min-imize the risk of data compromise or theft during data transportation from one device to another within the network infrastructure. This approach reduces the likelihood of potential vulnerabilities at any point in the net-work and ensures data security by processing and collecting information within the device itself [37].

Case 2

In today's fast-paced business world, gathering and analyzing information is time-consuming. This is particularly true for remote farming equipment. Businesses may be forced to choose between the quality of information they collect and the speed at which they process it. By analyzing the data collected by each network device and improving processor rates and understanding, businesses can improve the speed and accuracy of their decision-making processes.

Case 3

Economic complexity: The expenses of cloud computing generated by objects and delivered across the network are generally determined. Given the number of plans used by a solitary keen agricultural scheme and the volume of information delivered, the cost of the public cloud may quickly increase.

Various examples of smart agriculture range from nursing weather alteration and harvesting circumstances to autonomous house processes and IoT-enabled edge farm management services. The main opportunity lies in so-called "precise agriculture," which involves the use of advantage controls for keen farming.

5.10   Conclusion

In conclusion, intelligent IoT applications in fog computing have immense potential to revolutionize the way we interact with the digital world. By leveraging the power of edge computing, businesses can improve their operational efficiency, enhance customer experience, and even create new revenue streams.

In the future, the role of intelligent IoT applications in fog computing will only grow. As an increasing number of devices are connected to the Internet, the need for real-time data processing and analysis will only increase, driving the demand for fog computing solutions. Overall, the future of intelligent IoT applications in fog computing is exciting, and we expect to see significant advancements in this area in the years to come. With the potential to unlock new levels of efficiency and productivity, fog computing plays a crucial role in the digital transformation of businesses and society.

References

1. Hossain, M.S., Muhammad, G., Amin, M.B., Fog computing: An overview of big data analytics in IoT architectures. *J. Network Comput. Appl.*, 140, 30–42, 2019.
2. Taleb, T., Ksentini, A., Vidal, J., Fog computing architecture for the internet of things. *IEEE Commun. Mag.*, 55, 4, 22–29, 2017.
3. Zhang, Q., Liu, X., Chen, H., Fog computing: A review of concepts, technologies, and applications. *Commun. Surveys & Tutorials*, 21, 4, 3876–3907, 2019.
4. Al-Fuqaha, A., Guizani, M., Mohammadi, M., Aledhari, M., Ayyash, M., Internet of things: A survey on enabling technologies, protocols, and applications. *IEEE Commun. Surveys & Tutorials*, 17, 4, 2347–2376, 2015.
5. Varshney, U., Mobile edge computing: opportunities and challenges. *IEEE Comput.*, 50, 3, 54–62, 2017.
6. Zhang, Y., Zhang, Y., Zhou, X., Survey on security and privacy issues in fog computing. *J. Ambient Intell. Humaniz. Computing*, 10, 1, 107–121, 2019.
7. Shi, W., Cao, J., Zhang, Q., Li, Y., Xu, L., Edge computing: Vision and challenges. *IEEE Internet Things J.*, 3, 5, 637–646, 2016.
8. Bonomi, F., Milito, R., Zhu, J., Addepalli, S., Fog computing and its role in the internet of things, in: *Proceedings of the First Edition of the MCC Workshop on Mobile Cloud Computing*, ACM, pp. 13–16, 2012.
9. Ahmed, S.E. and Yaqoob, I., Intelligent IoT applications: current and future perspectives. *J. Ambient Intell. Humaniz. Computing*, 11, 1, 1–18, 2020.
10. Lu, R., Li, X., Liang, X., Lin, X., Shen, X., Fog computing: Focusing on mobile users at the edge. *IEEE Access*, 5, 8947–8960, 2017.
11. Whig, P., Velu, A., Naddikatu, R.R., The economic impact of ai-enabled blockchain in 6G-based industry, in: *AI and Blockchain Technology in 6G Wireless Network*, pp. 205–224, Springer, Singapore, 2022.
12. Alkali, Y., Routray, I., Whig, P., Strategy for reliable, efficient and secure IoT using artificial intelligence. *IUP J. Comput. Sci.*, 16, 2, 1–15, 2022.
13. Whig, P., Velu, A., Sharma, P., Demystifying Federated Learning for Blockchain: A Case Study, in: *Demystifying Federated Learning for Blockchain and Industrial Internet of Things*, pp. 143–165, IGI Global, USA, 2022.
14. Whig, P., Kouser, S., Velu, A., Nadikattu, R.R., Fog-IoT-assisted-based smart agriculture application, in: *Demystifying Federated Learning for Blockchain and Industrial Internet of Things*, pp. 74–93, IGI Global, USA, 2022.
15. Whig, P., Velu, A., Ready, R., Demystifying federated learning in artificial intelligence with human-computer interaction, in: *Demystifying Federated Learning for Blockchain and Industrial Internet of Things*, pp. 94–122, IGI Global, USA, 2022.
16. Whig, P., Velu, A., Bhatia, A.B., Protect nature and reduce the carbon footprint with an application of blockchain for IIoT, in: *Demystifying Federated Learning for Blockchain and Industrial Internet of Things*, pp. 123–142, IGI Global, USA, 2022.

17. Whig, P., Velu, A., Nadikattu, R.R., Blockchain platform to resolve security issues in IoT and smart networks, in: *AI-Enabled Agile Internet of Things for Sustainable FinTech Ecosystems*, pp. 46–65, IGI Global, USA, 2022.

18. Jupalle, H., Kouser, S., Bhatia, A.B., Alam, N., Nadikattu, R.R., Whig, P., Automation of human behaviors and its prediction using machine learning. *Microsystem Technol.*, 1–9, 2022.

19. Tomar, U., Chakroborty, N., Sharma, H., Whig, P., AI based smart agricuture system. *Trans. Latest Trends Artif. Intell.*, 2, 2, 1–12, 2021.

20. Whig, P., Nadikattu, R.R., Velu, A., COVID-19 pandemic analysis using application of AI, in: *Healthcare Monitoring and Data Analysis Using IoT: Technologies and Applications*, p. 1, 2022.

21. Anand, M., Velu, A., Whig, P., Prediction of loan behaviour with machine learning models for secure banking. *J. Comput. Sci. Eng. (JCSE)*, 3, 1, 1–13, 2022.

22. Alkali, Y., Routray, I., Whig, P., Study of various methods for reliable, efficient and Secured IoT using Artificial Intelligence, in: *Proceedings of the International Conference on Innovative Computing & Communication (ICICC)*, 2022, Available at SSRN: https://ssrn.com/abstract=4020364 or http://dx.doi.org/10.2139/ssrn.4020364.

23. Arun Velu, P.W., Impact of Covid vaccination on the globe using data analytics. *Int. J. Sustain. Dev. Computing Sci.*, 3, 2, 1–14, 2021.

24. Rupani, A., Whig, P., Sujediya, G., Vyas, P., A robust technique for image processing based on interfacing of Raspberry-Pi and FPGA using IoT. *2017 Int. Conf. Computer, Commun. Electron. (Comptelix)*, 2017, 350–353, 2017.

25. Sharma, A., Kumar, A., Whig, P., On the performance of CDTA based novel analog inverse low pass filter using 0.35 µm CMOS parameter. *Int. J. Science, Technol. & Manage.*, 4, 1, 594–601, 2015.

26. Whig, P. and Ahmad, S.N., Simulation of linear dynamic macro model of photo catalytic sensor in SPICE. *COMPEL: Int. J. Comput. Mathematics Electrical Electronic Eng.*, 14, 1–23, 2014.

27. Shi, W., Cao, J., Zhang, Q., Li, Y., Xu, L., Edge computing: Vision and challenges. *IEEE Internet Things J.*, 3, 5, 637–646, 2016.

28. Bonomi, F., Milito, R., Zhu, J., Addepalli, S., Fog computing and its role in the internet of things. *Proceedings of the first edition of the MCC workshop on mobile cloud computing*, pp. 13–16, 2012.

29. Gubbi, J., Buyya, R., Marusic, S., Palaniswami, M., Internet of things (IoT): A vision, architectural elements, and future directions. *Future Gener. Comput. Syst.*, 29, 7, 1645–1660, 2013.

30. Liang, X., Li, H., Li, Y., Li, F., Shen, X., Towards intelligent edge computing: A survey. *IEEE Internet Things J.*, 4, 5, 766–785, 2017.

31. Zhang, Y., Liu, C., Chen, J., Cheng, Y., Chen, H., A comprehensive survey on fog computing: State-of-the-art and research challenges. *IEEE Commun. Surveys & Tutorials*, 21, 2, 1664–1717, 2019.

32. Satyanarayanan, M., The emergence of edge computing. *Computer*, 50, 1, 30–39, 2017.
33. Saini, S. and Sharma, N., Intelligent IoT applications in smart city environments: Challenges and opportunities. *J. Ambient Intell. Humaniz. Computing*, 12, 2, 1507–1520, 2021.
34. Yu, W., Huang, X., Chua, S.-J., Zhang, Y., Fog computing with blockchain: Big data processing and management. *IEEE Internet Things J.*, 4, 6, 1717–1726, 2017.
35. Leng, S. and Li, X., Security and privacy issues in fog computing: A comprehensive review. *Future Gener. Comput. Syst.*, 97, 737–749, 2019.
36. Beloglazov, A., Abawajy, J., Buyya, R., Energy-aware resource allocation heuristics for efficient management of data centers for cloud computing. *Future Gener. Comput. Syst.*, 56, 534–551, 2016.
37. Zhou, X., Liu, H., Wu, X., A survey on fog computing security: Requirements and challenges. *IEEE Access*, 7, 117652–117669, 2019.

6

SaaS-Based Data Visualization Platform— A Study in COVID-19 Perspective

S. Majumder[1], A. Shaw[2]*, R. Keshri[2] and A. Chakraborty[2]†

[1]*Department of Computer Science and Engineering, Birla Institute of Technology and Science, Pilani, Rajasthan, India*
[2]*Department of Computer Science and Engineering, Swami Vivekananda University, Kolkata, West Bengal, India*

Abstract

Humans have a long history of essential information representation, which remains an interesting issue today. The historical backdrop of representation has been somewhat molded by accessible innovation. Information representation can be used to identify stowed-away signs and examples in informational collections found in information mining applications.

Currently, the world is grappling with the major pandemic issue of COVID, which has a severe impact on the lives of ordinary people. Dealing with COVID involves a plethora of factors that require extensive information and detail. People have suffered significantly because of a lack of proper information. The information can be anything like the doctor's details, oxygen supplier details, hospital details, and vaccine information.

To solve this scarcity of such information, we develop a working model named "Sahayak—An Initiative to help COVID Patients," which has all the necessary information related to COVID. The Sahayak dashboard will help the common people gather information on the basic needs related to COVID in a crisis. We used the Microsoft Power BI data visualization tool to build Sahayak, which has been publicly hosted in the cloud. Thus, any person with stable Internet will have access to Sahayak.

Corresponding author: aankitsshaw@gmail.com
†*Corresponding author*: amit13.ons@gmail.com

Chandan Banerjee, Anupam Ghosh, Rajdeep Chakraborty and Ahmed A. Elngar (eds.) Fog Computing for Intelligent Cloud IoT Systems, (119–136) © 2024 Scrivener Publishing LLC

Keywords: Pandemic, COVID, symptoms, vaccine, oxygen, lab, hospital, nGO

6.1   Introduction

This section presents background information on various COVID-related components using data visualization. In addition, we explain the motivation and objectives of our project.

6.1.1   Motivation and the Problem of Interest

The emergence of the novel coronavirus disease (COVID-19) in late 2019 has had a significant impact on virtually every aspect of our lives. Initial reports of COVID-19 emerged in Wuhan (Hebei Province, China) in December 2019. Following the outbreak, the virus rapidly spread to all provinces in China and quickly moved to other countries worldwide. More than 45 million cases of COVID-19 have been confirmed in over 180 countries, resulting in over 1 million deaths. Mostly people with existing health issues are the most affected as mentioned in reference [1].

While much of the literature on COVID-19 has focused on the outbreak in China, including the transmission of the disease, the risk factors of infection, and the biological properties of the virus, there is a dearth of information that can assist COVID-19 patients during difficult times.

Data visualization is a useful process that involves representing data as visual images created using a combination of points, lines, coordinate systems, numbers, symbols, words, shadings, and colors. This is a powerful tool for revealing patterns in large or complex datasets. Microsoft Power BI is a robust data-visualization tool that can be used to develop any type of dashboard or report.

With the help of data visualization, we can build a dashboard named SAHAYAK, consisting of several aspects of COVID that can eventually be very beneficial to COVID patients. For example, if a COVID patient wants to know the oxygen supplier details within his/her territory, then he might need to struggle a bit to get the consolidated information, whereas if we have a portal/dashboard that can have all this information consolidated at one place, it can be very helpful for the COVID patients.

6.2   Summary of Objectives

To summarize the research conducted, the following points can be highlighted:

First, we analyzed the pain points of COVID patients. In all phases of COVID patients, what is the major thing they require? Second, we collected data from different sources accordingly. Third, we built structured tabular data from the collected data from different sources. Fourth, we built a Power BI dashboard consisting of all the information to assist COVID patients in their difficult times.

6.3   What is a Pandemic?

A pandemic is an outbreak of a disease that spreads across countries or continents, affects a larger population and resulting in more fatalities than an epidemic. COVID-19 was classified as a pandemic by the World Health Organization (WHO) when it became apparent that the disease was severe and spread rapidly across a wide geographical region. The number of fatalities in a pandemic is determined by various factors, including the severity of the illness, number of people infected, and effectiveness of prevention measures [2]:

- Number of infected individuals
- The severity of the illness caused by the virus (virulence)
- The vulnerability of specific groups of people
- The effectiveness of prevention measures determines the number of lives lost during a pandemic.

The World Health Organization's pandemic alert system ranges from Phase 1, which indicates a low risk, to Phase 6, which signifies a complete pandemic as shown in Table 6.1.

6.4   COVID-19 and Information Gap

COVID-19 is an infectious disease caused by the SARS-CoV-2 virus. While most individuals infected with the virus will have mild-to-moderate respiratory symptoms and recover without any specific treatment, some

Table 6.1 The pandemic alert system of the World Health Organization (WHO) has varying levels of risk, ranging from low to full pandemic.

Phases	Description
Phase 1	There are no known cases of virus transmission from animals to humans.
Phase 2	A virus that originated in animals has infected humans.
Phase 3	There are isolated cases and small outbreaks of the disease in humans. However, if the illness is transmitted from humans to humans, it is not widespread enough to cause outbreaks at the community level.
Phase 4	The disease is transmitted from one person to another and outbreaks of the disease are confirmed at the community level.
Phase 5	The disease is spreading among humans in multiple countries within a region monitored by the World Health Organization (WHO).
Phase 6	There is at least one country in a region different from Phase 5, which has experienced community-level outbreaks.

may become severely ill and require medical attention. Individuals who are older or have underlying medical conditions, such as cardiovascular disease, diabetes, chronic respiratory disease, or cancer, are at a higher risk of developing severe illness. However, anyone, regardless of age, can contract COVID-19 and become seriously ill, or even die.

Apart from the basic details of COVID-19, certain mandate information needs to spread among the society to make them aware of resources that can be helpful for a person affected by COVID-19. Basic information such as hospital details, testing laboratories and helpline numbers, etc. can be very efficient at such times.

6.5   Data Visualization and its Importance

Data visualization is the practice of creating graphic displays to represent data. Depending on the type of data, each data point can be illustrated, as in a scatterplot, or statistical summaries can be shown, as in a histogram. These displays are primarily descriptive, focusing on 'raw' data and simple summaries; however, they can also include transformed data based on complex transformations. What one person considers statistical sum-maries? Another person may see it as raw data. The primary objective is to visualize the data and statistics and interpret the displays to extract information.

Collective COVID-19 information displayed through data visualization is a quick and effective solution.

6.6   Data Management with Data Visualization

Data management is the process of ingesting, storing, organizing, and maintaining data created and collected by an organization. The data man-agement process includes a combination of different functions that collec-tively aim to ensure that data in corporate systems are accurate, available, and accessible.

While working on Sahayak, integrating data management techniques with data visualization is a very important aspect. Because we are building a dashboard to help society, data integrity needs to have a solid data man-agement component. We rely heavily on Microsoft tools such as Excel for data management.

6.7   What is Power BI?

Microsoft's Power BI is a technology-driven business intelligence tool that enables the analysis and visualization of raw data to provide actionable information. It combines business analytics, data visualization, and best practices to assist organizations in making data-driven decisions. The tool can handle large volumes of data and construct dashboards. Therefore, Power BI was an ideal choice for our project [3, 4].

6.7.1   Data Collection & Wrangling

In this section, we understand the input data used to build the dashboard, and the raw input is handled and transformed into structured tabular data.

6.7.2   Data Description & Source

In this section, we understand the input data used to build the dashboard, and the raw input is handled and transformed into structured tabular data as shown in Table 6.2.

Table 6.2 Data table names.

Table name	
COVID Affected People	State-wise COVID Helpline Numbers
COVID Cases Information India	State-wise NGO Details
Day wise Symptoms	State-wise COVID Hospitals
Managing Symptoms	Testing Lab Information
Oxygen Supplier Information	Vaccinated People list
Post Vaccine Effects	Vaccination In India

6.7.3 Data Transformation

We used the data to build a repository with raw data in a transformed format. A few of the transformations used in the process are cleaning missing data, removing duplicates, removing junk characters, and fixing data types.

6.8   Output Data

As an output, we have a total of 12 different tables listed in Table 6.2.

6.9   Design & Implementation

6.9.1   Integration Design

Sahayak follows a simple design consisting of four components data, orchestration, analysis, and visualization as shown in Figure 6.1 and mentioned in references [3–5]. It starts with data collection, where several data sources, such as government websites and Internet scrapping, are involved. The collected data are then passed to the ingestion layer with it going to the flat files as the final data output following the data transformation process handled in Excel. The transformation is then passed to Power BI through data analytics to obtain the final dashboard.

6.9.2   High-Level Process Flow

The process flow as shown in Figure 6.2 also explains four processes: infrastructure and source identification, data integration, monitoring, and data

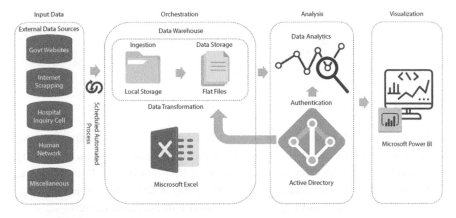

Figure 6.1 Integration design.

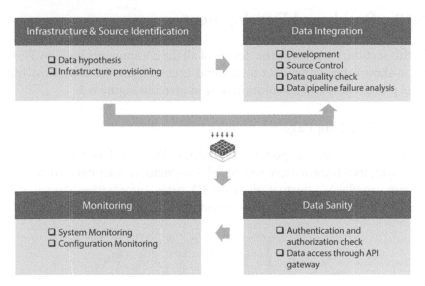

Figure 6.2 High-level process flow.

sanitation. Infrastructure and source identification requires data hypothesis and infrastructure provisioning, which requires development, source control, data quality check, and pipeline failure analysis. Monitoring is required for configuration and system followed by data sanity for data access through the API gateway.

6.9.3   Solution Flow

The solution flow as shown in Figure 6.3 comprises seven steps: data collection, data ingestion, data pre-processing, data transformation, data storage,

Figure 6.3 Solution flow.

data visualization, and end-user consumption. We followed data cleaning and transformation techniques such as cleaning missing data, removing duplicates, removing junk characters, fixing the data types, data mapping, labeling, and data conversion to the wrangling of the data. Table 6.2 illustrates the data tables and Figure 6.1 shows the integration design.

6.10 Dashboard Development

In this section, we provide the details of all the components built on Power BI to show informative data to the end users. Figure 6.2 shows the high level process flow and it's solution flow in given in Figure 6.3.

6.10.1 Landing Page

Here, we have eight components as shown in Figure 6.4: helpline information, symptom information, testing lab information, hospital information, oxygen supplier's information, COVID cases information, vaccination information, and patients' information. Each component has detailed

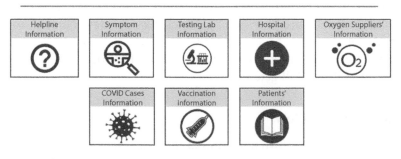

Figure 6.4 Landing page.

information that will help COVID people to do immediate action. We tried to put all the necessary information so that a COVID-positive patient could get help for themselves.

6.10.2   Approach and Design

Landing page design with a bookmark with hyperlinks for eight components. A bookmark is used to provide the current state of each page. This includes the settings we have made to filter, slicers, and visuals on that page. If we click on each component, it will navigate to another page where we can find detailed information about that component. Here, we used the image to better understand the components.

6.10.3   Helpline Information

Here we have six components in helpline information which are state, state wise NGO's name, state wise helpline number, NGO address, state wise helpline email, and back button as shown in Figure 6.5.

6.10.3.1   Approach and Design

Helpline information comprises of six components. The first component is State which is a Slicer with State names. If we can select a state according to that state, we can obtain the result. The second component is the State Wise NGO's Name which is a Card where we can show the name of the NGO.

Figure 6.5 Helping information.

The third component is the state-wise line number, which is also a card that shows Helpline numbers according to a State. COVID people can call the number and help. The fourth component is the NGO Address which is a Card that shows the address of each NGO. The fifth component is the State Wise Helpline Email which is also a Card on which we can see the mail address of the NGO. The sixth component is the back button when we click this button, and we can return to the landing page. Figure 6.4 is the landing page and Figure 6.5 gives the helping information of this model and implementation.

6.10.4   Symptom Detection

Symptom detection has five components as shown in Figure 6.6: symptom detection, day wise symptom detection, indication, physical symptoms, and the back button. This information is very important for COVID people to make them understand how critical or early stages they have, and they can take care of it according to the stages.

6.10.4.1   Approach and Design

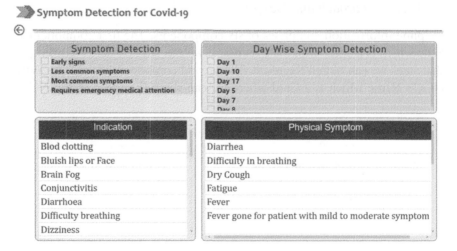

Figure 6.6 Symptom detection.

6.10.5   Testing Lab Information

Here, we have six components: state, state wise COVID testing lab details, testing labs counted by state, % of testing labs in test category, % of testing labs by institute type, and back button. Figure 6.6 shows the symptoms detection.

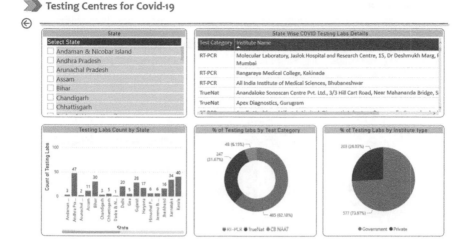

Figure 6.7 Testing centers for COVID-19.

6.10.5.1   Approach and Design

The first component is State which is a Slicer with State names in it. Second Component is State Wise Covid Testing Lab Details which is a Figure 6.7 where we can find the test category and institute name. The third component is the testing labs count by state, which is shown by a stacked column chart, where we can find a state-wise testing lab count. The fourth component is the percentage of testing by the test category, which is a donut chart. The fifth component is the percentage of testing laboratories by institute type, which is a pie chart where we can find government and private testing labs.

6.10.6   Hospital Information

Hospital Information has five components: state, state-wise hospital details, hospital count by state, hospital count by city, and back button.

6.10.6.1   Approach and Design

The first component is State which is a slicer where we can find the state's name. The second component is State Wise Hospital Details which is a Figure 6.8 showing the hospital address with the hospital name. The third component is hospital count by state which is a pie chart. The fourth component is hospital count by city which is a stacked column chart. The fifth component is the back button, which helps return to the landing page.

Covid Hospitals

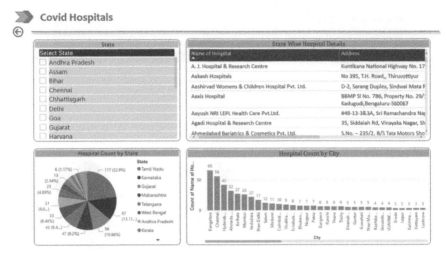

Figure 6.8 Hospital information.

6.10.7   Oxygen Suppliers Information

Here, we have four components: state, oxygen supplier count-by-state, and state-wise oxygen supplier details. COVID people who will suffer from breathing problems can take help from this page.

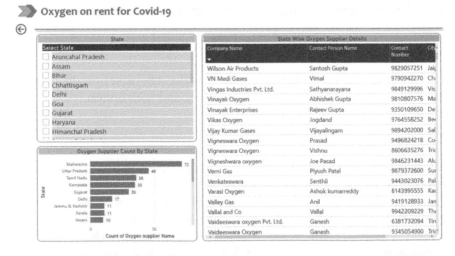

Figure 6.9 Oxygen supplier's information.

6.10.7.1   Approach and Design

The first component is State which is a Slicer which is showing State's name. The second component is State Wise Oxygen Supplier Details which is a Figure 6.9 where we can find the company name, contact person name, contact number, and city. The third component is the oxygen supplier count by state, which is shown in the clustered bar chart. The fourth component is the back button, which helps return to the landing page.

6.10.8   COVID Cases Information

COVID cases information has seven components: state/union territory, confirmed cases by year, deaths by year, recovery by year, confirmed, cured, and deaths by month, and total doses by year as shown in Figure 6.10.

6.10.8.1   Approach and Design

The first component is state/union territory, which is a slicer that shows the state name. The second component is confirmed cases by year, which is a donut of the years 2020 and 2021. The third component is death by year, which is a donut chart that shows the death count by year. The fourth component is the recovery by year, which is a donut chart that shows the recovery count by year. The fifth component was confirmed, cured, and death by month, which is a clustered column chart. The sixth component is

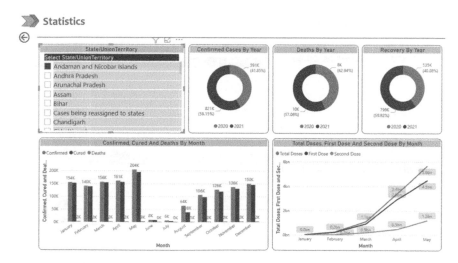

Figure 6.10 COVID cases information.

the total dose, first dose, and the second dose by month, which is a waterfall chart. The seventh component was the back button, which was used to return to the landing page.

6.10.9 Vaccination Information

Here, we have six components: state, state-wise vaccination center, post-vaccination effects, vaccination center count by state and vaccination name, people vaccinated with covaxin and covishield by month, and back button.

6.10.9.1 Approach and Design

The first component is State which is a Slicer that is showing State's name. The second component is State Wise Vaccination Centre which is a Figure 6.11 where we can find the vaccination center name, vaccination name, and address. The third component is the post-vaccination effect which is also shown in the table for post-vaccination effects such as abdominal pain, cold, and body ache. The fourth component is the vaccination center count by state and vaccination name, which is a stacked bar chart. The fifth component is people vaccinated with covaxin and covishield monthly. The sixth component is the back button, which helps return to the landing page.

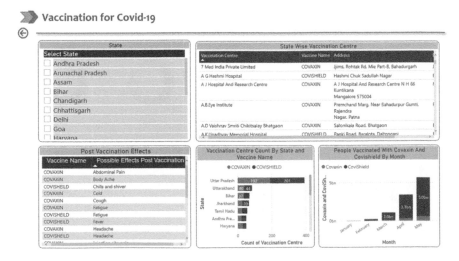

Figure 6.11 Vaccination information.

6.10.10   Patients' Information

Here, we have five components: state, information on vaccinated people, affected and vaccinated people count by state, people who have contracted COVID-19, and the back button.

6.10.10.1   Approach and Design

The first component is State which is a Slicer where we can find the state's name. The second component is Vaccinated People Information which is Figure 6.12 with name, contact, dose1, dose2, vaccine name, age, and vaccination center. The third component is affected, and vaccinated people count by state, which is a donut chart. The fourth component is people who have contracted COVID-19, which is a table. The fifth component is the back button that can be returned to the landing page.

6.11   Advantages and its Impact

COVID is spreading at a high speed in a short time. We need to prevent the transmission of this deadly virus. Sahayak helps people during pandemics in every possible way. It provides all the information a corona patient needs.

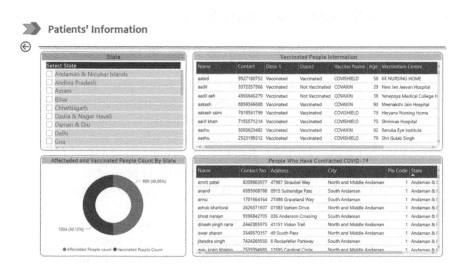

Figure 6.12 Patients' information.

Sahayak analyzed the importance of preventing the COVID-19 pandemic, what solutions people should follow, how to limit the transmission of this virus, and what we should do after getting infected as mentioned in reference [2]. Individuals have access to a vast array of information and options to safeguard themselves in the online environment [5]. However, caution and moderation are necessary. Some of the key advantages of Sahayak are as follows:

- Sahayak helps people understand the symptoms of COVID. If they are infected by the virus when they should admit to the hospital
- With the help of Sahayak people can get state-wise hospital information which helps people to take decisions quickly
- We can have a look at the rate of cured cases in India by month
- Oxygen Supplier details are provided by Sahayak. We can obtain phone numbers to communicate with dealers. Oxygen is very necessary for people who are seriously affected by the virus and have breathing problems
- People also can check information for vaccine and laboratories from Sahayak
- Sahayak also provides helpline numbers according to the city.

6.12   Conclusion and Future Scope

We used data visualization tools such as Power BI to build a very simple yet strong platform that can be beneficial to the needy. The approach of consolidating all multi-source information in one place simplifies the complexity of searching multiple places to gather information related to the same entity. We strongly feel that this dashboard is going to be a game changer for people who are affected, even those who are not affected by COVID. From having very basic details, such as helpline numbers to complex information, such as oxygen cylinder details, is present in the dashboard. With a simple and basic UI, it is very easy for users to traverse and see the information they want.

In the future, we will continue to update the data and plan to incorporate activities such as directly connecting to hospitals, alert systems, tracking the home quarantine COVID patients' details, etc. There is always a huge scope for improvement in such tools as this COVID keeps on changing and asking us to challenge ourselves to tackle it smoothly in our daily life, which leads to the path of continuous improvement.

References

1. Mishra, S., Biswas, S., Gupta, R., Cancer pain management in the era of COVID-19 pandemic: Concerns and adaptation strategies. *Asian Pac. J. Cancer Care*, 5, 83–94, 2020, http://waocp.com/journal/index.php/apjcc/article/view/485.
2. Brant, J.M., Fink, R.M., Thompson, C. *et al.*, Global survey of the roles, satisfaction, and barriers of home health care nurses on the provision of palliative care. *J. Palliat. Med.*, 22, 945–960, 2019, https://pubmed.ncbi.nlm.nih.gov/31380727/.
3. Shaw, A.K., Chakraborty, A., Mohapatra, D., Dutta, S., Scalable IoT solution using cloud services – An automobile industry use case. *2020 Fourth International Conference on I-SMAC (IoT in Social, Mobile, Analytics and Cloud) (I-SMAC)*, Palladam, India, pp. 326–331, 2020, https://doi.org/10.1002/9781119857686.ch6, doi: 10.1109/I-SMAC49090.2020.9243544.
4. Mohapatra, D., Chakraborty, A., Shaw, A.K., Exploring novel techniques to detect aberration from metal surfaces in automobile industries. *Proceedings of International Conference on Communication, Circuits, and Systems*. Lecture Notes in Electrical Engineering, Sabut, S.K., Ray, A.K., Pati, B., Acharya, U.R. (eds.), vol. 728, Springer, Singapore, 2021, https://doi.org/10.1007/978-981-33-4866-0_5.
5. Shaw, A.K. and Chakraborty, A., Secular trend analysis of extracted sentiment data for product positioning using TF-IDF NLP algorithm. *IJRAR - Int. J. Res. Anal. Rev. (IJRAR)*, 6, 2, 666–670, June 2019. E-ISSN 2348-1269, P-ISSN 2349-5138Available at : http://www.ijrar.org/IJRAR19K6116.pdf.

7

A Complete Study on Machine Learning Algorithms for Medical Data Analysis

Inderdeep Kaur* and Aleem Ali

Department of Computer Science and Engineering, Chandigarh University, Gharuan, Mohali, Punjab, India

Abstract

Machine learning (ML) algorithms have become increasingly important in healthcare because of their ability to analyze vast amounts of data from various patients and provide insights that can improve patient outcomes, reduce costs, and enhance overall efficiency. These algorithms may help in disease diagnosis, treatment optimization, prediction of treatment outcomes, and patient risk assessment. They can also assist in clinical decision making, resource allocation, and disease surveillance. Machine learning algorithms have been shown to be invaluable in the fight against COVID-19 in healthcare settings. These algorithms have been used in various ways, such as in developing models that accurately detect COVID-19 from medical images, predicting disease progression, and assisting with drug development. This chapter describes the current state-of-the-art machine learning algorithms used in medical data analysis, including supervised, unsupervised, and reinforcement learning. We also discuss the challenges in medical data analysis, such as the data quality, privacy concerns, and interpretability of ML algorithms. Finally, we highlight the potential of different machine-learning algorithms. Ultimately, the purpose of this chapter is to serve as a resource for academic and industry experts, as well as decision-makers and researchers in a variety of real-world circumstances and application domains, particularly from a technical standpoint.

Keywords: Supervised learning, unsupervised learning, medical data, healthcare and reinforcement learning

---

*Corresponding author: inderdeep.sgtb@gmail.com

Chandan Banerjee, Anupam Ghosh, Rajdeep Chakraborty and Ahmed A. Elngar (eds.) Fog Computing for Intelligent Cloud IoT Systems, (137–172) © 2024 Scrivener Publishing LLC

7.1   Introduction

Machine learning is a branch of artificial intelligence (AI), which is the study of algorithms and statistical models that allows computer systems to automatically learn from data without explicit programming. Machine learning aims to make it possible for machines to become better at a task by learning from experience, much like how people learn [1]. Machine learning algorithms are being rapidly used for medical data analysis enabling healthcare providers to make informed decisions, improve patient outcomes, and optimize treatment plans. These algorithms have a diverse variety of applications in medical data analysis and are increasingly being used to help healthcare providers make more knowledgeable decisions, improve patient outcomes, and optimize treatment plans [2]. From support vector machines (SVM) to artificial neural networks (ANN), random forests, naive Bayes, K-nearest neighbor (K-NN), deep learning, clustering, and principal component analysis, various kinds of machine learning algorithms can be used in medical data analysis, depending on the specific needs of the healthcare provider. From SVMs for medical imaging to ANNs for diagnosis and prognosis, a wide variety of machine learning algorithms are available for medical data analysis, each with its own strengths and limitations. As machine learning technology continues to grow and improve continuously, it is likely that these algorithms will become even more accurate and effective, making themindispensable tools for healthcare providers looking to leverage the power of data to improve patient care.

7.1.1   Importance of Machine Learning Algorithms in Medical Data Analysis

Machine learning has evolved as a critical tool for analyzing medical data because of its ability to process enormous amounts of complex data and recognize patterns and relationships that are challenging to detect using traditional statistical methods. With the explosion of digital health technologies, including EHRs, medical imaging, genomics, and sensor data, the volume, variety, and complexity of medical data are rapidly increasing [1, 3]. Machine learning algorithms offer a powerful alternative for analyzing complex data and generating insights that can improve medical diagnosis, treatment, and patient outcomes [4].

The main advantage of machine learning in medical data analysis is its ability to identify patterns and relationships that are not immediately clear to human analysts. Traditional statistical methods rely on *a priori* assumptions and hypotheses, limiting their ability to detect new and unexpected relationships in data. In contrast, machine learning algorithms are capable of analyzing massive volumes of data, pattern identification, and trend identification, and help in making accurate predictions. Machine learning algorithms, for example, may examine medical imaging data to discover early cancer symptoms that human observers may miss [5]. Similarly, machine learning can be used to analyze genetic data to identify new biomarkers for disease diagnosis and treatment. Figure 7.1 illustrates the various types of machine learning.

These algorithms can also be used to enhance medical diagnosis and treatment by predicting the outcomes of various patients, based on a range of clinical and biological factors. By analyzing patient data and identifying patterns of disease progression, these algorithms can generate personalized treatment plans that optimize treatment efficacy and reduce the risk of adverse events. For example, machine learning algorithms can analyze electronic health records to identify patients at high risk of developing complications and intervene before complications occur [6]. Similarly, machine learning algorithms can analyze genetic data to predict the risk of developing certain diseases and to develop personalized prevention strategies.

Another area in which machine learning has significant potential is drug discovery and development. Machine learning algorithms can be used to analyze vast amounts of data from preclinical studies, clinical trials, and post-market surveillance to identify potential drug targets and optimize drug development. For example, machine learning algorithms can analyze molecular data to identify potential drug targets and predict drug efficacies [6, 7]. Similarly, these algorithms can analyze EHR and clinical trial data to identify patient populations that are most likely to benefit from a particular drug and to optimize dosing and treatment schedules.

Despite the enormous potential of machine learning for medical data analysis, several challenges and limitations must be addressed to ensure the safe and ethical use of these algorithms in medical practice. One of the main challenges is the requirement for transparent and interpretable algorithms. Most of the time, machine-learning algorithms are black boxes, making it challenging to determine how they arrive at corresponding predictions [8]. This lack of transparency makes it challenging for healthcare providers to trust algorithms and incorporate them into clinical decision making. Interpretable algorithms that can provide insights into how they arrive at their predictions are essential for building trust in machine-learning algorithms and ensuring their safe and ethical use in medical practice.

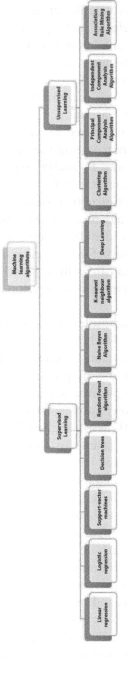

Figure 7.1 Types of machine learning algorithms.

Another problem is ensuring that machine learning algorithms are not biased. Machine-learning algorithms only perform well on the data on which they are trained, and if the data are skewed, the algorithm's predictions [9]. Biases can arise owing to several factors, including sampling, measurement, and algorithmic. Algorithmic bias can arise when a machine-learning algorithm is trained on data that reflect historical biases and inequities, leading to discriminatory predictions. Addressing bias in machine-learning algorithms is necessary to ensure that they are fair and equitable and do not perpetuate existing inequalities in healthcare.

Finally, machine-learning algorithms must be developed and used to protect patient privacy and confidentiality. Medical data are sensitive and protected by strict privacy regulations, including the Health Insurance Portability and Accountability Act (HIPAA) in the United States. Machine learning algorithms must be designed and implemented to ensure that patient data are secure and confidential and comply with applicable privacy regulations [10].

7.2   Pre-Processing Medical Data for Machine Learning

The machine learning process consists of four key steps: data collection, data pre-processing, model training, and model evaluation.

- In the first step, data are collected from various sources and prepared for use in a machine-learning model. This may involve cleaning and formatting the data as well as selecting the appropriate variables and features.
- In the second step, the data are transformed and manipulated to improve their quality and prepare them for use in a machine learning model. This involves tasks such as normalization, feature scaling, and dimensionality reduction.
- In the third step, model training, a machine-learning model was developed using preprocessed data. The goal of model training is to determine the best set of parameters or weights for the model that will allow it to accurately predict the output for new inputs.
- In the final step, the performance of the trained model was evaluated using a separate set of data that was not used in the training process. This allows the performance of the

model to be measured and compared with other models, and any necessary adjustments can be made to improve its performance.

Medical data collection and preparation are essential steps in building machine-learning models for healthcare applications. The quality and quantity of data are critical factors that can significantly affect the accuracy and reliability of models. The key steps involved in collecting and preparing medical data for machine learning are as follows:

- **Identify the data sources**: Medical data can be obtained from different sources such as EHRs, medical imaging devices, wearable devices, and mobile apps. It is essential to identify the relevant sources for the specific healthcare problem that the machine learning model intends to solve.
- **Data cleaning and preprocessing**: Medical data often contain missing values, outliers, and inconsistencies. Data cleaning and pre-processing involve identifying, removing, or correcting these issues to ensure that the data are accurate and ready for analysis. This step may also involve standardizing data formats and handling categorical variables.
- **Feature selection and engineering**: Feature selection involves selecting the relevant variables that are most useful for predicting the target variable. To increase the model performance, feature engineering entails generating new variables or changing existing ones. These steps are critical for improving the model accuracy and reducing the risk of overfitting.
- **Data labeling and annotation**: In certain cases, medical data may need to be labeled or annotated to indicate specific features or characteristics. For example, medical images may need to be labeled to identify specific anatomical structures or pathological features.
- **Data privacy and security**: Medical data are sensitive and subject to strict privacy regulations. It is crucial to ensure that patient data are anonymized and protected to maintain patient privacy and comply with legal requirements.
- **Data augmentation**: This is the process of producing new synthetic data from existing data by applying modifications. This strategy can expand the dataset and enhance model generalization.

- **Collecting and preparing medical data** for machine learning requires careful planning, attention to detail, and thorough understanding of the particular healthcare problem. It is a complex and iterative process that can significantly impact the success of machine-learning models in healthcare applications.

7.3   Supervised Learning Algorithms for Medical Data Analysis

In medical-data analysis, supervised learning algorithms are widely used to create predictions based on labeled data. These algorithms were trained on a dataset with known results before being used to predict fresh unknown data. Support vector machines (SVMs), artificial neural networks (ANNs), random forests, naive Bayes, and k-nearest neighbors are some examples of supervised learning techniques used in medical data processing (KNN) [11]. These algorithms can be used to forecast illness diagnosis, identify risk factors for particular medical disorders, and predict patient outcomes. Healthcare practitioners can make better judgements, offer better patient care, and ultimately save lives by employing supervised learning algorithms. Supervised Learning algorithms are described as follows.

7.3.1   Linear Regression Algorithm

Linear regression is a widely used machine learning method in the medical profession for analyzing and predicting various health outcomes. Linear regression is a supervised learning method that uses one or more predictor variables to predict a continuous variable. The algorithm is based on a linear equation that relates the predictor variables to the dependent variable [12].

$$y = \beta 0 + \beta 1 x1 + \beta 2 x2 + \ldots e$$

Here, y is the dependent variable, x1, x2, ..., xn are the predictor variables, $\beta 0$ is the intercept, $\beta 1$, $\beta 2$, ..., βn are the coefficients for the predictor variables, and e is the error term.

The goal of linear regression is to determine the best-fit line that describes the relationship between the predictor variables and the dependent variable. In medical data analysis, the dependent variable is usually the clinical outcome, such as patient survival, disease progression, or treatment efficacy. The predictor variables included various clinical parameters, such as age, sex, body mass index (BMI), laboratory values, and medical imaging data. There are two types of linear regression: simple linear regression and multiple linear regression. A single predictor variable was used in the simple linear regression, but two or more predictor variables were used in the multiple linear regression. In medical data analysis, multiple linear regression is more commonly used because it allows us to analyze the relationship between multiple predictor variables and the dependent variable simultaneously [13]. For example, we can use multiple linear regression to analyze the relationship between age, sex, BMI, and laboratory values and patient survival.

Linear regression can be performed using different software packages, such as MATLAB, R, and Python. Input data can be in various formats, such as CSV, Excel, or SQL databases. Before applying linear regression to medical data, it is essential to preprocess the data to ensure that they are clean, accurate, and ready for analysis. This involves handling missing values, removing outliers, and normalizing the data if necessary [14]. In addition, it is important to select features to identify the most relevant predictor variables for the analysis. This can be achieved using various techniques such as correlation analysis, forward selection, and backward elimination. Once the data are preprocessed and the relevant predictor variables are identified, the linear regression model can be trained using the input data. The model can then be used to predict new data. Linear regression can be used in various medical applications such as predicting patient survival, analyzing disease progression, and evaluating treatment efficacy.

For example, linear regression can be used to predict patient survival based on various clinical parameters such as age, sex, BMI, and laboratory values. The model can be trained on a dataset of patients with known survival outcomes, and then used to predict the survival of new patients [15]. Similarly, linear regression can be used to analyze the relationship between various clinical parameters and disease progression. For example, linear regression can be used to analyze the relationship between age, sex, BMI, and laboratory values and the progression of a particular disease. Finally, linear regression can be used to evaluate treatment efficacy by analyzing the relationship between treatment variables such as drug dosage, treatment duration, and clinical outcome.

7.3.2   Logistic Regression Algorithm

Logistic regression is a widely used classification algorithm in machine learning that is commonly applied in medical data analysis to predict binary outcomes, such as disease diagnosis and treatment response. In this article, we discuss the use of logistic regression in medical data analysis, and how it can be used to predict binary outcomes [16]. Logistic regression is a sort of supervised learning technique that uses one or more predictor variables to predict a binary outcome (i.e., a yes/no or 0/1 outcome). This approach is based on a logistic function, which converts a linear equation into a probability value ranging from 0 to 1.

$$p(y = 1) = 1/(1 + expn(-z))$$

Where p(y = 1) is the probability of the binary outcome being 1, expn is the exponential function, and z is a linear equation that combines the predictor variables:

$$z = \beta 0 + \beta 1x1 + \beta 2x2 + ... + \beta nxn$$

Where x1, x2, ..., xn are the predictor variables, β0 is the intercept, β1, β2, ..., βn are the coefficients for the predictor variables.

The logistic regression model calculates the coefficients (β1, β2,..., βn) that best explain the connection between predictor variables and binary outcomes. This is accomplished by maximizing the likelihood function, which indicates the probability of witnessing the data given the parameters of the logistic regression model.

Various techniques can be used to estimate the coefficients of the logistic regression model, including maximum likelihood estimation (MLE) and gradient descent. In addition, various regularization techniques that can be used to prevent overfitting, such as L1 and L2 regularization. In medical data analysis, LR is commonly used to predict binary outcomes such as disease diagnosis and treatment response. For example, logistic regression can be used to predict whether a patient has a particular disease based on various clinical parameters, such as age, sex, BMI, and laboratory values.

Logistic regression can also be used to predict treatment response by analyzing the relationship between treatment variables, such as drug dosage and treatment duration, and binary outcomes. Before applying logistic regression to medical data, it is essential to preprocess the data to ensure that it is clean, accurate, and ready for analysis. This involves handling missing values, removing outliers, and normalizing the data if necessary. In addition, it is important to select features to identify the most relevant predictor variables for the analysis. This can be achieved using various techniques such as correlation analysis, forward selection, and backward elimination.

Once the data are preprocessed and the relevant predictor variables are identified, the logistic regression model can be trained using the input data. The model can then be used to predict new data.

Similar to linear regression, LR can be performed using various software packages such as MATLAB R and Python. Input data can be in various formats, such as CSV, Excel, or SQL databases. It is critical to analyze the performance of the logistic regression model in medical data analysis to guarantee that it is accurate and dependable [17]. This may be accomplished using multiple assessment criteria such as accuracy, precision, recall, and F1 score. Additionally, it is important to validate the model on an independent dataset to ensure that it generalizes well to new data. This can be achieved using techniques such as cross validation and bootstrapping.

Logistic regression can also be extended to multiclass classification problems using techniques such as one-vs.-all and multinomial logistic regression. In addition, logistic regression can be combined with other machine-learning algorithms, such as decision trees and random forests to improve its performance. In medical data analysis, logistic regression has been used in various applications, such as prediction of disease diagnosis, analysis of treatment response, and evaluation of the effectiveness.

7.3.3   Decision Trees Algorithm

The decision tree method is a supervised learning strategy that can be used for classification and regression. It is a well-known method used in machine learning, data mining, and medical data analysis. Decision trees are used to construct a model that predicts the class or value of a target variable by learning the fundamental choice rules generated from the data properties.

A decision tree is a hierarchical model that shows a series of decisions and their possible results. A decision tree is a supervised learning model that connects the input data attributes to their matching output class labels. The nodes of a decision tree represent features, and each branch indicates a potential value for that feature [18]. The leaf nodes represent the output class labels.

The decision tree algorithm is a top-down recursive approach for building a decision tree using training data. The algorithm selects the feature that provides the most information regarding the target variable and constructs a node around it. The algorithm then divides the data into subsets based on the value of the chosen feature and repeats the process until a stopping requirement, such as the preset depth of the tree or the minimum number of samples at a node, is fulfilled.

In medical data analysis, decision trees can be used for various applications, such as disease diagnosis, prediction of treatment outcomes, and identification of risk factors. For instance, decision trees can be used to predict the possibility of a patient having a certain disease, based on their symptoms and medical history. The decision tree approach partitions the data recursively into subsets based on the value of a characteristic that optimizes information gain [18].

The algorithm selects the characteristic that offers the most information about the target variable and builds a node around it. This procedure is repeated until a stopping requirement, such as the preset depth of the tree or the minimum number of samples in a node, is fulfilled [18, 19]. The generated decision tree may be understood as a set of decision rules that can be used to forecast the class or value of the target variable. The use of decision trees has the benefit of being simple to read, and capable of handling both categorical and continuous data. Nevertheless, decision trees are prone to overfitting, particularly when the tree depth or the number of features is excessive.

7.3.3.1 Advantages of Decision Tree Algorithm

Decision tree algorithms have several advantages in the context of medical data analysis.

a) Easy to interpret: The decision-tree algorithm produces a graphical representation of the decision-making process. The resulting tree can be easily interpreted by medical professionals and provide insights into the factors that influence the outcome.

b) Handles both categorical and continuous data: The decision-tree algorithm can handle both categorical and continuous data. This is important in medical data analysis, as some features may be binary, such as the presence or absence of a symptom, whereas others may be continuous, such as blood pressure.

c) Handles missing data: The decision tree algorithm can handle missing data by imputing missing values using the mode or mean of the feature.

d) Can handle irrelevant features: The decision tree algorithm can handle irrelevant features by ignoring them during the feature-selection process.

e) Can handle interactions between features: The decision tree algorithm can capture interactions between features, which may be important for medical data analysis.

7.3.3.2   Limitations of Decision Tree Algorithm

The decision tree algorithm has several limitations in medical data analysis.

a) Decision trees can overfit training data, resulting in poor performance on new, unseen data. Pruning is necessary to avoid overfitting; however, this is a subjective process.
b) Decision trees work best with categorical variables and may not handle continuous variables or missing data well. Discretization and imputation techniques can be used; however, they introduce uncertainty and can result in biased predictions.
c) The order in which variables are included in a tree can have a significant impact on its structure and accuracy. Different variable selection methods can be used to address this limitation; however, they are not fool-proof.
d) Decision trees may not be suitable for analyzing complex medical data involving the interactions between multiple variables. More complex machine-learning algorithms may be more appropriate in these cases.

Overall, decision trees are useful and widely used machine-learning algorithms in medical data analysis, but their limitations must be considered to avoid biased results and ensure accurate predictions.

7.3.4   Random Forest Algorithm

Random forest is a popular machine learning algorithm used in various fields, including medical data analysis. Random forest is an ensemble approach for creating a more accurate and stable model by combining numerous decision trees.

To train each decision tree, the algorithm randomly selects a subset of features and data. This technique continues until a decision tree forest is formed. The random forest model output is the mode of the forecasts produced by individual decision trees. The random forest algorithm has two main components: tree construction and tree selection. In the tree-construction phase, the algorithm builds a decision tree from a random subset of features and data. Feature selection was performed by randomly selecting a subset of features from the total set of features. Data selection was performed by randomly sampling a subset of the total set of data. In the tree-selection phase, the algorithm selects the best subset of trees that provide the highest accuracy [20]. The algorithm uses a method called "Out-of-Bag" (OOB) to estimate the accuracy of each tree. In this method, each tree was evaluated using data that were not used in the tree-construction phase. The algorithm then selects trees with the highest accuracy to form the final model.

7.3.4.1   Advantages of Random Forest Algorithm

The random forest algorithm has several advantages for medical data analysis.

a) High accuracy: The random forest algorithm provides high accuracy compared with other machine learning algorithms, especially when the data has many features.
b) Robustness to outliers: The RF algorithm is robust to outliers, which are common in medical data analysis.
c) Handling of missing data: The random forest algorithm can handle missing data by imputing missing values using the mode or mean of the feature.
d) Can handle irrelevant features: Random forest algorithm can handle irrelevant features by ignoring them during the feature selection process.
e) Capture interactions between features: The random forest algorithm captures the interactions between features, which may be important in medical data analysis.
f) Reduce overfitting: The random forest algorithm reduces overfitting by averaging the predictions of multiple decision trees.

7.3.4.2   Limitations of Random Forest Algorithm

The random forest algorithm has several limitations in medical data analysis.

a) Computationally expensive: The random forest algorithm can be computationally costly, in case, when the number of features is high.

b) Difficult to interpret: The random forest algorithm produces a model that is difficult to interpret because it involves multiple decision trees.
c) Bias towards features with many levels: The random forest algorithm can be biased towards features with many levels because it may overemphasize their importance in the model.

7.3.4.3   Applications of Random Forest Algorithm in Medical Data Analysis

The random forest algorithm has several applications in medical data analysis, including disease diagnosis, the prediction of treatment outcomes, and the identification of risk factors.

a) Disease diagnosis: The random forest algorithm can be used to identify illnesses based on patient symptoms and medical history. For example, given a patient's age, family history, and other clinical factors, the random forest algorithm may be used to identify breast cancer.
b) Prediction of treatment outcomes: The random forest algorithm can be used to predict the outcomes of various treatments based on the patient characteristics. For example, the random forest algorithm can be used to predict the response to chemotherapy based on the patient age, tumor size, and other clinical features.
c) Identification of risk factors: The random forest algorithm can be used to identify the risk factors for various diseases based on patient characteristics.

7.3.5   Support Vector Machine Algorithm

Support Vector Machine (SVM) is a well-known supervised learning technique that has been used effectively in a variety of applications, including medical data processing. The SVM works by applying a kernel function to map data points to a high-dimensional feature space [21]. The kernel function converts the data points into a space in which a linear decision boundary can be used to partition the data points into classes. The kernel function used was determined by the nature of the data and the situation at hand.

The SVM algorithm comprises of three main steps:

1. Training: With a labeled dataset, the SVM method trains the model by locating the hyperplane that maximizes the margin between classes.
2. Testing: The SVM algorithm tests the model on a new set of data points to predict class labels.
3. Tuning: The SVM algorithm can be tuned by adjusting the kernel function and hyperparameters, such as the regularization parameter and kernel coefficient.

7.3.5.1   Advantages of SVM Algorithm

The SVM algorithm has several advantages for medical data analysis.

a) Effective for high-dimensional data: The SVM algorithm is effective for high-dimensional data where the number of features is much larger than the number of data points. This is often the case in medical data analysis, where hundreds or thousands of features may exist.
b) Robust to overfitting: The SVM algorithm is robust to overfitting, which is a problem of fitting the model too closely to the training data, resulting in poor generalization to new data. The SVM algorithm achieves this by maximizing the margin between classes.
c) Can handle nonlinear data: The SVM algorithm can handle nonlinear data by using a kernel function to map the data points to a high-dimensional feature space where a linear decision boundary can be used to separate the data points of different classes.
d) Can handle unbalanced data: The SVM algorithm can handle unbalanced data, where one class has significantly fewer data points than the other class. This is often the case in medical data analysis, in which rare diseases may have fewer cases than common diseases.
e) Can handle noisy data: The SVM algorithm can handle noisy data by ignoring outliers and focusing on support vectors, which are the closest data points to the hyperplane.

7.3.5.2   Limitations of SVM Algorithm

The SVM algorithm has several limitations in medical data analysis.

a) Computationally expensive: The SVM algorithm is computationally expensive and can take longer to train than other machine-learning algorithms. This may be a limitation when using large datasets.

b) Sensitivity to kernel function: The performance of the SVM algorithm depends on the choice of kernel function, which can be difficult to determine in practice. The choice of the kernel function depends on the nature of the data and the problem at hand [21].

c) Difficult to interpret: The SVM algorithm produces a hyperplane that separates the data points of different classes, which can be difficult for medical professionals to interpret.

7.3.5.3   Applications of SVM Algorithm in Medical Data Analysis

The SVM algorithim has several applications in medical data analysis.

a) Disease diagnosis: SVM can be used to predict the likelihood of a patient having a certain disease based on their symptoms and medical history.

b) Identification of biomarkers: SVM can be used to identify associated biomarkers.

7.3.6   Naive Bayes Algorithm

This algorithm is a powerful machine-learning technology used for classification tasks in a variety of applications, including medical data analysis. The NB algorithm is based on Bayes' theorem, and is known for its simplicity, speed, and accuracy in predicting the likelihood of a particular outcome based on a set of features. Medical data analysis involves the prediction of the possibility of a patient having a particular disease based on certain symptoms or risk factors.

The Naive Bayes method can be used to assess medical data and forecast a patient's chance of having a certain ailment. For example, it can be used to forecast a patient's chance of developing diabetes based on their age, sex, BMI, blood sugar level, and other characteristics. The Naive Bayes technique assumes that categorization features are independent of one another, which may not be the case in real-world medical data. Despite this disadvantage, the Naive Bayes algorithm is commonly employed in medical data analysis because it produces correct findings in a wide range of situations and is reasonably simple to apply [22].

The Naive Bayes technique can be used in medical data analysis for two types of classification tasks: binary classification and multi-class classification. The process of predicting whether a patient has a specific condition is known as a binary classification. The first step in using Naive Bayes algorithm for medical data analysis is to collect and preprocess the data. This involves collecting data on patients, including their symptoms, medical history, and other relevant factors [23]. The data were then preprocessed to remove any noise or outliers and to ensure the suitability as per the format for analysis.

In the case of medical data analysis, the most used variation of Naive Bayes algorithm is Gaussian Naive Bayes. This variation assumes that the features are normally distributed, which is often the case with medical data. However, if the features are not normally distributed, other variations of Naive Bayes algorithm, such as multinomial Naive Bayes or Bernoulli naive Bayes, may be more appropriate. The performance of Naive Bayes algorithm for medical data analysis depends on several factors, including the size and quality of the dataset, choice of features and classes, and choice of Naive Bayes variation. However, the Naive Bayes algorithm is known for its simplicity, speed, and accuracy, making it a popular choice for medical data analysis.

7.3.7   KNN (K-Nearest Neighbor Algorithm)

The K-nearest neighbor (K-NN) method is a machine-learning technique used in medical data analysis for classification and regression problems. The K-NN technique works by determining the K-nearest neighbors for a given data point and predicting the data point's class or value based on the class or values of its K-nearest neighbors. The K-NN method in medical data analysis can be used to estimate the possibility of a patient having a certain disease based on their symptoms, medical history, and other relevant characteristics.

It can also be used in medical image analysis to predict the diagnosis of a disease based on the features of medical images. The K-NN algorithm is simple to understand and implement, making it a popular choice for medical data analysis. However, the choice of the number of neighbors K is critical to the performance of the algorithm and choosing an appropriate value for K requires experimentation and domain knowledge. The first step was to collect and preprocess the data using K-NN algorithm for medical data analysis. This involves collecting data on the patients, including their symptoms, medical history, and other relevant factors. The data are then preprocessed to remove any noise or outliers and ensure that they are in a suitable format for analysis [23].

When the data have been preprocessed, they are divided into training and testing datasets. The K-NN model was trained using the training dataset and its performance was evaluated using a testing dataset. The K-NN technique computes the distance between the predicted data points and all the data points in the training dataset. The distance is often determined using either the Euclidean or Manhattan distance. The K-NN method then chooses the k-nearest neighbors to the anticipated data point and assigns it to the class or value of the majority of those neighbors.

One important consideration when using the K-NN algorithm for medical data analysis is the choice of distance metric. The distance measure used was determined by the nature of the data and the problem being solved. For example, Euclidean distance may be more suitable for continuous data, whereas Manhattan distance may be more suitable for discrete data.

Another important consideration when using K-NN algorithm for medical data analysis is the choice of K. The choice of K depends on the complexity of the problem being solved and size of the dataset. If K is too small, the algorithm may be too sensitive to noise and outliers, whereas if K is too large, it may not capture the true structure of the data [24]. The performance of the K-NN algorithm for medical data analysis depends on several factors, including the size and quality of the dataset, choice of distance metric and K value, and choice of features and classes. However, in general, K-NN algorithm is known for its simplicity and interpretability, making it a popular choice for medical data analysis.

7.3.7.1   Applications of K-NN Algorithm

Disease prediction is typically used in the analysis of medical data. Based on symptoms, medical history, and other relevant information, the K-NN algorithm can be used to forecast the chance of a patient having a certain condition. For example, the K-NN method may be used to estimate the probability of a patient acquiring diabetes based on age, BMI, blood pressure, and other parameters. Medical image analysis is another popular use of the K-NN method in medical data analysis. The K-NN algorithm can be used to predict illness diagnoses based on the aspects of medical imagery. For example, depending on the characteristics of the cells, the K-NN algorithm can be used to predict the presence of malignant cells in a breast biopsy image. The K-NN algorithm has also been used in other medical data analysis tasks, such as drug discovery, drug toxicity prediction, and medical signal processing.

7.3.8 Deep Learning Algorithm

Deep learning is a subset of machine learning that employs multi-layered artificial neural networks [25]. Deep learning algorithms can learn complicated data representations and extract high-level features for use in prediction or classification. Deep learning algorithms have shown great potential in many areas of medical data analysis, including medical image analysis, natural language processing, and predictive modeling. One of the most successful applications of deep learning in medical data analysis is medical image analysis.

Deep learning algorithms maybe trained to detect and classify objects in medical images, such as tumors in MRI scans, abnormalities in X-rays, or retinal diseases in fundus images [26]. These algorithms can also be used to segment medical images into different regions of interest, allowing doctors to identify and measure specific features within the image.

7.3.9 Deep Learning Application

Convolutional neural networks (CNNs) are used for skin lesion classification in medical image analysis. A CNN is a type of deep neural network that can learn the spatial hierarchies of features by convolving image patches with a set of learned filters. For skin lesion classification, a CNN can be trained to detect and classify different types of skin lesions, such as melanoma or benign lesions. These algorithms have shown high levels of accuracy in detecting skin lesions, sometimes outperforming dermatologists [27].

Another application of deep learning in medical data analysis is natural language processing (NLP). NLP is another field of AI that focuses on the interaction between humans and computers using natural language. In medical data analysis, NLP can be used to analyze electronic medical records (EMRs) or patient reviews. These algorithms can extract relevant information from unstructured texts, such as patient symptoms or treatment outcomes, and use this information to make predictions or recommendations.

One example of the successful application of NLP in medical data analysis is the use of recurrent neural networks (RNNs) for predicting patient readmissions. RNNs are a type of deep neural network that can model sequential data by processing them one element at a time and maintaining the memory of previous inputs. In the case of patient readmissions, an RNN can be trained to predict the likelihood of a patient being readmitted based on their medical history and treatment plan [28]. These algorithms have shown high levels of accuracy in predicting patient readmissions, allowing doctors to take preventive measures to avoid unnecessary hospitalization.

Another application of deep learning in medical data analysis is predictive modeling. Deep learning algorithms can be used to predict patient outcomes, such as mortality or readmission rates, based on patient data, such as demographics, medical history, and treatment plans. These algorithms can also be used to identify patients at risk of developing certain conditions, allowing for early intervention and treatment.

One example of the successful application of deep learning in predictive modeling is the use of neural networks to predict the onset of Alzheimer's disease. Researchers have used deep neural networks to analyze brain scans and identify subtle changes in brain structure that are indicative of Alzheimer's disease [29]. These algorithms have shown high levels of accuracy in predicting Alzheimer's disease onset, allowing for early intervention and treatment.

In conclusion, deep learning algorithms have shown great promise for medical data analysis, particularly in the areas of medical image analysis, natural language processing, and predictive modeling. These algorithms have the potential to improve patient outcomes by providing doctors with more accurate and timely information, thereby allowing for early intervention and treatment. However, it is important to note that deep learning algorithms require large amounts of data and computational resources, and their performance can be highly dependent on the quality of the data and design of the algorithm. Nonetheless, deep learning is a rapidly evolving field, with great potential for advancing medical research and improving patient care.

7.4   Unsupervised Learning Algorithms for Medical Data Analysis

Unsupervised learning algorithms are used in medical data analysis to identify patterns and groupings within datasets, without the need for labeled data. Clustering is one of the most popular unsupervised learning algorithms, which groups similar data points based on their characteristics [30]. Another popular unsupervised learning algorithm is principal component analysis (PCA), which is used for dimensionality reduction by recognizing the most important features in a dataset. Unsupervised learning algorithms can be particularly useful in medical data analysis to identify patient subgroups, detect anomalies, and find hidden patterns in the data [31]. By leveraging the power of unsupervised learning algorithms, healthcare providers can improve patient care and outcomes, and develop new insights into complex medical conditions. Unsupervised learning algorithms are explained as follows.

7.4.1   Clustering Algorithm

Clustering is a type of unsupervised learning in which similar data points are grouped into clusters based on their similarity or distance from each other. Clustering algorithms can be used in medical data analysis to identify patterns and relationships in large datasets such as electronic medical records, genetic data, and medical images.

An example of clustering in medical data analysis is the use of clustering algorithms to stratify cancer patients based on their molecular characteristics [28]. Figure 7.2 illustrates the clustering algorithms. Cancer is a complex disease with multiple subtypes that differ in their genetic and molecular profiles, which makes it difficult to develop effective treatments

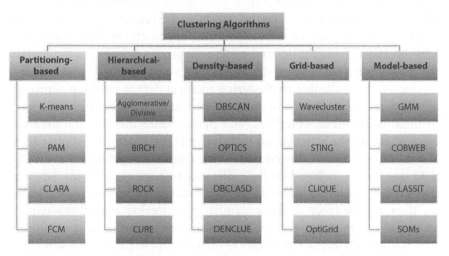

Figure 7.2 Types of clustering algorithms [35].

for all patients. By clustering cancer patients based on their molecular characteristics, researchers can identify subgroups of patients that may respond better to specific treatments such as targeted therapies or immunotherapies. This approach has been used successfully for several types of cancers, such as breast cancer, lung cancer, and melanoma [28].

Another example of clustering in medical data analysis is the use of clustering algorithms to identify subgroups of patients with similar disease phenotypes [32]. For instance, clustering algorithms can be used to group patients with certain diseases based on their clinical characteristics, such as age, sex, disease duration, and comorbidities. This approach can help clinicians develop personalized treatment plans for patients with similar disease phenotypes, as well as identify risk factors and biomarkers associated with disease progression and treatment response.

Clustering algorithms can also be used in medical image analysis to segment medical images into different regions of interest, such as tumors, organs, and blood vessels. Image segmentation is an essential step in many medical imaging applications such as diagnosis, treatment planning, and monitoring. Clustering algorithms can be used to identify and segment similar regions in medical images based on their intensity, texture, and spatial relationships [33]. This approach has been used successfully in several imaging modalities such as computed tomography (CT), magnetic resonance imaging (MRI), and positron emission tomography (PET).

Another application of clustering in medical data analysis is the identification of adverse drug reactions (ADRs). ADRs are unwanted or unexpected side effects of medications that can have serious consequences on patient safety and health outcomes. Clustering algorithms can be used to identify patterns of ADRs in large datasets, such as electronic health records or pharmacovigilance databases [34]. This approach can help researchers and clinicians identify drugs and patient subgroups that are at a higher risk for ADRs, as well as develop strategies to prevent or mitigate these events.

One of the challenges in clustering medical data is selecting appropriate clustering algorithms and parameters. Clustering algorithms can vary in their assumptions, objectives, and performance metrics, and different algorithms may be better suited to different types of data and applications. For instance, k-means clustering is a very common algorithm that divides data into k clusters based on their distance to a set of centroids, whereas hierarchical clustering builds a tree-like structure of nested clusters based on their similarity or distance. Similarly, clustering algorithms require careful selection of parameters, such as the number of clusters, similarity or distance metric, and initialization method. These parameters can affect the quality, stability, and interpretability of the clustering results.

In conclusion, clustering algorithms are powerful tools in medical data analysis, enabling researchers and clinicians to identify patterns and relationships in large and heterogeneous datasets. Clustering algorithms can be used for patient stratification, disease subtyping, image segmentation, and ADR detection, among other applications [18]. However, clustering medical data requires careful consideration of the appropriate algorithms and parameters, as well as validation and interpretation of the clustering results. Future research on clustering medical data may focus on the development of novel algorithms and techniques that can handle the complexity and heterogeneity of medical datasets, as well as the integration of clustering with other machines.

7.4.2   Principal Component Analysis Algorithm

Principal Component Analysis (PCA) is a technique used for data analysis and dimensionality reduction. PCA can be applied to medical data to identify the most important features or variables that explain variability in the data. PCA is particularly useful in medical data analysis, where the number of features can be very large and there is a need to reduce the dimensionality of the data to facilitate visualization, modeling, and interpretation.

PCA is a linear transformation method that converts a high-dimensional dataset into a lower-dimensional one, although it preserves most of the variability of the original data. PCA achieves this by identifying a set of orthogonal axes, called principal components, which capture powerful patterns and inequality in the data. The first principal component accounts for the maximum amount of variability in the data, and each subsequent principal component accounts for the remaining variability in descending order.

PCA can be applied to different types of data, such as continuous, discrete, or categorical data, and it can handle missing data and outliers. The study of medical imaging data is one use of PCA for medical data analysis. Medical imaging data, such as magnetic resonance imaging (MRI) or computed tomography (CT) scans, can be extremely high dimensional and complicated, making visualization and interpretation challenging. PCA can be used to reduce the dimensionality of imaging data by identifying the most significant patterns and variations in images [35]. For instance, PCA can be used to identify the most important voxels or regions of interest (ROI) in an MRI scan that differentiates between healthy and diseased tissues, or to identify the most informative imaging features that predict treatment response or disease progression.

PCA can also be applied to electronic medical records (EMRs) and other types of clinical data to identify the most important variables that explain variability in the data. For example, PCA can be used to identify the most relevant demographic, clinical, and laboratory variables that predict patient outcomes such as hospitalization, mortality, and disease recurrence. This approach can help clinicians and researchers develop predictive models that use a reduced set of variables, reduce the computational complexity, and improve the interpretability of the model.

Another application of PCA in medical data analysis is in the analysis of genetic data. Genetic data can be very high-dimensional, with thousands or millions of genetic variants or single-nucleotide polymorphisms (SNPs). PCA can be used to identify the most important genetic variants that explain the genetic variability in a population or disease. For example, PCA can be used to identify genetic variants associated with a particular disease, such as cancer or diabetes, and to identify genetic subtypes associated with different disease phenotypes or responses to treatment.

PCA has several advantages for medical data analysis. First, PCA can reduce the dimensionality of data, making it easier to visualize and interpret. Second, PCA can identify the most important features or variables that explain the variability in data, enabling researchers and clinicians to focus on the most relevant information. Third, PCA can remove redundant or irrelevant features from the data, reducing the noise and improving the accuracy of the analysis [35, 36]. Finally, PCA can help identify patterns and relationships in the data that may not be apparent from the original data.

However, PCA has some limitations in the analysis of medical data. First, PCA assumes that the data are linearly correlated, which may not always be the case in medical data, where the relationships between variables may be complex and nonlinear. Second, PCA may not be appropriate for categorical or binary data, which may require other dimensionality reduction techniques, such as correspondence analysis or factor analysis. Third, PCA may not always preserve the interpretability of data, as the principal components may not have a direct biological or clinical meaning.

7.4.3   Independent Component Analysis Algorithm

Independent Component Analysis (ICA) is a popular machine learning technique that can be applied to medical data to identify underlying sources or components that contribute to the observed data. ICA is a blind source separation technique that can be used to separate mixed signals into independent components, based on the statistical independence criteria.

ICA is very effective for medical data analysis because the observed data may be a combination of several physiological signals or sources, such as electroencephalography (EEG) or functional magnetic resonance imaging (fMRI). ICA can be used to decompose mixed signals into their underlying sources or components, which can provide insight into the underlying physiological processes and aid in the diagnosis and treatment of various medical conditions.

ICA works by presuming that the observed data are a linear combination of independent sources and seeks to find a set of uncorrelated and independent components that explain the observed data [36]. ICA can be performed using various algorithms such as FastICA, Infomax, or JADE, which optimize different criteria for independence, such as mutual information, kurtosis, or negentropy. An application of ICA in medical data analysis is the analysis of EEG data. EEG signals can be very complex and may contain various sources such as brain waves, muscle artifacts, and electrooculogram (EOG) signals.

ICA can be used to separate these sources and identify the underlying brain activity related to various cognitive or clinical states, such as attention, sleep, or epilepsy. For example, ICA can be used to identify independent components related to epileptic seizures and aid in the diagnosis and treatment of epilepsy [37]. ICA can also be applied to fMRI data to identify the underlying neural activity associated with various cognitive or clinical states such as emotions, pain, and depression. fMRI data can be very complex and may contain various sources of noise such as head motion, physiological artifacts, and scanner drift.

ICA can be used to separate these sources and identify the underlying neural activity related to a task or condition of interest. For example, ICA can be used to identify the independent components related to the brain networks involved in the processing of pain, and aid in the development of new treatments for chronic pain. ICA can also be applied to other types of medical data, such as electrocardiography (ECG), electroretinography (ERG), and magnetoencephalography (MEG) data, to identify the underlying physiological sources or components.

ICA can also be used in combination with other machine-learning techniques, such as clustering or classification, to further analyze and interpret the independent components. ICA has several advantages in medical data analysis. First, ICA can separate mixed signals into their independent components, providing insights into the underlying physiological processes and aiding in the diagnosis and treatment of various medical conditions [36]. Second, ICA can handle non-Gaussian and non-stationary data, which are common in medical data, and remove sources of noise and artifacts from the data. Third, ICA can be used to analyze data from multiple sensors or modalities, such as EEG and fMRI, and can integrate information from various sources to provide a more comprehensive picture of the underlying physiological processes.

However, ICA has some limitations for medical data analysis. First, ICA assumes that the sources are statistically independent, which may not always be the case in real-world data where the sources may be correlated or mixed in complex ways. Second, ICA may not always preserve the temporal or spatial structure of the data, because the independent components may not have a direct physiological or clinical meaning. Third, ICA may be sensitive to the choice of algorithm and parameters, and may require careful tuning and validation.

7.4.4   Association Rule Mining Algorithm

Association rule mining (ARM) is a popular machine-learning algorithm that can be applied to medical data to discover interesting patterns or relationships between different variables or features. ARM is a type of unsupervised learning that involves finding frequent itemsets or combinations of variables and then generating rules that describe the associations or dependencies between them.

The ARM is particularly useful in medical data analysis, where the observed data may consist of many variables or features that are related to various clinical or physiological outcomes. ARM can be used to identify the variables or combinations of variables that are most strongly associated with a particular outcome, and to generate rules that can be used to predict or explain the occurrence of the outcome.

ARM first identifies frequent itemsets, which are combinations of variables that occur together frequently in the data. This can be achieved using algorithms such as Apriori, FP-growth, or Eclat, which use different techniques to efficiently search for frequent itemsets [37]. Once the frequent itemsets are identified, association rules can be generated that describe the relationships between the variables in the itemsets. The quality of the rules can be evaluated using metrics, such as support, confidence, or lift, which measure the frequency, strength, or significance of the associations.

The study of electronic health records is one use of ARM in medical data analyses (EHRs). EHRs provide a variety of patient information such as medical history, diagnosis, prescriptions, and test findings. ARM can be used to identify patterns or associations between different variables in EHRs, and to generate rules that can be used to predict or explain various clinical outcomes, such as readmission rates, medication adherence, and mortality. For example, ARM can be used to identify the variables or combinations of variables that are most strongly associated with readmission rates for patients with heart failure and to generate rules that can be used to identify high-risk patients and develop targeted interventions to reduce readmissions.

ARM can also be applied to other types of medical data such as imaging or genomic data. For example, ARM can be used to identify genetic mutations or combinations of mutations that are most strongly associated with a particular disease, and to generate rules that can be used to predict the risk of developing the disease. ARM can also be used to identify imaging features or combinations of features that are most strongly associated with a particular condition, such as cancer or Alzheimer's disease, and to generate rules that can be used to improve diagnosis and treatment [38].

ARM has several advantages for medical data analysis. First, using traditional statistical methods, ARM can identify interesting patterns or associations between variables that may not be apparent. Second, ARM can handle large and complex datasets, including those with many variables or features. Third, ARM can generate rules that are easy to interpret and provide insights into the underlying relationships between variables.

However, the ARM has some limitations in the analysis of medical data. First, the ARM can generate many rules, which may be difficult to interpret and validate. Second, ARM may not capture all the important relationships between variables, as it relies on identifying frequent itemsets rather than looking for more complex or subtle associations. Third, ARM may be sensitive to the choice of algorithm and parameters and may require careful tuning and validation. In conclusion, ARM is a powerful technique for discovering interesting patterns or associations in medical data, and can be used to improve the diagnosis, treatment, and outcomes of various medical conditions. However, careful attention should be paid to the choice of the algorithm and parameters, as well as the interpretation and validation of the generated rules.

7.5   Applications of Machine-Learning Algorithms in Medical Data Analysis

These algorithms have various applications in medical data analysis, and their use has the potential to revolutionize medical diagnosis, treatment, and outcomes. Some of the main and popular applications of machine-learning algorithms in medical data analysis are included in Table 7.1:

Table 7.1 Applications of machine-learning algorithms in medical data analysis.

Application	Description
Diagnosis	Machine-learning algorithms can be used to develop models that accurately diagnose various medical conditions. For example, machine-learning models have been developed to diagnose skin cancer, heart disease, and other conditions with high accuracy. These models can analyze patient data, such as medical images or laboratory results, to make diagnoses quickly and accurately.
Disease prognosis	ML algorithms can be used to develop models that predict the progression of various medical conditions. For example, machine learning models can predict the likelihood of disease recurrence or prognosis of a particular cancer.
Drug discovery	Machine-learning algorithms can be used to identify potential drug candidates and predict their efficacies. By analyzing large datasets of molecular structures, machine-learning models can identify compounds that are likely to be effective in treating specific medical conditions. This can significantly accelerate the drug discovery process and reduce costs.
Clinical decision support	These algorithms can be used to provide clinical decision-making support to healthcare providers. By analyzing patient data and providing recommendations based on those data, machine learning models can help healthcare providers make more informed decisions about patient care.
Remote patient monitoring	These algorithms can be used to monitor patients remotely, such as through wearable devices or mobile applications. By analyzing patient data in real time, machine-learning models can alert healthcare providers to potential problems before they become serious.
Predictive modeling	These algorithms can be used to generate models that predict the likelihood of various medical events such as hospital readmissions or the onset of a medical condition. These models can help healthcare providers identify patients who are at risk of adverse events and intervene before an event occurs.

(Continued)

Table 7.1 Applications of machine-learning algorithms in medical data analysis. (*Continued*)

Application	Description
Patient stratification	These algorithms can be used to stratify patients based on their risk factors or medical history. This can help healthcare providers identify critical patients who are at high risk of adverse events and prioritize their care accordingly.
Personalized medicine	These algorithms can be used to create individualized treatment recommendations for individuals based on their unique traits, such as genetics, medical history, and lifestyle variables. Machine learning models, for example, can be used to predict therapy response and optimize treatment programs for specific patients.
Medical image analysis	Medical images, such as X-rays, MRIs, and CT scans, are rich sources of data that can be analyzed using machine-learning algorithms. ML models can be used to identify abnormalities in medical images, such as tumors or other lesions, and make accurate diagnoses based on these findings.
EHRs	Electronic health records (EHRs) contain a wealth of data that can be analyzed using machine-learning algorithms [40]. Machine-learning models can be used to identify patterns in EHR data, such as risk factors for certain medical conditions or efficacy of specific treatments.

Overall, the applications of machine-learning algorithms in medical data analysis are vast and varied. By analyzing large and complex datasets, machine-learning algorithms can identify patterns, predict outcomes, and improve patient care. As the field of machine learning continues to evolve, its applications in medical data analysis are likely to become even more diverse and impactful.

7.6 Limitations and Challenges of Machine Learning Algorithms in Medical Data Analysis

Machine learning has shown significant results in medical data analysis. However, several challenges and limitations are associated with machine learning. One challenge is the need for large amounts of high-quality data to train and evaluate machine learning models [37]. Machine-learning algorithms may suffer from bias or overfitting, which can lead to inaccurate or unfair predictions. Several limitations and challenges must be addressed to maximize their potential.

a. **Data quality and quantity**: The accuracy of machine-learning models depends on the quality and quantity of the data used to train them. In medical data analysis, data may be limited in quantity or quality, which makes it difficult to train accurate models.

b. **Bias and fairness**: Machine learning models are susceptible to bias if the training data is not representative of the population being studied. This can lead to unfair and inaccurate predictions, particularly in medical data analysis, where fairness and ethical considerations are crucial.

c. **Interpretability and explainability**: Machine learning models are often considered "black boxes," making it difficult to understand how the models arrive at their predictions. In medical data analysis, this lack of interpretability and explainability can be a significant barrier to adoption by healthcare providers [38].

d. **Ethical and privacy concerns**: Medical data are highly sensitive, and there are significant ethical and privacy concerns associated with their use in machine learning. It is important to ensure that patient privacy is protected, and ethical considerations are considered when developing and deploying machine learning models.

e. **Generalizability**: Machine learning models developed using one dataset may not necessarily be generalized to other datasets or patient populations. This can limit the utility of machine learning in medical data analysis because models that work well in one context may not be effective in others.

f. **Regulatory compliance**: In many countries, medical data are subject to strict regulatory requirements, which can make it difficult to develop and deploy machine-learning models. Compliance with regulatory requirements is essential to ensure that machine-learning models are safe and effective in clinical practice.

g. **Integration with clinical workflows**: Machine learning models must be integrated into clinical workflows to be useful in medical data analysis [39]. This can be challenging because it requires collaboration between clinicians, data scientists, and other stakeholders to ensure that the models are seamlessly integrated into clinical practice.

To address these challenges, researchers and practitioners are developing new techniques and approaches to improve the accuracy and fairness of machine-learning models. These include techniques such as transfer learning, which allows a model to leverage knowledge from one task to another, and adversarial training, which involves training a model to be robust to adversarial attacks.

Overall, addressing these limitations and challenges is essential for the successful adoption of machine learning in medical data analysis. This will require collaboration between stakeholders from multiple disciplines and a focus on ensuring that machine learning is used ethically, fairly, and effectively in clinical practice.

7.7 Future Research Directions and Machine Learning Developments in the Realm of Medical Data Analysis

The field of machine learning for medical data analysis is evolving rapidly, with new algorithms, techniques, and applications emerging on a regular basis. Some of the key areas of future research and potential advancements in this field include the following:

- **Integration of multiple data sources**: In medical data analysis, it is often necessary to collect data from multiple sources such as electronic health records, imaging data, and genomic data. Future research should focus on developing new algorithms and techniques to integrate these different data sources and identify the most relevant features or variables for predicting clinical outcomes.
- **Explainable AI**: One of the challenges in using machine learning in medical data analysis is the difficulty in interpreting the results and understanding how the models make predictions. Future research could focus on developing

new techniques for making machine learning models more transparent and explainable, so that clinicians and researchers can better understand and trust the predictions.

- **Transfer learning**: Transfer learning is a technique that allows ML models to leverage knowledge learned from one dataset to improve performance on a different dataset. Future research could focus on developing transfer learning techniques for medical data analysis, which could allow models to learn from large, publicly available datasets and then apply that knowledge to smaller, more specialized datasets.
- **Deep learning for imaging data**: Deep learning has shown great potential for analyzing medical imaging data, and future research could focus on developing new architectures and techniques for improving the accuracy and speed of deep learning models for this application.
- **Personalized medicine**: Personalized medicine uses patient characteristics such as genetics to tailor medical treatment and care. Machine learning could play a key role in personalized medicine by identifying the most relevant features or variables for predicting clinical outcomes for individual patients, and by developing models that can be used to guide treatment decisions.
- **Mobile health**: Mobile health (mHealth) is a rapidly growing field that involves the use of mobile devices such as wearable sensors and smartphones for health monitoring and management. Machine learning can be used to analyze the data collected by these devices and develop models that can predict and prevent adverse health events.
- **Reinforcement learning**: Reinforcement learning is a type of machine learning in which models are trained to make decisions based on feedback from their surroundings. The development of reinforcement learning models for medical decision-making, such as therapy selection or medication dosage, should be the focus of future studies.

7.8   Conclusion

In conclusion, machine learning for medical data analysis is a rapidly evolving and exciting area of research. With the emergence of new algorithms, techniques, and applications, machine learning has tremendous potential to improve medical diagnosis, treatment, and outcomes. However, there are many challenges and opportunities for future research, including the integration of multiple data sources, explainable AI, transfer learning, deep learning for imaging data, personalized medicine, mobile health, and reinforcement learning. By addressing these challenges and developing new techniques and applications, machine learning has great potential for revolutionizing healthcare and improving patient outcomes.

References

1. Oladimeji, O., Machine learning in smart health research: A bibliometric analysis. *Int. J. Inf. Sci. Manage.*, 21, 119–128, 2023, 10.22034/ijism.2022.1977616.0.
2. Sachdeva, S., Ali, A., Khalid, S., Telemedicine in healthcare system: A Discussion Regarding Several Practices, in: *Telemedicine: The Computer Transformation of Healthcare. TELe-Health*, T. Choudhury, A. Katal, J.S. Um, A. Rana, M. Al-Akaidi (eds.), Springer, Cham, pp. 295–310, 2022, https://doi. org/10.1007/978-3-030-99457-0_19.
3. Jujjavarapu, C., Suri, P., Pejaver, V. *et al.*, Predicting decompression surgery by applying multimodal deep learning to patients' structured and unstructured health data. *BMC Med. Inform. Decis. Mak.*, 23, 1, 2, 2023, https://doi. org/10.1186/s12911-022-02096-x.
4. Mohsen, F., Ali, H., El Hajj, N. *et al.*, Artificial intelligence-based methods for fusion of electronic health records and imaging data. *Sci. Rep.*, 12, 17981, 2022, https://doi.org/10.1038/s41598-022-22514-4.
5. Hobensack, M., Song, J., Scharp, D., Bowles, K., Topaz, M., Machine learning applied to electronic health record data in home healthcare: A scoping review. *Int. J. Med. Inf.*, 170, 104978, 2022, 10.1016/j.ijmedinf.2022.104978.
6. Sachdeva, S., Ali, A., Khan, S., Secure and privacy issues in telemedicine: Issues, solutions, and standards, in: *Telemedicine: The Computer Transformation of Healthcare. TELe-Health*, T. Choudhury, A. Katal, J.S. Um, A. Rana, M. Al-Akaidi (Eds.), Springer, Cham, pp. 321–331, 2022, https://doi. org/10.1007/978-3-030-99457-0_21.
7. Mustafa, A. and Rahimi Azghadi, M., Automated machine learning for healthcare and clinical notes analysis. *Computers*, 10, 24, 2021, https://doi. org/10.3390/computers10020024.
8. Sachdeva, S. and Aleem, A., Advanced approach using deep learning for healthcare data analysis in IOT system. *Emergent Converging Technologies and Biomedical Systems: Select Proceedings of ETBS 2021*, pp. 163–172, Springer, Singapore.
9. Alizadehsani, R., Roshanzamir, M., Hussain, S. *et al.*, Handling of uncertainty in medical data using machine learning probability theory techniques:

A review of 30 years (1991–2020). *Ann. Oper Res.*, 2021, https://doi.org/10.1007/s10479-021-04006-2.

10. Antonello, F., Baraldi, P., Shokry, A., Zio, E., Gentile, U., Serio, L., Association rules extraction for the identification of functional dependencies in complex technical infrastructures. *Reliab. Eng. Syst. Saf.*, 209, 2021, https://doi.org/10.1016/j.ress.2020.107305, Elsevier.

11. Alloghani, M., Al-Jumeily, D., Mustafina, J., Hussain, A., Aljaaf, A.J., A systematic review on supervised and unsupervised machine learning algorithms for data science, in: *Supervised and Unsupervised Learning for Data Science*, M. Berry, A. Mohamed, B. Yap (Eds.), pp. 3–21, Springer, US, 2020.

12. Polignano, M., Suriano, V., Lops, P., de Gemmis, M., Semeraro, G., A study of machine learning models for clinical coding of medical reports at CodiEsp 2020, in: *Proceedings of the Working Notes of Conference and Labs of the Evaluation (CLEF) Forum, CEUR Workshop Proceedings*, Thessaloniki, Greece, 2–25 September 2020.

13. Huang, S.C., Pareek, A., Seyyedi, S. *et al.*, Fusion of medical imaging and electronic health records using deep learning: A systematic review and implementation guidelines. *NPJ Digit. Med.*, 3, 136, 2020. https://doi.org/10.1038/s41746-020-00341-z\.

14. Sakagianni A, Feretzakis G, Kalles D, Koufopoulou C, Kaldis V. Setting up an Easy-to-Use Machine Learning Pipeline for Medical Decision Support: A Case Study for COVID-19 Diagnosis Based on Deep Learning with CT Scans. *Stud. Health Technol. Inform.*, 272, 13–16, 2020 Jun. doi: 10.3233/SHTI200481. PMID: 32604588.

15. Yala, A., Lehman, C., Schuster, T., Portnoi, T., Barzilay, R., A deep learning mammography-based model for improved breast cancer risk prediction. *Radiol.*, 292, 60–66, 2019.

16. Malasinghe, L.P. *et al.*, Remote patient monitoring: A comprehensive study. *J. Ambient Intell. Hum. Comput.*, 10, 57–76, 2019.

17. Seetharam, K. *et al.*, Application of mobile health, telemedicine and artificial intelligence to echocardiography. *Echo Res. Pract.*, 6, 2, 41–52, 2019.

18. Bardou, D., Zhang, K., Ahmad, S.M., Classification of breast cancer based on histology images using convolutional neural networks. *IEEE Access*, 6, 24680–24693, 2018.

19. Kamiński, B., Jakubczyk, M., Szufel, P., A framework for sensitivity analysis of decision trees. *Cent. Eur. J. Oper. Res.*, 26, 1, 135–159, 2018, doi: 10.1007/s10100-017-0479-6.

20. Najafabadi, M.K., Mahrin, M.N., Chuprat, S., Sarkan, H.M., Improving the accuracy of collaborative filtering recommendations using clustering and association rules mining on implicit data. *Comput. Hum.*, 67, 113–128, 2017. https://doi.org/10.1016/j.chb.2016.11.010, Elsevier.

21. Salcedo-Bernal, Villamil-Giraldo, M.P., Moreno-Barbosa, A.D., Clinical data analysis: An opportunity to compare machine learning methods. *Proc.*

Comput. Sci., 100, 731–738, 2016. ISSN 1877-0509, https://doi.org/10.1016/j. procs.2016.09.218.

22. UmaRani, P. *et al.*, A case study on telemedicine practices implemented with respect to Apollo hospitals. *Int. J. Appl. Environ. Sci. (IJAES)*, 10, 1, 23–28, 2015.

23. Herland, M.,.T., Khoshgoftaar, M., Wald, R., A review of data mining using big data in health informatics. *J. Big Data*, 1, 1, 1–35, 2014.

24. Azar, A.T. and El-Said, S.A., Performance analysis of support vector machines classifiers in breast cancer mammography recognition. *Neural Comput. Appl.*, 24, 1163–1177, 2014.

25. Ali, A., A concise artificial neural network in data mining. *Int. J. Res. Eng. & Appl. Sci.*, 2, 2, 418–428, 2012.

26. Sadiq, M., Mariyam, F., Alil, A., Khan, S., Tripathi, P., Prediction of software project effort using fuzzy logic. *2011 3rd International Conference on Electronics Computer Technology*, Kanyakumari, India, pp. 353–358, 2011, doi: 10.1109/ICECTECH.2011.5941919.

27. Lundereng, E.D., Nes, A.A.G., Holmen, H., Winger, A., Thygesen, H., Jøranson, N., Borge, C.R., Dajani, O., Mariussen, K.L., Steindal, S.A., Health care professionals' experiences and perspectives on using telehealth for home-based palliative care: Scoping review. *J. Med. Internet Res.*, 25, e43429, 2023 Mar 29.

28. Khan, Javed, *et al.*, Classification and diagnostic prediction of cancers using gene expression profiling and artificial neural networks. *Nat. Med.*, 7, 6, 673–679, 2001.

29. Ardabili, S.F., Mosavi, A., Ghamisi, P., Ferdinand, F., Varkonyi-Koczy, A.R., Reuter, U., Rabczuk, T., Atkinson, P.M., Covid-19 outbreak prediction with machine learning. *Algorithms.*, 13, 10, 249, 2020.

30. Fatima, M., Pasha, M. *et al.*, Survey of machine learning algorithms for disease diagnostic. *J. Intell. Learn Syst. Appl.*, 9, 01, 1, 2017.

31. Kushwaha, S., Bahl, S., Bagha, A.K., Parmar, K.S., Javaid, M., Haleem, A., Singh, R.P., Significant applications of machine learning for covid-19 pandemic. *J. Ind. Integr. Manage.*, 5, 4, 453–479, 2020.

32. Lalmuanawma, S., Hussain, J., Chhakchhuak, L., Applications of machine learning and artificial intelligence for covid-19 (sarscov-2) pandemic: A review. *Chaos Sol Fract.*, 110059, 2020.

33. Mohammed, M., Khan, M.B., Bashier Mohammed, B.E., *Machine learning: algorithms and applications*, CRC Press, 2016.

34. Mehta, V., Bawa, S., Singh, J., Analytical review of clustering techniques and proximity measures. *Artif. Intell. Rev.*, 53, 1–29, 2020, 10.1007/s10462-020-09840-7.

35. Nilashi, M., Ibrahim, O.B., Ahmadi, H., Shahmoradi, L., An analytical method for diseases prediction using machine learning techniques. *Comput. Chem. Eng.*, 106, 212–23, 2017.

36. Perveen, S., Shahbaz, M., Keshavjee, K., Guergachi, A., Metabolic syndrome and development of diabetes mellitus: Predictive modeling based on machine learning techniques. *IEEE Access.*, 7, 1365–75, 2018.

37. Gökhan, S. and Nevin, Y., Data analysis in health and big data: A machine learning medical diagnosis model based on patients' complaints. *Commun. Stat. Theory Methods*, 50, 7, 1–10, 2019.

38. Zheng, T., Xie, W., Xu, L., He, X., Zhang, Y., You, M., Yang, G., Chen, Y., A machine learning-based framework to identify type 2 diabetes through electronic health records. *Int. J. Med. Inform.*, 97, 120–7, 2017.

39. Woldaregay, A.Z., Årsand, E., Botsis, T., Albers, D., Mamykina, L., Hartvigsen, G., Data-driven blood glucose pattern classification and anomalies detection: Machine-learning applications in type 1 diabetes. *J. Med. Internet Res.*, 21, 5, 11030, 2019, doi: 10.2196/11030.

40. Rao, S.R., Desroches, C.M., Donelan, K., Campbell, E.G., Miralles, P.D., Jha, A.K., Electronic health records in small physician practices: Availability, use, and perceived benefits. *J. Am. Med. Inform. Assoc.*, 18, 3, 271–275, 2011, doi: 10.1136/amiajnl-2010-000010.

Part II
APPLICATIONS AND ANALYTICS

Fog Computing in Healthcare: Application Taxonomy, Challenges and Opportunities

Subrata Datta[1]* and Priyanka Datta[2]

[1]Department of AIML, Netaji Subhash Engineering College, Kolkata, West Bengal, India
[2]Department of CSE, Kalinga Institute of Industrial Technology, Bhubaneswar, Odisha, India

Abstract

Advancements in science and technology have commenced the era of the Internet of Things (IoT). Service-related activities with the IoT generate a large volume of heterogeneous data. Storing and processing a high volume of data using traditional techniques increases production costs. Therefore, fog computing (FC) paradigm has been introduced to mitigate the production costs. This fact makes fog computing an emerging area of research in recent time. Technically, FC functions as an initial computing paradigm in the domain of cloud computing (CC). The fog computing paradigm covers a wide variety of applications in different sectors such as transportation, navigation, and agriculture. Among the several applications of fog computing, healthcare is the most promising. Rapid global population growth has created new challenges for healthcare services. In this respect, traditional healthcare services suffer from scarcity of doctors and medical equipment. This also increases the cost of treatment. To eliminate this, the fog computing paradigm has been applied in healthcare services such as diagnosis and monitoring. Fog computing provides real-time remote solutions to medical problems or services at a low cost. This has boosted the healthcare industry. Recently, there has been an era of Healthcare 4.0, which demands smooth, secure, and accurate healthcare services. Traditional FC-based healthcare systems suffer from several problems in the context of data processing, data transmission, data security and authenticity, and power consumption. Several researchers have contributed different proposals to uplift FC-based healthcare services. This paper presents a systematic literature review on FC-based healthcare from 2019 to 2023 to highlight the recent and

*Corresponding author: subrataju2008@gmail.com

Chandan Banerjee, Anupam Ghosh, Rajdeep Chakraborty and Ahmed A. Elngar (eds.) Fog Computing for Intelligent Cloud IoT Systems, (175–202) © 2024 Scrivener Publishing LLC

pioneering contributions of researchers. The review first proposes an application taxonomy for fog computing in the healthcare sector. Second, it identifies critical challenges in the implementation of FC-based healthcare services. Finally, this study draws a limelight on the opportunities in FC-based healthcare services for future research.

Keywords: Fog computing, cloud computing, internet of things, healthcare, application taxonomy

8.1   Introduction

The use of Internet of Things (IoT) [1, 2] based devices in different application areas has increased significantly in recent times. Naturally, these devices generate large volumes of data at every moment. However, dealing with a large volume of data is a typical task and suffers from different kinds of challenges, especially in the context of data storage management. This has inspired researchers to introduce cloud-based data-storage-management policies. Cloud computing (CC) [3, 4] offers different kinds of services and management schemes. This technique is highly efficient in data storage and management. However, cloud computing is highly expensive when dealing with heterogeneous [5] type of data. However, IoT-based devices often generate heterogeneous data. This fact has motivated researchers to introduce fog computing (FC) [6–11] to ease cloud computing services. Fog computing is an extension of the cloud computing paradigm. The relationship between fog computing, cloud computing, and the IoT [12–14] is shown in Figure 8.1. The essential characteristics of fog computing [15–18] are illustrated in Figure 8.2. The basic architecture of fog computing includes different layers [19, 20], such as physical and virtualization, monitoring, pre-processing, temporary storage, security, and transport layers. Table 8.1 summarizes the activities of each layer.

There are different applications of FC in the current world. Healthcare [21–23] is one of the most promising applications of FC. Due to the increase in population, it has become an important issue for government and non-government organizations in different countries to properly maintain public health. Several infrastructural factors, such as poor communication systems, lack of human resources, and low budgets, often disrupt healthcare services. Moreover, unscientific, additional, and illegal diagnoses are serious threats to the health of people. These factors also lead to an increase in medical expenses. Therefore the poorer sections find it very difficult to obtain proper healthcare services. The fog computing paradigm helps the

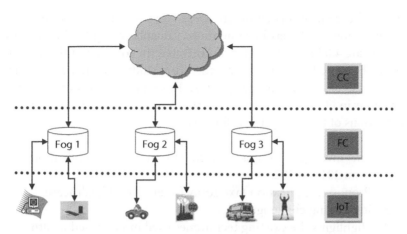

Figure 8.1 Relationship between cloud computing, fog computing, and Internet of Things.

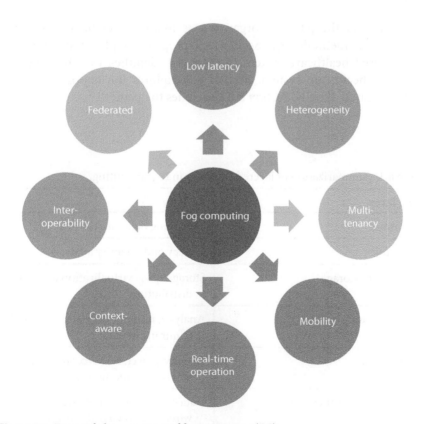

Figure 8.2 Essential characteristics of fog computing (FC).

people and organizations eliminate these types of problems to an extent. The application of FC has become more valuable owing to the inception of Healthcare 4.0 [24, 25]. This fact motivated me to conduct this research work on FC-based healthcare systems. This study presents a systematic review of FC-based healthcare systems. This study focuses on the recent innovations in FC-based healthcare systems from 2019 to 2023. The major contributions of this study are as follows.

1. The investigation was carried out in recent publications from 2019 to 2023.
2. Proposed application taxonomy for FC-based healthcare.
3. Identifying challenges.
4. Highlights the existing techniques used in FC-based healthcare systems.
5. Exploring opportunities for future research in FC-based healthcare systems.

The rest of the paper is organized as follows. *Section 8.2* describes the research methodology. *Section 8.3* proposes application taxonomy of FC-based healthcare system. *Section 8.4* identifies the challenges in FC-based healthcare system. *Section 8.5* explores the opportunities for future research. Finally, *Section 8.6* concludes the paper.

Table 8.1 Summarization of layered activities in fog computing.

Fog layer	Activity
Transport	Uploading data into cloud
Security	Privacy and integrity analysis
Temporary storage	Storage space virtualization and data distribution
Pre-processing	Analysis, mining, reconstruction and trimming of data
Monitoring	Activity, power, resource, response, and service monitoring
Physical and Virtualization	Data collection with physical, wireless, and virtual sensors

8.2 Research Methodology

This section discusses our research methodology in detail. The review work is carried out in the time span of 2019 to 2023. The keyword search method was used to identify current publications published in referred journals and conferences. The investigated string words are ("Healthcare" OR "Health" OR "ECG" OR "EEG" OR "Diabetics" OR "Heart" OR "Cardio" OR "Monitoring" OR "e-health," OR "Disease" OR "Diagnosis," OR "Detection" OR "Smart hospital") AND ("Fog computing" OR "Fog service" OR "Fog"). This study follows the Systematic Literature Review (SLR) method to investigate existing works. In this case, review questions were set to accelerate the investigation process. The research questions are presented in Table 8.2. The SLR process considers the inclusion and exclusion of publications based on the following criteria.

(a) Papers published between January 2019 and May 2023 were included.
(b) Journal papers indexed in SCI, SCIE, SSCI, ESCI or Scopus indexed are included.
(c) Conference or book chapters published by renowned publishers such as IEEE, Elsevier, Springer, Willy, ACM, and MDPI.
(d) Papers with non-English language are excluded.

Table 8.2 Research question.

Research question no	Question
RQ1	What are the scopes of FC in healthcare system?
RQ2	What are the challenges in FC-based healthcare system?
RQ3	What are the FC-based techniques used in healthcare system?
RQ4	Which techniques are most effective ones?
RQ5	What are the opportunities for future work?

A sketch of the review process is shown in Figure 8.3. Finally, 38 research papers published between January 2019 and May 2023 for this review. The papers were published by renowned publishers, such as IEEE, Elsevier, Springer, MDPI, Wiley, ACM, Emerald, and SAGE. Figure 8.4 shows the number of papers published by the different publishers. Table 8.3 presents a summary of review papers on FC-based healthcare systems and compares them in different contexts, such as application taxonomy, number of accounted papers, timeframe, and review methodology.

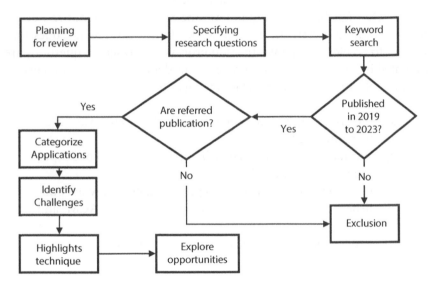

Figure 8.3 Sketch of review process.

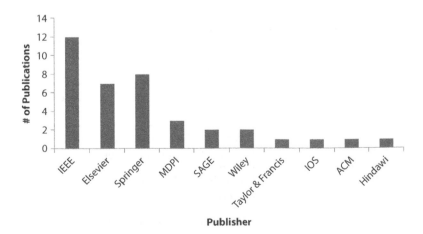

Figure 8.4 Number of publications made by the publishers.

8.3   Application Taxonomy in FC-Based Healthcare

This study first proposes an application taxonomy for FC-based healthcare services. The advancement of fog-based IoT paradigms [34] has opened new application areas in healthcare. Figure 8.5 presents the application taxonomy of the FC-based healthcare. Application taxonomy provides a clear view to readers to understand implementation challenges of the FC paradigm in healthcare. This study primarily identified three major categories of application areas of the FC paradigm in healthcare: diagnosis, monitoring, and notification.

8.3.1   Diagnosis

Medical diagnosis [35–37] is another application of FC in healthcare. The primary objectives of FC-based medical diagnosis in healthcare are (a) minimizing the cost of treatment, (b) easy access to opinions from experts throughout the globe, and (c) enhanced reliability from authentic diagnostic organizations. This study identifies different sub-application areas of the FC paradigm under medical diagnosis, such as cardiovascular diagnosis (CVD), outbreak disease detection (ODD) and cancer cell diagnosis (CCD). Cardiovascular diagnosis refers to the investigation of a heart's health condition. The outcome of CVD helps doctors make quick and reliable decisions regarding clinical treatment. Outbreak diseases are mainly caused by insects or animals, such as mosquitoes, flies, rats, and bats. This type of disease often creates a pandemic in our society, and hence, it may affect many people. Therefore, ODD is an important subapplication area in fog-based healthcare systems.

Cancer cell diagnosis is another sub-application of the FC-based medical diagnosis system. The CCD under the FC paradigm provides more accurate and reliable clinical results that help doctors and authorities of hospitals arrange necessary medical facilities for the betterment of the cancer patients. Table 8.4 presents recent publications on diagnoses in FC-based healthcare.

8.3.2   Monitoring

Health monitoring [53] is a popular application of FC. The necessity for health monitoring in today's society is highly appreciated. In many cases, elderly people must live home alone; hence, it becomes difficult for them to attend routine check-ups periodically. Sudden requirements of medicine,

Table 8.3 Summary of review papers on FC-based healthcare.

Ref.	Aim of review	Application taxonomy	Review time frame	# of papers included	Method
[26]	Identification of different technologies for FC in healthcare	No	2007–2017	99	SLR
[27]	Implementations of FC in healthcare	No	2015–2020	5	SLR
[28]	Development of taxonomy for FC	No	2010–2019	44	PICOCO
[29]	Identification of recent trends, key constraints application areas of FC in healthcare	No	2017–2022	46	PRISMA
[30]	Systematic analysis of FC techniques for health management system	No	2014–2019	50	SLR
[21]	Comparison among the FC technologies in healthcare.	No	2019–2021	13	SLR
[31]	Exploration and classification of FC-based healthcare systems in addition to performance evaluation methods and metrics	No	2015–2020	34	SLR
[32]	Explores the strategies for e-health applications	No	Undefined	48	SLR
[33]	Explores techniques, challenges, and monitoring system in FC-based healthcare system	No	2016–2021	40	AMSTAR
Proposed	Introduction of application taxonomy in FC-based healthcare in addition to exploration of challenges, techniques, and opportunities	Yes	2019–2023	38	SLR

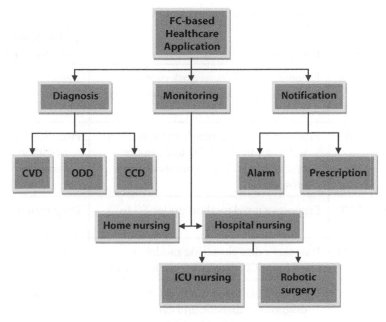

Figure 8.5 Application taxonomy in FC-based healthcare.

medical equipment, and ambulances are additional problems. In this case, the FC-based health monitoring system has brought hope to them by providing healthcare support remotely. This scenario is also true for pregnant women and people with disabilities. These patients require nursing facility care at home. Critical patients at hospitals need intensive care; hence, they are admitted to the intensive care unit (ICU). Continuous and real-time monitoring of patients in the ICU is necessary to improve patient health. In addition, the FC-based healthcare paradigm can be implemented in robotic surgical operations at a smart hospital. Table 8.5 presents the recent publications on monitoring in FC-based healthcare.

8.3.3   Notification

Another application area in FC-based healthcare is the real-time notification of patients regarding their health condition. Notification was sent to the patients in two primary cases. The first case was related to the issue of doctors or medical experts' prescriptions. The FC-based paradigm analyzes the medical conditions of the patient, such as body temperature, heartbeat, and pressure in real time, and quickly notifies the patient regarding which medicine/diet he/she should take to overcome the problem. The second case is related to a real-time alarm to the patient whenever his/

Table 8.4 Recent publications on diagnosis in FC-based healthcare.

Ref.	Year	Proposal	Technology/ device used
[38]	2020	Proposes a novel framework named HealthFog for automatic heart disease analysis	Deep Learning
[39]	2019	Proposes a social network analysis (SNA) technique in cloud-fog to compute probability of disease outbreak from mosquito	Fuzzy k-nearest neighbor classifier
[40]	2020	Proposes a novel method under FC to identify oral cancer	Deep neural network
[41]	2020	Proposes a data clustering model to analyze ECG data in FC environment	Raspberry Pi
[42]	2021	Proposes a FC-based method for diagnosis of diabetic and cardio diseases	Blockchain
[43]	2022	Proposes a smart model in FC paradigm to control outbreak of Encephalitis	Temporal-Recurrent Neural Network (TRNN)
[44]	2022	Proposes a cardiac health detection framework under FC paradigm to maintain quality of service (QoS) in healthcare	Deep Learning
[45]	2022	Proposes a FC, Priority Queue and Certainty Factor (CF) based model to analyze heart disease patients' condition in Clinical Decision Support System	Raspberry Pi
[46]	2022	Proposes a model called FETCH to monitor and diagnosis of heart disease under FC paradigm	Deep Learning

(Continued)

Table 8.4 Recent publications on diagnosis in FC-based healthcare. (*Continued*)

Ref.	Year	Proposal	Technology/ device used
[47]	2022	Proposes an efficient FC paradigm to detect osteosarcoma cancer from histopathology images	Deep Learning
[48]	2022	Proposes a lossless EEG data compression technique in FC paradigm for diagnosis of heart disease	Agglomerative hierarchical clustering and Huffman encoding
[49]	2022	Proposes an edge-fog-enabled lossless EEG data compression technique to detect epileptic seizure situation of patients	K-Means clustering, Huffman encoding and Naive Bayes classifier
[50]	2023	Proposes a fog empowered framework named FRIEND for real time data access and diagnosis of heart disease	Ensemble Machine Learning and Ensemble Deep Learning
[51]	2023	Proposes an ECG data analysis model in fog environment called FedSDM for diagnosis of heart disease	Federated Learning
[52]	2023	Proposes an efficient EEG data compression technique (ECoT) to analyze heart disease in FC paradigm	DBSCAN clustering, Huffman encoding and Delta encoding

her health is going to fall at risk. Activities such as running, walking, playing, and traveling may increase/decrease standard body vital parameters, which cause illness later in life. In such a case, the FC-based healthcare paradigm notifies the person of a warning message. After receiving the warning messages, a person can easily decide when to stop the activities.

Table 8.5 Recent publications on monitoring in FC-based healthcare.

Ref.	Year	Proposal	Technology/ device used
[54]	2019	Proposes a new health monitoring system architecture under FC paradigm based on physiological and environmental signals	WSN and Lambda cloud architecture
[55]	2019	Proposes a novel fog-based health monitoring system for promotion of patient-centric treatment	LoRa WSN
[56]	2019	Proposes a fog-based user-centric healthcare system called HEART to monitor patient's health condition at home	Machine Learning
[57]	2020	Proposes a remote pain monitoring system under FC paradigm based on bio-signals captured by various sensors	iFogSim toolkit
[58]	2020	Proposes an energy-efficient fog computing architecture for health monitoring applications	Gigabit Passive Optical Network (GPOT) and Mixed Integer Linear Programming (MILP)
[59]	2021	Proposes an efficient wireless communication management technique for FC based health monitoring system	Non-orthogonal multiplexing assess (NOMA)
[60]	2021	Proposes a fog-based health monitoring system with efficient load balancing computational paradigm	iFogSim toolkit
[61]	2022	Proposes jeopardy prophylaxis model to monitor health condition under FC paradigm	Machine Learning

(Continued)

Table 8.5 Recent publications on monitoring in FC-based healthcare. (*Continued*)

Ref.	Year	Proposal	Technology/ device used
[62]	2022	Proposes a fog-based patient monitoring system at intensive care unit (ICU) to help doctors and hospital authorities to take quick decision	MongoDB Atlas
[63]	2023	Proposes a fog-based monitoring system for heart disease diagnosis purpose	Modified Salp Swam Optimization (MSSO) and Adaptive Neuro-Fuzzy Inference System (ANFIS)
[64]	2023	Proposes a fog-based internet of medical things (IoMT) framework to monitor patient's diabetic hazards	SVM and ANN
[65]	2023	Proposes an energy efficient fog-based heath monitoring system	Swarm intelligence
[66]	2023	Proposes a fog-based patient monitoring system	Blockchain

The notification service also helps the person follow a special diet or medicine to obtain immediate relief from the illness. Table 8.6 shows the recent publications on notification services in FC-based healthcare.

8.3.4 Zest of Applications of FC in Healthcare

This section presents the latest applications of fog computing in healthcare.

A. Disease diagnosis
1. Heart disease diagnosis using ECG and EEG data.
2. Outbreak or infectious disease diagnosis for community health preservation.
3. Cancer diagnosis for better treatment.

Table 8.6 Recent publications on notification in FC-based healthcare.

Ref.	Year	Proposal	Technology/ device used
[67]	2019	Proposes an activity monitoring and recognition framework in FC paradigm to alert the patient regarding their health	Blockchain
[68]	2019	Proposes a real-time notification service using FC	Smart Google
[69]	2019	Proposes a job scheduling algorithm in FC paradigm for emergency notification to the doctor's for treatment	iFogSim toolkit
[70]	2019	Proposes a e-health system in FC paradigm that can monitor elderly people and provide notifications to the doctors and administrators	MySignals HWV2 and Android App
[71]	2019	Proposes a 3-layer fog architecture, heterogeneous fog network and fog-enabled healthcare service that can send notification to the hospitals for ambulance service	Cloudlet server, gateways, routers, Smartphone, Zigbee
[72]	2019	Proposes a system architecture in FC-paradigm for real-time alerts and notification	LSTM Recurrent neural network
[73]	2020	Proposes a fall detection and notification system in FC paradigm for elderly people	SVM
[74]	2021	Proposes the concept of health zone based on fog enabled body vital data analysis to monitor health hazards for the athletes	LSTM
[75]	2022	Proposes a fog-based framework for real-time monitoring and notifying the patient as well as doctors or caregivers	Wearable device and Machine learning technique
[76]	2023	Proposes a new Priority-Queue service in fog-layer to prioritize events such as warning to the patients whenever required	iFogSim toolkit

B. Health monitoring
1. Home nursing monitoring.
2. Hospital nursing monitoring.
3. ICU nursing monitoring.
4. Robotic surgery monitoring

C. Health notification
1. Alarm/Warning
2. Medicine prescription

8.4   Challenges in FC-Based Healthcare

Implementation of the FC paradigm in healthcare faces several challenges. This study revealed the crucial challenges in FC-based healthcare. This section highlights the major challenges faced by fog-based healthcare services. An outline of the major challenges in FC-based healthcare systems is presented in Figure 8.6.

8.4.1   QoS Optimization

The fog-based healthcare paradigm requires maintenance of Quality of Service (QoS) [77]. In the healthcare sector, QoS is hampered by poor

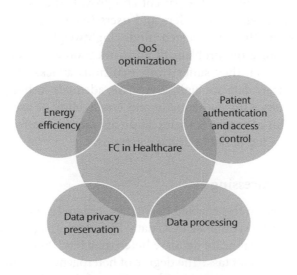

Figure 8.6 Major challenges in FC-based healthcare system.

latency and response time. Latency refers to the closeness of IoT devices or sensors to the users. High latency often creates problems in the acquisition of real-time and accurate patient data. This misguides the FC paradigm for disease diagnosis and monitoring services. Therefore, the devices or sensors should be kept close to the user. However, in reality, it sometimes becomes difficult to organize all IoT devices or sensors close to the user because of several factors such as space, disability, and network issue. Moreover, obtaining fast data access by IoT devices or sensors in real time is a real problem in healthcare. Health data, especially data related to vital body parameters, are time variant in nature. For example, the pulse rate of a person may differ owing to changes in time. Therefore, if IoT devices or sensors cannot acquire data on time, it becomes difficult for doctors to make fast and accurate decisions. This type of problem is known as the response time problem. Real-time diagnosis and monitoring require fast response times. In such a case, it is necessary to optimize the closeness of the IoT devices or sensors to achieve low latency and minimize the response time. Scholars have taken few initiatives to optimize latency and response time. Although the application of machine learning and deep learning techniques solves the problem in some sort, it remains a challenge for researchers to optimize QoS.

8.4.2   Patient Authentication and Access Control

In the domain of fog-based healthcare applications, it is necessary to authenticate the identity of the patient and provide the right to access the service [78]. Fog-service providers and users (patients) want to communicate with each other in a trusted mode. Lightweight protocols [66] are introduced to solve the problem of authentication and access control at an extent. However, they suffer from malicious attacks from intruders. Because healthcare data are highly sensitive, adequate techniques are necessary to guarantee the authenticity and creditability of users. Therefore, the development of patient authentication and access control mechanisms is challenging in fog-based healthcare systems.

8.4.3   Data Processing

Disease diagnosis in fog-enabled healthcare systems is a data-driven process. Healthcare data comprise ECG data, EEG data, image data, numerical data, etc. Hence, healthcare data are heterogeneous. Processing heterogeneous data is a difficult task. The degree of heterogeneity hampers the performance of the processing algorithms. One of the actions in this case is data filtering [40–42]. Filtering not only reduces the degree of heterogeneity but also the volume of data. Classification and clustering techniques are popular methods used for filtering data, but they face the problem of missing data. This leads to an improper diagnosis of the disease. Context data processing is required to collect data from sensors [79]. Smart data processing is required to issue final decisions in healthcare monitoring. The application of machine-learning techniques and big data analysis has solved this problem to an extent. However, further improvements in data processing techniques are required to optimize this task. Therefore, data processing is a challenge in fog-based healthcare systems.

8.4.4   Data Privacy Preservation

Fog nodes within the vicinity of patients can collect sensitive patient information, such as identity, location, and body statistics. Fog nodes with loose security are the most lucrative for intruders. Within the vicinity of the fog network, an intruder can steal the personal information of the patient and dispatch it to a third-party for some interests. This fact definitely damages personal and social lives of patients. Therefore, it is mandatory to preserve data privacy. Cryptography-based privacy preservation is common practice in healthcare. Tight encryption and decryption mechanisms have also been implemented to preserve the security and privacy of the data [80]. Data-size partitioning is another option for preserving privacy. However, a restricted partitioning size may hamper the optimum QoS latency. Therefore, preserving data privacy is a challenge in fog-based healthcare systems.

8.4.5   Energy Efficiency

Energy consumption is a vital issue in fog-based healthcare systems. Primarily, two types of energy consumption occur in fog-based healthcare systems. The first is networking energy consumption and the second is processing energy consumption. A higher energy consumption increases the cost of production. Architectural failure is the prime reason for the high energy consumption of fog nodes. Similarly, the processing of heterogeneous and voluminous data requires considerable energy. Therefore, optimization of the energy consumption by fog nodes is required. Some scholars [81] proposed solutions to this problem. However, this remains a challenge in fog-based healthcare systems.

8.5   Research Opportunities

The fog-computing paradigm is a popular technology used in the health-care industry. Owing to the commencement of Healthcare 4.0, the application of the FC paradigm has increased. This review thoroughly examines the applications of fog computing techniques to different variants of health-care services. Simultaneously, this review identifies crucial challenges in the implementation of fog computing in healthcare. This section addresses research opportunities in FC-based healthcare systems. Research opportunities were addressed from four perspectives: such as computing, security, services, and applications. To improve FC-based healthcare systems, scholars should first focus on computing paradigms to mitigate the power consumption. In this case, green computing is highly appreciable. Computation should follow a security perspective. Security is concerned with data security and data filtration processes. In this case, blockchain-based data security and lossless data processing are limited. Once computing and security perspectives are satisfied, researchers may investigate the matter of new services. There is plenty of research on community healthcare services and e-healthcare in rural areas. The implementation of FC-based services by end-users is another research opportunity. This necessitates the development of user-friendly interfaces. A chronological summary of the research opportunities is shown in Figure 8.7.

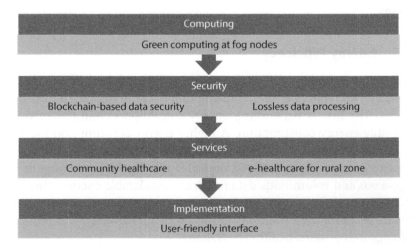

Figure 8.7 A chronological view of research opportunities in FC-based healthcare system.

8.5.1   Research Opportunity in Computing

- **Green computing at fog nodes:** Power consumption by fog networks and nodes is an important issue in FC-based healthcare systems. Complex data processing techniques increase power consumption, which in turn increases the cost of service. In addition, high energy consumption is unsuitable for a sustainable environment. This encourages the incorporation of green computing [82] at fog nodes. Green computing significantly reduces power consumption. Therefore, the incorporation of green computing into the FC-based healthcare domain is an opportunity for future research.

8.5.2   Research Opportunity in Security

- **Blockchain-based data security:** Data security is a primary issue in FC-based healthcare services. The medical and body vital data were highly sensitive. Leakage or theft of data may hamper patients' personal and social lives. Traditional techniques use encryption and decryption mechanisms for data security. However, it has been observed that intruders sometimes hack traditional mechanisms and steal the data. Blockchain technology [83] is a light method in this respect. Blockchain provides high security between two blocks. In addition, malicious attacks on the chain or linkage are difficult. Therefore, blockchain-based fog-enabled healthcare is a promising research area.
- **Lossless data processing:** The data filtration mechanism at the fog node sometimes rejects valuable data, which is called loss of data. Information loss is not good for any type of analysis. Fog-based healthcare services rely on the data processed at fog nodes and sent to the cloud. Decision-making on lossy data leads to improper knowledge discovery [84]. This is not good for healthcare services. Therefore, a data quality examination is required before the filtration process. The fog nodes should only send quality data into the cloud from where decision-making may be performed. Therefore, it may be an opportunity to develop a data-qiality-checking process to obtain lossless data.

8.5.3 Research Opportunity in Services

- **Community healthcare:** Fog computing-based healthcare techniques are mostly used for disease diagnosis at the individual level. However, sometimes a group of people binds with zone, ethnicity, or work falls in the same disease. This type of group forms a community. This may be due to the spread of infectious bacteria or viruses. Naturally, the symptoms and effects of the disease on the human body are the same for all patients. In this situation, it is better to protect community health. Government organizations and NGOs can monitor disease severity using fog-based community healthcare.

- **e-healthcare for rural zones:** People living in rural areas suffer from medical infrastructure such as doctors, medicine, oxygen, diagnosis centers, and ambulances. In addition, scarcity or distance from good hospitals is another problem for them at the time of emergency. These factors often cause patient death. The fog computing-based e-healthcare paradigm can help in this respect. Fog-based diagnosis and notification can help them book a seat at a smart hospital and arrange ambulances to carry the patients. This can save lives in rural areas. Therefore, the expansion of fog-based e-healthcare is an important and promising research topic.

8.5.4 Research Opportunity in Implementation

- **User-friendly interface:** Fog-based real-time notification is sent to doctors, medical experts, patients, and caregivers. A user-friendly interface is required to receive notification in the form of a prescription or any other medical suggestions at the user's end. Research and development in the interface design for Android gadgets is highly promising.

8.6 Conclusion

Healthcare is a rapidly growing global industry. Fog computing is used in healthcare to access allied medical services to people electronically and remotely. This accelerates the growth of e-healthcare on a daily basis. This has become more important due to the commencement of the era of

Healthcare 4.0. This paper presents a systematic literature review of fog computing in healthcare to highlight recent innovations from January 2019 to April 2023. First, this study presents the application taxonomy of FC-based healthcare system. The taxonomy shows the scope of the application areas of the fog-computing paradigm in the healthcare sector. Diagnosis, monitoring, and notification are the three primary services of FC-based healthcare systems. Second, this study identifies and discusses some crucial challenges in FC-based healthcare systems. Third, this study addresses some important opportunities for FC-based healthcare systems. Therefore, researchers should consider the application taxonomy, challenges, and opportunities for further development of fog computing-based healthcare systems.

References

1. Mohindru, G., Mondal, K., Banka, H., Internet of things and data analytics: A current review. *WIREs Data Min. Knowl. Discov.*, 10, 3, 1341, 2020.
2. Junior, F.M.R. and Kamienski, C.A., A survey on trustworthyness for the Intenet of Things. *IEEE Access*, 9, 42493–42514, 2021.
3. Kunal, S., Saha, A., Amin, R., An overview of cloud-fog computing: Architectures, applications with security challenges. *Secur. Priv.*, 2, 4, 72, 2019.
4. Hamid, K., Iqbal, M.W., Abbas, Q., Arif, M., Brezulianu, A., Geman, O., Cloud computing network empowered by modern topological invariants. *Appl. Sci.*, 13, 1399, 2023.
5. Nazabal, A., Olmos, P.M., Ghahramani, Z., Valera, I., Handling incomplete heterogeneous data using VAEs. *Pattern Recognit.*, 107, 107501, 2020.
6. Sabireen, H. and Neelanarayanan, V., A review on fog computing: Architecture, fog with IoT, algorithms and research challenges. *ICT Express*, 7, 162–176, 2021.
7. Songhrobadi, M., Rahimi, M., Farid, A.M.M., Kashani, M.H., Fog computing approaches in IoT-enabled smart cities. *J. Network Comput. Appl.*, 211, 103557, 2023.
8. Laroui, M., Nour, B., Moungla, H., Cherif, M.A., Afifi, H., Guizani, M., Edge and fog computing for IoT: A survey on current research activities & future directions. *Comput. Commun.*, 180, 210–231, 2021.
9. Bellavista, P., Berrocal, J., Corradi, A., Das, S.K., Foschini, L., Zanni, A., A survey on fog computing for the internet of things. *Pervasive Mob. Comput.*, 52, 71–99, 2019.

10. Caiza, G., Saeteros, M., Onate, W., Garcia, M.V., Fog computing at industrial level, architecture, latency, energy and security: A review. *Heliyon*, 6, 03706, 2020.

11. Singh, J., Singh, P., Gill, S.S., Fog computing: A taxonomy, systematic review, current trends and research challenges. *J. Parallel Distrib. Comput.*, 157, 56–85, 2021.

12. Habibi, P., Farhoudi, M., Kazemian, S., Khorsandi, S., Leon-Garcia, A., Fog computing: A comprehensive architectural survey. *IEEE Access*, 8, 69105–69133, 2020.

13. Donno, M.D., Tange, K., Dragoni, N., Foundations and evaluation of modern computing paradigms: Cloud, IoT, edge and fog. *IEEE Access*, 7, 150936–150948, 2019.

14. Koohang, A., Sargent, C.S., Nord, J.H., Paliszkiewicz, J., Internet of Things (IoT): From awareness to continued use. *Int. J. Inf. Manage.*, 62, 102442, 2022.

15. Brogi, A., Forti, S., Guerrero, C., Lera, I., How to place your apps in the fog state of the art and open challenges. *Softw.: Pract. Exper.*, 20, 5, 719–740, 2020.

16. Costa, B., Bachiega Jr., J., Carvalho, L.R.D., Araujo, A.P.F., Orchestration in fog computing: A comprehensive survey. *ACM Comput. Surv.*, 55, 2, 29, 2022.

17. Das, R. and Inuwa, M.M., A review on fog computing: Issues, characteristics, challenges and potential applications. *Telemat. Inform. Rep.*, 10, 100049, 2023.

18. Abdulkareem, K.H., Mohammed, M.A., Gunasekaran, S.S., Al-Mhiqani, M.N., Mutlag, A.A., Mostafa, S.A., Ali, N.S., Ibrahim, D.A., A review of fog computing and machine learning: Concepts, applications, challenges and open issues. *IEEE Access*, 7, 153123–153140, 2019.

19. Roy, S., Li, J., Bai, Y., A two-layer-fog-cloud intrusion detection model for IoT networks. *Internet Things*, 19, 1000557, 2022.

20. Mann, Z.A., Notions of architecture in fog computing. *Computing*, 103, 51–73, 2021.

21. Quy, V.K., Hau, N.V., Anh, D.V., Ngoc, L.A., Smart healthcare IoT applications based on fog computing: Architecture, applications and challenges. *Complex Intell. Syst.*, 8, 3805–3815, 2022.

22. Chengoden, R., Victor, N., Huynh-The, T., Yenduri, G., Jhaveri, R.H., Alazab, M., Bhattacharya, S., Hegde, P., Maddikunta, P.K.R., Gadekallu, T.R., Metaverse for healthcare: A survey on potential applications, challenges and future directions. *IEEE Access*, 11, 12765–12795, 2023.

23. Gopinath, A.R., Singh, Y.P., Narawade, N.S., Design of fog computing system for health care applications based on IoT. *IEEE 3rd International Conference on Emerging Technology*, Belgaum, India, 2022.

24. Jain, R., Gupta, M., Nayyar, A., Sharma, N., Adoption of fog computing in healthcare 4.0, in: *Fog Computing for Healthcare 4.0 Environments. Signals and Communication Technology*, S. Tanwar, (Ed.), pp. 3–36, Springer, Cham, Switzerland, 2021.

25. Krishnamoorthy, S., Dua, A., Gupta, S., Role of emerging technologies in future IoT-driven healthcare 4.0 technologies: A survey, current challenges and future directions. *J. Ambient Intell. Hum. Comput.*, 14, 361–407, 2023.

26. Mutlag, A.A., Ghani, M.K.A., Arunkumar, N., Mohammed, M.A., Mohd, O., Enabling technologies for fog computing in healthcare IoT systems. *Future Gener. Comput. Syst.*, 90, 62–78, 2019.

27. Ijaz, M., Li, G., Lin, L., Cheikhrouhou, O., Hamam, H., Noor, A., Integration and applications of fog computing and cloud computing based on the internet of things for provision of healthcare services at home. *Electronics*, 10, 1077, 2021.

28. Costa, H.J.M., Costa, C.A., Righi, R.R., Antunes, R.S., Fog computing in healthcare: A systematic literature review. *Health Technol.*, 10, 1025–1044, 2020.

29. Gupta, A. and Singh, A., Healthcare 4.0: Recent advancements and futuristic research directions. *Wirel. Pers. Commun.*, 129, 933–952, 2023.

30. Fu, C., Lv, Q., Badrnejad, R.G., Fog computing in health management processing systems. *Kybernetics*, 49, 12, 2893–2917, 2020.

31. Ahmadi, Z., Kashani, M.H., Nikravan, M., Mahdipour, E., Fog based healthcare system: A systematic review. *Multimedia Tools Appl.*, 80, 36361–36400, 2021.

32. Vilela, P.H., Rodrigues, J.J.P.C., Righi, R.R., Kozlov, S., Rodrigues, V.F., Looking at fog computing for E-health through the lens of deployment challenges and applications. *Sensors*, 20, 2553, 2020.

33. Kashyap, V., Kumar, A., Kumar, A., Hu, Y.C., A systematic survey on fog and IoT driven healthcare: Open challenges and research issues. *Electronics*, 11, 2668, 2022.

34. Hazra, A., Rana, P., Adhikari, M., Amgoth, T., Fog computing for next-generation internet of things: fundamental, state-of-the-art and research challenges. *Comput. Sci. Rev.*, 48, 100549, 2023.

35. Singh, P.D., Kaur, R., Singh, K.D., Dhiman, G., Soni, M., Fog-centric IoT based smart healthcare support service for monitoring and controlling an epidemic of swine flu virus. *Inf. Med. Unlocked*, 26, 100636, 2021.

36. Alshehri, F. and Muhammad, G., A comprehensive survey of the Internet of Things (IoT) and AI-based smart healthcare. *IEEE Access*, 9, 3660–3678, 2021.

37. Javaid, H., Saleem, S., Wajid, B., Khan, U.G., Diagnosis a disease: A fog assisted disease diagnosis framework with bidirectional LSTM, in: *Proceedings of IEEE International Conference on ICoDT2*, Islamabad, Pakistan, 2021.

38. Tuli, S., Basumatary, N., Gill, S.S., Kahani, M., Arya, R.C., Wander, G.S., Buyya, R., HealthFog: An ensemble deep learning based smart healthcare system for automatic diagnosis of heart diseases in integrated IoT and fog computing environments. *Future Gener. Comput. Syst.*, 104, 187–200, 2020.

39. Vijayakumar, V., Malathi, D., Subramaniyaswamy, V., Saravanan, P., Logesh, R., Fog computing-based intelligent healthcare systems for the detection and prevention of mosquito-brone diseases. *Comput. Hum. Behav.*, 100, 275–285, 2019.

40. Rajan, J.P., Rajan, S.E., Martis, R.J., Panigrahi, B.K., Fog computing employed computer aided cancer classification system using deep neural network in internet of things based healthcare system. *J. Med. Syst.*, 44, 34, 2020.

41. Kahani, P. and Padole, M., Analyzing ECG waves in fog computing environment using Raspberry Pi clustering, in: *Proceedings of IEEE 4th I-SMAC*, Palladam, India, 2020.

42. Shynu, P.G., Menon, V.G., Kumar, R.L., Kadry, S., Nam, Y., Blockchain-based secure healthcare application for diabetic-cardio disease prediction in fog computing. *IEEE Access*, 9, 45706–45720, 2021.

43. Bhatia, M. and Kumari, S., A novel IoT-fog-cloud based healthcare system for monitoring and preventing encephalitis. *Cogn. Comput.*, 14, 1606–1626, 2022.

44. Iftikhar, S., Golec, M., Chowdhury, D., Gill, S.S., Uhlig, S., FogDLearner: A deep learning based cardiac health diagnosis framework using fog computing. *Proceedings of the 2022 Australasian Computer Science Week*, Brisbane, Australia, pp. 136–144, 2022.

45. Golkar, A., Malekhosseini, R., Zadeh, K.R., Yazdani, A., Beheshti, A., A priority-queue based telemonitoring system for automatic diagnosis of heart diseases in integrated fog computing environments. *Health Inf. J.*, 28, 4, 1–18, 2022, doi: 10.1177/14604582221137453.

46. Verma, P., Tiwari, R., Hong, W.C., Upadhyay, S., Yeh, Y.H., FETCH: A deep-learning-based fog computing and IoT integrated environment for healthcare monitoring and diagnosis. *IEEE Access*, 10, 12548–12563, 2022.

47. Nasir, M.U., Khan, S., Mehmood, S., Khan, M.A., Rahman, A., Hwang, S.O., IoMT-based osteosarcoma cancer detection in histopathology images using transfer learning empowered with blockchain, fog computing, and edge computing. *Sensors*, 22, 5444, 2022.

48. Idress, S.K. and Idress, A.K., New fog computing enabled lossless EEG data compression scheme in IoT network. *J. Ambient Intell. Hum. Comput.*, 13, 3257–3270, 2022.

49. Idress, A.K., Idress, S.K., Couturier, R., Ali-Yahiya, T., An edge-fog computing-enabled lossless EEG data compression with epileptic seizure detection in IoMT networks. *Internet Things*, 9, 15, 13327–13337, 2022.

50. Pati, A., Parhi, M., Alnabhan, M., Pattanayak, B.K., Habboush, A.K., Al. Nawayseh, M.K., An IoT-fog-cloud integrated framework for real-time remote cardiovascular disease diagnosis. *Informatics*, 10, 21, 2023.

51. Rajagopal, S.M., Supriya, M., Buyya, R., FedSDM: Federated learning based smart decision making module for ECG data in IoT integrated Edge–Fog–Cloud computing environments. *Internet Things*, 22, 100784, 2023.

52. Idress, A.K. and Khlief, M.S., Efficient compression technique for reducing transmitted EEG data without loss in IoMT networks based on fog computing. *J. Supercomput.*, 79, 9047–9072, 2023.

53. Khullar, V., Singh, H.P., Miro, Y., Anand, D., Mohamed, H.G., Gupta, D., Kumar, N., Goyal, N., IoT fog-enabled multi-node centralized ecosystem for real time screening and monitoring of health information. *Appl. Sci.*, 12, 9845, 2022.

54. Debauche, O., Mahmoudi, S., Manneback, P., Assila, A., Fog IoT for health: A new architecture for patients and elderly monitoring. *Proc. Comput. Sci.*, 160, 289–297, 2019.

55. Kharel, J., Reda, H.T., Shin, S.Y., Fog computing-based smart health monitoring system deploying LoRa wireless communication. *IETE Tech. Rev.*, 36, 1, 69–82, 2019.

56. Akrivopoulos, O., Amaxilatis, D., Mavrommati, I., Chatzigianna, I., Utilising fog computing for developing a person-centric heart monitoring system. *J. Ambient Intell. Smart Environ.*, 11, 237–259, 2019.

57. Hassan, S.R., Ahmad, I., Ahmad, S., Alfaify, A., Shafiq, M., Remote pain monitoring using fog computing for E-healthcare: An E_cient architecture. *Sensors*, 20, 6574, 2020.

58. Isa, I.S.B.M., El-Gorashi, T.E.H., Musa, M.O., II, Elmirghani, J.M.H., Energy efficient fog-based healthcare monitoring infrastructure. *IEEE Access*, 8, 197828–197852, 2020.

59. Qiu, Y., Zhang, H., Long, K., Computation offloading and wireless resource management for healthcare monitoring in fog-computing based internet of medical things. *Internet Things*, 8, 21, 15875–15883, 2021.

60. Asghar, A., Abbas, A., Khattak, H.A., Khan, S.U., Fog based architecture and load balancing methodology for health monitoring systems. *IEEE Access*, 9, 96189–96200, 2021.

61. Suggala, R.K., Krishna, M.V., Swain, S.K., Health monitoring jeopardy prophylaxis model based on machine learning in fog computing. *Trans. Emerging Telecommunication Technol.*, 33, 7, 4497, 2022.

62. Mudawi, N.A., Integration of IoT and fog computing in healthcare based the smart intensive units. *IEEE Access*, 10, 59906–59918, 2022.

63. Khan, M.A. and Algarni, F., A healthcare monitoring system for the diagnosis of heart disease in the IoMT cloud environment using MSSO-ANFIS. *IEEE Access*, 8, 122259–122269, 2020.

64. Yildirim, E., Cicioglu, M., Calhan, A., Fog-cloud architecture-driven internet of medical things framework for healthcare monitoring. *Med. Biol. Eng. Comput.*, 61, 5, 1133–1147, 2023.

65. Ali, H.M., Bomgni, A.B., Bukhari, S.A.C., Hameed, T., Liu, J., Power-aware fog supported IoT network for healthcare infrastructure using swarm intelligence-based algorithms. *Mobile Networks Appl.*, 28, 824–838, 2023. https://doi.org/10.1007/s11036-023-02107-9.

66. Cheikhrouhou, O., Mershad, K., Jamil, F., Mahmud, R., Koubaa, A., Moosavi, S.R., A lightweight blockchain and fog-enabled secure remote patient monitoring system. *Internet Things*, 22, 100691, 2023.

67. Islam, N., Paheem, Y., Din, I.U., Talha, M., Guizani, M., Khalil, M., A blockchain-based fog computing framework for activity recognition as an application to E-Healthcare services. *Future Gener. Comput. Syst.*, 100, 569–578, 2019.

68. Mani, N., Singh, A., Nimmagadda, S.L., An IoT guided healthcare monitoring system for managing real-time notifications by fog computing services. *Proc. Comput. Sci.*, 167, 850–859, 2020.

69. Jamil, B., Shojafar, M., Ahmed, I., Ullah, A., Munir, K., Ijaz, H., A job scheduling algorithm for delay and performance optimization in fog computing. *Concurrency Computation: Pract. Experience*, 32, 7, 5581, 2020.

70. Hassen, H.B., Dghais, W., Hamdi, B., An E-health system for monitoring elderly health based on internet of things and fog computing. *Health Inf. Sci. Syst.*, 7, 1, 24, 2019.

71. Tang, W., Zhang, K., Zhang, D., Ren, J., Zhang, Y., Shen, X., Fog-enabled smart health: Toward cooperative and secure healthcare service provision. *IEEE Commun. Mag.*, 57, 5, 42–48, 2019.

72. Queralta, J.P., Gia, T.N., Tenhunen, H., Westerlund, T., Edge-AI in LoRa-based health monitoring: Fall detection system with fog computing and LSTM recurrent neural networks, in: *Proceedings of IEEE 42nd TSP*, Budapest, Hungary, 2019.

73. Srivastava, R. and Pandey, M., Real time fall detection in fog computing scenario. *Cluster Computing*, 23, 2861–2870, 2020.

74. Hussain, A., Zafar, K., Baig, A.R., Fog-centric IoT based framework for healthcare monitoring, management and early warning system. *IEEE Access*, 9, 74168–74179, 2021.

75. Elhadad, A., Alanazi, F., Taloba, A., II, Abozeid, A., Fog computing service in the healthcare monitoring system for managing the real-time notification. *J. Healthcare Eng.*, 2022, 5337733, 2022.

76. Yazdani, A., A fog-assisted information model based on priority queue and clinical decision support systems. *Health Inf. J.*, 29, 1, 1–21, 2023.

77. Saurabh, and Dhanaraj, R.K., Enhance QoS with fog computing based on sigmoid NN clustering and entropy-based scheduling. *Multimedia Tools Appl.*, 83, 305–326, 2023, doi: 10.1007/s11042-023-15685-3.

78. Ke, C., Zhu, Z., Xiao, F., Huang, Z., Meng, Y., SDN-based privacy and functional authentication scheme for fog nodes of smart healthcare. *Internet Things*, 9, 18, 17989–18001, 2022.

79. Islam, M.S.U., Kumar, A., Hu, Y.C., Context-aware scheduling in fog computing: A survey, taxonomy, challenges and future directions. *J. Network Comput. Appl.*, 180, 103008, 2021.

80. Alzoubi, Y., II, Osmanaj, V.S., Jaradat, A., Al-Ahmad, A., Fog computing security and privacy for the Internet of Thing applications: State-of-the-art. *Secur. Priv.*, 4, 2, 145, 2021.

81. Keshavarznejad, M., Rezvani, M.H., Adabi, S., Delay-aware optimization of energy consumption for task offloading in fog environments using meta-heuristic algorithms. *Cluster Comput.*, 24, 1825–1853, 2021.

82. Srivastava, A., Singh, A., Joseph, S.G., Rajkumar, M., Borole, Y.D., Singh, H.K., WSN-IoT clustering for secure data transmission in E-health sector using green computing strategy, in: *Proceedings of 9th IEEE CITSM*, Bengkulu, Indonesia, 2021.

83. Huynh-The, T., gadekallu, T.R., Wang, W., Yenduri, G., Ranaweera, P., Pham, Q.V., da Costa, D.B., Liyanage, M., Blockchain for the metaverse: A review. *Future Gener. Comput. Syst.*, 143, 401–419, 2023.

84. Datta, S., Mali, K., Das, S., Kundu, S., Harh, S., Rhythmus periodic frequent pattern mining without periodicity threshold. *J. Ambient Intell. Hum. Comput.*, 14, 8551–8563, 2023.

IoT-Driven Predictive Maintenance Approach in Industry 4.0: A Fiber Bragg Grating (FBG) Sensor Application

Dipak Ranjan Nayak[1,2], Pramod Sharma[3], Ambarish G. Mohapatra[4*],
Narayan Nayak[4], Bright Keswani[5] and Ashish Khanna[6]

[1]University of Technology, Jaipur, Rajasthan, India
[2]Department of Electrical and Electronics Engineering, Silicon Institute of
Technology, Bhubaneswar, Odisha, India
[3]Electronics & Communication Engineering, University of Technology, Jaipur,
Rajasthan, India
[4]Department of Electronics and Instrumentation Engineering, Silicon Institute of
Technology, Bhubaneswar, Odisha, India
[5]Department of Computer Science & Engg, Poornima University, Jaipur,
Rajasthan, India
[6]Department of Computer Science and Engineering, Maharaja Agrasen Institute of
Technology, Delhi, India

Abstract

Industry 4.0 entails, it is explained how vision, physical sensing, chemical sensing, and sensor multiplexing can help the development of cutting-edge industrial solutions. Industry 4.0 and IIoT have created a digital lean in manufacturing that has increased productivity, improved workflow, and automated processes. Optical sensing technology is preferred in high-precision sensing and control applications. Furthermore, the applications of passive sensing technologies such as Fiber Optic Sensors, are growing, and several industrial solutions have introduced widespread adaptation of such technologies. These fiber-optic sensors are highly sensitive and widely accepted in solutions where conventional sensors cannot be used owing to their limitations. A brief overview of such fiber-optic sensing technologies is discussed in this chapter, and real-time use cases are highlighted with detailed technological implementations. In addition to the above aspects, new trends in

Corresponding author: ambarish.mohapatra@gmail.com; ambarish.mahapatra@silicon.ac.in

Chandan Banerjee, Anupam Ghosh, Rajdeep Chakraborty and Ahmed A. Elngar (eds.) Fog Computing for Intelligent Cloud IoT Systems, (203–228) © 2024 Scrivener Publishing LLC

fiber Bragg grating (FBG) are portrayed with detailed practical implementations. Some of the major applications discussed in this article are the use of FBGs in magnetic fluid (MF), fiber optic Fabry–Perot (FP) cavity, etc. The last section of this chapter highlights the broad concept of predictive maintenance and the use of FBG sensors to solve various PM techniques.

Keywords: Industry 4.0, IIoT, predictive maintenance, passive sensing, fiber optic sensors, fabry–perot cavity, magnetic fluid, fBG

9.1   Introduction

The industrial revolution is based on technological innovation in industry and machine manufacturing, which helps in various fields that affect production, resources, and labor. These technical advancements have created new modes of living and working that fundamentally altered civilization. With the invention of machines, water power, and steam power in the 18th century, human and animal labor was transformed into machinery technology, beginning with the first industrial revolution (Industry 1.0). The 18th century saw the beginning of the first industrial revolution (Industry 1.0), which was characterized by the development of mechanization, water power, and steam power. The second industrial revolution (Industry 2.0), which began in the 19th century and was centered on mass production and assembly lines employing electricity, followed. The introduction of electronics, information technology, and automation signaled the beginning of the third industrial revolution (Industry 3.0) in the 1970s of the 20th century. The fourth industrial revolution (Industry 4.0) is a leading trend in data exchange in cyber-physical systems. The broad concept of the Industrial Revolution is shown in Figure 9.1 as mentioned below. The different automations and technologies used in manufacturing industries are listed below.

  a) Cyber-Physical Systems (CPS)
  b) The Internet of Things (IoT)
  c) The Industrial Internet of Things (IIoT)
  d) Smart Manufacture Practices (SMP)
  e) Cognitive Computing (CC)
  f) Smart Factories
  g) Cloud Computing
  h) Artificial Intelligence (AI)

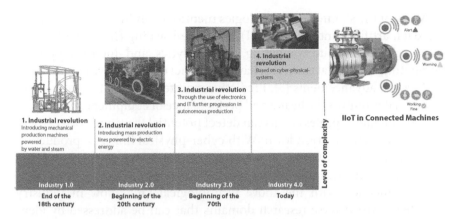

Figure 9.1 Broad concept of Industrial Revolution and Industry 4.0.

The technological revolution was directly influenced by the fourth industrial revolution. Both robots and supervisors must use a large amount of data and customization to make judgments daily during the manufacturing process. Predicting the requirements for asset maintenance at a specific future time is one of the hardest challenges in this domain. The business must be able to carry out its industrial activities uninterrupted or with minimal disruption to survive in tough competitive environments. This necessitates equipment maintenance to avoid issues such as employment loss, production loss, and increased product costs [1].

In a similar context, reactive, preventive, and predictive maintenance are three different categories of machine maintenance. The type of care given after a break is known as reactive maintenance [2]. Reactive maintenance involves pushing a piece of equipment to its breaking point and only making repairs after that. When low-cost systems such as light bulbs and fans are used, the reactive technique can make sense. Consider a complex system with high-priced components such as an aircraft engine. You cannot risk causing it to fail because repairing heavily damaged pieces is prohibitively expensive. However, crucially, it is a matter of life and death. Routine maintenance is based on preventive maintenance, which is used to prevent the machines from breaking down.

Further, the ability to undertake predictive maintenance helps reduce machine downtime, minimize costs, increase control action, and enhance production quality. Industry 4.0 surveys and tutorials mostly discuss data analytics and machine learning approaches for changing manufacturing procedures, excluding predictive maintenance methods and their implementation.

Many of the significant technologies mentioned in Industry 4.0, such as big data, artificial intelligence (AI), machine learning (ML), the Internet of Things (IoT), cloud computing, data analytics, and, increasingly, edge computing and digital twin, etc., have an impact on predictive maintenance and related advancements [3]. Predictive maintenance is a type of maintenance that monitors the health and performance of equipment while it is in use. Maintenance professionals can detect potential flaws and correct them before they cause a breakdown. With cyber-physical linkages, production can be done in Industry 4.0 without the need for humans, with a lot fewer mistakes and considerably higher reliability [4].

In connection with the above technological know-how in Industry 4.0, there exist diverse research domains that can be addressed by identifying the appropriate scheme for sensing and post-processing of sensor signals. Further, the accuracy of the sensors and the installation of such sensing devices inside industrial machines are also challenging domains of research. This report presents a summary of research directions in the domain of predictive maintenance using IoT and the use of high-precision flexible sensors to address maintenance-related issues in a real-time fashion. Hence, fiber Bragg grating (FBG) sensors are such high-precision and flexible sensors that can be used in various critical applications. These sensors are very rugged and can be fitted into critical locations like the shaft of the motors, the pento of the electric rails, the coil of the transformers, reinforced concrete, etc. The speed of data transmission is also another important parameter that influences the measurement. Further, the speed of internet technology is improving day by day using new emerging technologies like 4G and 5G. Also, the backbone of these emerging communication technologies relies on fiber optic communication systems due to their high network throughput, minimum error during data transmission, etc. Therefore, the cutting-edge FBG sensing system is one of the potential technological advancements to address the fastest sensing solution for a variety of industrial monitoring applications.

This literature survey is prepared to showcase a new research direction for the monitoring of machine conditions using cutting-edge FBG sensors and integrating the monitoring system with IoT technologies. This will enable real-time monitoring of industrial machines, processing of large-scale data samples, prediction of future issues using current machine conditions, generating adequate notifications and alerts during emergencies, etc. A detailed analysis of similar predictive analyses of machines is discussed further.

Electric motors are utilized in various industrial and household applications, including electric vehicles, escalators, pumps, process industries, manufacturing, and production plants. There are two basic failures of the motors, such as mechanical and electrical failures [5]. Susceptible and crucial damage in motors occurs due to the connection between the rotor, stator, and bearing [6]. The main aim of condition monitoring is to reduce failure, increase reliability, minimize cost, and safely keep industry running [7], which has drawn more attention from researchers [8]. Real-time data is continuously gathered from the operating machine by the sensors and compared with a reference value for online condition monitoring. IoT solutions have increased the use of online CMS in the sector. The Industrial Internet of Things (IIoT) can create innovative and dependable solutions for systems that are aimed at improving operational effectiveness in today's new breed of smart factories [9].

Traditional maintenance has been replaced by IIoT based on CMS in Industry 4.0. The IIoT idea allows for more convenient and reliable maintenance. It developed a low-cost CMS that is compatible with Industry 4.0 and is based on the IIoT. The preparation of the experimental setting, IIoT-based condition monitoring applications (CMAs), and finally machine learning (ML) models and their evaluation make up its three main elements.

The learning system is developed based on the use of new methodologies and strategies. Predictive maintenance is a recent topic in Industry 4.0. Technology such as IoT, cloud computing, machine learning, and management systems are used to create innovative and effective systems [10]. In the article by Girdhar et al. (2004), numerous methods for performing predictive maintenance are proposed [11]. Vibration monitoring, corrosion monitoring, particle analysis, oil analysis, thermography, acoustic emission, and performance monitoring are among these approaches. Similarly, Chu et al. (2018) analyzed the health of a bearing by determining vibration data to postulate defective or similar conditions. In the above research article, the study examines the vibration data from bearing components such as the inner bearing, outer bearing, and rolling element [12].

In recent years, support vector machines (SVMs) for the monitoring and diagnosis of bearing conditions have been applied in various predictive maintenance applications [13]. The reason for such highly accepted technological applications of SVM in predictive maintenance applications is due to the higher classification success rate and easy tracking of the machine's health [14]. Yadav et al. (2013) examined the SVM algorithm using rotational speed, voltage, and current as input parameters to identify bearing deterioration in a three-phase induction motor [15]. Moosavian et al. (2013) explained the vibration data collected from the journal-bearing in three distinct circumstances to discover faults by performing a motor experiment [16]. They compared the results of vibration data analysis by using the machine learning tools kNN and ANN. Similarly. RuizGonzalez *et al.* (2014) have proposed the SVM method to study the vibration on agricultural industrial machinery, achieving an average cross-validation accuracy of 85% [17]. Similarly, Sun *et al.* (2011) have utilized SVM to evaluate bearing life [18]. The predictive maintenance experiment was introduced to identify the fault in the problematic bearing. The Internet of Things (IoT) capability has been included and adapted in the Industry 4.0 system. The condition monitoring software is applicable in the industry and integrated with monitoring, recording, and notification tools, as well as other low-cost and open-source facilities. Machine learning techniques were used to categorize the real-time data gathered from the experiment setting, and the effectiveness of the classifier models was evaluated.

The transition to Industry 4.0 is made easier by IoT-based monitoring and warning systems. The use of non-conventional FBG sensors for predictive maintenance has plenty of scope for the researcher, which was explained briefly above. In the literature review section, a thorough review of various predictive maintenance schemes is discussed in *Section 9.2* of this chapter. The potential research gaps from various research articles are identified and discussed in the next section of the chapter, followed by emerging research techniques. Further, a broad concept of PM technique using FBGs in Industry 4.0 is discussed further with a conceptual block diagram.

9.2   Review of Related Research Articles

Predictive maintenance techniques were created to assess the state of the equipment that is currently in use and predict when maintenance should be performed. In comparison to normal or time-based preventative maintenance, these strategies aid in cost reduction. It is therefore seen as condition-based maintenance that is carried out in response to projections of an item's degree of degradation. The basic objectives of predictive maintenance are to prevent unexpected equipment failures and to make scheduling corrective maintenance simple. The literature review of the related research articles based on various predictive and condition maintenance methods is shown in Table 9.1.

The key features are enhanced plant safety, increased equipment lifetime, eliminated accidents with negative impacts on the environment, and improved handling of spare parts. This concept of handling the equipment

Table 9.1 Literature review of related research articles.

Authors	Proposed work	Findings
Wang et al. [2]	Predictive Maintenance (PM) technique.	To track and assess the machine's condition, a practical and scientific maintenance approach has been created.
Nandi et al. [5]	Electrical motor condition monitoring and fault analysis.	Axial flux-based measurements, vibration analysis, transient current and voltage monitoring, and other theoretical analyses and models of machine problems.
Khuntia et al. [9]	Big Data and the Future of Smart Asset Management for Electric Utilities.	Effective maintenance will result from data that is reliable, timely, accurate, and thorough when it comes to machine degradation state.
Chu et al. [12]	A technique for tracking bearing vibration and identifying defects.	A method based on statistical information on the peak coordinates of faults for predicting prospective machine tool failures.
Yadav et al. [15]	SVM-based Bearing Fault Detection of Induction Motor.	The successful identification of lubrication issues in bearings and the detection of the induction motor defect was made possible by the superb classification tool known as LS-SVM.
Moosavian et al. [16]	k-NN and ANN for fault diagnosis on a main engine.	Using two classifiers, KNN and ANN with PSD methodology, a method for diagnosing the main engine journal-bearing condition was presented.

smartly and efficiently has been proposed by various researchers. Several research articles have been reported to showcase the concept.

The prototype CMS systems are shown in Figure 9.2, which include a microcontroller, an electric motor, non-oil ORS 6203 type bearings, a Wi-Fi module, a Bluetooth module, and several sensors [58]. A three-axis

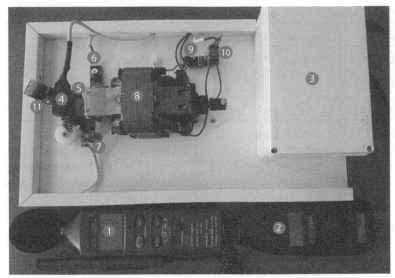

1: Sound Meter 2: Digital Tachograph 3: Control Box (Arduino UNO + NodeMCU) 4: Vibration Sensor
5: Bearing 6: Microphone 7: Hall Sensor 8: Direct Current Machine 9: Current Sensor 10: Voltage Sensor
11: Contactless Temperature Sensor

Figure 9.2 Snapshot of a prototype version of a CMS. [Source: Cakir *et al.* (2021)].

accelerometer, a microphone, a voltage sensor, a current sensor, a Hall sensor, and a non-contact temperature sensor are among the sensors used. This setup yielded data from both the healthy and non-oil-bearing bearings. Connecting the microcontroller platform to the peripherals is the initial stage in building the setup (sensors and communication modules). The second stage involved the use of highly precise measuring devices to calibrate all the sensors. The final stage involved testing non-oil ball bearings while collecting data via PLX-DAQ from the PC-interfaced microcontroller platform. A Wi-Fi module was used to send the data to the cloud. The CMA interface was built in the fourth step to monitor, notify, and control the system using a computer program. The Bluetooth module helps the smartphone visually display the data collected from the sensors. All the sensor data were collected in the designed CMA. CMA software was used to produce notifications (e-mail and SMS) for maintenance team members based on the threshold values acquired. According to the testing, the pivotal threshold values established in the system were crossed by real-time data collection from a non-oil ball bearing. In this case, the CMA contacted the maintenance team via email and SMS. The final step involved analyzing the data using ML toolkits in the R-Studio environment. The LDA, DT, kNN, SVM, and RF algorithms were employed to create the models.

These models' performance evaluations were then carried out. Figure 9.3 depicts these procedures [58]. An experimental setup for IoT-based predictive maintenance applications is developed in this study. A mobile CMA was also developed to work with the experimental setup. The threshold settings for the detection of bearings were determined according to the results acquired from the DT classifier. Employees in the maintenance unit are given a CMA to send SMS messages and email notifications concerning bearing status.

Similarly, the development of fiber Bragg grating (FBG) sensors in the middle of the 1990s was a wide-selection innovation that gave rise

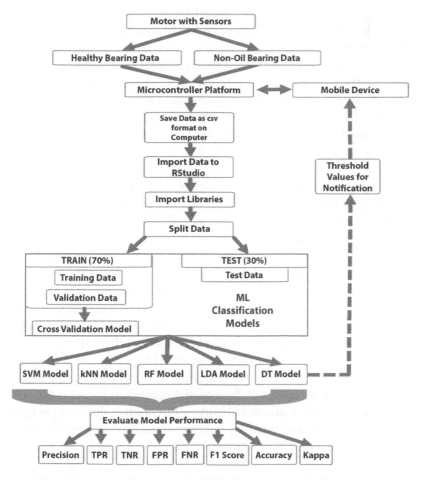

Figure 9.3 Procedure to evaluate CMS model built using R-studio environment. [Source: Cakir *et al.* (2021)].

to research in the field of wavelength-encoded sensors. The FBG sensors are more sensitive to parameters such as strain and temperature, so with the proper interface, they can measure a variety of parameters, such as temperature, strain, pressure, vibration, displacement, acceleration, and load. For both static and dynamic mode operations, the FBG sensor can be applicable, and it produces excellent performance in the presence of various industrial, biomedical, and chemical substances. For a wide range of applications, the FBG can be used as a superb signal shaping and filtering element. The CMS-based approach is one of the challenging areas where FBG sensors play a vital role in measuring critical machine or system parameters with very high accuracy. Another application of magnetic field sensors using FBGs is discussed further. The creation and authentication of a magnetic field sensor based on an FBG array immersed in a magnetorheological fluid (MR fluid, or MRF) were presented in this study. MRF is a smart fluid that is suspended in a carrier fluid, usually oil. When a strong magnetic field is applied to the fluid, it becomes a viscoelastic solid because of the increase in apparent viscosity. The active state of the fluid can be adjusted by adjusting the magnetic field intensity. Ulasyar *et al.* [19] have used MR fluids as dampers and shock absorbers. Similarly, Attia *et al.* [20] have used MR fluids as brakes, Andrade *et al.* [21] used clutches, and Kaluvan *et al.* [22] used actuators utilizing the shear stress generated when the magnetic field intensity in the fluid region increases.

Dispersions of micron-sized particles of magnetizable materials spread in a liquid make up MR fluids. When magnetic fields are applied, scattered particles get magnetized. As a result, they feel attraction forces and develop particle structures that obstruct the flow.

Because of variations in stress, the application of a magnetic field to MR fluid causes an axial strain on the FBGs. As a result, there is a wavelength shift that is inversely related to the strength and location of the magnetic field. To test and validate this strategy, a 4-FBG array was positioned in the middle of a container filled with the MR 140-DG fluid (LORD, USA), as shown in Figure 9.4. The FBGs have a physical length of 10 mm, a physical spacing of 5 mm, a wavelength range of 1,535–1,551 nm, and a reflectivity of 90%. The sensor's spatial resolution is dependent on the distance between FBGs. As a result, excellent spatial resolution is produced, which depends on the shorter distances between FBGs when detecting magnetic field positions. The fiber and MR fluid are contained in a polylactic acid container with a diameter of 10 mm and a length of roughly 80 mm.

The disadvantages of today's magnetic field and electromagnetic current sensors are their high cost, ease of explosion, complex insulating structure, and difficulty in digitizing. Using the right methods, such as optical fiber

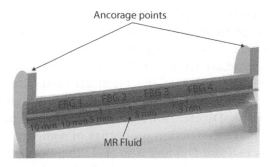

Figure 9.4 Multiple FBGs are embedded inside an MR fluid container. [Source: Leal-Junior *et al.* (2020)].

magnetic field sensors and optical fiber current sensors, it is possible to eliminate the drawbacks. This study describes the most recent developments in optical fiber current sensors and magnetically sensitive optical fiber magnetic field sensors. When materials are exposed to a magnetic field, the materials themselves are treated as a medium. The terms magnetostrictive materials, magneto-optical (MO) materials, and magnetic fluid (MF) materials are used to describe three different types of magnetically sensitive materials.

9.2.1   Studies on FBG Sensors and Their Role in Industry 4.0

The use of FBG sensors in Industry 4.0-based applications is very well experimented with by many researchers throughout the globe. There are some critical applications where the sensing device is designed with more sophisticated methodologies and technologies. In a similar context, the use of FBG sensors for the precise measurement of electrical and magnetic parameters is the most critical industrial application. Some of these applications are discussed in the subsequent sections of this article. The key aspect in the design of such FBG sensors is the required sensing material, which is influenced by electrical and magnetic parameters. Various magnetic materials are being experimented with in FBG sensor-related research works reported to date. Some of the important materials reported in the sensor design process are discussed further.

9.2.1.1   Magnetostrictive Material

Magnetostrictive materials can transfer potential energy between two states, such as elastic and magnetic. Also, magnetostrictive materials can be used for both sensing and actuation. If L and ΔL are the original length and change in length of the magnetostrictive material, then ΔL / L = γ, where γ is the magnetostriction coefficient. Went [23] analyzed the magnetostriction coefficients of different elements. The magnetostriction coefficient of the materials varies from material to material. For Ni, the coefficient γ is very low and it is high for rare earth materials such as Tb, Dy, etc. However, a high magnetic field is required to increase the magnetostriction properties of some materials, such as rare earth alloys (Tb and Dy) and iron (Fe). Therefore, the applications of magnetostrictive materials are limited. Clark *et al.* investigated gigantic magnetostrictive materials (GMM) in 2002. To increase the synthesis of Terfenol-D (TD), also known as the GMM and having the chemical formula Tb0.27Dy0.73Fe1.95 [24], the decrease of magneto-crystalline anisotropy relies on the doping concentration of Tb and Dy. These magnetostrictive materials have the inherent property of changing their shape due to the application of an external magnetic field. The use of FBG sensors to sense the change in the shape of the material will result from a shift in the reflected wavelength. This principle is used in most of the magnetostriction-based FBG sensors for various industrial applications. Some of the interesting industrial applications, such as robotics and factory automation, power distribution units (PDUs), etc., require precise sensing with better accuracy. The use of FBG sensors for magnetic field sensing will meet industrial requirements with better accuracy and precision.

9.2.1.2   Magneto-Optical (MO) Materials

Material is referred to as magneto-optical (MO) in the article by Li *et al.* [25] if it affects the characteristics of light propagation when an external magnetic field is applied to it. Glass, crystal, and ceramic materials are among the MO materials. The demerits of MO glasses are a larger value of absorption, lower thermal conductivity, etc. Aldbea *et al.* [26] studied MO materials as one type of garnet crystal. Garnet crystal, a ferrimagnetic material with the chemical formula $X_3Fe_5O_{12}$, belongs to the body-centered cubic (bcc) crystal system. Typically, X is a rare earth element or the yttrium (Y) element. The substance is known as yttrium iron garnet when X is yttrium and has the chemical formula $Y_3Fe_5O_{12}$ (YIG). MO material-based sensors are the most cutting-edge technologies, and very limited applications have been presented to date. Similarly, the FBG sensor based on MO materials is the most challenging and innovative approach, and plenty of research directions can be explored.

9.2.1.3   Magnetic Fluid (MF) Materials

To create magnetic fluid (MF), a stable colloid, magnetic nanoparticles (such as Fe3O4), and a surfactant must be highly dispersed in a liquid carrier, usually water or an organic solvent. The Faraday effect, birefringence, tunable transmittance, and tunable refractive index are the interesting optical properties of magnetic fluid. MF has fluidity and the ability to interact with the magnetic field. The characteristics of their components (dispersion medium, solid magnetic phase, and stabilizer) depend on magnetic fluid properties; a wide range of changes in those characteristics allow for changes in magnetic fluid parameters.

In the work by Miao *et al.* [27], magnetic fluid was identified as a distinct class of magnetic substance that exhibits several MO properties, such as the Faraday magneto-optical effect and a variable refractive index (RI). In a similar vein, magnetic fluid with field-relevant transmission magnetron dichroism and MO properties was studied by Zhao *et al.* [28]. The metal particles in MF are nickel (Ni), cobalt (Co), and iron (Fe), as well as their alloys Ni-Fe and Fe-Co [29–31]. The ferrite particles in MF are Fe3O4, Fe2O3, and MeFe2O4 (Me = Co, Mn, and Ni). The stated MF material principle can be used to detect magnetic field impact through optical phenomena.

9.2.1.4   Magnetically Sensitive Materials and Their Application

Optical fiber sensing, which generally consists of two components, optical fiber magnetic field sensors and optical fiber current sensors, uses magnetically sensitive materials. Similarly, precise measurement of the current inside a highly magnetic field environment, such as transformers, and motors, is possible using cutting-edge FBG sensors. A brief discussion of this a current sensing approach using FBGs is presented in the subsequent section.

9.2.1.5   Optical Fiber Current Sensors

These types of sensors are magnetostrictive materials, which combine with magnetostrictive materials and fiber gratings. Thus, with the shifting of the magnetic field, the substance approaches expanding and compressing. Further, the grating's distance in the FBG is modified, and finally, the current is measured using the electro-magnetism principle.

Mora *et al.* proposed the use of spliced Terfenol-D and MONEL400 alloy rods with an FBG on each rod as the material for current sensors in 2000 [32]. Direct current (DC) and temperature could both be detected concurrently by this substance. Then, in 2005, Satpathi *et al.* created the Terfenol-D material and FBG-related current sensor, which could measure alternating current (AC) in the 10–1,000 A range [33].

Because the material employed in the sensor is impacted by rising temperatures, the accuracy of the current sensor has decreased. The dual-parameter measurement of current and temperature is now being implemented. Using a dual-fiber grating structure, Han *et al.* presented a method for temperature modification in 2017 [34]. Dante *et al.* created a current sensor with fiber Bragg gratings and two different weights of Terfenol-D materials in 2019 using finite element simulation (FES) methods [35].

Using magnetostrictive materials, Zhao *et al.* [36] created an optical fiber current sensor (shown in Figure 9.5). When the current was raised from −170 A to 170 A, it was discovered that the sensor's linearity was within −0.3 nm to 0.3 nm. Two magnetostrictive films were applied to two fiber Bragg gratings (FBGs) that had equal beginning Bragg wavelengths. These FBGs were inserted into the magnetic circuit with the same bias but in opposite directions. One half was compressed while the other was expanded because of the magnetic field's strength in its ability to detect electricity.

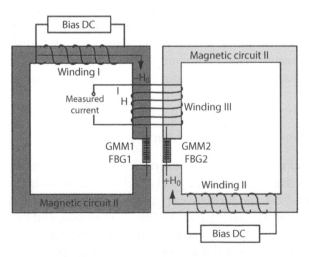

Figure 9.5 The sensor units comprised FBG and Terfenol-D with opposing magnetic circuits. [Source: Liu *et al.* (2021)].

For the FBGs wavelength to be moved in the direction of both shorter and longer wavelengths, respectively. The changing wavelength distance was used to measure the sensor current.

Figure 9.6 shows how optical fiber current sensors built with MO materials for wire current monitoring [36]. The performance analysis and control facets of various optical fiber current sensor components reflecting MO glass rods were studied by Rogers [37].

Two approaches, dual-channel optical light polarization and signal processing, were described by Shao *et al.* in 2008 as part of their investigation into a passive current sensor based on MO crystals [38]. Low-cost optical fiber current sensors were covered by Zubia Zaballa in 2013 [39]. The magnetic field generated a current in the MO material SF2, which changed the rotation of the beam. This prototype sensor exhibited excellent linearity and sensitivity for detecting currents ranging from 0 to 800 A [40]. In 2015, Wang *et al.* created a sensing system that used an MF-filled Fabry–Perot cavity. A long-tail optical fiber current sensor was created based on the adjustable magnetic refractive index, attenuation spectrum, and magnetic tunable transmission qualities. The sensor exhibited a 14.88 mA/s sensitivity.

Scientists from the United States, Yariv, and Winsor, explained in 1980 that the optical fiber and magnetostrictive materials were systematically connected to sense the weak magnetic fields through the phase modulation of the optical signal [41]. Theoretically, the magnetic field detection may be detected up to 10–16 T, according to the paper. The first weak magnetic field optical fiber sensor was proposed by Dandridge and colleagues from the U.S. Naval Laboratory [42]. The Mach-Zehnder interferometer was used to build the system (MZI). To vary the magnetostrictive effect of the interferometer, the magnetostrictive materials on one of its arms were coated with Ni or metallic glass. The strains transferred to the fiber from the magnetostrictive jacket that generates magnetically induced changes

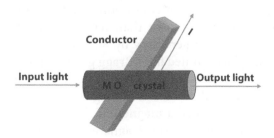

Figure 9.6 The configuration of optical fiber current sensors fabricated using MO materials. [Source: Liu *et al.* (2021)].

in optical path length were detected using an all-fiber Mach-Zender inter-ferometer (MZI), and its magnetic field sensitivity was increased up to 8×10^8 Oe/m.

Picon *et al.* [43] created four separate sensor arms connected by optical wire made of magnetostrictive materials in 1994 using the MZI principle. The lowest magnetic flux density (B) measured by the sensor was 0.3 mG.

Temperature compensation techniques were proposed by Yi *et al.* [44]. In the first, a single magnetostrictive plate has two FBGs that are mutually perpendicular and joined together. In the second, two FBGS were joined with two different magnetostrictive rods, which displayed comparable magnetostriction and thermal expansion coefficients with the opposite sign. The two temperature compensation systems offered to enhance the magnetic field sensitivity were lowered by the 10th time in the two meth-ods. A polymer magnetostrictive material-based optical fiber magnetic field sensor was proposed by Wang *et al.* in 2008. This sensor is used to measure magnetic fields that are produced by a ferromagnetic poly-mer (WCS-NG1) that has a magnetostrictive coating [45]. In addition, Nguyen *et al.* developed a magnetic field measuring model in 2011 using composite materials made of piezoelectric and magnetostrictive compo-nents using a two-dimensional finite element simulation (FES) method. The three-dimensional FES model was the subject of further research by the authors [46]. An optical fiber magnetic field sensor using a magneto-strictive composite material and FBG as the sensing unit was proposed in a separate study by Liu *et al.* in 2012 [46]. These Terfenol-D and epoxy resin composite compositions were identified as magnetically sensitive substances [47]. The aforementioned sensor, when exposed to an exter-nal magnetic field of 146 kA/m, showed a significant quasi-static peak wavelength drift of 0.68 nm. Distributed magnetic field sensors with a long range are another option. In the same year [48], Alisafaee *et al.* discussed how to improve a whole garnet magnetic field sensor using a genetic algorithm (GA) and a non-quarter wave. The outcomes sug-gested that a genetic algorithm could enhance the MO impact. A tiny optical fiber magnetic field sensor that made use of a filtering mecha-nism was proposed in another study by Shao *et al.* [49]. On a TbDyFe rod, a narrow-gap phase-shifted fiber Bragg grating (PS-FBG) sensor was placed. By monitoring variations in PS-FBG reflection intensity, the sen-sor could determine the distribution of magnetic intensity.

In 2018 [50], Zhou created a magnetic field sensor that combined an optical fiber and an EMG507-type magnetic field sensor. The magneto-strictive strain induces a wavelength drift, leading to magnetic intensity demodulation, and the sensor's detecting process is based on the conversion of this magnetic intensity demodulation into edge filtering. According to the sensor's results, it was able to detect magnetic fields between 2.43 mT and 22.54 mT with a resolution of 0.023 mT. Between 0 and 349 G, the sensor appeared to have a sensitivity of 303 pm/G. There is a tremendous use case for FBGs in sensing magnetostrictive strains [51–53]. Similarly, Wang *et al.* developed a dual-parameter sensor made of a serial structure of PCF and FBG that could measure temperature and magnetic field [54]. Figure 9.7 shows that the PCF was filled with different concentrations of MF and surfactants [55]. It was found that temperature and magnetic field strength had a good linear relationship with wavelength drift. The sensitivity increased with increasing magnetic particle concentration and reached 924.63 pm/mT [56].

Surface plasmon resonance (SPR)-based optical fiber magnetic field sensors were created in 2021 by Zhu *et al.* [55]. The sensors showed extraordinary sensitivity to refractive index, ranging from 1,973.72 nm/RIU to 3,223.32 nm/RIU, by covering the structure with 10 nm chromium (Cr) and 50 nm gold (Au). The research proved that when the same materials were used to cover the SMF structure, the performance of the sensor based on SPR was superior in the range of 1.3326 nm/RIU to 1.3680 nm/RIU. The sensor unit has a range of 0 mT–24 mT and a sensitivity of 4.42 nm/mT. The above study on optical fiber magnetic field sensing mechanisms has a large potential machine monitoring applications. Special-purpose machines (SPMs) are such industrial machines where precise measurement of magnetic fields is an important parameter. Therefore, there exists a large scope of research in the domain of FBG sensors for the monitoring

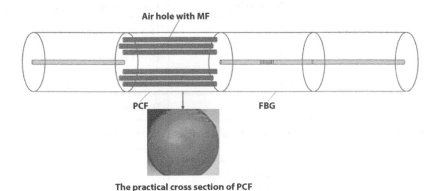

Figure 9.7 A dual-parameter sensor for both magnetic field and temperature. [Source: Liu *et al.* (2021)].

of important parameters like vibration, temperature, pressure, strain, magnetic field, etc.

9.3   Research Gaps

There is plenty of research scope in the domain of FBG sensing for critical sensing applications. Most of the magnetic field and current sensing approaches were discussed in the previous sections of this chapter. Another important aspect of industrial sensing in the domain of FBG sensors is vibration measurement with a very high level of accuracy. These vibration monitoring schemes are mostly applicable to rotating machines where conventional sensors cannot be used. Rotating machinery parts need careful balancing to prevent premature damage from vibrations. Vibration analysis is used to detect the causes of vibration, and it is useful for predictive maintenance. Vibration is not a steady one, and it varies from instrument to instrument and from time to time [57]. Even the same instrument will sense and produce different sets of vibrations. Hence, there is no fixed method for measuring and controlling vibration. An analysis must be done on a vibration body before framing a method to control or minimize it. Table 9.2 represents a few pieces of equipment and processes that generally require vibration analysis and monitoring of their continuous operations.

It is postulated that vibration monitoring of industrial machines is one of the important parameters that requires continuous measurement

Table 9.2 Equipment and processes monitored by vibration analysis.

Centrifugal	Reciprocating	Continuous process
Pumps	Pumps	Hot and Cold strip lines
Compressors	Compressors	Paper machines
Blowers/Fans	Engines	Continuous casters
Motors/Generators	Cylinders	Printing machines
Ball mills/Rotary dryers	Hobbling machines	Process flow lines (Chemical, Petroleum, etc.)
Mixers	Metal working machines	
Gearboxes	Temper mills	

and analysis. In some machines and locations, conventional vibration sensors are not suitable to be installed. Therefore, passive sensors like FBG sensors are very suitable for these types of applications. There are very few studies reported regarding vibration monitoring of industrial machines using FBG sensors. Adequate sensors and sensing mechanisms for the FBG sensors need to be identified through a proper study of the design as well as installation schemes. Nowadays, various fiber optic sensors are available on the market based on their principle of operation. These sensors have some limitations in their application field, but they can be used in harsh environments as well as in environments with high electromagnetic fields. In a similar context, other parameters like surface temperature and surface strain are useful in machine diagnostic applications. Therefore, the identification of an adequate type of sensor element is one of the major points of this research work. The FBG sensor is also influenced by temperature and strain parameters. The implementation of an appropriate signal processing technique to nullify the effect of strain and temperature on the vibration sensor signal and the calibration of the sensor element is also a challenging task, as these devices respond to both strain and temperature. There are several signal processing techniques proposed by many researchers to extract relevant information signals from a noisy one. The performance of these signal processing methods and a comparative analysis of these methodologies need to be evaluated. A comprehensive analysis of these signal-processing methods has not yet been reported in any article. The application of the Internet of Things (IoT) and the use of a cloud computing environment to perform data storage, backups, testing and development, big data analytics, and disaster recovery mechanisms have not been reported. Further, a robust architecture of such internet-enabled measurement and analysis schemes to remotely visualize real-time machine conditions must be formulated. Further, there is a need for a Decision Support System (DSS) mechanism for generating suitable alerts, notifications, and suggestions during the running of the machine under predictive monitoring. There are limited research outcomes reported to date on such DSS mechanisms in predictive maintenance-based research.

9.4   Emerging Research Directions

To simulate, develop, and test an appropriate sensing device suitable for vibration monitoring of a machine and allow the fabrication of a passive sensor embedded with suitable packaging material, the device characteristics need to be studied using the Finite Element Analysis (FEA) tool.

Appropriate mechanism for the installation of an FBG sensor for the measurement of machine vibration and the development of algorithms for nullifying the effect of temperature and strain on the vibration signature. Application of various signal processing, classification, and feature extraction techniques for the estimation of machine-related issues from the processed signals needs to be simulated, developed, and evaluated for the better performance of the sensing device. The use of a learning-based fuzzy logic classification approach must apply for classifying the rotating machinery vibrations with admissible performance. To design a model for identifying faults from the FBG sensor data and then perform predictive maintenance on that machine. To formulate the architecture of a Decision Support System (DSS) model for the generation of adequate alerts, notifications, and suggestions during the running of the machine under predictive monitoring and formulate a complete IoT-based distributed machine monitoring scheme using the proposed DSS model and FBG sensors.

9.5   The Broad Concept of FBG Sensor Applications in Industry 4.0

A broad picture of the predictive maintenance techniques using FBG sensors in the Industry 4.0 scenario is presented in Figure 9.8, as shown below.

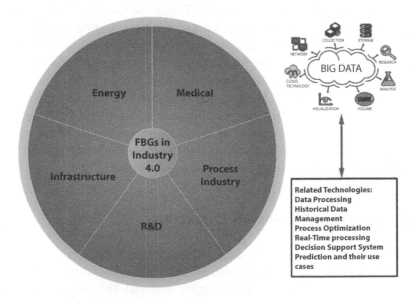

Figure 9.8 A broad understanding of FBG sensing in Industry 4.0.

Industry 4.0-based applications require the use of big data and related technologies where data handling is the primary concern. The real-time data from the sensor needs to be processed so that further actions can be initiated. The FBGs are suitable for various industrial and scientific applications such as energy, medical, infrastructure, process industries, R&D, etc. In every case of application, the use of data-related technologies is the highest priority. Some of the data-related technologies are data processing, historical data management, process optimization, real-time processing, decision support systems (DSSs), predictive models, etc.

9.6   Conclusion

The application of FBG sensing technology is widely accepted in many industrial applications. The Industry 4.0 implementation needs a very high-precision and high-speed sensing approach where the devices/systems are mostly based on optical fibers. Various critical use cases exist in which conventional sensors cannot be installed. Therefore, various cutting-edge industrial applications are thoroughly discussed to address the use of high-precision and high-speed sensing approaches in a real Industry 4.0 scenario. Similarly, the applications of FBGs in magnetic fields and current sensing have been discussed in detail. The concepts of magnetostrictive, magneto-optical (MO), magnetic fluid (MF), magnetically sensitive materials, and optical fiber current sensors are discussed thoroughly in this chapter. These sensing methodologies are critical where the assembly of sensor parts and integration of FBGs into the sensing region are much more difficult tasks to perform. Furthermore, some of the most important aspects of industrial monitoring are discussed as research gaps, where plenty of research scope is present. Finally, a broad understanding of FBGs in the Industry 4.0 scenario is presented in this chapter.

References

1. Fitch, E.C., *Proactive maintenance for mechanical systems*, Elsevier Science Ltd, Elsevier, 1992.
2. Wang, H., Ye, X., Yin, M., Study on predictive maintenance strategy. *Int. J. U- e-Service, Sci. Technol.*, 9, 4, 295–300, 2016. https://doi.org/10.14257/ijunesst.2016.9.4.29.
3. Gültekin, Ö.,Cinar, E., Özkan, K., Yazıcı, A., Real-time fault detection and condition monitoring for industrial autonomous transfer vehicles utilizing

edge artificial intelligence. *Sensors,* 22, 3208, 2022. https://doi.org/10.3390/s22093208

4. Altuntas, S., II, Dereli, T., Kusiak, A., Assessment of corporate innovation capability with a data-mining approach: Industrial case studies. *Comput. Ind. Eng.,* 102, 58–68, 2016.

5. Nandi, S., Toliyat, H.A., Li, X., Condition monitoring and fault diagnosis of electrical motors - A review. *IEEE Trans. Energy Convers.,* 20, 4, 719–729, 2005. https://doi.org/10.1109/TEC.2005.847955.

6. Gebraeel, N., Lawley, M., Liu, R., Parmeshwaran, V., Residual life predictions from vibration-based degradation signals: A neural network approach. *IEEE Trans. Ind. Electron.,* 51, 3, 694–700, 2004. https://doi.org/10.1109/TIE.2004.824875.

7. Harris, T.A., *Rolling bearing analysis,* Second Edition, p. 1086, CRC Press, 1984.

8. Chiter, A., Zegadi, R., Bekka, R.E., Felkaoui, A., A new method for automatic defects detection and diagnosis in rolling element bearings using Wald test. *J. Theor. Appl. Mechanics,* 56, 1, 123, 2018.

9. Khuntia, S.R., Rueda, J.L., M., A.M.M., Smart asset management for electric utilities: Big data and future. *Lect. Notes Mech. Eng.,* 311–322, 2019. https://doi.org/10.1007/978-3-319-95711-1_3.

10. Zhou, H., The internet of things in the cloud: A middleware perspective, in: *The Internet of Things in the Cloud: A Middleware Perspective,* 2012, https://doi.org/10.1201/b13090.

11. Girdhar, P., Scheffer, C., Mulrow, C.D., Williams, J.W., Gerety, M.B., Ramirez, G., Kerber, C., Predictive maintenance techniques: Part 1 predictive maintenance basics, in: *Practical machinery vibration analysis and predictive maintenance,* pp. 1–10, 2004, https://doi.org/10.1016/ B978-075066275-8/50001-1.

12. Chu, Y.C., Pham, T.N., Hsu, F.R., Tuw, M.J., Tan, C.W., Chay, M.C., Tsai, M.F., An effective method for monitoring the vibration data of bearings to diagnose and minimize defects. *MATEC Web of Conferences,* vol. *189,* pp. 10–15, 2018, https://doi. org/10.1051/matecconf/201818903019.

13. Konar, P. and Chattopadhyay, P., Bearing fault detection of induction motor using wavelet and Support Vector Machines (SVMs). *Appl. Soft Computing J.,* 11, 6, 4203–4211, 2011, https://doi.org/10.1016/j. asoc.2011.03.014.

14. Widodo, A. and Yang, B.S., Support vector machine in machine condition monitoring and fault diagnosis. *Mechanical Syst. Signal Process.,* 21, 6, 2560–2574, 2007. https://doi.org/10.1016/j.ymssp.2006.12.007.

15. Yadav, O.P., Joshi, D., Pahuja, G.L., Support vector machine-based bearing fault detection of induction motor. *Indian J. Advanced Electron. Eng.,* 1, 1, 34–39, 2013.

16. Moosavian, A., Ahmadi, H., Tabatabaeefar, A., Khazaee, M., Comparison of two classifiers; K-nearest neighbor and artificial neural network, for fault diagnosis on a main engine journal-bearing. *Shock Vib.,* 20, 2, 263–272, 2013, https://doi.org/10.3233/SAV-2012-00742.

17. Ruiz-Gonzalez, R., Gomez-Gil, J., Gomez-Gil, F.J., Martínez-Martínez, V., An SVM-Based classifier for estimating the state of various rotating components in Agro-Industrial machinery with a vibration signal acquired from a single point on the machine chassis. *Sensors*, *14*, 11, 20713–20735, 2014, https://doi.org/ 10.3390/s141120713.

18. Sun, C., Zhang, Z., He, Z., Research on bearing life prediction based on support vector machine and its application. *J. Physics: Conf. Ser.*, *305*, 1, 1–9, 2011, https://doi.org/10.1088/1742-6596/305/1/012028.

19. Ulasyar, A. and Lazoglu, I., Design and analysis of a new magneto rheological damper forwashing machine. *J. Mech. Sci. Technol.*, 32, 4, 1549–1561, 2018.

20. Attia, E.M., Elsodany, N.M., El-Gamal, H.A., Elgohary, M.A., Theoretical and experimentalstudy of magneto-rheological fluid disc brake. *Alexandria Eng. J.*, 56, 2, 189–200, 2017.

21. Andrade, R.M., Filho, A.B., Vimieiro, C.B.S., Pinotti, M., Optimal design and torquecontrol of an active magnetorheological prosthetic knee. *Smart Mater. Struct.*, 27, 10, 105031, 2018.

22. Kaluvan, S., Thirumavalavan, V., Kim, S., Choi, S.B., A novel magnetorheologicalactuator for micro-motion control: Identification of actuating characteristics. *SmartMater. Struct.*, 24, 10, 1–8, 2015.

23. Went, J.J., Linear magnetostriction of homogeneous nickel alloys. *Phy*, 17, 2, 98–116, 1951.

24. Clark, A.E. and Wun-Fogle, M., Modern magneto-strictive materials - Classical and non-classical alloys. *Smart Structures Mater. 2002: Active Materials: Behav. Mechanics*, 4699, 421–436, 2002.

25. Li, J., Dai, J.W., Pan, Y.B., Research progress on magneto-optical transparent ceramics. *J. Inorganic Mater.*, 33, 1, 1–8, 2018.

26. Aldbea, F.W., Ibrahim, N.B., Yahya, M., Effect of adding aluminum ion on the structural, optical, electrical and magnetic properties of terbium doped yttrium iron garnet nanoparticles films prepared by sol-gel method. *Appl. Surface Sci.*, 321, 150–157, 2014.

27. Miao, Y.P. and Yao, J.Q., Temperature sensitivity of microstructured optical fiber filled with ferrofluid. *AcPSn*, 62, 4, 044223, 2013.

28. Zhao, Y., Lv, R.Q., Wang, D., Wang, Q., Fiber optic fabry-perot magnetic field sensor with temperature compensation using a fiber Bragg grating. *IEEE Trans. Instrum. Measur.*, 63, 9, 2210–2214, 2014.

29. Chen, B., Fan, Y.G., Zhou, S.P., Study on Preparation of Oil-Based Fe3O4 Nano Magnetic Fluid. *Trans. Tech Publ.*, 148, 808–811, 2011.

30. Zheng, H., Shao, H.-P., Lin, T., Zhao, Z.-F., Guo, Z.-M., Preparation and characterization of silicone-oil-based γ-Fe 2 O 3 magnetic fluid. *Rare Met.*, 37, 9, 803–807, 2018.

31. Huang, W., Wu, J.M., Guo, W., Li, R., Cui, L.Y., Study on the magnetic stability of iron-nitride magnetic fluid. *J. Alloys Comp.*, 443, 1–2, 195–198, 2007.

32. Mora, J., Diez, A., Cruz, J.L., Andres, M.V., A magneto-strictive sensor inter-rogated by fiber gratings for DC-current and temperature discrimination. *IPTL*, 12, 12, 1680–1682, 2000.
33. Satpathi, D., Moore, J.A., Ennis, M.G., Design of a terfenol-D based fiber-op-tic current transducer. *IEEE Sens. J.*, 5, 5, 1057–1065, 2005.
34. Han, J.H., Hu, H.F., Wang, H., Zhang, B.W., Song, X.W., Ding, Z.Y., Zhang, X.Z., Liu, T.G., Temperature-compensated magneto-strictive current sensor based on the configuration of dual fiber Bragg gratings. *JLwT*, 35, 22, 4910–4915, 2017.
35. Dante, A., Lopez, J.D., Carvalho, C.C., Allil, R.C.D.B., Werneck, M.M., A compact FBG-based magneto-strictive optical current sensor with reduced mass of terfenol- D. *IPTL*, 31, 17, 1461–1464, 2019.
36. Zhao, H., Sun, F.F., Yang, Y.Q., Cao, G.Y., Sun, K., A novel temperature-com-pensated method for FBG-GMM current sensor. *OptCo*, 308, 64–69, 2013.
37. Rogers, A.J., Optical technique for measurement of current at high voltage. *Proc. Inst. Elect. Eng.*, 120, 2, 261–267, 1973.
38. Shao, J., Liu, W., Liu, C.Q., Xu, D., Ieee, A., Passive Optical Fiber Current Sensor Based on YIG, 2008.
39. Zubia Zaballa, J.A., Casado, L., Aldabaldetreku Etxeberria, G., Montero, A., Zubia, E., DuranaApaolaza, G., Design and development of a low-cost opti-cal current sensor. *Sensors*, 13, 10, 13584–13595, 2013.
40. Wang, Q., Liu, X., Xia, J., Zhao, Y., A novel long-tail fiber current sensor based on fiber loop ring-down spectroscopy and fabry-perot cavity filled with magnetic fluid. *IEEE Trans. Instrum. Meas.*, 64, 7, 2005–2011, 2015.
41. Yariv, A. and Winsor, H.V., Proposal for detection of magnetic fields through magneto-strictive perturbation of optical fibers. *Optics Lett.*, 5, 3, 87, 1980.
42. Dandridge, A., Tveten, A.B., Sigel, G.H., West, E.J., Giallorenzi, T.G., Optical fiber magnetic field sensors. *Electron. Lett.*, 16, 11, 408–409, 1980.
43. Picon, L.L., Bright, V.M., Kolesar, E.S., Detecting low-intensity magnetic-fields with a magneto-strictive fiber optic sensor. *Proceedings of the IEEE 1994 National Aerospace and Electronics Conference, Naecon*, vol. 1, IEEE, pp. 1034–1039, 1994.
44. Yi, B., Chu, B.C.B., Chiang, K.S., Temperature compensation for a fiber-Bragg- grating-based magneto-strictive sensor. *MiOTL*, 36, 3, 211–213, 2003.
45. Wang, W.C., Hua, W.S., Lin, W.H., Wu, W.J., Development of a polymeric magneto-strictive fiber-optic sensor system. *Health Monitoring Struct. Biol. Syst.*, 635, 579–587, 2008.
46. Nguyen, T.T., Bouillault, F., Daniel, L., Mininger, X., Finite element modeling of magnetic field sensors based on nonlinear magnetoelectric effect. *J. Appl. Phys.*, 109, 8, 084904, 2011.
47. Liu, H., Or, S.W., Tam, H.Y., Magneto-strictive composite–fiber Bragg grat-ing (MC–FBG) magnetic field sensor. *Sens. Actuat. A Phys.*, 173, 1, 122–126, 2012.

48. Alisafaee, H. and Ghanaatshoar, M., Optimization of all-garnet magne-to-optical magnetic field sensors with genetic algorithm. *Appl. Optics*, 51, 21, 5144–5148, 2012.

49. Shao, Z.H., Qiao, X.G., Rong, Q.Z., Sun, A., Fiber-optic magnetic field sensor using a phase-shifted fiber Bragg grating assisted by a TbDyFe bar. *Sens. Actuat. A Phys.*, 261, 49–55, 2017.

50. Zhou, X., Li, X., Li, S., An, G.-W., Cheng, T., Magnetic field sensing based on SPR optical fiber sensor interacting with magnetic fluid. *IEEE Trans. Instrum. Meas.*, 68, 1, 234–239, 2018.

51. Wei, F., Liu, D., Mallik, A.K., Farrel, G., Wu, Q., Peng, G.D., Semenova, Y., Magnetic field sensor based on a tri-microfiber coupler ring in magnetic fluid and a fiber Bragg grating. *Sensors (Basel)*, 19, 23, 5100, 2019.

52. Jiang, J., Wu, Z., Sheng, J., Zhang, J., Song, M., Ryu, K., Li, Z., Hong, Z., Jin, Z., A new approach to measure magnetic field of high-temperature supercon-ducting coil based on magneto-optical faraday effect. *ITAS*, 31, 1, 1–5, 2020.

53. Zhao, Y., Wang, X.-X., Lv, R.-Q., Li, G.-L., Zheng, H.-K., Zhou, Y.-F., Highly sensitive reflective Fabry-Perot magnetic field sensor using magnetic fluid based on Vernier effect. *IEEE Trans. Instrumen. Meas.*, 70, 1–8, 2020.

54. Wang, J., Pei, L., Wang, J., Ruan, Z., Zheng, J., Li, J., Ning, T., Magnetic field and temperature dual-parameter sensor based on magnetic fluid materials filled photonic crystal fiber. *Opt. Express*, 28, 2, 1456–1471, 2020.

55. Zhu, L., Zhao, N., Lin, Q., Zhao, L., Jiang, Z., Optical fiber SPR magnetic field sensor based on photonic crystal fiber with the magnetic fluid as cladding. *Meas. Sci. Technol.*, 32, 7, 075106, 2021.

56. Liu, C., Shen, T., Wu, H.-B., Feng, Y., Chen, J.-J., Applications of magne-to-strictive, magneto-optical, magnetic fluid materials in optical fiber cur-rent sensors and optical fiber magnetic field sensors. *Opt. Fiber Technol.*, 65, 1–19, 2021.

57. Leal-Junior, A.G., Campos, V., Díaz, C., Andrade, R.M., Frizera, A., Marques, C., A machine learning approach for simultaneous measurement of mag-netic field position and intensity with fiber Bragg grating and magnetorheo-logical fluid. *Opt. Fiber Technol.*, 56, 1–7, 2020.

58. Cakir, M., Guven, M.A., Mistikoglu, S., The experimental application of pop-ular machine learning algorithms on predictive maintenance and the design of IIoT based condition monitoring system. *Comput. Ind. Eng.*, 151, 1–14, 2021.

10

Fog Computing-Enabled Cancer Cell Detection System Using Convolution Neural Network in Internet of Medical Things

Soumen Santra[1]*, Dipankar Majumdar[2] and Surajit Mandal[3]

[1]Department of MCA, Techno International New Town, Kolkata, West Bengal, India
[2]Department of CSE, RCC Institute of Information Technology, Kolkata, West Bengal, India
[3]Department of ECE, B.P. Poddar Institute of Management and Technology, Kolkata, West Bengal, India

Abstract

Computer-enabled smart home management systems are very flexible in nature and easy to use as hand-held devices. This type of feature selection device is currently used in health management systems. The health management system is a service or HaaS that provides all kinds of facilities to the patient by which they can understand the status of the disease, just like medical practitioners. Convolutional neural networks (CNNs) are a special subset of deep learning (DL), which is used to fetch hidden features through multiple hidden layers from images and produce optimum output. Because cancerous images contain huge amounts of information, these large-scale datasets require high computational power to process properly and provide proper output within a short span of time. The CNN model is implemented in Google Collaboratory (Colab) where we import a large-scale dataset through a customized model. This model contains a CNN layer, average pool layer, and MaxPool layer through which we pass the image dataset. The Deep CNN (DCNN) fetches mostly hidden features that are omitted by the normal machine learning (ML) model. Using this model, we obtain the proper classification of cells, whether carcinoma or not, and the status of the propagation rate

*Corresponding author: soumen70@gmail.com

Chandan Banerjee, Anupam Ghosh, Rajdeep Chakraborty and Ahmed A. Elngar (eds.) Fog Computing for Intelligent Cloud IoT Systems, (229–244) © 2024 Scrivener Publishing LLC

by which the malignancy percentage is evaluated. If the proper malignancy percentage is evaluated at a proper time, it will be helpful for medical practitioners to process it properly. Using fog computing, the model works very close to the cluster range of data rather than edge devices, which will result in network tolerance in edge computing. The fog metaphor works closer to a datacenter. The high propagation rate of this disease in terms of the exponential equation can be easily calculated using fog-computing methodologies. Here, the model works as a smart health management tool that works between the patient and doctor and reduces the communication gap between them for better monitoring and understanding of the disease status, which helps them to properly treat and save life more accurately.

Keywords: Computer vison, deep neural network, medical imaging, edge computation, Internet of Medical Things (IoMT)

10.1   Introduction

Real-world examples where fog computing is used are in IoT devices, sensors, cameras (IIoT—Industrial Internet of Things), etc. It provides online computing activities, which makes high-computing tasks easier. With this development of applications and technology, most companies are becoming interested in processing and computing power. Due to the risk analysis of data and the many connected devices, cloud computing is obsolete. Devices are incurring unavoidable costs to sustain in the market due to the increasing complexity of software. Edge computing divides the computing load among the servers and the device. This facility helps the cloud provide its services to more users, and the device never needs to require changes to its detailed design. A lot of real-time applications now call for a lot of processing power. The objective of this paper is to create a workable and practical real-time picture classification system. This paper investigated three setups, including the cloud concept, image processing methods, and the fundamentals of deep neural networks. Our studies' findings demonstrate that the technological market, whose size and complexity are expanding exponentially, cannot be satisfied by cloud computing and edge computing alone. Instead of concentrating on a single model, the same results are encouraging when looking for the best configurations for systems in terms of a mix of end device power consumption, application runtime, and server latency. Overall, it is preferable to take each computer architecture's advantages and disadvantages into account.

The Internet of Things (IoT) is a network of disparate gadgets connected to the internet through wi-fi access points and Bluetooth technology. It provides a variety of online services that are now in use due to the volume of users. The idea was to make it possible for any user to access their records properly from any location with an internet connection. The resulting shift in data storage gave rise to options like Dropbox and Google Drive. Every individual who has a smart device (such as a phone, laptop, etc.) gets online storage space from their suppliers. IOT is a group of interconnected devices that connect to the Internet using wi-fi technologies like Bluetooth and wi-fi. The idea was to leverage this IoT application to let any user subscribe to any records anywhere. With the use of online storage, this storage technology gives clients the ability to save, retrieve, or back up their information. With the usage of cluster applications, community technologies, distributed file systems, and several additional online resources, it is advantageous. When combined with IoT, cloud computing will develop into a cutting-edge tool for devices that rely on online servers for data storage.

A server that can only fully manage a small number of devices cannot be scaled up. As a result, when scaling up a cloud-based structure, its workability will always be limited; its functionality defines the volume of clients a company can manage. Managing the data traffic internal to a server will emerge as more tedious if the community funnels all the resources into one centralized unit.

The massive amounts of data generated by IoT are growing exponentially as a result of its constant operational states. These Internet of Things devices are creating an information deluge that interferes with the cloud's ability to predictably handle predictable data processing and analytics. These disruptions are dealt with by the fog computing structure, which is based on the deployment of micro clouds (fog nodes) at the immediate edge of data sources [1].

Massive IoT data analytics utilizing a fog computing architecture are still in their infancy and require in-depth research to deliver better knowledge and help make wiser judgments. In the context of extensive IoT data analytics, this survey provides an overview of the opportunities and issues associated with fog networking. It also emphasizes how the underlying characteristics of various proposed research efforts make fog computing a suitable platform for new IoT services, goods, and applications [3, 4].

According to the perspective of the computing architect, fog computing is the best structure. It is also connected to several nodes that receive data in real-time. Additionally, the live data computation technique is run and handled in multiple seconds. The nodes send an overall summary of the cloud structure on a regular basis. Most businesses and organizations find IoT security challenging, and some devices with limited resources also restrict security measures [4–6]. As a result, the primary purpose of fog computing is to serve as a middleman to update the software within security credential formations to alleviate the issues associated with data privacy.

Emerging ideas in fog computing are now receiving greater consideration and interest from both industry and academia. Fog computing enables the extension of cloud computing components, such as storage, networking, and compute, onto the edge of networks, reducing the pressure on cloud data centers and lowering the latency of delivering services to users. These fog systems can be installed on many different types of hardware and analyze huge amounts of data locally. Fog is a suitable fit for time- and place-based applications, such as those found in Internet of Things (IoT) devices that can process a lot of data [1].

The centralized cloud computing (CC) paradigm was proposed as the core idea for creating massive data center architectures in response to the growing demand for centralized computing services. Even if CC was successfully migrated to the IoT, the cloud server itself continued to use a lot of CPU resources [7]. All data that generates files of a specific type and is stored in video files, log files, or other places was used in the cloud.

10.2   Fog Computing: Approach of IoMT

The amount of data being processed was so large that it could only be done on an extremely high-performance computer cluster. Today, most large-scale fog computations are conducted using cloud computing—an approach where an individual or group rents computer resources from a service provider. Cloud computing allows users to take advantage of the collective power of many computers without having to manage or own those resources themselves [3]. In practice, this results in increased efficiency and optimal resource use by allowing more scalability than centralized cloud computing would allow. Fog computing is a way to process large amounts of data in the form of distributed computing, which can run on multiple computers at once rather than just one. Fog computing allows for the processing of images, videos, and other large files to take place on remote servers. This is done using cloud computing technology, which allows multiple computers to communicate with each other over the internet. The result is faster processing times for large amounts of data. Fog computing overcomes any barrier between the cloud and end gadgets (e.g., IoT hubs) by empowering computing, capacity, organizing, and information for the executives on network hubs inside the nearby area of IoT gadgets [4]. Significantly, calculation, capacity, organizing, decision-making, and information on the board happen in the cloud, yet likewise happen along the IoT-to-cloud way as information crosses to the cloud (ideally near the IoT gadgets). For example, packing the GPS information can occur at the edge before transmission to the cloud in Intelligent Transportation Systems (ITS). Fog computing is characterized by the Open Fog Consortium as "a flat-framework level engineering that appropriates computing, capacity, control, and organizing capabilities nearer to the clients along a cloud-to-thing continuum." The "flat" stage in fog computing permits computing capabilities to be conveyed between various stages, furthermore, enterprises, while an upward stage advances siloed applications. An upward stage might be a serious area of strength for an offer for a single sort of use (storehouse); however, it does not represent stage-to-stage collaboration in other in an upward-centered stage. In addition to working with even engineering, fog computing provides an adaptable stage to meet the information-driven necessities of administrators and clients. Fog computing is planned to an area of strength for the Internet of Things. More often, due to the complexity of the fog computing process, professionals do not understand the storing and analyzing procedures of any data structure. In the total fog infrastructure, there are many sophisticated fog nodes, which create complications within the large imagery structure of any data processor [5].

Edge or fog computing can be used to offload computations and storage from IoT devices as an alternative to cloud computing. The main difference between fog computing and cloud computing is that fog computing employs a local component or a side device, whereas cloud computing uses a server. It is an IoT network-unconnected end-user device. Files, alternative methods, and other data are no longer fully available. In fog computing, decisions are made and calculations are completed by the end-user device. The administrative workload is distributed towards its edges using component computing.

It is feasible to offload computations from the IoT community by using cloudlets. A tiny piece of hardware known as a cloudlet stands between the server and the information source. In the context of computers, the cloud efficiently performs the responsibilities of processing, storing, caching, and load balancing the data transferred to and received from it [7].

The calculation can be disseminated to the edges in this intermediate statistics processing area. An illustration of an Internet of Things civilization with various outstanding qualities is shown in Figures 10.1 and 10.2 where Figure 10.1 has explained the basic model and Figure 10.2 has explained the featured model [1–6]. This computing diagram emphasizes the benefits and advancements of the present cloud computing architecture.

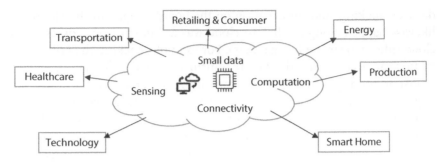

Figure 10.1 Fog computing block diagram.

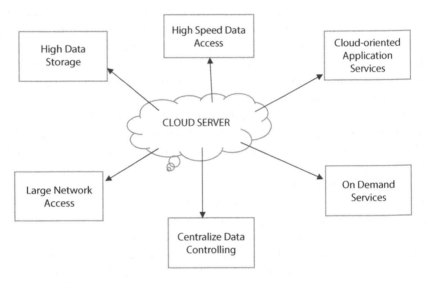

Figure 10.2 Wings of fog computation application.

Fog computing [7] typically involves extending cloud computing in a non-trivial way from the core network to the sting network, where the application, storage, compute, and data are distributed between the source and the cloud. Application servers, edge routers, and portable end devices like smartwatches and sensors act as the points closest to the user in the crucial world. Fog nodes are autonomous machines that eat the information generated [1]. Fog nodes, [8] fog servers, and fog gateways are the three different types of fog nodes. Fog gateways act as a data conduit between the various fog devices and servers, whereas fog servers calculate the information, and fog devices are essentially connected to them [2]. Fog computing is frequently used to regulate the level of privacy. Instead of transferring sensitive data to a centralized cloud infrastructure, it is analyzed locally. It might be used to monitor and manage the specific device. Depending on the resources, the bandwidth needed to send the information may be very expensive. They may be handled at the nearby data source, which would be much closer to the user. Customers will use fog computing if they need to modify the machine so that it operates according to their needs. The network requires additional maintenance because controllers and storage are dispersed across several locations [2, 3]. One of the computation-heavy functions stated earlier was classification. Image classification is a type of large-scale classification that can be used in cities as a smart city application.

However, medical image categorization was previously selected because it is a more distinctive subset. In this approach, a medical image (such as a CT or PET CT scan) is normalized inside each individual area using a vast array of quiet devices. The accumulated sound is then categorized into distinct patterns and occurrences in each region of interest (ROI). Every computer would need to utilize more resources if it were required to continuously calculate image data, which would shorten the lifespan of the system. Additionally, better approaches recommend a longer software runtime, which should lead to unreasonable wait times for the data to reach the server. Because there is no longer a real-time depiction of the big picture inside the area that the device is classifying, this wait period should reduce the integrity of the incoming facts. Additionally, if most of the processing occurs in the cloud, the server should become overloaded and unresponsive to the load of data processing.

10.3   Relationship Between IoMT and Deep Neural Network

We define our category of distributed, large-scale fog applications as such. This is due to the fact that it is busy when you take into account the dynamic nature of edge devices (like mobile phones and smart automobiles) and how many of them there are (like thousands), all of which are dispersed over a sizable physical region. These characteristics provide our class of fog applications with a very strong link to the actual physical setting of the computing infrastructure. Our fog apps are so firmly connected to the device on which they are placed, in contrast to standard distributed applications that run in the cloud with no understanding of the underlying infrastructure. Figure 10.1 depicts how our class of applications are positioned in relation to three characteristics: the size of system deployment, the degree of connection with the physical setting, and the system's dynamic nature [1–4].

The breadth of system deployment may include everything from smart homes to smart industries, offices, and cities. We contend that each deployment size has a distinct issue and, as a result, a unique solution. Device naming and identification, for instance, could be an intriguing issue in a limited environment such as a smart home. This issue is becoming less significant with respect to the wider implementation of smart cities.

Fog computing is a new paradigm that combines traditional client-server computing with the clouds. This enables a large amount of CPU power and storage to be used efficiently across many client devices rather than being located on a single server or computer. This can be used for image recognition tasks where this scale is required, or to increase the speed at which images can be analyzed by decreasing the processing time. Fog computing allows large-scale image processing and analysis tasks to be executed on demand when computers are not otherwise being used. If a computer is idle and has adequate computing power (e.g., in the cloud), it can be directed to perform tasks that would otherwise require additional resources, such as heavy computations for AI training or deep learning [9–14].

10.4   Fog Computing Enabled CNN for Medical Imaging

A widely utilized computational device that has the capacity to perform practical categorization where functions are called artificial neural locals. It is a natural neuronal conduct that computerized algorithms have placed and used. Neural networks come in a wide variety of amazing forms, especially when considered in the context of their purported learning to be aware flow. Each neighbor creates a shared computer that chooses an output based entirely on the input it is supplied with. Enter layers, output layers, and hidden layers are the three types of layers that can make up a neural community. Over a huge geographical area, the function of fog computing is to generate a total process with low latency and location awareness [1]. Additionally, the characteristics that fog computing mostly carries forward during the data processing procedures support mobility without compromising any widespread nodes. It mainly tried to support mobility for delivering the data in different places. Moreover, at the edge of the network system, the location or position of the delivered date is calculated through the fog computing procedure. Fog computers are predominantly accessible via wireless devices and have a strong presence in real-time and streaming applications. It can be mentioned that heterogeneity is the main objective that can differentiate the characteristics of fog computing from the cloud computing structure. Information processing is easily converted from the local level to the global aspect through distributed, decentralized infrastructure. Fog computing is an effective intermediary between a remote server and computing hardware [2–5]. Fog computing is a large imager and an embedded application format on a production line, and in this aspect, an edge server is connected to a temperature sensor that further measures the total temperature every single second.

All the doable items, or parameter values, are first found in the entry layer. Neural networks base their decisions on these values. The output layer then contains every possible outcome that the mannequin may provide based on the potential inputs. Machine learning (ML) has a branch known as neural networks, where the model consists of three layers: input, hidden, and output. The hidden layers receive input parameters with weighted input from the input layers. The number of middle-level or hidden layers is not determined. In a neural network, as per the McCulloch–Pitts model, the summative input parameters are passed to the computation unit and processed based on threshold values. There is a biased function that is working to generate perception-based output. When the input layers accept image parameters, it is relevant to convolutional neural networks (CNNs). A medical image contains a variety of features in terms of pixels. These pixels contain both general features and special features. These special features are visible or invisible in nature. The invisible features are known as hidden ones, which play significant role in understanding the nature of the image. The medical image is big in terms of volume, variety in terms of features, and rapidly growing content. The image segregates into several small image sets and passing them as input parameters [7–10]. Each image set's region of interest (ROI) is taken into consideration when choosing which features to include in the input layers. Perceptron's feed forward, radial basis networks, deep feed forward, recurrent neural networks, long or short-term memories, gated recurrent, auto encoder, variational auto encoder, denoising auto encoder, sparse auto encoder, competitive, Jordan, etc. are some examples of different types of neural network models based on their architecture. The output layer generates output, which is again treated as input and computed in another hidden layer to produce new and better output [12–15].

10.5   Algorithm Approach of Proposed Model

Here, as per above the Figure 10.2, the cloud server is segregated into small fog metaphors. The target image is computing in cloud architecture, but it

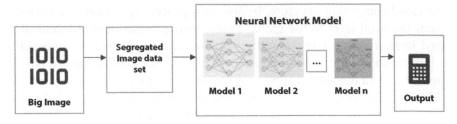

Figure 10.3 CNN-based fog computation model.

is accessed through edge devices. Figure 10.3 shows the basic model of neural network based on our approach. There are several activities of fog metaphor, such as:

10.6   Parallel programming of devices.
10.7   Data sensing of presence of devices.
10.8   Find location of devices and indicating the presence of it.
10.9   Distribute the load of computation of devices.
10.10   Large scale IoT application support to Device.
10.11   Real-time data gathering from a device.

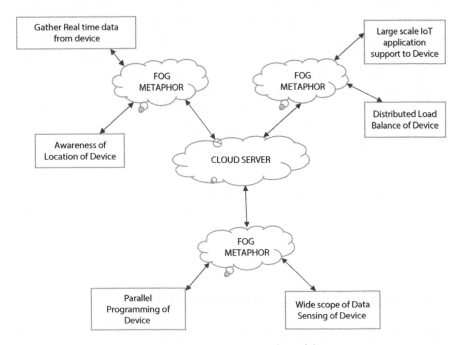

Figure 10.4 Deep learning based algorithmic approach model.

The target image is stored as a small segment in the fog metaphor and then computed through the neural network model [16, 17]. Here, we apply the deep Gaussian mixture model (DGMM) through the whole image set and collect their corresponding output. DGMM is a special Gaussian mixture model based on a neural network. Figure 10.4 have shown deep learning based model where the algorithm is stated below. All sample metaphors pass through the Gaussian distribution model and apply neural network essence to the image sets. Here the algorithmic approach is discussed below:

Step 1. Import NumPy

Step 2: Import cv2

Step 3: Import Gaussian Mixture from sklearn mixture.

Step 4: Read image using CV.

Step 5: Normalize the image using reshape function and store into another image.

Step 6: Fit into Deep Gaussian mixture model (DGMM).

Step 7: Apply predict function of DGMM model.

Step 8: Labels the output using np into unsigned integer form (8 bit)

Step 9: Using shape function store the image into matrix form.

Step 10: Store the matrix form of image into result image.

Step 11: Apply the threshold strategy upon the image:

```
for i in range(row):

    for j in range(column):
        if result [i, j] == 0:result
        [i, j] = 0

    elif result [i, j] == 1:
        result [i, j] = 85

    elif result [i, j] == 2:
        result [i, j] = 170

    elif result [i, j] == 3:
        result [i, j] = 255
```

Step 12: Display the result image.

As per the algorithm the target image is computed in a settings of MATLAB software. the target image brain3.png is used and the result image is shown in Section 10.6.

10.6   Result and Analysis

The whole image, brain3.png, is segregated into small portions. Each segregated image is sent to the Gaussian distribution model. A neural network approach is applied to each image set and converted into a binary version. There is a threshold applied through this model to all the image sets. Therefore, all the result image sets are merged and produce the actual target output. The target output is located in a portion that is indicated as a gray zone. This gray zone is indicated as a cancerous zone. This kind of large image computation is taken care of by the cloud platform, but it is also seen on edge device like mobile.

The DGMM is a form of neural network model that works on images. The convolutional neural network (CNN) or deep convolutional neural network (DCNN) is the basic platform of DGMM. The gray zone is all indicated as carcinoma, except where it is indicated as metastasis. Because metastases are a propagated form of cancer, Figure 10.5 has shown all gray zones throughout the target image. Here, the novelty of the study is to

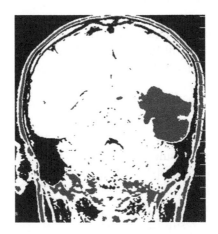

Figure 10.5 Result image of DGMM computation model.

reduce the computation time over the cloud platform, indicating all very small portions that are affected by metastasis.

10.7   Conclusion

The main difference is that while fog computing uses a local component or a small device, cloud computing uses a server. Cloud computing offloads data management to the server, whereas component computing spreads the administrative load closer to its edges. A cloudlet is a tiny computing unit placed between a server and an archive storage. This middle-ground data processing location enables the distribution and offloading of computations to the edges. New developments in fog computing are attracting increasing attention from both businesses and academia. A fog is a good fit for time- and location-based applications, such as Internet of Things (IoT) gadgets that can process a large amount of data.

References

1. Awad, A.I., Fouda, M.M., Khashaba, M.M., Mohameda, E.R., Hosny, K.M., Utilization of mobile edge computing on the Internet of Medical Things: A survey. *ICT Express*, 9, 3, 473–485, 2023, https://doi.org/10.1016/j.icte.2022.05.006, 2405-9595/c 2022.

2. Elhoseny, M., Bianc, G.-B., Lakshmanaprabud, S.K., Shankar e, K., Singhf, A.K., Wu, W., Effective features to classify ovarian cancer data in internet of medical things. *Comput. Networks*, 159, 147–156, 2019, https://doi.org/10.1016/j.comnet.2019.04.016 1389-1286.

3. Nagendra Singh, S.P., Sasirekha, A.D., Sai Thrinath, B.V., Ramya, D., Thiagarajan, R., IOT enabled hybrid model with learning ability for E-health care systems. *Measurement: Sensors*, 24, 100567, December 2022, https://doi.org/10.1016/j. measen.2022.100567.

4. Kashani, M.H., Madanipour, M., Nikravan, M., Asghari, P., Mahdipour, E., A systematic review of IoT in healthcare: Applications, techniques, and trends. *J. Network Comput. Appl.*, 192, 103164, 2021, https://doi.org/10.1016/j.jnca.2021.103164.

5. Sworna, N.S., Muzahidul Islam, A.K.M., Shatabda, S., Islam, S., Towards development of IoT-ML driven healthcare systems: A survey. *J. Network Comput. Appl.*, 196, 103244, 15 December 2021.

6. Mohapatra, S.K. and Mohanty, M.N., Big data classification with IoT-based application for e-health care. *Cogn. Data Sci. Sustain. Comput.*, 7, 147–172, 2022, https://doi.org/10.1016/B978-0-323-85117-6.00014-5, chapter 7.

7. Kai, K. and Tao, L., Fog computing for vehicular Ad-hoc networks: paradigms, scenarios, and issues. *J. China Universities Posts Telecommunications*, 23, 2, 56–65, 96, 2016.

8. Kashani, M.H., Madanipour, M., Nikravan, M., Asghari, P., Mahdipour, E., A systematic review of IoT in healthcare: Applications, techniques, and trends. *J. Network Comput. Appl.*, 192, 103164–74, 2021.

9. Santra, S., Dey, H., Majumdar, S., A survey with proposed approach on dynamic load balancing: Via VM migration strategy in cloud computing, in: *IEEE Sponsored conference CONFLUENCE 2013*, Amity University, Noida, 27-28, September 2013, pp. 27–29, ISBN: 978-93-83083-30- 5.

10. Santra, S. and Mandal, S., A new approach towards invariant shape descriptor tools for shape classification through morphological analysis of image, in: *2nd International Conference on Computational Advancement in Communication circuit and System (ICCACCS-2018)*, Narula Institute of Technology, Agarpara, Kolkata, India, 23rd November - 24th November 2018, Accepted for publication in Springer Lecture Note entitled "Computational Advancement in Communication Circuits and Systems.

11. Santra, S., Mukherjee, P., Sardar, P., Mandal, S., Deyasi, A., Object detection in clustered scene using point feature matching for non-repeating texture pattern, in: *Conference on Control, Signal Processing and Energy System (CSPES 2018)*, accepted in Lecture Note of Electrical Engineering by Springer, Kolkata, India, 16-18 November 2018.

12. Santra, S., Majumdar, D., Mandal, S., Identification of Shape using Circularity approach for Medical Image Analysis, in: *IEEE AMPHE 2020 (Advances in Medical Physics and Health Engineering 2020*, Springer, LNBE, 2020, https:// link. springer.com/book/10.1007/978-981-33-6915-3.

13. Santra, S., Mandal, S., Das, K., Bhattacharjee, J., Deyasi, A., A comparative study of Z-Transform and Fourier transform applied on medical images for detection of cancer segments. *3rd International Conference on Electronics, Materials Engineering & Nanotechnology*, IEEE Xplore, August 2019, ISBN:978-1-7281-5542-5.

14. Santra, S., Mandal, S., Das, K., Bhattacharjee, J., Roy, A., A modified canny edge detection approach to early detection of cancer cell. *3rd International Conference on Electronics, Materials Engineering & Nanotechnology*, IEEE Xplore, August 2019, ISBN: 978-1-7281-5542- 5.

15. Santra, S. and Mali, K., Pixel variation problem identification in image segmentation for big image data set in cloud platform. *IEEE International Conference on Advances in Computer Applications*, IEEE Xplore, ISBN:978-1-5090-3769-8.

16. Santra, S. and Mali, K., A new approach to survey on load balancing in vm in cloud computing: using CloudSim. *IEEE International Conference on*

Computer, Communication and Control, IEEE Xplore, 2015, doi: 10.1109/IC4.2015.7375671.

17. Santra, S., Dey, H., Majumdar, S., Jha, G.S., New simulation toolkit for comparison of scheduling algorithm on cloud computing, in: *2014 International Conference on Control, Instrumentation, Communication and Computational Technologies (ICCICCT),* vol. 1, pp. 466–469, IEEE at ICCICCT-2014, 2014, 978-1-4799-4190-2/14.

Application of IoT in Smart Farming and Precision Farming: A Review

Suparna Biswas* and Soumik Podder

Faculty of Electronics & Communication Engineering Department, Guru Nanak Institute of Technology, Kolkata, India

Abstract

Agriculture is an important source of living and vital part of the Indian economy. As per survey, nearly 70% Indian people are dependent on agriculture. Agriculture industry has adopted different new technologies to meet the demands of the growing population. New technologies like Internet of Things (IoT) are now widely applied in the agriculture industry to improve the operational efficiency, quality of product and diminish the waste. There are different applications of IOT in agriculture such as smart farming, precision farming, agricultural drones etc.

Smart farming is basically the application of ICT (Information and Communication Technologies) in the field of agriculture. In IoT-based smart farming a system is constructed to monitor the crop field by using different sensors to measure light, temperature, humidity, moisture of soil etc. and to develop automatic irrigation systems. On the other hand, precision farming is another important application of IoT which is related to CropMetrics.

In this paper we have first reviewed the IOT based smart farming system in detail and then in the next section precision farming is reviewed. All the existing techniques are reviewed along with their merits and demerits. At last we have discussed the other scope of research in future to improve the performance of industry of agriculture.

Keywords: Internet of things, smart farming, cropmetrics, smart sensor, operation research, precision farming

Corresponding author: suparna.biswas@gnit.ac.in

Chandan Banerjee, Anupam Ghosh, Rajdeep Chakraborty and Ahmed A. Elngar (eds.) Fog Computing for Intelligent Cloud IoT Systems, (245–278) © 2024 Scrivener Publishing LLC

11.1   Introduction

As the population is increasing year after year, the challenge of production of food is a big matter of concern. So for the fulfilment of increasing demands of food, agriculture is undergoing a fourth revolution by incorporating different technologies like Internet of Things (IoT), robotics, Artificial Intelligence, drones etc. in the traditional farming process [1, 2]. IoT is one of the hot technologies utilized in agriculture, which converts conventional farming practices into a new era of smart farming and precision farming or jointly Farming 4.0 [3–5].

The main objective behind smart farming is to improve the quantity and quality of agriculture products and optimize the labor requirement for the production. It is a new concept of farming which integrates different techniques at different stages of agriculture to solve the problem of food production and the manpower.

Precision agriculture is described as the implementation of modern technologies to administer the agricultural production in order to improve the crop quality and environmental serenity. It is associated with spatial and temporal variability on agricultural production. Precision agriculture is technologically impacted viz. genetic engineering, process automation, information technology, telecommunications, Global Positioning System (GPS), integrated circuit technology, remote sensing, advanced information processing, mobile computing etc. transform conventional agricultural scenario into precision agriculture. This technologically empowered precision agriculture is characterized by low input, high level of efficiency and sustainability [6].

Conventional approaches viz. integrated pest management system that is employed in agriculture is not well standard and the extensive usage of chemical pesticides puts adverse effects on living beings and environment. The ingredients present in the fertilizers such as potassium, nitrogen and phosphorous will not be absorbed by the plants and lost to the environment. This oddness essentially welcomes precision agriculture by which farmers can produce good quality of crops with state of the art production. The step wise conventional farming is depicted in Figure 11.1.

In traditional agriculture there are six grouped variability such as

    i.   Yield variability
    ii.   Field variability
   iii.   Soil variability
   iv.   Crop variability

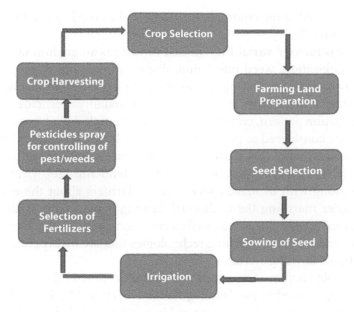

Figure 11.1 Flowchart of conventional farming.

v.   Anomalous factors' variability
vi.   Management variability.

Yield variability is considered as dependent variability and the other variability are considered as independent variability [7].

Yield variability: This is achieved from past and recent yield distributions

Field variability: In the field variability field topography like elevation, slope, aspect, terrace, proximity to field boundary and streams are influential in deciding the crop production.

Soil variability: The presence of different element such as nitrogen, Phosphorous, Potassium, Calcium, Magnesium, Carbon (C), Iron, Manganese, Zinc, and Copper define the soil fertility. The physical properties of soil viz. texture, mechanical strength, density, moisture component, electrical conductivity and the different chemical properties such as pH, salinity etc., soil depth, the water-capturing capacity of soil-plant and hydraulic property are considered as soil variable that can bias the agricultural productivity.

Crop variability: The crop variability factors are categorized as crop density, crop nutrient stress for different element present in soil, crop water requirement, crop height, leaf-area index, biomass, intercepted photo synthetically radiation, chlorophyll content in the crop leaf and the quality of crop grain [7].

Anomalous factors' variability: In case of various anomalous factors like parasite infestation, weed infestation, disease infestation, damage due to wind, hay damage are playing role in controlling the crop production.

Management variability: In management variability, pesticide application, irrigation pattern, crop rotation, fertilizer employment, crop seeding rate etc. are considered as prime factors in deciding crop production.

The motivation of this study is to reshape the traditional agriculture in regards of transparent utilization of farming land and crop yield for the farmers along with to make concern of the farmers about the emerging technologies marrying the traditional farming system. This study might be guidance for the farmers as well as common people to be accustomed with IoT and Machine Learning technologies that are incorporated in the conventional farming system.

The whole chapter is arranged as follows: Section 11.2 described the methodologies used in precision agriculture. Section 11.3 highlighted the contribution of IoT in Agriculture and in Section 11.4, IoT enabled Smart farming methods are summarized. Section 11.5 provides a detail review of various methods of IoT enabled precision farming and Section 11.6 presents the machine learning approaches applied in precision farming. In Section 11.7 we have reported the operational research (OR) based farming techniques. Finally Section 11.8 concludes the chapter and in Section 11.9 we have discussed the future scope of the research.

11.2   Methodologies Used in Precision Agriculture

In this section, we are emphasizing different methodologies frequently employed in precision agriculture. The methodologies are finely linked up with site specific management. Site specific management is important to enhance profitability in crop production, enhancement incrop quality and to protect the nature from pollution. There are two types of methodologies for site specific management and they are grouped as:

A. Map based technique
B. Sensor based technique

In Map based technique Global Positioning System (GPS), remote sensing, and soil sampling are the popular technologies used for precision agriculture. At first an agricultural land is subjected to grid sampling followed by laboratory analysis of soil samples. Finally GPS is employed to control the variable rate applicator [7].

The GPS receiver is employed for locating and navigating agricultural vehicles within a target field. The GPS also determines the geographic coordinate's viz. latitude and longitude and the data is useful to calculate the slope, aspect of the landscape. Here a map is generated and processed along with spatial information.

In the sensor based technique the soil and plant properties are measured using 'on-the-go' fashion based real time sensors to control variable-rate applicator. The sensor based approach has proven itself as inexpensive and rapid measurement of soil variabilities. The 'on-the-go' soil sensors produce the data related to mechanical and physico-chemical properties of soil. These real time sensors are electromagnetic, optical, electrochemical, radiometric, electrical, and pneumatic in principle of operation but the electromagnetic and electrical sensors are extensively used for measurement of soil variability in rapid and inexpensive fashion [8].

The parameters of soil that can be measured by sensor based approaches are:

(a) Electrical resistivity/conductivity: This parameter can be measured by electrical and electromagnetic sensors.

(b) Quality of soil by energy absorption/reflection: In this case optical and radiometric sensors are used.

(c) Force developed from a tool associated with soil: In this case mechanical sensors are employed.

(d) Sound produced by a tool interacting with the soil: Acoustic sensors are employed to quantify the sound.

(e) Quantity of air into the soil: Pneumatic sensors are used to measure the air injection into the soil.

(f) Measurement of ions (H^+, K^+, $NO3^-$, Na^+): In this case electrochemical sensors are used by incorporating the ion-selective membranes. They produce a voltage at the cost of activity of the selected ions.

In last few decades, innumerable researchers have contributed in the field of IoT based farming system. So it is very much important to collect, analyze and summarize these studies to classify the different research methods in this field. The main focus of this work is to find the applications of IoT in the field of agriculture.

11.3 Contribution of IoT in Agriculture

In this section we have surveyed different application area of IoT in agriculture. The main applications area can be divided broadly into three categories: monitoring, controlling and tracking. These applications can be classified into ten different classes as shown in Figure 11.2.

Humidity Monitoring
Humidity is an important factor for plant growth [9]. By using humidity sensors humidity level of air is measured to control the cell growth of plant.

Temperature Monitoring
Temperature of soil plays a vital role for crop development and production. In a particular field which crop will be cultivated can be decided by measuring the temperature range of soil. Different temperature sensors provide the information about the temperature and alerts if the temperature level is greater or lower than the threshold. Widely used temperature sensor is p-n junction diode of CMOS technology [10]. In an IoT based low cost prediction method has been presented in [11].

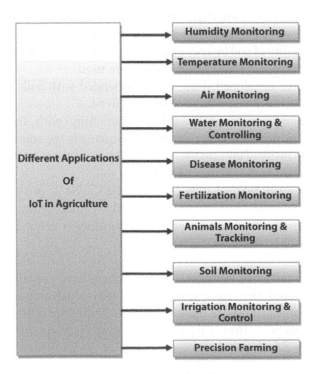

Figure 11.2 Different applications of IoT in agriculture humidity monitoring.

Air Monitoring or Wind Speed Monitoring

Air condition or wind speed sensors are used to measure the surface wind speed of a particular field to save from the damaging effect due to high speed. This type of sensor is generally mounted at a suitable height [12] to measure the direction and speed of the wind depending on the crop types.

Water Monitoring and Controlling

Soil water is another important parameter for the growth of plant. It is measured by the sensor which computes the ratio of water presents in soil to the amount of test soil. It is computed in terms of capacitance value [13].

Disease Monitoring

Detection of plant diseases is highly necessary for the growth of agriculture. There are different leaf diseases [14, 15] like a) Bacterial disease b) Fungal diseases c) Viral disease d) Diseases due to insects, etc. which indirectly affect the production of crops.

Fertilization Monitoring

Fertilizing failure directly affects the productivity and which is very difficult to correct the failure. In [16] authors reported a climate monitoring process for green houses to monitor fertilization, pests, irrigation and climate. Authors have used WSN to collect and analyze data.

Animals Monitoring and Tracking

To save the crops from animals, different IoT based animals monitoring and tracking systems are implemented. In [17] authors presented an IoT based animal monitoring system which observes the behavior of swamp deer. In [18] authors reported a real time cattle monitoring system using RFID and WSN.

Soil Monitoring

In [19] authors reported a soil monitoring system to measure and control the moisture and temperature of soil utilizing WSN. Here [19] authors have used different communication techniques like GPRS, ZigBee, internet service and web applications [20, 21].

Irrigation Monitoring and Control

It is a vital part of agriculture which helps to optimizing water budget, irrigation schedule or helps to take timely all decisions or services [22]. Presented an IoT based technique to monitor and control the growths of grapes. In [23] authors reported an apple orchards monitoring system which provide suggestions based on the sensed data.

Precision Farming

Precision farming is defined as the implementation of modern techniques to administer the agricultural production in order to improve the crop quality and environmental serenity. This technologically empowered precision agriculture is characterized by low input, high level of efficiency and sustainability [6].

The findings narrated in this section, is represented in tabular structure (Table 11.1).

Table 11.1 Contribution of IoT in agriculture.

Sl. no.	Parameters to be monitored	Contribution of IoT in agriculture
1	Humidity	Humidity sensors gives the estimation of humidity level of air is to control the cell growth of plant [9].
2	Temperature	Different temperature sensors (CMOS compatible p-n junction sensor) provide the information of atmospheric temperature and generates necessary alert for any temperature variation with respect to the threshold value [10, 11].
3	Wind speed (Air)	Wind speed sensors (often called air condition sensor) are exercised to quantify the surface wind speed of a particular field to save crops from the high speed induced scratch [12].
4	Water	The water sensor computes the ratio of water presents in soil via soil's capacitance owing to its dielectric constant [13].
5	Disease	IoT enabled image processing technology detects different leaf diseases [14, 15].
6	Fertilization	Wireless Sensor Network (WSN) will monitor and collect the data regarding climate changes due to green house effect as green house essentially affects fertilization process [16].
7	Animals	Different IoT based animal-monitoring and tracking systems including RFID and WSN are employed to navigate the behavior of swamp deer as well as cattle [17, 18].

(Continued)

Table 11.1 Contribution of IoT in agriculture. (*Continued*)

Sl. no.	Parameters to be monitored	Contribution of IoT in agriculture
8	Soil	Various soil monitoring systems including WSN, GPRS, ZigBee, internet service and web applications are exercised to measure and control the moisture and temperature of soil utilizing WSN [19–21].
9	Irrigation	IoT based system is used to monitor and control water budget, irrigation schedule and helps to take timely decisions or services [22, 23].

11.4   IoT Enabled Smart Farming

In this section we have reviewed different sensors which were used in IoT based smart farming in different literature. A sensor is basically a device which can detect different types of physical parameters, like heat, pressure, light, humidity, level of pollution, wind etc. For the further processing, these sensors convert the detected parameters into electrical signal and then transmitted to microcontroller or other devices or network. With the advancement of technology, different intelligent sensors are also developed. IoT enabled smart farming techniques are summarized in Table 11.2.

Table 11.2 List of smart farming systems with functional sensors and communication network.

Reference	Year	Major contribution	Sensor/Devices	Protocols/ Network type
[17]	2008	Tracking system to monitor the behavior of animals in the field.	Wild CENSE Node	GPS/WSN
[24]	2009	Method to measure the temperature and humidity of a vast area.	Microclimate Sensor	ZigBee/WSN
[25]	2009	Proposed a low-cost wireless irrigation system.	Sensor Node and Microcontroller	GPRS/WSN

(*Continued*)

Table 11.2 List of smart farming systems with functional sensors and communication network. (*Continued*)

Reference	Year	Major contribution	Sensor/Devices	Protocols/ Network type
[26]	2009	Sensor network to measure soil moisture.	Soil Moisture Sensor	ZigBee/WSN
[27]	2010	Proposed a IoT based system to control the parameters, humidity and temperature.	Temperature and Humidity Sensor	SMS, Wireless application protocol
[28]	2013	Presented a climate controlling system for greenhouse.	Sensor Nodes	ZigBee/WSN
[29]	2014	Presented a decision support system for irrigation Scheduling.	Weather Station	WSN
[30]	2014	Designed a method to measure soil moisture and temperature.	Core Ship CC2530	WSN
[31]	2017	Designed a wireless mobile robot to perform multiple controlling and monitoring tasks.	Many Sensors/ Raspberry PI	WIFI, ZigBee
[32]	2017	IoT based system to monitor the different environment parameters.	Temperature and Moisture Sensor	RFID
[33]	2017	Developed an IoT based low-cost irrigation system.	Soil Moisture Sensor	MQTT
[34]	2018	Presented an innovative system for monitoring the agricultural system.	Humidity and Temperature Sensor	LoraWAN
[35]	2018	Discussed various challenges and benefits for monitoring temperature, air, humidity, moisture.	Multiple Sensors and Devices	Sigfox, Lora, NB-IoT, Wi-Fi
[36]	2018	Developed an IoT based system to monitor various parameters which are humidity, light, water and pesticide.	Soil Moisture, Temperature, and Humidity Sensor	Microcontroller GPS, Wi-Fi
[37]	2019	To monitor various application like water, fertilization, heat and gas a framework has been designed.	Various Sensors/ Gateway	ZigBee, MQTT/ WSN

11.5   IoT Enabled Precision Farming

With the advent of information technology and computer science, Internet is used extensively to associate things (objects) of real world through Wireless Sensor Networks, Bluetooth, Long Term Evolution (LTE), Radio-frequency Identification (RFID) etc. for smarter communication. This unimaginable technology is termed as Internet of Things (IoT). This benchmark in technology helps to transform the things of real world into smarter devicesthat may reshape the world in a fantastic way. IoT facilitates the transfer of information from smarter devices to the destination over the Internet. According to recent survey industry 4.0 isentirely associated with IoT technology. In industrial revolution 5.0, IoT can be associated with sensing devices, big data along with patterns of connected devices within different network configurations. This advancement in IoT is called upon IoT 2.0. Recently Artificial Intelligence, Cloud Computing and Data Science are emerging in IoT 2.0 to make it more powerful [38].

As Precision Agriculture is a farm management system for crop and soil ensuring what they actually need for optimum well being and productivity so modern technologies are more involving for this purpose. The new age farmers are migrating from traditional farming methodologies to modernized attempts only to produce qualitative crops with sustainability and profitability.

IoT encourages the farmers to install smart devices for monitoring the crop growth and health and after that based on observations, agricultural activities should be performed. The IoT inclusion in agriculture is increasing day by day as compared sensor based agriculture (depicted in Figure 11.3) as the sensor based agriculture has stopped at one end where the

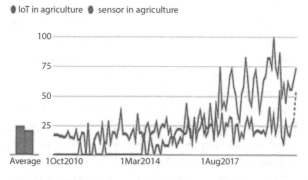

Figure 11.3 Google survey on IoT and sensor-based agriculture. [Courtesy: M. Torkya, A. Ella Hassanein, Integrating blockchain and the internet of things in precision agriculture: Analysis, opportunities, and challenges, https://doi.org/10.1016/j.compag.2020.105476.]

remote user cannot get the sufficient data to monitor and administer the farming land to enhance the agro-economics.

Remote Monitoring System (RMS) with wireless Internet connections is manifested to monitor the plant growth and health in green house and the technique was easy to operate as compared to open field. The devices used for monitoring the plant growth are WSN, RFID, Autonomous sensors etc. and these devices were communicating with each otherthrough TCP based communication technology [39].

Bo and Wang *et al.* had proposed cloud computing and IoT enabled precision agriculture in order to analyze the future prospect and their study revealed that the conjugation of these two techniques may resolve the bottlenecks of precision agriculture. Their work employed WSN and Zigbee with IP based infrastructure and UDP based communication technologies [40] but farmers are lagging behind such technological concepts. Farm Management System utilizes several smart devices viz. Zigbee, RFID, Sensors in a farming land for getting necessary information and coordinating tractors with suitable management [41].

Message Queue Telemetry Transport is a useful technique in IoT based precision agriculture where the request for pushing data in cloud is overcome and the system is easierto install, maintain and control. In this approach, smart phone and Wi Fi router are used with 4G LTE, Bluetooth and Wi-Fi technologies for storing the data of crop production, quality control etc. directly to the cloud [42]. Smart Farm Net Application is used to predict crop performance of crop forecasts. Different agricultural and environmental sensors were employed with OpenIoT X-GSN communication technology [43].

In regards of crop health and crop disease monitoring unmanned vehicle draws enormous attention to farmers. Basically India's 70% economy depends on agriculture. So the agricultural prosperity should be a prime concern for us. Agricultural prosperity depends on the health of crop viz. height of crop, quality of crop etc., crop production. IoT based precision farming facilitates the transfer of crop related data over internet to all farmers after installation of smart devices but the entire technology is not well versed to farmers. Again themonitoring of the crop health and crop production from outside is very important to administer the farming process. Manual pesticide spray to protect the crop against attack frompests and insects is not satisfactory as the process could not be able to maintain the optimized level of pesticides. As a result of which human health is at stake. World Health Organization (WHO) has announced one million ill health effects due to uncontrolled pesticide spray manually. So Unmanned Aerial Vehicle (UAV)-aircraft based spray technique becomes popular for avoiding the human health problem. There are 250 models of UAV are established for this purpose and these models have incorporated advanced aerodynamicmodeling using PID (proportional integral derivative) controlling algorithm, autonomous flight controlling using laser beaming technology, software system, image collection platform, NDVI system, sensors and vision system etc. [44]. According to existing literature the sprayer system is mounted on UAV for pesticides spray and this model becomes a successful attempt in regards of pest management and vector control. One significant aspect of this model is that this has large accuracy with higher speed on site specificity for a large crop field but this open loop UAV lacks the coverage of the crop field particularly for overlapped crop areas and outer edge of the crop field. Such shortcoming is overcome by SWARM UAV where a feedback system is incorporated that is working with the principles of WSN. The WSN send messages to the UAV regarding the dimension of crop field and the possible route for full coverage along with indication to increase the speed. Thus the UAV can cover the entire farming land with continuum in spraying. Additionally the closed loop UAV controls the wastage of pesticides. With PWM system installed in this UAV may enhance the operational speed due to reduced power consumption and switching mechanism. In the WSN conjugated UAV the system may get some time to analyze the data sent from WSN and decide the next route due to provision of delay. With pesticide spray at minimal wastage is the employment of blimp integrated quad copter aerial automated pesticide sprayer based on the GPS coordinates [45]. There is a substantial development of UAV system for multiplexed operation in precision agriculture. Android app based low cost user friendly drone puts a significant signature in pesticide spraying at a controlled rate [44]. Another breakthrough model of UAV based pesticide sprayer is depicted as presence of automated drone system with multispectral camera [44]. The working protocol of this system is based on

1. Scanning of the field including crop production by multispectral camera throughreflectance mechanism.
2. Controlling the coordinates of the pictures by GPS
3. Generation of a spatial map through telemetry
4. Monitoring the crop health condition using the spatial map in terms of Normalized Difference Vegetation Index (NDVI)
5. Taking decision of applying the suitable pesticides or fertilizers on crop by farmers

The reflectance of the vegetation is recorded at five different wavelengths viz.

    (a)   440–510 nm (Blue wavelength)
    (b)   520–590 nm (Green wavelength)
    (c)   630–685 nm (Red wavelength)
    (d)   690–730 nm (Red edge wavelength)
    (e)   760–850 nm (Near infrared wavelength)

NDVI: NDVI is one kind of geographic indicator that is defined as:

$$NDVI = \frac{(R_{INR} - R_{RED})}{(R_{INR} + R_{RED})}$$

R_{INR} = Reflectance of near infrared band
R_{RED} = Reflectance of red band
NDVI defines the vegetation density of the crop. If the NDVI is equal to zero then no vegetation. If NDVI = 0.8–0.9 (~1) then there is highest vegetation in terms of green leaves onthe crop. The findings narrated in this section, is represented in tabular structure (Table 11.3).

11.6   Machine Learning Enable Precision Farming

Machine Learning (ML) is a branch of computer science that imposes some abilities in computers to learn without being explicitly programmed [46]. Applying ML, the computer becomes intelligent device that can (a) learn and extract knowledge from the available dataset, (b) applying the knowledge to build up framework and (c) may give predictions or take intelligent decisions. The generalized model of ML is depicted in Figure 11.4. The difference between the conventional computer algorithm and ML algorithm is absence of training. The popularity of ML algorithms is due to its instantaneous decision for any type of complex problems viz. disease identification in plants, pattern recognition, weather forecasting, spam filtering etc.

The ML algorithms are classified into three categories such as (1) supervised learning technique (2) unsupervised learning technique (3) reinforcement learning (shown in Figure 11.5).

Table 11.3 Contribution of IoT in precision farming.

Sl. no.	Parameters to be monitored	Contribution of IoT in precision farming
1	Plant growth and health	Remote Monitoring System (RMS) with wireless Internet including WSN, RFID, and Autonomous sensors is employed to monitor the plant growth and health. The information is communicated to different devices via TCP based communication technology [39].
2	Coordination between tractors with suitable management	WSN and Zigbee with IP based infrastructure and UDP based communication technologies and Zigbee, RFID, Sensors are exercised to record necessary information of smart farming as well as coordinate the tractors with suitable management [40, 41].
3	Crop production data storage and quality control	Message Queue Telemetry Transport (MQTT) involving smart phone, Wi-Fi router with 4G LTE, Bluetooth and Wi-Fi technologies were used to store crop production data and provide quality control [42].
4	Prediction of crop performance and computation of crop forecasting	Different agricultural and environmental sensors were employed with OpenIoT X-GSN communication technology [43].
5	Crop health and crop disease monitoring, Scanning of the field, Controlling the coordinates of the image, Generation of a spatial map through telemetry, Decision taking	Unmanned Aerial Vehicle (UAV)-aircraft based spray technique including PID (proportional integral derivative) controlling algorithm, autonomous flight controlling using laser beaming technology, software system, image collection platform, NDVI system, sensors and vision system, blimp integrated quad copter aerial automated pesticide sprayer with GPS were exercised to monitor crop health and crop disease [44, 45].

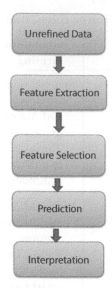

Figure 11.4 Generalized model of machine learning.

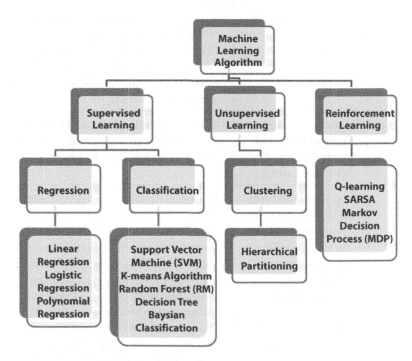

Figure 11.5 Different machine learning algorithms.

1. Supervised learning is defined as ML algorithm based on labeled data set (there exists an output for every input). This guided framework enables the computer to make decision on unseen input. There exist two types of supervised algorithm viz. (a) Classification-Prediction on categorical value for any unknown input, (b) Regression-Prediction on numerical value.

2. Unsupervised learning is dealing with untrained dataset, extracting hidden knowledge from trained data set and finally making prediction of any object by the principle of cohesiveness or clustering mechanism.

3. Reinforcement learning is regarded as most complicated algorithm that can learn fromthe environment mediated by reward and punishment based system.

Significance of ML in Crop Yield Prediction

For agro-economic countries such as India crop yield is considered to be the most effective indicator of economical status of the country. Nevertheless the crop yield is dependent on several factors including pH value, qualitative figure of soil, temperature, humidity, rainfall, the effective sunshine hours, fertilizers, pesticides and harvesting schedules. So in case of anyanomaly in these parameters may affect the crop yield. The manual agriculture system has feedback system which can detect any setback in order to correct the methodologies in farming but such system limits itself in regards of momentary failure in detection of setbackin anyone of the parameters discussed earlier. Such unobserved and uncorrected error may affect the crop production. ML based agriculture fosters feed forward system that can anticipate anyone of the factors that may hamper the crop yield. Thus any anomaly can be rectified after detection. The ML based agriculture system is depicted in Figure 11.6.

In perspective of ML algorithms, Random Forest (RF), MLP, Gaussian Process, k-NN, and Multivariate Adaptive Regression, Boosted Regression tree are extensively used in prediction of crop yield based on superfine yield map [47].

BBI model as suggested by Chu and Yu, operates in three stages where the initial stage entertains the pre-processing the data followed by extraction of deep spatial and transform domain features from the first stage data outperformed by BPNN and recurrent neural network (RNN) at the second stage. The BPNN correlates the deep features and the crop yield and

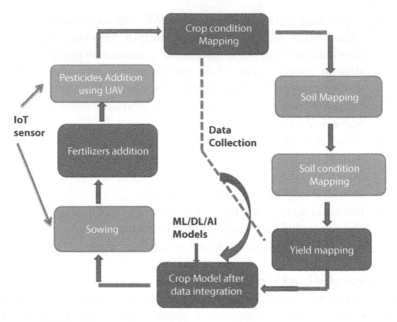

Figure 11.6 ML-based agriculture system.

predicts the summer and winter rice yield. The model produced a prediction error with MAE of 0.0044 and RMSE of 0.0057 for summer rice [48].

Regression models have larger impact on crop yield prediction as
observed by Aghighi *et al.* 28,000 hectares' area of Moghan Agro-Industrial
and Animal Husbandry Company (MAIAHC) is selected in Iran for such
purpose. At first crop yield data set was collected for around 40 maize
lands. Then time-series data was collected from Landsat8 OLI satellite for
the year of 2013-2015. The data were fed to several regression models such
as (a) Gaussian Regression (b) SVR (c) Boosted Regression and (d) RF
Regression models. The comparative analysis of the prediction produced
from each model revealed that the boosted regression produced best result
with an average R-value higher than 0.87 and RMSE with a mean value of
9.5. The optimum yield was observed during the time span of 2013–14.
[49] The crop yield can also be predicted from climate data and satellite
data of NDVI with the help of SVM, RF, and NN models. In this case the
yield prediction with R^2 of around 0.75 [50]. The Deep Learning (DL)
Model such as Convolutional Neural Network (CNN) was employed to
predict wheat and barley yield at Pori, Finland. Here UAV based system
was installed for pesticide spraying and to monitor the crop health. The
cameras in UAV took photos of crop and the field and send the data to

UAV for NDVI analysis. Interestingly here the prediction based on NDVI dataset is fully based on DL model wherethe six-layer CNN was trained by NDVI and RGB data set.

Multiplexed Crop development prediction with crop health monitoring could be possible by installing IoT smart sensors in green houses along with processing the dataset throughBayesian Network [51].

Soil Variability and Weather Prediction by ML Models

Soil is regarded as the platform for crop growth as it is enriched with several nutrients [47] that are essential for crop health. The nutrients are enlisted in Table 11.4.

Table 11.4 List of nutrients in soil.

Name of the element	Type of the nutrient	Primary form of the nutrient
Carbon	Non mineral elements	CO_2 (g)
Hydrogen		$H_2O(l)$, H^+
Oxygen		H_2O (l), O_2 (g)
Nitrogen	Primary Macronutrients- Mineral elements	NH_4^+, NO_3^-
Phosphorous		HPO_4^{2-}, $H_2PO_4^-$
Potassium		K^+
Calcium	Secondary Macronutrients- Mineral elements	Ca_2^+
Magnesium		Mg_2^+
Sulphur		SO_4^{2-}
Iron	Micronutrients- Mineral elements	Fe^{3+}, Fe^{2+}
Manganese		Mn^{2+}
Zinc		Zn_2^+
Copper		Cu_2^+
Boron		$B(OH)_3$
Molybdenum		MoO_4^{2-}
Chlorine		Cl^-
Nickel		Ni^{2+}

As discussed earlier that soil variability such as pH of the soil, nutrients level, soil type, soil moisture level etc. play important role in agriculture as these properties influence the crop yield, land choice, selection of seed, type of fertilizers to be added, land geographic location etc. Manual monitoring of all these properties may lead error and also the addition of excessive fertilizers may cause adverse effect on environment.

Therefore the automatic monitoring of soil properties is an optimum need to maximize the production.

ML models play an important role in case of automatic monitoring of soil properties henceforth there are plenty of documentations regarding ML based automatic soil properties control. Table 11.5 depicts the present scenario of soil properties control using ML based prediction mechanism.

11.7 Application of Operational Research Method in Farming System

The operation research (OR) method is a new branch of mathematics to solve real-world problems or we can define it as a decision-making method which is useful in the managementof organizations. The basic block diagram of OR method to solve real world problems is shown in Figure 11.7.

This method basically combines the management process in IoT-based advanced agriculture or farming system. It actually integrates planting, processing, tracking, production, and selling [60] or indirectly each and every important step or process related to agriculture with management processes. There are very few works available in the literature which integrate IoT-based agriculture with the OR method.

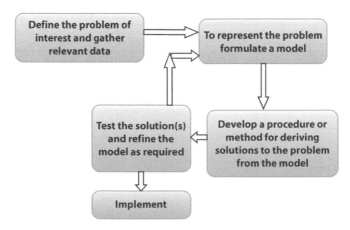

Figure 11.7 Basic flow diagram of OR method to solve real world problems [59].

Table 11.5 Depicts the present scenario of soil properties control using ML-based prediction mechanism.

Sl. no.	Soil properties and weather condition to be investigated	ML algorithm employed	Data set	Performance	References
01	Soil surface humidity	Extreme Learning Machine (ELM) based Regression Model	Polarimetric Radarsat-2 data	Root Mean Square Error (RMSE) = 2.19%	[52]
02	Soil nitrogen and organic carbon (SOC)	Ensemble learning modeling algorithm	NIR spectroscopic data	R^2 = 0.96, RMSE = 1.92, Performance to deviation (RPD) = 4.87 for SOC R^2 = 0.94, RMSE = 0.57, Performance to deviation (RPD) = 4.91 for soil nitrogen	[53]

(Continued)

Table 11.5 Depicts the present scenario of soil properties control using ML-based prediction mechanism. (*Continued*)

Sl. no.	Soil properties and weather condition to be investigated	ML algorithm employed	Data set	Performance	References
03	Total nitrogen content, cation exchange capacity, soil organic component	Random Forest, Ordinary Least Squares Regression Model, Cubist Regression Model, XGBoost Model	Portable X-Ray Fluorescence Spectrophotometric data	$R^2 = 0.50$ for total nitrogen $R^2 = 0.75$ for cation exchange capacity $R^2 = 0.56$ for soil organic matter	[54]

(*Continued*)

Table 11.5 Depicts the present scenario of soil properties control using ML-based prediction mechanism. (*Continued*)

Sl. no.	Soil properties and weather condition to be investigated	ML algorithm employed	Data set	Performance	References
04	pH, Mg content, K content, soil organic matter, crop yield	Support Vector Machine (SVM), RF, Neural Network (NN), Cubist, Gradient Boosting Model (GBM)	Aerial image of agricultural land collected with the help of remote sensing.	NN predicts highest accuracy for soil organic matter depicted as: $R^2 = 0.64$, RMSE = 0.44 SVM produces highest prediction for K and Mg content as: $R^2 = 0.21$, RMSE = 0.49 for K $R^2 = 0.22$, RMSE of 4.57 for Mg For pH value, GBM predicts highest accuracy as: $R^2 = 0.15$, RMSE = 0.62	[55]

(*Continued*)

Table 11.5 Depicts the present scenario of soil properties control using ML-based prediction mechanism. (*Continued*)

Sl. no.	Soil properties and weather condition to be investigated	ML algorithm employed	Data set	Performance	References
05	SO_4^{2-}, $H_2PO_4^-$	ELM	Auxiliary Measurement	RMSE = 1.2414 for predictions in SO42– RMSE = 0.8892 for prediction of $H_2PO_4^-$	[56]
06	Soil temperature at various soil depths such as 5, 10, 50 and 100 cm	ELM, ANN, classification and regression trees	Dataset was obtained from Mersin station that was operated by Turkish Meteorological Service	ELM provides best prediction RMSE: 1.914, 1.429 and 1.456 for 5, 10 and 50 cm R^2 = 0.977, 0.980, 0.984 for 5, 10 and 50 cm	[57]
07	Rainfall	SVM, Knn, Clustering, RF	Atmospheric synoptic pattern	NN produces best prediction with F score = 0.4	[58]

The operation research is an appropriate decisiveness for scarce and uncertain world. There are two popular approaches for taking decision in intelligent farming based on IoT viz. a) Mathematical Programming where linear fractional functioning and programming is employed b) Game Theory.

In mathematical programming technique, objective function can be expressed in terms of mathematical model and its solution is obtained by programming. Linear Programming (LP) is the most popular technique amongst the family of mathematical programming.

In LP the following parameters are used to solve the problem. They are defined as

Z = Objective function that is to be maximized, for agriculture it is net income.X_j = Input Variables

C_i = Cost coefficients of the objective function Z_{bi} = Maximum limit of the constraints.

A_{ij} = Coefficients of the functional constraint equations where i = crop combination and j = arable land. In [61] simplex problem, smaller iterations are used to solve the problem. The importance of LP in IoT based agriculture is to maximize the profit and minimize the cost of the macro-level agriculture.

In this regards Dos Santos et al. [62] had defined a production problem associated with known demand of crops. The decisive nature of the problem lies in 1) identification of the available heterogeneous areas in plots in order to meet the demand and 2) determination of the crop production schedule for every plot. Ecological based constraints are taken into consideration during the problem settlement. A linear program is used to model the problem resolution and the problem was solved with the help of a column-generation approach. A set of computational tests ran using real data comprising of 24 crops that yield good result.

Osama et al. [63] had reported significant increase in net return in crop production after the application linear optimization model. The model was designed on 28 crops based sample from 2008 to 2012. The ecological constraints are socio-economic status of Egypt where the security of food, scarcity of water resources etc. The operation research is applied in order to achieve food security, effective utility of water resources and availability arable land and self-affluence in order to increase the strategic crops. Consequently non strategic crop productionhas decreased and the strategic crops such as wheat, sugarcane, maize, rice yield were remained constant in order to satisfy the country's food requirements. Tomatoes that are treated as high net return are yielded substantially. The operational research thus depicted thatdeclining non strategic crop farming land, saturating the strategic crop allocation areas and increasing tomato production affects the net return of the country.

The operation research was also applied to overcome the deficit of water resources. This implication of operation research in water deficit and to enhance the crop yield despite the ecological constraint was observed in southern part of Iran. Multi-objective programming approach is applied in the LP based operation research. The objectives in this LP based operation research were gross margin, water use and risk in terms of gross margins variance. Target MOTAD and Min Variance risky are the approaches used in the programming [61]. In this case study it was observed that at high level of risk wheat production increases. Additionally the water consumption is reduced by 14.7%.

Bhattacharya *et al.* [64] had designed a pre-harvest prediction of sugarcane production. According to his prediction mechanism, a goal programming formulation was employed for this purpose. The basic parameters of this formulation were plant height, cane's girth per plot, number of canes, and width of third leaf from the top. This methodology is advantageous from ML induced conventional precision farming in regards of absence of strong assumptions.

Another utility of operation research in agriculture is found in water crisis problem in the Saudi Kingdom. The operation research was based on water quality and quantity. In Saudi Arab, farmers often face the limited water supply. For accessing value of water in irrigation system good decision in regard to water price and its availability in different regions is necessary. The mathematical model such as mixed-integer programming model was developed. The ecological constraints in this model were water and land availability constraints, mass balance constraints, market constraints, time constraints [61].

11.8   Conclusion

In this chapter we have reviewed IoT based smart farming and precision farming in detail. In the first part of review IoT enabled precision farming is highlighted where IoT encourages the farmers to install smart devices for monitoring the crop growth and health and after that based on observations, agricultural activities should be performed. Different environmental sensors especially smart devices are installed at farming land to monitor the precision agriculture variability and at the same time the output of the sensors are processed with data acquisition system and uploaded to cloud through IoT based network. This sophisticated system may enable the farmers to correctly decide how to manage the agricultural system.

In the next part of the review automated crop health monitoring system with pesticide spraying technique is discussed. UAV is depicted as that kind of automated device that can administer the crop health and pesticide spray in a well defined manner. UAV based spray system is intervening into precision agriculture as manual pesticide spray system experience lots of limitations like expertise, knowledge of proper dosage of pesticide, scarcity of human resource etc. This UAV system turns the pesticide spraying more convenient and faster. The review has highlighted different UAV based spraying system with multispectral camera, association of PWM system in order to elucidate the sophisticated operation such analysis of captured pictures by GPS and a spatial map is generated by telemetry. This analysis becomes helpful to navigate the area where the pesticide is to be sprayed. NDVI identifies the density of vegetation and henceforth the spraying will be modulated that would result the save in water and chemicals.

There are still some sorts of setback in IoT and UAV based precision farming as they could not enable farmers to predict crop yield and economical strength in a forecasting manner. The intelligent computer can administer all these things and to be very honest the machine learning model can perform such activities. In this context several machine learning models along with CNN and ANN are well described with prediction accuracy. The machine learning models can predict the crop yield, soil parameters, weather conditions which are playing important role in deciding the annual turnover from precision farming.

Thus the present chapter enables the readers to accumulate the corrected knowledge regarding the smart farming and precision farming with a zeal to advance the field.

Despite of emergence of IoT in agriculture there is no remarkable improvement in agriculture. The IoT enabled agriculture is scattered and incomplete in production and management perspectives. Intelligent agriculture although is very much popular but it lacks complete exploration in agricultural development. Importantly with the growing demands of modern society for transparent, specialized and integrity functionalized agricultural production, conventional intelligent agriculture is not efficient. In this regards operational management enabled intelligent agriculture is at utmost priority. From farming point of view several ecological constraints such as consumption of water, quality of water, soil, climate etc. do impact the agriculture industry in great extent. There is substantial delay in getting net return or profit from agriculture and this time lag is the major concern for agriculture development. Also the selling issues on bulky products are also a commendable factor for agriculture saturation. In this regards decision making on selling agricultural products, making annual returns in a good figure are important to turn the farming in profitable sector. The operational research based agriculture mold the farming in a profitable sector with the high selectivity and forecasting.

11.9 Future Scope

Blockchain technology may be related to futuristically intelligent and precise farming. Blockchain can be used to more intelligently manage supply networks, soils, and warehouses. It can be used as a vital tool to send real-time data regarding livestock and crops. Moreover, it can be applied to controlling money transactions, logistics, and food safety. Blockchain technology has the potential to advance a number of processes and increase their accuracy. agriculture, including monitoring and traceability, transparency, and efficiency for both farmers and consumers.

References

1. Sundmaeker, H., Verdouw, C., Wolfert, S., Prez Freire, L., Digitising the industry - Internet of things connecting physical, digital and virtual worlds. *IoF 2020*, vol. 2, pp. 129–151, Aug, 2016.
2. Wolfert, S., Ge, L., Verdouw, C., Bogaardt, M.-J., Big data in smart farming a review. *Agric. Syst.*, 153, 69–80, May, 2017, doi: 10.1016/j. agsy.2017.01.023.
3. Walter, A., Finger, R., Huber, R., Buchmann, N., Opinion: Smart farming is key to developing sustainable agriculture. *Proc. Natl. Acad. Sci. U.S.A.*, 6148–6150, 2017, doi: 10.1073/pnas.1707462114.
4. Phupattanasilp, P. and Tong, S.R., Augmented reality in the integrative internet of things (AR-IoT): Application for precision farming. *Sustainability*, 11, 2658, 2019, [CrossRef].
5. Wong, S., *Decentralised, off-grid solar pump irrigation systems in developing countries—are they pro-poor, pro-environment and pro-women*, pp. 367–382, Springer International Publishing, Cham, Swiss Publisher, The University of Edinburgh, Word Meteorological Organization, Switzerland, 2019, doi: 10.1007/ 978-3-319-75004-0_21, URL: http://www.precisionfarming.com.
6. Gibbons, G., Turning a farm art into science-an overview of precision farming, Studio Di Ingegneria Terradat Di Paolo Dosso Via Andrea Costa, Italy, 2000, URL: http://www.precisionfarming.com.
7. Zhang, N., Wang, M., Wang, N., Precision agriculture-a worldwide overview. *Comput. Electron Agric.*, 36, 113–132, Nov, 2002.

8. Adamchuk, V.I., Hummel, J.W., Morgan, M.T., Upadhyaya, S.K., On-the-go soil sensors for precision agriculture. *Comput. Electron. Agric.*, 44, 71–91, Jul, 2004.

9. Krishna, K.L., Silver, O., Malende, W.F., Anuradha, K., Internet of things application for implementation of smart agriculture system, in: *Proc. 2017 International Conference on I-SMAC (IoT in Social, Mobile, Analytics and Cloud) (I-SMAC)*, Palladam, India, pp. 54–59, 10–11 Feb. 2017.

10. Futagawa, M., Iwasaki, T., Takao, H., Ishida, M., Sawada, K., Takao, H., Ishida, M., Sawada, K., Fabrication of a multi-modal sensor with PH, EC and temperature sensing areas for agriculture application. *Sensors*, 1, 2013–2016, 2009, doi: 10.1109/ICS.

11. dos Santos, U.J.L., Pessin, G., da Costa, C.A., da Rosa Righi, R., AgriPrediction: A proactive internet of things model to anticipate problems and improve production in agricultural crops. *Comput. Electron. Agric.*, 161, 202–213, Jun, 2019.

12. W.M. Organization (Ed.), *Guide to Meteorological Instruments and Methods of Observation*, pp. 1.5–1–1.5–14, Chairperson, Publications Board World Meteorological Organization (WMO), Word Meteorological Organization, Switzerland, 2018.

13. Lakhankar, T., Ghedira, H., Temimi, M., Sengupta, M., Khanbilvardi, R., Blake, R., Non-parametric methods for soil moisture retrieval from satellite remote sensing data. *Remote Sens.*, 1, 3–21, Mar, 2009, doi: 10.3390/rs1010003.

14. Johannes, A., Picon, A., Alvarez-Gila, A., Echazarra, J., RodriguezVaamonde, S., Navajas, A.D. *et al.*, Automatic plant disease diagnosis using mobile capture devices, applied on a wheat use case. *Comput. Electron. Agric.*, 138, 200–209, June, 2017, https://doi. org/10.1016/j.compag.2017.04.013.

15. Islam, M., Dinh, A., Wahid, K., Bhowmik, P., Detection of potato diseases using image segmentation and multiclass support vector machine. *Can. Conf. Electr. Comput. Eng.*, 1, 8–11, 2017, https://doi.org/10.1109/CCECE.2017.7946594.

16. Pahuja, R., Verma, H.K., Uddin, M., A wireless sensor network for greenhouse climate control. *IEEE Pervasive Comput.*, 12, 49–58, April, 2013.

17. Jain, V.R., Bagree, R., Kumar, A., Ranjan, P., WildCENSE: GPS based animal tracking system, in: *Proc. of the 2008 International Conference on Intelligent Sensors, Sensor Networks and Information Processing*, Sydney, Australia, pp. 617–622, 15–18 Dec. 2008.

18. Ehsan, S., Bradford, K., Brugger, M., Hamdaoui, B., Kovchegov, Y., Johnson, D., Louhaichi, M., Design and analysis of delay-tolerant sensor networks for monitoring and tracking free-roaming animals. *IEEE Trans. Wirel. Commun.*, 11, 1220–1227, Feb., 2012.

19. Chen, K.T., Zhang, H.H., Wu, T.T., Hu, J., Zhai, C.Y., Wang, D., Design of monitoring system for multilayer soil temperature and moisture based on WSN,

in: *Proc. of the 2014 International Conference on Wireless Communication and Sensor Network*, Wuhan, China, pp. 425–430, 13–14 Dec. 2014.

20. Thorat, A., Kumari, S., Valakunde, N.D., An IoT based smart solution for leaf disease detection, in: *Proc. of the 2017 International Conference on Big Data, IoT and Data Science (BID)*, Pune, India, pp. 193–198, 20–22 Dec. 2017.

21. Jayaraman, P.P., Palmer, D., Zaslavsky, A., Salehi, A., Georgakopoulos, D., Addressing information processing needs of digital agriculture with ope-nIoT platform, in: *Interoperability and Open-Source Solutions for the Internet of Things*, pp. 137–152, Springer: Cham, Switzerland, 2015.

22. Lee, J., Kang, H., Bang, H., Kang, S., Dynamic crop field analysis using mobile sensor node, in: *Proc. of the 2012 International Conference on ICT Convergence (ICTC)*, Jeju Island, Korea, pp. 7–11, 15–17 Oct., 2012.

23. Feng, C., Wu, H.R., Zhu, H.J., Sun, X., The design and realization of apple orchard intelligent monitoring system based on internet of things technology. *Adv. Mat. Res.*, 546, 898–902, Trans Tech Publications, Stafa-Zurich, Switzerland, 2012.

24. Watthanawisuth, N., Tuantranont, A., Kerdcharoen, T., Microclimate real-time monitoring based on ZigBee sensor network, in: *Proc. of the SENSORS*, Christchurch, New Zealand, IEEE, pp. 1814–1818, 25–28 Oct. 2009.

26. Khandani, S.K. and Kalantari, M., Using field data to design a sensor network, in: *Proc. of the 2009 43rd Annual Conference on Information Sciences and Systems*, pp. 219–223, Baltimore, MD, USA, 18–20 Mar. 2009.

27. Zhao, J.C., Zhang, J.F., Feng, Y., Guo, J.X., The study and application of the IOT technology in agriculture, in: *Proc. of the 2010 3rd International Conference on Computer Science and Information Technology*, Chengdu, China, pp. 462–465, 9–11 July 2010.

28. Pahuja, R., Verma, H.K., Uddin, M.A., Wireless sensor network for greenhouse climate control. *IEEE Pervasive Comput.*, 12, 49–58, Jun, 2013.

29. Fourati, M.A., Chebbi, W., Kamoun, A., Development of a web-based weather station for irrigation scheduling, in: *Proc. of the 2014 Third IEEE International Colloquium in Information Science and Technology (CIST)*, Tetouan, Morocco, pp. 37–42, 20–22 Oct. 2014.

30. Chen, K.T., Zhang, H.H., Wu, T.T., Hu, J., Zhai, C.Y., Wang, D., Design of monitoring system for multilayer soil temperature and moisture based on WSN, in: *Proc. of the 2014 International Conference on Wireless Communication and Sensor Network*, Wuhan, China, pp. 425–430, 13–14 Dec 2014.

31. Krishna, K.L., Silver, O., Malende, W.F., Anuradha, K., Internet of things application for implementation of smart agriculture system, in: *Proc. of the 2017 International Conference on I-SMAC (IoT in Social, Mobile, Analytics and Cloud) (I-SMAC)*, Palladam, India, pp. 54–59, 10–11 February 2017.

32. Wasson, T., Choudhury, T., Sharma, S., Kumar, P., Integration of RFID and sensor in agriculture using IoT, in: *Proc. of the 2017 International Conference on Smart Technologies for Smart Nation (SmartTechCon)*, Bangalore, India, pp. 217–222, 17–19 Aug, 2017.

33. Kodali, R.K. and Sarjerao, B.S., A low cost smart irrigation system using MQTT protocol, in: *Proc. of the 2017 IEEE Region 10 Symposium (TENSYMP)*, Cochin, India, pp. 1–5, 14–16 July 2017.

34. Davcev, D., Mitreski, K., Trajkovic, S., Nikolovski, V., Koteli, N., IoT agriculture system based on LoRaWAN, in: *Proc. of the 2018 14th IEEE International Workshop on Factory Communication Systems (WFCS)*, Imperia, Italy, 13–15 June 2018, pp. 1–4.

35. Elijah, O., Rahman, T.A., Orikumhi, I., Leow, C.Y., Hindia, M.N., An overview of internet of things (IoT) and data analytics in agriculture: Benefits and challenges. *IEEE Internet Things J.*, 5, 3758–3773, June, 2018.

36. Dholu, M. and Ghodinde, K.A., Internet of things (IoT) for precision agriculture application, in: *Proc. of the 2018 2nd International Conference on Trends in Electronics and Informatics (ICOEI)*, Tirunelveli, India, pp. 339–342, 11–12 May 2018.

37. Liu, S., Guo, L., Webb, H., Ya, X., Chang, X., Internet of things monitoring system of modern eco-agriculture based on cloud computing. *IEEE Access*, 7, 37050–37058, March, 2019.

38. Khanna, A. and Kaur, S., Evolution of internet of things (IoT) and its significant impact in the field of precision agriculture. *Comput. Electron Agric.*, 157, 218–231, Feb. 2019.

39. Zhao, J.-C., Zhang, J.-F., Feng, Y., Guo, J.-X., The study and application of the IoT technology in agriculture, in: *Computer Science and Information Technology (ICCSIT), 2010 3rd IEEE International Conference*, vol. 2, pp. 462–465, 2010.

40. Bo, Y. and Wang, H., The application of cloud computing and the internet of things in agriculture and forestry, in: *Service Sciences (IJCSS), 2011 International Joint Conference*, IEEE, pp. 168–172, 2011.

41. Kaloxylos, A., Eigenmann, R., Teye, F., Politopoulou, Z., Wolfert, S., Shrank, C., Dillinger, M., Lampropoulou, I., Antoniou, E., Pesonen, L. *et al.*, Farm management systems and the future internet era. *Comput. Electron. Agric.*, 89, 130–144, Jan. 2014.

42. Ferrández-Pastor, F.J., García-Chamizo, J.M., Nieto-Hidalgo, M., Mora-Pascual, J., MoraMartínez, J., Developing ubiquitous sensor network platform using internet of things: Application in precision agriculture. *Sensors*, 16, 7, 1141, Jul. 2016.

43. Jayaraman, P.P., Yavari, A., Georgakopoulos, D., Morshed, A., Zaslavsky, A., Internet of things platform for smart farming: experiences and lessons learnt. *Sensors*, 16, 11, 1884, Nov. 2016.

44. Rao Mogili, U.M. and Deepak, B.B.V.L., Review on application of drone systems in precision agriculture. *Proc. Comput. Sci.*, 133, 502–509, 2018.

45. Spoorthi, S., Shadaksharappa, B., Suraj, S., Manasa, V.K., Freyr drone: Pesticide/fertilizers spraying drone-an agricultural approach, in: *IEEE 2nd International Conference on Computing and Communications Technologies (ICCCT - 2017)*, pp. 252–255, 2017.

46. Samuel, A.L., Some studies in machine learning using the game of checkers. *IBM J. Res. Dev.*, 3, 3, 210–229, Jul. 1959.

47. Sharma, A., Jain, A., Gupta, P., Chowdary, V., Machine learning applications for precision agriculture: A comprehensive review. *IEEE Access*, 9, 4843–4873, Jan. 2021.

48. Chu, Z. and Yu, J., 'An end-to-end model for rice yield prediction using deep learning fusion. *Comput. Electron. Agricult.*, 174, 105471, Jul. 2020.

49. Aghighi, H., Azadbakht, M., Ashourloo, D., Shahrabi, H.S., Radiom, S., Machine learning regression techniques for the silage maize yield prediction using time-series images of landsat 8 OLI. *IEEE J. Sel. Topics Appl. Earth Observ. Remote Sens.*, 11, 12, 4563–4577, Dec. 2018.

50. Cai, Y., Guan, K., Lobell, D., Potgieter, A.B., Wang, S., Peng, J., Xu, T., Asseng, S., Zhang, Y., You, L., Peng, B., Integrating satellite and climate data to predict wheat yield in Australia using machine learning approaches. *Agricult. For. Meteorol.*, 274, 144–159, Aug. 2019.

51. Kocian, A., Massa, D., Cannazzaro, S., Incrocci, L., Lonardo, S.D., Milazzo, P., Chessa, S., 'Dynamic bayesian network for crop growth prediction in greenhouses'. *Comput. Electron. Agricult.*, 169, 105167, Feb. 2020.

52. Acar, E., Ozerdem, M.S., Ustundag, B.B., Machine learning based regression model for prediction of soil surface humidity over moderately vegetated fields, in: *Proc. 8th Int. Conf. Agro-Geoinformat. (AgroGeoinformat.)*, Istanbul, Turkey, pp. 1–4, Jul. 2019.

53. Reda, R., Saffaj, T., Ilham, B., Saidi, O., Issam, K., Brahim, L., El Hadrami, E.M., A comparative study between a new method and other machine learning algorithms for soil organic carbon and total nitrogen prediction using near infrared spectroscopy. *Chemometric Intell. Lab. Syst.*, 195, 103873, Dec. 2019.

54. Andrade, R., Silva, S.H.G., Weindorf, D.C., Chakraborty, S., Faria, W.M., Mesquita, L.F., Guilherme, L.R.G., Curi, N., Assessing models for prediction of some soil chemical properties from portable X-ray fluorescence (pXRF) spectrometry data in brazilian coastal plains. *Geoderma*, 357, 113957, Jan. 2020.

55. Khanal, S., Fulton, J., Klopfenstein, A., Douridas, N., Shearer, S., Integration of high resolution remotely sensed data and machine learning techniques for spatial prediction of soil properties and corn yield. *Comput. Electron. Agricult.*, 153, 213–225, Oct. 2018.

56. Wang, X., Hu, W., Li, K., Song, L., Song, L., Modeling of soft sensor based on DBN- ELM and its application in measurement of nutrient solution composition for soilless culture, in: *Proc. IEEE Int. Conf. Saf. Produce Informatization (IICSPI)*, pp. 93–97, Chongqing, China, Dec. 2018.

57. Alizamir, M., Kisi, O., Ahmed, A.N., Mert, C., Fai, C.M., Kim, S., Kim, N.W., El-Shafie, A., "Advanced machine learning model for better prediction accuracy of soil temperature at different depths. *PloS One*, 15, 4, e0231055, Apr. 2020.

58. Diez-Sierra, J. and Jesus, M.D., Long-term rainfall prediction using atmospheric synoptic patterns in semi-arid climates with statistical and machine learning methods. *J. Hydrol.*, 586, 124789, Jul. 2020.

59. Carravilla, M.A. and Oliveira, J.F., Operations research in agriculture: Better decisions for a scarce and uncertain world. *Agris On-line Pap. Econ. Inform.*, 5, 1–10, Jun. 2013.

60. Bo, L.J., Yang, F., Fei, Z., Wang, S.R., Research on agricultural management system based on internet, vol. 5, pp. 55–56, Agriculture of Henan, China, April 2020.

61. Thakkar, U., Chachan, V., Gupta, V., Vedak, V., Basit, Y., Shah, H., Application of operations research in agriculture. *Int. J. Sci. Eng.*, 10, 10, 250–256, Oct. 2019.

62. Santos, D., M. R., L., Costa, A.M., Arenales, M.N., Santos, R.H.S., Sustainable vegetable crop supply problem. *Eur. J. Oper. Res.*, 204, 639–647, Aug, 2010.

63. Osama, S., Elkholy, M., Kansoh, R.M., Optimization of the cropping pattern in Egypt. *Alexandria Eng. J.*, 56, 4, 557–566, Dec. 2017.

64. Bhattacharya, A., A goal programming approach for developing pre-harvest forecasts of crop yield. *J. Oper. Res. Soc.*, 57, 1014–1017, Dec. 2017.

Big IoT Data Analytics in Fog Computing

Manash Kumar Mondal¹*, Riman Mandal² and Utpal Biswas¹

¹Department of Computer Science and Engineering, University of Kalyani, Kalyani, WB, India
²Department of Computer Science and Engineering, Annasaheb Dange College of Engineering and Technology, Ashta, Sangli, Maharashtra, India

Abstract

IoT data analysis is a significant role in economic growth, social development and people's life. So, IoT data analysis is the combination of artificial intelligence, machine learning and big data. Fog computing is a way of bringing to market the growing amounts of data gathered for Internet-of-Things (IoT) devices. It works by pooling the computational power from multiple nodes connected through the cloud, each node being able to support the requests generated by its IoT sensors. The more devices you add to the network, the more powerful it becomes, but it has its limits in terms of memory and processing speed. In this chapter, we have discussed a new model by combining these technical methods and it has a strong function in the effective analytics of IoT-generated big data in fog computing environments. This chapter highlights a brief introduction to fog computing, the generation of big data, sources of big data, and how fog computing is used to analyze IoT-generated big data. The chapter also covers the regions of choosing fog computing for big data analytics over the cloud. Additionally, this chapter highlights big data characteristics and various applications of big data. The fog engine is used to analyze data in the fog node.

Keywords: Big data, IoT, fog computing, big data analytics, fog-engine

12.1 Introduction

Fog computing is the future of data analytics and one of the most significant innovations in recent years. This new paradigm shifts the way we think about data storage, processing and analysis away from the traditional infrastructure

*Corresponding author: manashkumarmondal@gmail.com

Chandan Banerjee, Anupam Ghosh, Rajdeep Chakraborty and Ahmed A. Elngar (eds.) Fog Computing for Intelligent Cloud IoT Systems, (279–308) © 2024 Scrivener Publishing LLC

such as server farms to a much more distributed cloud architecture that can be managed at any scale. Fog computing is a widely used, most efficient and cost-effective approach to deploying big data analytics. With thousands of systems all operating inside the cloud, the application moves from local computations to distributed computation. This makes it feasible for large-scale dimension data mining and analysis. But the problem that remains unsolved is how to do big data analytics fast, to get insights in a short time frame.

Fog computing is a mechanism for processing data in which the information is not contained in any single place. Data is placed in another place and analyzed. This helps to make it cost-efficient as well as more secure than traditional centralized computing where all data processing occurs at a specific place. Fog computing can be used for many applications such as social media, marketing, financial services etc. Furthermore, fog computing has seen some interesting use cases such as smart cities, big data analytics, network management, etc. The third one is a graphical user interface (GUI). The GUI is needed for managing smart devices and applications [1, 2].

A typical Internet of Things system collects and exchanges data in real-time. There are three parts to an IoT system. The first one is a smart device. Smart devices like security cameras, television or other devices experience computational capabilities [3]. These devices collect data from the environments, taking inputs from the users and sharing data via the internet using IoT applications. The second one is the internet of things application. The IoT application uses machine learning or AI technology to analyze the data generated by smart devices to make proper decisions [4–6].

IoT devices produce an enormous amount of data for several reasons:

High Volume of Connected Devices
IoT networks can consist of thousands or even millions of devices that are interconnected and constantly communicating with each other. Each device generates a stream of data, which accumulates over time and leads to massive amounts of data.

High Frequency of Data Collection
IoT devices often collect data at high frequencies, such as every second or even every millisecond. This means that data is generated rapidly, leading to large volumes of data being collected in a short period.

Richness of Data
IoT devices can generate a variety of data types, including sensor data, video data, audio data, location data, and more. This data can be highly

detailed and provide valuable insights, but it also requires a lot of storage and processing power.

Continuous Data Generation
IoT devices are always on and always collecting data, generating a continuous stream of data that can quickly add up.

Edge Computing
Numerous IoT devices are furnished with sensors and computing capabilities that allow them to process and analyze data at the network's edge, instead of sending it all to a central location for processing. This guides to better data being produced at the edge and the need for more storage and processing capabilities. Edge computing cloud computing and machine learning are the three main technologies that are widely used in IoT systems. Edge computing corresponds that the technology that makes smart devices more computationally capable. In this edge computing paradigm, smart devices are not only used for sending and receiving data but also used for computing purposes. It reduces the data transfer latency and decreases response time. In IoT systems, cloud computing is used for data repository and managing of IoT devices. It also provides data access to all other smart devices over the network. Machine learning represents the collection of software or algorithm which is used to process the data to make a suitable judgement in real-time [2, 7].

To process and analyze big data, fog computing and cloud computing are two essential concepts that can be used. However, in some scenarios, fog computing may offer advantages over cloud computing. Here are some reasons why:

Lower Latency
The most useful feature that makes the fog an edge over the cloud is latency. Fog computing brings the computing power closer to the edge devices of the grid, which can decrease the latency of data transfer and processing. This is particularly critical for real-time applications, such as autonomous vehicles or industrial IoT, where milliseconds can make a significant difference.

Bandwidth Optimization
It is one of the most useful features of fog computing. By processing data locally, the fog computing can decrease the quantity of data that requires to be transferred to the cloud for processing. This can help optimize network

bandwidth and reduce the cost of data transfer, especially for applications that generate large volumes of data.

Security
Fog computing can offer improved security compared to cloud computing, as data can be computed and analyzed locally (near the sources) without transmitting over the internet. This can be particularly important for applications that deal with sensitive data, such as healthcare or financial services.

Resilience
Fog computing can provide greater resilience in the face of network disruptions or failures, as the local processing capability can continue to function even when connectivity to the cloud is lost.

Overall, fog computing is more promising than cloud computing for big data analytics in scenarios where low latency, bandwidth optimization, security, and resilience are critical factors. However, it is essential to mention that fog computing is not a substitute for cloud computing but relatively a complementary technology that can work alongside cloud computing to deliver more efficient and effective big data processing and analysis.

The rest of the sections of the chapter are organized as follows: Section 12.2 contains some related studies regarding big data analytics in fog computing. The main motivation behind the writing of this chapter describes in Section 12.3. Section 12.4 gives a concise idea of fog computing, the characteristics of fog computing, the fog nodes and various deployment and services models. A brief discussion of big data and various sources for the generation of big data discusses in Section 12.5. Section 12.6 illustrates the details of big data analytics in fog computing. Ultimately, the conclusion and future dimensions of research are covered in Section 12.7.

12.2   Literature Review

A significant amount of literature has been published on big IoT data analytics in fog computing. These studies contribute a lot to this literature. The cloud is one of the prominent options for analyzing big data. Most of the investigation regarding big data analytics is carried out in cloud computing environments [8–11]. Big data analytics (BDA) using machine learning (ML) and cloud computing is proposed in the article. Large amounts of data are produced by smart homes, the article proposed a big data analytics system using fog computing [12]. To provide the services of smart cities with a huge number of infrastructure management using hierarchical fog computing is proposed in studies [13, 14]. FogGIS a fog computing-based framework is proposed for geo-positional data mining and analytics [15]. FogData a telehealth monitoring model using fog computing is suggested by Dubey *et al.* [16]. A multiple-tier fog computing is proposed for large-scale data analytics in various smart city applications. The study used the Raspberry Pi system for deploying the fog model for resource management and tackling problems like pollution, traffic management, public budget, and health data. A novel state-of-the-art regarding fog computing is highlighted in article [17]. Liu *et al.* suggested an outline of fog computing and explain several architectures and cover many latency-sensitive applications [18]. This paper provided an outline of fog computing and its application to IoT. The authors discussed various fog computing architectures and the challenges and opportunities of using fog computing for IoT data analytics [19]. The authors discussed various smart city scenarios, such as traffic management, energy management, and public safety, and how fog computing can enable real-time data analytics and decision-making [20]. Ahmed *et al.* proposed a fog computing-based framework for real-time IoT data analysis. The researchers described a case study involving a smart healthcare system and demonstrate how fog computing can provide timely and accurate insights for healthcare professionals [21]. Collectively this literature supports the importance of the study. These papers demonstrate the potential of fog computing for IoT data analytics and provide insights into the challenges and opportunities of using fog computing in various IoT applications. The researchers described a case study involving a power plant and demonstrated how fog computing can reduce maintenance costs and downtime by enabling real-time predictive analytics [22].

12.3   Motivation

The Internet of Things (IoT) is nothing but a device that attaches to networks that allow communication and exchange of information with other intelligent devices via the internet. The Internet of Things (IoT) has been one of the numerous exciting developments in recent years. This technology has allowed companies to reimagine how and what they do, mainly for their business strategy. With IoT and cloud technologies, businesses can create better products, improve customer relationships and increase revenue.

The IoT becomes a part of daily life. IoT provides several applications including agriculture, consumer applications, healthcare, Insurance, Manufacturing, Retail, transportation, Utilities/Energy, traffic monitoring, hospitality, water supply, fleet management, smart pollution control, smart cities etc.

Intelligent Internet of things devices produces an enormous amount of data. Generally, a massive amount of data refers to as big data. Using cloud computing generally analysts such big data for better decision makings. The main motivation behind this chapter that how such big data can be analyzed near the source. Cloud computing encountered some limitations like data loss or theft, data leakage, service hijacking, DoS attack, technology vulnerabilities high latency time etc. Cloud computing generally follows *pay-as-you-go* service model or subscription-based model. Although, deploying a fog environment requires a high establishment cost but in long run, it will be more cost-effective than the cloud [23, 24].

The motivation behind writing a chapter on IoT-generated Big Data analytics using fog computing is driven by the growing importance of these technologies in modern business operations. With the proliferation of IoT devices, organizations are producing massive amounts of data that can be analyzed to gain valuable insights into customer behaviour, product performance, and operational efficiency.

However, processing and analyzing this data can be a significant challenge, as it requires powerful computing resources and high-speed connectivity. Moreover, the conventional approach of processing data in the cloud can lead to latency and network congestion, which can impede real-time insights and hinder decision-making.

Fog computing has emerged as a profitable resolution to these challenges, by bringing computing aids nearer to the boundary of the network, where the data is generated by some intelligent devices. However, in processing data near the edge, fog computing can reduce latency and network congestion, enabling faster and more efficient data analysis. Moreover, fog computing can also help diminish the cost of IoT Big Data analytics by minimizing the need for data transmission and storage.

The potential advantages of IoT-generated big data analytics using fog computing are vast and include enhanced customer experience, improved operational efficiency, and increased innovation. As more organizations adopt IoT technologies and generate massive amounts of data, the need for efficient and cost-effective data processing and analysis will only continue to grow.

Thus, the motivation behind writing a chapter on IoT big data analytics using fog computing is to deliver a comprehensive overview of this important and emerging field and to highlight the potential benefits and challenges associated with its adoption. By doing so, we hope to contribute to a better insight into the role that big IoT data analytics and this fog computing can play in driving innovation and improving business operations.

12.4   Fog Computing

A layered approach called fog computing enables universal access to shared computational resources. The concept of fog computing consists of computational units called fog nodes, placed halfway between intelligent end-edge-devices and the topmost layered cloud services, creates it more effortless to develop dispersed, latency-aware apps and services [25]. The fog nodes support a standard data management and communication framework and it is also context-aware. They can be grouped either vertically (to promote solitariness), horizontally (to facilitate association), or in relation to the latency space between fog nodes and the intelligent end devices. The fog computing reduces the time it takes for subsidized apps to receive requests and respond, and it gives end devices access to regional computing resources and, if necessary, grid connectivity to centralized services [26, 27].

Figure 12.1 illustrates a layered architecture of fog computing in the larger context of a cloud-based environment supporting intelligent edge devices. Both the centralized (cloud) service and fog computing are not thought to be necessary layers for these ecosystems in order for smart end-device capabilities to be supported. Depending on the best method for enabling end device functionality, various use case scenarios could have various architectural designs. The decision to use this model was made with the goal of accurately portraying a complicated architecture that uses fog computing services [28, 29].

Cloud computing can offer significant benefits for IoT data analytics, such as scalability, flexibility, and cost savings. However, there are also limitations to consider, including:

Latency: IoT devices often generate large volumes of data in real time, which requires fast processing to provide timely insights. However, cloud computing can introduce latency due to data transmission and processing delays, which can affect the accuracy and relevance of the analytics results.

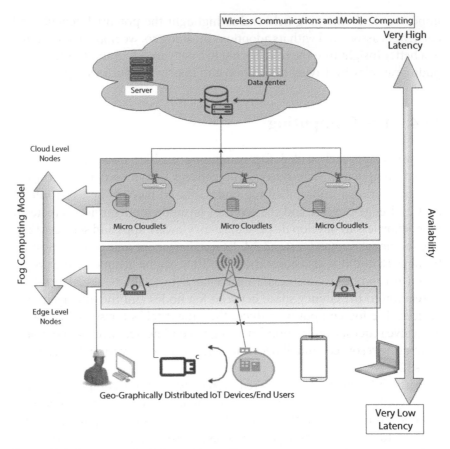

Figure 12.1 Fog computing in larger perspective.

Network bandwidth: IoT devices can produce a huge amount of data, which requires high bandwidth networks to transport data to the cloud for processing. However, many IoT devices operate in remote areas or have limited network connectivity, which can result in data transmission issues.

Security: IoT devices often collect sensitive data, such as private or economic statements, which requires secure storage and processing. However, cloud computing introduces potential security risks, such as data breaches and unauthorized access.

Data privacy: IoT devices may generate personal or sensitive data that is subject to privacy regulations, such as GDPR or CCPA. Cloud computing introduces the possibility of data exposure or unauthorized sharing, which can result in legal or reputational consequences.

Cost: Cloud computing can be expensive, especially for large-scale IoT deployments that require high-performance computing resources. The cost of keeping and processing enormous volumes of data can quickly add up, which can impact the ROI of IoT analytics projects.

To mitigate these limitations, organizations may need to consider hybrid cloud solutions that combine on-premises and cloud-based computing resources, or edge computing solutions that process data locally on the IoT devices themselves.

12.4.1   Fog Node

The fog node is a crucial component in fog architecture. The fog nodes provide computing resources to smart endpoints or access networks through close connections. Routers, switches, gateways, servers, etc. are examples of physical fog nodes, whereas virtual fog nodes are examples of virtualized switches, virtualization software, cloudlets, etc. A fog node is aware of its cluster's physical location as well as its logical position inside it. Moreover, the fog nodes deliver several types of data governance and communication services as needed between the edge layers of the network, where end smart devices are located, and the centralized (cloud) computing resources. To serve the service, fog nodes can be set up as independent fog nodes that are in contact with one another, or they can be unified to form groups that offer horizontal scalability over-dispersed geo-locations via mirroring or extension mechanisms [30]. To deploy a specific fog computing facility, the fog nodes might work centrally or decentralized.

Fog computing is a fully distributed computational instance that expands cloud computing to the edge or middle layer of the network, closer to where data is generated and consumed. It provides a service model that is created to support the deployment of applications and assistance in distributed circumstances, such as the IoT, where there are large numbers of connected devices generating data that requires to be analyzed in real-time [31].

The fog computing service model is based on the principles of resource sharing, virtualization, and service-oriented architecture. It consists of the following components [32]:

Fog Nodes: These are the physical computing instruments that make up the fog computing infrastructure. They can be any type of computing device, such as routers, networking switches, gateways, or servers that have the sufficient processing power, memory, and storage capacity to support fog computing applications.

Fog Services: These are the software applications and services that are deployed on fog nodes. They can be custom-built applications or off-the-shelf software that provides a specific functionality, such as data analytics, machine learning, or security.

Fog Broker: This is a software component that acts as an intermediary between fog nodes and cloud services. It helps to manage the allocation of fog services across the fog computing infrastructure and provides a unified interface for users and applications to access fog services.

Fog Orchestrator: This is a software component that manages the deployment, configuration, and monitoring of fog services. It ensures that fog services are deployed to the appropriate fog nodes based on their resource necessities and workload characteristics.

The fog computing service model provides several benefits, including lower latency, reduced network bandwidth, improved security, and greater resilience. It enables the deployment of real-time applications and benefits that need fast processing and analysis of huge volumes of data, while also providing a more cost-effective and scalable alternative to traditional cloud computing.

12.4.2   Characteristics of Fog Computing

Fog computing can be differentiated from other computer paradigms by the following six features. An intelligent end-device or Internet of Things user does not necessarily have to utilize every feature when using fog computing benefits.

Low latency and location awareness Generally real-time applications require a low latency system. Fog computing achieves low latency by using the location awareness feature. The logical location of edge devices is known to the fog node, it is associated with the overall system context. The end device may contain some sensor or actuator. Due to the clear understanding of each device's location for communicating with those devices with a low latency path. It makes an optimal path between end devices and the fog node before transferring data. Location awareness is a great feature that helps the system to achieve the low latency feature.

Geographically distributed The services and applications that fog computing is designed to support require widely dispersed installations that may yet be uniquely identified by their geographic location, in sharp contrast to the more centralized cloud. For instance, fog computing will actively participate in supplying high-quality data streaming features to moving automobiles via proxy servers and access points strategically placed along roadways and railroads.

Heterogeneity It enables the collection and analysis of data in various forms obtained through a variety of network communication methods.

Interoperability and federation Being a distributed system the fog system allows federation. The collaboration of several suppliers is necessary for the seamless provision of some services (real-time streaming services are an excellent example). As a result, users must be united across fields and fog computing elements must be able to communicate with one another.

Real-time communication Nowadays all IoT applications become a time-sensitive applications. Time-sensitive applications need to respond in a moment. Applications of fog computing entail real-time interactions as opposed to batch processing methods. In fog computing data is processed at the prime component called fog nodes. The fog node is generally placed near the end devices. Whereas the cloud is not suitable for this type of application. Due to the implementation of hardware near the end devices, it processes faster than the cloud.

Agility and scalability Agility means how quickly and easily data move from the source and the destination. Whereas scalability defines the ability of a computing process to be used or produced in a range of capabilities. Fog computing is adaptable in nature, providing elastic computing, pooling of hardware resources, data-load management, and variations in the network state, to name a few of the supported flexible services, at the cluster level.

Some additional features of fog computing are

Wireless access In general, fog computing is utilized in wired systems, however, the extensive use of wireless sensors in the IoTs necessitates distributed analytics and computing. Fog computing is hence a perfect fit for wireless IoT access networks.

Mobility Various fog computing applications must be capable to interface with moving portable devices directly, thus they must support mobility approaches like the LISP, which separates host identification from location originality along with necessitating a distributed directory approach.

Fog computing provides a platform for deploying IoT applications in a more efficient and cost-effective way than traditional cloud computing.

There are several reasons why fog computing is suitable for IoT applications:

Low Latency IoT applications require low latency because they often involve real-time interactions between devices. Fog computing reduces latency by processing data closer to the location where data is created, at the network's edge.

Reduced Network Congestion With fog computing, data processing is distributed between the edge and the cloud, which reduces network congestion and lowers the amount of data that needs to be sent to the cloud for processing.

Improved Security IoT devices are often vulnerable to cyber attacks, and fog computing can provide an auxiliary layer of security by allowing data to be processed and stored locally, reducing the quantity of data that requires to be transferred over the network.

Cost-Effective With fog computing, data processing and storage can be distributed between the edge and the cloud, which reduces the demand for expensive data centers and infrastructure.

Increased Scalability Fog computing allows IoT applications to scale more easily by distributing data processing and storage across a larger number of devices.

Overall, fog computing is a suitable platform for deploying IoT applications due to its low latency, reduced network congestion, improved security, cost-effectiveness, and increased scalability.

12.4.3   Attributes of Fog Node

Fog nodes must support one or more of the following qualities to make it easier to create a fog computing capability that demonstrates the six key traits listed.

Autonomy The fog nodes can function autonomously at the single node or cluster of nodes level, making local decisions.

Hierarchical cluster The fog nodes follow hierarchical systems, wherein a continuum of interconnected service functions is provided by several service levels.

Heterogeneity The fog nodes are available in a range of form factors and can be set up in a combination of settings.

Manageability Complex systems that are capable of doing the majority of ordinary tasks automatically organize and orchestrate the fog nodes.

Programmability Programmability is a great feature of any system. Customization is an obvious feature for better flexibility. Fog nodes can naturally be programmed at various levels by a variety of parties, including network administrators, subject matter experts, equipment suppliers, and end users.

12.4.4   Fog Computing Service Model

Fog computing provides a scalable and efficient way to process data and run applications in a decentralized way. Like cloud computing, fog computing also supports service-based models. The fog computing architecture can be implemented in several layers of network topology. The following service model types can be used. Figure 12.2 depicts the service model architecture of fog computing.

Software as a Service (SaaS) It is the topmost layer of the service-layered architecture. Software as a service delivers software services to the user. The user can only use the software in this layer. Platform and infrastructure layers are abstract at this layer. Utilizing the apps of the fog service provider operating on a cluster of confederate fog nodes maintained by the provider is the capacity offered to the customer of the fog service. This form of service indicates that the end-device or smart devices access the service as applications of fog node's using a thin client junction or an application program interface (API), akin to cloud computing's software as a service. With the probable exception of a small number of user-specific application configuration parameters, the end users have no grant of access to the network components, operating systems, servers, storage units, or even the other specific operation abilities of the underlying fog node. In this model, the fog computing infrastructure provides software applications to the users over the network. The applications are typically hosted and managed by the fog computing infrastructure, and the users can access them using various devices and platforms.

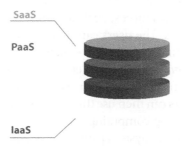

Figure 12.2 Fog node architectural service model.

Platform as a Service (*PaaS*) PaaS is the second layer of the service-layered architecture. The underlying layer of PaaS is infrastructure as a service layer. PaaS provide a platform base related environment to the users. In simple form, the user got key access to the virtual machine (VM). Users can customize the platform as per their needs. These layer users are also capable of deploying the SaaS layer in the platform layer. The features of SaaS can be achieved by installing the required software. The platform as a service capability offered to the fog service consumer is comparable to cloud computing and enables the deployment of customer-created or developed applications utilizing programming languages, services, libraries, and equipment endorsed by the fog service provider onto the platforms of federated fog nodes forming a cluster. The customer of the fog service does not manipulate or have authority over the network, servers, operating systems, or storage of the underlying fog platform(s), but does have control over the distributed applications and perhaps some arrangement options for the app hosting environment. In this model, the fog computing infrastructure provides a platform for the users to develop, deploy, and control their applications without worrying about the underlying infrastructure. The platform typically includes tools and libraries for application development, as well as middleware for managing application deployment and scaling.

Infrastructure as a Service (*IaaS*) SaaS is the bottom layer of the service-layered architecture. The IaaS users have no restrictions on any platform or service. Using the infrastructure of the fog nodes constituting a federated cluster, the fog service customer is given the capacity to require processing units, massive amounts of storage, networks, and other basic computing aids. The customer is capable to deploy and execute any application software, which can contain operating systems and specific application software, such as cloud computing IaaS services. The consumer has limited control over some networking components but does not manage or control the fog nodes cluster's underlying architecture. Rather, the client has full authority over the installed application softeners, storage, and operating systems. In this model, the fog computing infrastructure provides virtualized computing resources, such as processing power, storage, and networking, to the users. The users can then deploy their applications and services on these resources and manage them as per their requirements.

Data as a Service (*DaaS*) In this model, the fog computing infrastructure provides access to data from various sources, such as sensors, IoT devices, and cloud services. The users can then use this data for analysis, machine learning, or other purposes. The fog computing infrastructure typically provides data storage, processing, and analysis capabilities for efficient data management. The following advantages come from using DaaS (Data as a Service):

Agility The DaaS is based on a service-oriented architecture (SOA), and it offers a lot of flexibility when it comes to accessing vital data through cloud or fog services. Data may be accessed quickly thanks to the architecture that supports them. Changes to the data are also simple to implement when the data structure needs to be altered or when there are geographic requirements.

High-quality data The DaaS provider ensures that consumers have access to high-quality data by enforcing a strict method of data control and processing (collection, purification, accumulation, and enrichment).

Simple access The DaaS paradigm enables simple access to data via a variety of devices, including desktops PC, tablets, laptops, and smartphones, wherever and whenever they are needed.

Preventing provider lock-in with DaaS The DaaS paradigm makes it possible to move data quickly from one platform to another.

Function as a Service (FaaS) In this model, the fog computing infrastructure provides a server-less environment for running code snippets or functions. The users can upload their code to the fog computing infrastructure, and the infrastructure automatically handles the scaling and execution of the code as per the incoming requests.

12.4.5   Fog Computing Architecture

Instead of processing data in data centers as in the traditional cloud computing paradigm, this new extent of big data necessitates processing the data close to the sensors at the edge. The fog computing model allows for rapid control loops because the data is not transferred to the cloud it is generally processed at the edge.

Figure 12.3 depicts a four-layer fog computing design. The sensing network is located at Layer 4 of the network, which has a lot of sensory nodes. These sensors are low-cost, extremely dependable, and non-invasive, allowing them to be widely installed in different general infrastructures to track changes in their state from time to time.

Be aware that these sensors provide enormous sensing data streams that are spatially dispersed and must be handled as a unit [13].

The edge nodes transmit the unprocessed data to the third layer, which is made up of several low-power and highly-performance computing nodes or intelligent edge devices. Low-powered smart edge device are various devices, including desktops PC, tablets, laptops, and smartphones, wherever and whenever it covers a small community or area. The output generated by the edge device includes moving data quickly from one platform

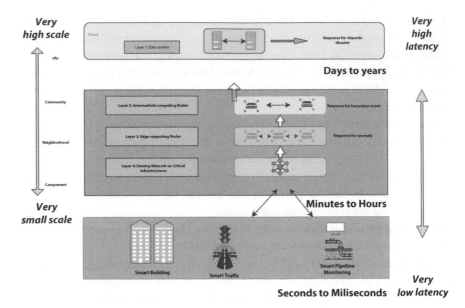

Figure 12.3 Fog computing architecture.

to other possible outcomes to a middle computing node at its subsequent higher layer, and the second is straightforward and speedy response controls to regional infrastructure to react to disjoined and minor hazards to the overseas infrastructure elements.

In order to identify potentially dangerous events, Layer 2 comprises a number of intermediary computational nodes that are individually associated with a pool of end-edge devices at Layer 3. When dangerous events are discovered, the infrastructure can be controlled quickly [33].

Layers 2 and 3 immediate feedback controls serve as localized "reflex" judgements to avert probable harm. For more intricate and extensive behaviour analysis and circumstances observation, the top layer receives reports on all data analysis findings from the bottom two layers.

In conclusion, the four-layered fog computing framework facilitates rapid reaction at neighborhood, community, and metropolis levels, offering high computing enactment and intelligence in the hereafter.

12.4.6   Data Flow and Control Flow in Fog Architecture

Solving the problems of huge data processing, the layered fog computing architecture enables high-performance computing and connectivity. It also delivers quick responses. It is demonstrated that data analysis workloads can be worked parallel across vast edge devices and computing nodes. Since only lightweight computations are carried out by each edge device or middle computer node, their extensive parallel utilization provides high-performance computing capacity for citywide data processing. However, the main benefit of such parallel computing systems is their simplicity in balancing throughput and loading all computer nodes and edge devices to prevent potential computing bottlenecks. The data and control flow enable architecture is depicted in Figure 12.4.

At Layer 4, an extended number of sensors are used to generate an enormous amount of data. The hierarchically dispersed edge devices and intermediary computer nodes at Layers 3 and 2 only upload high-level data depiction while carrying out interrelated computing operations, which can significantly decrease the amount of data transported to the cloud [34]. In order to exchange data with their neighbors, sensor nodes or computing nodes can communicate with other nodes in the same layer. Depending on the exact uses of a smart city, conveyed information between neighboring levels and within a layer may be wireless or wired. Wireless networks have numerous crucial uses in isolated and portable observation, and wired networks can offer stable and dependable connections between various devices. Additionally, when abnormalities and dangerous occurrences are discovered, the computing machines in each layer can send command signals (dashed line) in a convenient fashion to the depicted infrastructures to guarantee their protection (see Figure 12.4). A large number of computers are linked together at the top layer to create clouds, which are used for data storage and city-scale computation [35, 36].

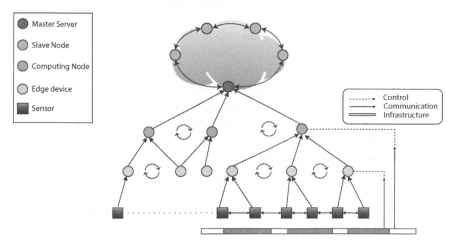

Figure 12.4 Data and control flow for layered fog computing architecture.

12.4.7   Fog Deployment Models

The following deployment strategies are also supported because fog computing is recognized and described as an addition to the conventional cloud-based computing model:

Public fog Users can avail of the services without restrictions. The fog node is made available for open use by everyone. A business, academic, or governmental body, or an assortment of them, may own, administer, and run it. It is present on the grounds of the fog service supplier. The public fog node is nearly similar to the public cloud.

Private fog This fog node is designated only for use by one company with numerous consumers (e.g., business units.) It may establish on or off premises and be owned. Private fog nodes are controlled and handled by the self-organization, third-party organizations, or some collaboration of both (self and third-party). It provides the same functionality and services as the private cloud.

Community fog This fog node is designated for service only by a particular group of clients from companies with similar concerns (such as tasks, safety needs, guidelines, and obedience issues). It may be owned, controlled, and run by one or more community associations, a third party, or a combination. It may also be located on or off-site. Community fog is sometimes identical to community cloud.

Hybrid fog This fog node is made up of two or more different fog nodes (public or private, community), each of which is distinct and continues to exist as a separate entity, but which are connected by standardized or proprietary technology that allows for the portability of data and applications.

12.5   Big Data

Terabytes of data are gathered by businesses, organizations, and research facilities from a variety of origins, including emails, social media, survey answers from various customers, call logs, click-stream data from the Internet, web server logs, and sensors. Massive amounts of continuously flowing unstructured, semi-structured, or organized data are referred to as "big data" in businesses. The idea of big data has been around for a while, and most organizations today are aware that they may use analytics to their data to generate understandings that can be put to use. Advanced analytics for big data includes complicated applications with elements like statistical models, what if analyses, and predictive analytics that are supported by high-performance analytics platforms. Business analytics is used to provide basic insights into business operations and performance. Large volumes of data are analyzed using big data analytics to find undiscovered patterns, correlations, and other insights. Both batch and streamlined methods can be used to process big data. This indicates that for various applications, data analysis and result generation are based on the store-and-process approach. Many time-sensitive applications, like stock market data processing, generate data continually and anticipate the processed result in real time [37].

12.5.1 What is Big Data?

A data set is a collection of data values that are related in meaningful and specific ways. Big Data is an umbrella term for structured, unstructured and semi-structured data sets. Big data is a massive data set which provides valuable information to organizations in order to run businesses efficiently.

Big data can be described as a set of large, complex structured and unstructured data items that are readily available, but too voluminous or diverse to be stored or manipulated with conventional database systems. Thus, the processing of big data requires advanced high-performance computing (HPC) capabilities and technologies [38].

Big data refers to enormous amounts of information that may or may not be organized in a specific way. Typically, in big data, the individuals involved are less concerned with identifying each piece of information as unique and individually important, but instead, seek to identify patterns using these data.

The application of big data has been one of the most significant technological innovations in recent decades. It is expected to be a key factor in the coming expansion of artificial intelligence (AI) and machine learning (ML) techniques, which are also anticipated to guide to further refinements in many other scopes such as health care and natural or social science research [39].

Big data includes a broad range of applications across different industries and domains, including:

Healthcare: Big data is used in healthcare to enhance patient results, decrease expenses, and optimize healthcare delivery. It can help identify high-risk patients, predict disease outbreaks, and personalize treatments based on individual patient data.

Finance: Big data is used in finance to analyze market trends, manage risks, and detect fraudulent activities. It can help financial institutions make informed investment decisions and improve customer experience.

Retail: Big data is used in retail to analyze consumer behavior, predict sales trends, and optimize supply chain management. It can help retailers personalize marketing campaigns, improve inventory management, and increase customer satisfaction.

Manufacturing: Big data is used in manufacturing to optimize production processes, reduce costs, and improve quality control. It can help manufacturers detect defects in real-time, predict maintenance needs, and optimize production schedules.

Transportation: Big data is used in transportation to optimize routes, reduce congestion, and improve safety. It can help transportation companies predict traffic patterns, optimize logistics, and improve fuel efficiency.

Education: Big data is used in education to personalize learning experiences, improve student outcomes, and optimize educational programs. It can help educators identify at-risk students, predict student performance, and improve curriculum design.

Energy and Utilities: Big data is used in energy and utilities to optimize energy consumption, reduce costs, and improve sustainability. It can help utility companies monitor energy usage, predict demand, and optimize energy production.

These are just a few examples of how big data is being used to solve complex problems and drive innovation across different industries. The possible applications of big data are virtually limitless, and as the amount of data persists to increase, its impact will only become more significant.

12.5.2   Source of Big Data

As per McKinsey Global Institute, the potential source of big data includes [40]:

Public sector: The governments and other non-governmental organizations promote digital systems. They move to digital platforms for creating transparency, data accessibility, better data discovery, and performance improvements making decisions for product services-related activity. It is one of the main sources of big data in recent days.

Manufacturing: The manufacturing industry generates and analytics big data for efficient demand prediction, supply chain management, sales support, production operations etc.

Personal location data: Personal location data refers to the data generated by each person's geographical location using GPS. That data is used by Geo tagged advertising, for emergency purposes, smart urban planning etc.

Retail: Retail industry generates a huge amount of data every single second. By using this data the organization analyze store behaviour, labor management, product placement strategies etc.

Healthcare: Healthcare sector is one of the finest sources of big data generation. Nowadays data is everywhere in the medical field like patient profiles, clinical decision support data, and analysis of diseases by pattern recognition, performance-based price options etc.

12.5.3   Characteristic of Big Data

Big data is generally characterized by the following four attributes, commonly referred to as the "4 Vs of Big Data":

Volume: Big data refers to very large data sets, typically in the terabytes or petabytes range. This vast amount of data often requires specialized hardware and software tools to store, manage, and process.

Velocity: Big data is often generated and collected at high speed and in real-time, such as data from sensors, social media feeds, or financial transactions. This requires fast processing and analysis to provide timely insights.

Variety: Big data comes in many forms, including structured, semi-structured, and unstructured data. This data may be generated from a variety of sources, such as text, images, audio, or video. This variety of data requires flexible and adaptable tools to process and analyze it effectively.

Veracity: Big data is often characterized by its quality and accuracy, which can vary depending on the source and collection methods. Big data may contain errors, inconsistencies, or biases that can affect the analysis and interpretation of the data. It is essential to validate and verify the accuracy of the data before making any decisions based on it.

In addition to these four characteristics, big data may also exhibit the following characteristics:

Variability: Big data may exhibit high variability or fluctuation over time, making it challenging to analyze and interpret.

Complexity: Big data may be complex, with many interrelated variables and relationships, making it challenging to model and analyze.

Privacy and Security: Big data may contain sensitive or confidential information, which requires appropriate security measures to protect against

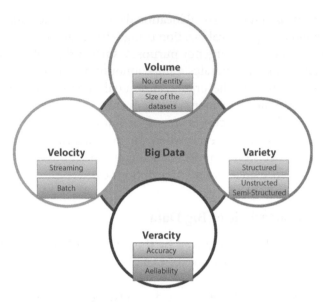

Figure 12.5 Characteristic of big data.

unauthorized access or disclosure. Figure 12.5 depicts the characteristics of big data.

12.6   Big Data Analytics Using Fog Computing

"Big data" is the phrase utilized to define the vast quantities of unstructured, semistructured, or organized data that are constantly flowing through and around companies. Enormous amounts of data are gathered by businesses, organizations, and research institutes from a wide range of sources, such as social networking sites, consumer emails and questionnaire replies, telephone records, Internet user behaviour data, IoT devices, and sensors. The idea of big data has been around for a while; currently, the majority of enterprises are aware that they may use analytics to big data to obtain useful ideas. Large volumes of data are processed using big data analytics to find undiscovered patterns, relationships, and other truths. Both batch and streamlined methods may be used to analyze big data. Many applications use store-and-process schemes to analyze and produce results from data. Some real-time applications regenerate a mass of data continuously and anticipate the possible result in a real-time manner like health data, stock market data etc.

Big data analytics has some advantages. Firstly, quick and efficient decision-making is one of the excellent advantages of big data analytics. Secondly, discovering new opportunities to improve business leads to higher profit. Finally, new services and products can be introduced based on data analytics results.

Typical big data analytics consists of several components like a platform, storage scheme, data management scheme, core analytics and its operations, add-on tools, and presentation. Hadoop is the most popular platform that acts as an underlying foundation of core analytics. It acts like a big data processing engine [41].

Big data analytics is a complicated analytical job on massive data. Figure 12.6 highlights a typical outflow of big data processing [42]. Data collection from numerous sources is done in the first step. The second step is responsible for data cleaning. This step requires a large processing time additionally this step reduces the data size by discarding impurities, missing values and redundant data. It also detects and removes inconsistencies from data. As a result, the next step requires less effort and time for data analytics [43]. Data is stored in a storage database before processing. Generally, raw data is unstructured data, before processing it is mandatory

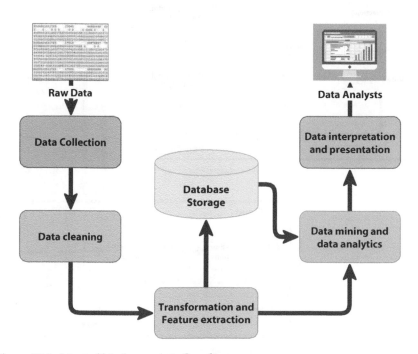

Figure 12.6 A typical big data analytic flow diagram.

to transform the data into semi-structured or structured data. Data processing is one of the most crucial jobs of data mining. How to deal with the data, and what kind of information need to be extracted from the data set, are determined by a rule-based model [44]. To discover knowledge from the data, the job of data analysts comes into account. They run several queries, machine learning algorithms, and other techniques to visualize the data as per requirements and extract information from them.

Fog engine support complete solution data analytics near the data sources device and, exchange information among other devices and the cloud. Figure 12.7 shows data transmission among the fog engines and the cloud. Generally, the data generated from the different sources are gathered, cleaned and processed at the fog-engine on-premise of data source devices. But when data become significantly large and the fog engine is unable to process the data, it transfers the data to the cloud.

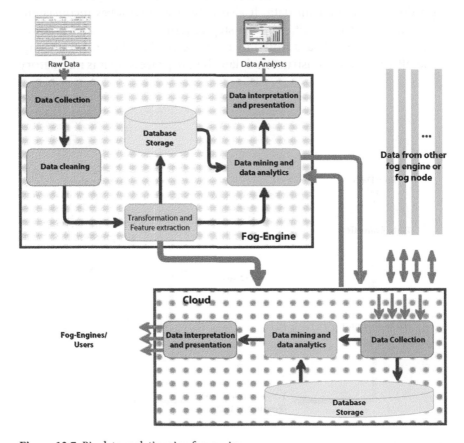

Figure 12.7 Big data analytic using fog-engine.

In Figure 12.7, the data collection step of the cloud collects and integrates the data from all the fog-engine. Data can be stored in the database for future use. After mining the data knowledge can be exchanged between the fog engine and the cloud. Real-time applications like continuous monitoring require real-time processing. So, that kind of analytical model can be deployed in the fog engine. Although the fog-engine limited computing capabilities and storage capacity than cloud. Fog-engine may consist of different types of hardware such as FPGA, and graphics processing units, the multi-core processor for real-time processing. Cloud is not capable of real-time processing due to several dependencies like location, bandwidth, latency etc. Finally, process information sent back to fog engines or users from the cloud through proper channels.

12.7   Conclusion

In conclusion, IoT big data analytics is a critical component of modern business operations, providing valuable insights into customer behaviour, product performance, and operational efficiency. However, processing and analyzing large amounts of IoT data can be a challenging task that requires powerful computing resources and high-speed connectivity.

Fog computing has appeared as an optimal solution to address the challenges of IoT big data analytics, by bringing computing resources nearer to the edge of the network, where the IoT data is generated. By processing data closer to the origin, fog computing reduces latency and network congestion, enabling faster and more efficient data analysis.

Moreover, fog computing can also help decrease the cost of IoT big data analytics by minimizing the need for data transmission and storage. By processing data at the edge, fog computing can filter out irrelevant data and only send relevant insights back to the cloud, reducing the amount of data that needs to be stored and transmitted.

Overall, IoT big data analytics using fog computing has the potential to revolutionize business operations, enabling real-time insights that can drive innovation, improve efficiency, and enhance customer experience. As more organizations adopt IoT technologies and generate massive amounts of data, fog computing is poised to become an increasingly essential tool for unlocking the full possibility of IoT big data analytics.

References

1. Dastjerdi, A.V. and Buyya, R., Fog computing: Helping the internet of things realize its potential. *Computer*, 49, 8, 112–116, 2016.
2. Dastjerdi, A.V., Gupta, H., Calheiros, R.N., Ghosh, S.K., Buyya, R., Fog computing: Principles, architectures, and applications, in: *Internet of things*, pp. 61–75, Elsevier, USA, 2016.
3. Banerjee, A., Dutta, B., Mandal, T., Chakraborty, R., Mondal, R., Blockchain in IoT and beyond: Case studies on interoperability and privacy, in: *Blockchain based Internet of Things*, pp. 113–138, Springer, Singapore, 2022.
4. Atlam, H.F., Walters, R.J., Wills, G.B., Fog computing and the internet of things: A review. *Big Data Cogn. Comput.*, 2, 2, 10, 2018.
5. Saharan, K. and Kumar, A., Fog in comparison to cloud: A survey. *Int. J. Comput. Appl.*, 122, 3, 10–12, 2015.
6. Alrawais, A., Alhothaily, A., Hu, C., Cheng, X., Fog computing for the internet of things: Security and privacy issues. *IEEE Internet Comput.*, 21, 2, 34–42, 2017.
7. Mandal, R., Mondal, M.K., Banerjee, S., Chakraborty, C., Biswas, U., A survey and critical analysis on energy generation from datacenter, in: *Data Deduplication Approaches*, pp. 203–230, Elsevier, USA, 2021.
8. Buyya, R., Ramamohanarao, K., Leckie, C., Calheiros, R.N., Dastjerdi, A.V., Versteeg, S., Big data analytics-enhanced cloud computing: Challenges, architectural elements, and future directions, in: *2015 IEEE 21st International Conference on Parallel and Distributed Systems (ICPADS)*, pp. 75–84, IEEE, 2015.
9. Trovati, M., Hill, R., Anjum, A., Zhu, S.Y., Liu, L., *Big-Data Analytics and Cloud Computing*, Springer, Derby, UK, 2015.
10. Gupta, R., Gupta, H., Mohania, M., Cloud computing and big data analytics: what is new from databases perspective?, in: *Big Data Analytics: First International Conference, BDA 2012, New Delhi, India, December 24-26, 2012. Proceedings 1*, pp. 42–61, Springer, Berlin, Heidelberg, 2012.
11. Yetis, Y., Sara, R.G., Erol, B.A., Kaplan, H., Akuzum, A., Jamshidi, M., Application of big data analytics via cloud computing, in: *2016 World Automation Congress (WAC)*, pp. 1–5, IEEE, 2016.
12. Singh, S. and Yassine, A., IoT big data analytics with fog computing for household energy management in smart grids, in: *Smart Grid and Internet of Things: Second EAI International Conference, SGIoT 2018, Niagara Falls, ON, Canada, July 11, 2018, Proceedings 2*, pp. 13–22, Springer, Rio Grande, PR, USA, 2019.
13. Tang, B., Chen, Z., Hefferman, G., Pei, S., Wei, T., He, H., Yang, Q., Incorporating intelligence in fog computing for big data analysis in smart cities. *IEEE Trans. Ind. Inf.*, 13, 5, 2140–2150, 2017.

14. Tang, B., Chen, Z., Hefferman, G., Wei, T., He, H., Yang, Q., A hierarchical distributed fog computing architecture for big data analysis in smart cities, in: *Proceedings of the ASE BigData & SocialInformatics 2015*, pp. 1–6, 2015.

15. Barik, R.K., Dubey, H., Samaddar, A.B., Gupta, R.D., Ray, P.K., Foggis: Fog computing for geospatial big data analytics, in: *2016 IEEE Uttar Pradesh Section International Conference on Electrical, Computer and Electronics Engineering (UPCON)*, pp. 613–618, IEEE, 2016.

16. Dubey, H., Yang, J., Constant, N., Amiri, A.M., Yang, Q., Makodiya, K., Fog data: Enhancing telehealth big data through fog computing, in: *Proceedings of the ASE BigData & SocialInformatics 2015*, pp. 1–6, 2015.

17. Mouradian, C., Naboulsi, D., Yangui, S., Glitho, R.H., Morrow, M.J., Polakos, P.A., A comprehensive survey on fog computing: State-of-the-art and research challenges. *IEEE Commun. Surv. Tutor.*, 20, 1, 416–464, 2017.

18. Liu, Y., Fieldsend, J.E., Min, G., A framework of fog computing: Architecture, challenges, and optimization. *IEEE Access*, 5, 25445–25454, 2017.

19. Puliafito, C., Mingozzi, E., Longo, F., Puliafito, A., Rana, O., Fog computing for the internet of things: A survey. *ACM Trans. Internet Technol. (TOIT)*, 19, 2, 1–41, 2019.

20. Vimal, S., Suresh, A., Subbulakshmi, P., Pradeepa, S., Kaliappan, M., Edge computing-based intrusion detection system for smart cities development using IoT in urban areas, in: *Internet of Things in Smart Technologies for Sustainable Urban Development*, pp. 219–237, 2020.

21. Ahmed, A., Arkian, H., Battulga, D., Fahs, A.J., Farhadi, M., Giouroukis, D., Gougeon, A., Gutierrez, F.O., Pierre, G., Souza Jr., P.R. *et al.*, Fog computing applications: Taxonomy and requirements, Cornell University, preprint arXiv:, 1, 1907, 2019, arXiv preprint arXiv:1907.11621.

22. Teoh, Y.K., Gill, S.S., Parlikad, A.K., Iot and fog computing based predictive maintenance model for effective asset management in industry 4.0 using machine learning. *IEEE Internet Things J.*, 10, 2087–2094, 2021.

23. Mandal, R., Mondal, M.K., Banerjee, S., Srivastava, G., Alnumay, W., Ghosh, U., Biswas, U., MECpVmS: An SLA aware energy-efficient virtual machine selection policy for green cloud computing. *Cluster Comput.*, 26, 651–665, 1–15, 2022.

24. Mandal, R., Mondal, M.K., Banerjee, S., Chatterjee, P., Mansoor, W., Biswas, U., PbV mSp: A priority-based Vm selection policy for Vm consolidation in green cloud computing, in: *2022 5th International Conference on Signal Processing and Information Security (ICSPIS)*, pp. 32–37, IEEE, 2022.

25. Luan, T.H., Gao, L., Li, Z., Xiang, Y., Wei, G., Sun, L., Fog computing: Focusing on mobile users at the edge, Cornell University, 1, 2015, arXiv preprint arXiv:1502.01815.

26. Mondal, M.K. and Bandyopadhyay, M., A comparative study between cloud computing and fog computing. *Brainwave: Multidiscip. J.*, 2, 1, 36–42, 2021.

27. Mondal, M.K., Mandal, R., Banerjee, S., Biswas, U., Lin, J.C.-W., Alfarraj, O., Tolba, A., Design and development of a fog-assisted elephant corridor over a railway track. *Sustainability*, 15, 7, 5944, 2023.

28. Gupta, H. and Vahid Dastjerdi, A., Ifogsim: A toolkit for modeling and simulation of resource management techniques in the internet of things, edge and fog computing environments. *Softw.: Pract. Exper.*, 47, 9, 1275–1296, 2017.

29. Mondal, M.K., Mandal, R., Banerjee, S., Sanyal, M., Ghosh, U., Biswas, U., Fog assisted tiger alarming framework for saving endangered wild life, in: *SoutheastCon 2023*, IEEE, pp. 798–803, 2023.

30. Mondal, M.K., Mandal, R., Banerjee, S., Biswas, U., Chatterjee, P., Alnumay, W., A cps based social distancing measuring model using edge and fog computing. *Comput. Commun.*, 194, 378–386, 2022.

31. Chang, Y.-C.P., Chen, S., Wang, T.-J., Lee, Y., Fog computing node system software architecture and potential applications for NB-IoT industry, in: *2016 International Computer Symposium (ICS)*, pp. 727–730, IEEE, 2016.

32. Mukherjee, M., Shu, L., Wang, D., Survey of fog computing: Fundamental, network applications, and research challenges. *IEEE Commun. Surv. Tutorials*, 20, 3, 1826–1857, 2018.

33. Bonomi, F., Milito, R., Natarajan, P., Zhu, J., Fog computing: A platform for internet of things and analytics, in: *Big Data and Internet of Things: A Roadmap for Smart Environments*, pp. 169–186, 2014.

34. Yi, S., Li, C., Li, Q., A survey of fog computing: concepts, applications and issues, in: *Proceedings of the 2015 Workshop on Mobile Big Data*, pp. 37–42, 2015.

35. Mandal, R., Mondal, M.K., Banerjee, S., Chatterjee, P., Mansoor, W., Biswas, U., Design and implementation of an SLA and energy-aware VM placement policy in green cloud computing, in: *2022 IEEE Globecom Workshops (GC Wkshps)*, IEEE, pp. 777–782, 2022.

36. Chakraborty, R., Ghosh, A., Mandal, J.K., Balamurugan, S., *Convergence of Deep Learning in Cyber-IoT Systems and Security*, John Wiley & Sons, USA, 2022.

37. Davenport, T.H., Barth, P., Bean, R. *et al.*, How'big data'is different. *MIT Sloan Manage. Rev.*, 54, 1, 22–24, 2012.

38. Daas, P.J., Puts, M.J., Buelens, B., van den Hurk, P.A., Big data as a source for official statistics. *J. Off. Stat.*, 31, 2, 249–262, 2015.

39. Fan, J. and Liu, H., Challenges of big data analysis. *Natl. Sci. Rev.*, 1, 2, 293–314, 2014.

40. Manyika, J., Chui, M., Brown, B., Bughin, J., Dobbs, R., Roxburgh, C., Hung Byers, A. *et al.*, *Big data: The Next Frontier for Innovation, Competition, and Productivity*, McKinsey Global Institute, USA, 2011.

41. White, T., *Hadoop: The Definitive Guide*, M. Loukides (Ed.), O' Reilly Media, Inc., USA, 2009.

42. Mehdipour, F., Noori, H., Javadi, B., Chapter two energy-efficient big data analytics in datacenters, in: *Advances in Computers Energy Efficiency in Data*

Centers and Clouds, vol. 100, A.R. Hurson and H. Sarbazi-Azad (Eds.), pp. 59–101, Elsevier, USA, 2016.

43. Rahm, E. and Do, H.H., Data cleaning: Problems and current approaches. *IEEE Data Eng. Bull.*, 23, 4, 3–13, 2000.

44. Analytics, B.D., Extract, transform, and load big data with apache hadoop, Intel White paper, Big Data, 1, 1–8, 2013.

13

IOT-Based Patient Monitoring System in Real Time

Suparna Biswas[1]*, Tirtha Chakraborty[2], Souvik Mitra[2], Shubham Banerjee[2], Tuhin Sarkar[2] and Sourav Paul[2]

[1]Faculty of Electronics and Communication Engineering Department Guru Nanak Institute of Technology Kolkata, India
[2]Student of Electronics and Communication Engineering Department Guru Nanak Institute of Technology, Kolkata, India

Abstract

This work presents an Internet of things (IOT)-based patient monitoring system utilizing Node MCU (microcontroller unit), which is enabled with an ESP8266 chip, and two sensors' modules attached externally. These two modules are used to determine the pulse rate and temperature of the patient. With the help of Node MCU's Wi-Fi capabilities especially the ESP-12E (Wi-Fi) module, the data captured by the sensors from the patient's body are directly uploaded or fed into a cloud platform, ThingSpeak, in real time. Aside from the 24-hour patient monitoring without manpower, this system is also capable of detecting any serious abnormality in the vital signs of the patient and in real time, the doctor and nurses will be informed. Apart from that, the reading that the sensor collected from the patient can be put under study and could be analyzed remotely by a doctor.

This work would reduce the workload for medical staff or nurses in hospitals. Conventional methods that require nurses to check up each patient to record measurement of vital signs is time-consuming and hectic at times, so with this system, such data can be exported in real time. It can also be used in multiple applications and implementations in the field of medical sciences.

Keywords: IoT, Node MCU, ThingSpeak, Wi-Fi, patient monitoring

*Corresponding author: suparna.biswas@gnit.ac.in

Chandan Banerjee, Anupam Ghosh, Rajdeep Chakraborty and Ahmed A. Elngar (eds.) Fog Computing for Intelligent Cloud IoT Systems, (309–330) © 2024 Scrivener Publishing LLC

13.1   Introduction

As we know, doctors and nurses are always running in a hurry to save lives and improve patient conditions. In the last 2 years, we have seen that in most hospitals, there has been a shortage of doctors, nurses, and medical equipment due to COVID-19 pandemic. Sometimes 24-hour observation of somepatients is very much required at the severe stages and in this crisis period, sometimes, it also happens that numerous patients are required to be observed by the medical staff at a time. But due to the crisis in the number of nurses and doctors, it has become unmanageable and had often led to death at the height of COVID-19.

Datuk, the health director of the Kuching, Sarawak, conveyed his concern for the ratio of nurse to patient [1]. He mentioned that this ratio of nurses to patients in 2015 was one nurse to 250 patients [1]. This ratio of nurse to patient is too large a value and it is a matter of concern. A new or modified system needs to be implemented to complete nurses' work in an efficient way and save time. There are some vital parameters usually checked as important measurements of the patient's body. These vital parameters are weight, height, blood pressure, pulse rate, and body temperature [2, 3], which are needed every monitoring time. In every hospital, we have seen that to check these parameters, a health care professional is always required. It is the basic drawback of a health monitoring system. This drawback can be solved by the integration of IOT with the health monitoring system [4, 5].

The term IOT indicates the collective network of different connected devices or sensors and the technology that provides communication among the devices and the cloud. In the case of IOT-based health monitoring system, it works as a centralized process that uses a wireless technique for the transmission of different patient data after collecting them using various sensors and software over the Internet. In any emergency, if the collected parameters are out of range or not in normal range and the patient needs the presence of a doctor or other support, this IOT-based system may locate the patient [6]. As a result, they can get emergency support without wasting time [7] and keep patients healthy and safe.

A health monitoring system utilizing IoT is a demanding topic of research. Some recent works on IOT-based health tracking techniques are found in [8–10]. In [8], authors reported a remote, IOT-based health monitoring/tracking method. Their method [8] or IOT-based gadget can measure temperature, circulatory strain, and electro-cardiogram signal parameters, and it can send an alarm if any abnormality or crisis arises.

Their setup is assembled by integrating thermometer, sphygmomanometer, and electrocardiogram sensors attached to an Arduino that sends its collected information to servers utilizing a WiFi module. A. M. Ghosh *et al.* [9] also presented a remote, IOT-based health monitoring system. In another work [10], authors reported an IOT-based remote health monitoring system utilizing wearable sensors using online as well as offline modes for android systems based on mobile platforms.

Recently, operational research (OR) is widely used in different fields of research. For public health, it was first implemented in 1952 for hospital planning in UK, and in India, it was introduced in 1962 at the National Tuberculosis (TB) Institute for the development of national TB program. It is a field of mathematics, which provides a scientific foundation for management and can process informed decisions to resolve detected problems. This OR model minimizes errors or dangerous situations, which may occur in conventional methods of thumb rules or guessing [11]. In general, we analyze any problem in terms of cost and execute the method or solution without hampering human, social, or political power [12].

In the case of public health, researchers of the OR model provide solutions that help to upgrade the performance of a program or technique and select the best program/technique or provide the best solution and identify diagnostic and therapeutic constraints. It is a quantitative approach that also depends on qualitative elements and always has a great impact on program managers or decision-making management. As per the application variety, different researchers have defined OR in different ways [13, 14]. In 2008, in a global meeting at Geneva, in the context of public health issue, the OR method was defined as any research constructing practically functioning knowledge that can upgrade the implementation of a plan or program in any case of the category of research methodology. The overall OR process is shown in Figure 13.1. Various existing applications of the OR method in health care systems are given in the literature [16–21].

The motivations of the present work are mentioned below:

i) At the time of COVID-19 pandemic, we have faced a lot of crises of medical staff and doctors. Our technique will solve this problem in an optimized way.

ii) Health care facilities in rural hospitals are limited. This technique will solve this problem with very low cost investments from the government.

In this work, we have focused on body temperature and pulse rate. In Celsius scale, the normal body temperature is 37°C. Here, we have used

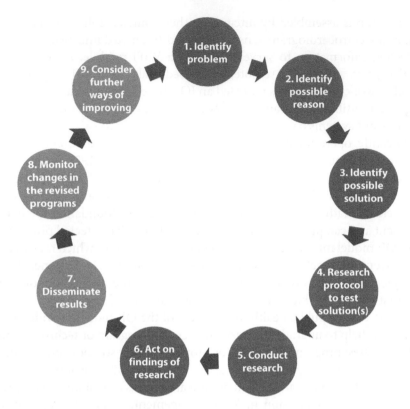

Figure 13.1 Flow diagram of the database search, selection, and the review process of an article [15].

TEMPERATURE SENSOR and HEART RATE PULSE SENSOR. After measuring these parameters, the data are fed into a centralized cloud server. These data can be analyzed and can be used to inform doctors or nurses if any abnormality is detected.

The whole chapter is arranged as follows: Section 13.2 explains all the components used in this work. Section 13.3 represents the information about the IoT platform. Section 13.4 describes the proposed method in detail. Section 13.5 explains the setup of the experiment and results. Section 13.6 concludes the paper.

13.2 Components Used

This section provides the detailed explanation of the different components used to design the proposed technique.

13.2.1   Node MCU

Node MCU is an IoT-based platform, which comprises firmware that works on the ESP8266 Wi-Fi SoC from Espressif Systems, and the hardware is as depicted in Figure 13.2. The term "Node MCU" indicates the firmware. This firmware works on the language of Lua scripting. It combines "node" and "MCU" (micro-controller unit). In addition, it also provides the most vital features of micro-controllers such as GPIO, PWM, and ADC.

This module contains an ESP8266 chip associated with Tensilica Xtensa 32-bit LX106 RISC microprocessor as depicted in Figure 13.3.

There is also a 128-KB RAM and a flash memory size of 4 MB for the data storage and programming. This module also integrates an 802.11b/g/n HT40 Wi-Fi transceiver.

Its operating voltage range is 3V–3.6V. Power requirement pins are shown in Figure 13.4.

Figure 13.2 Node MCU.

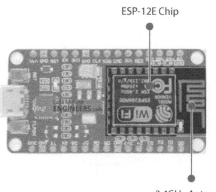

Figure 13.3 ESP-12E module in Node MCU.

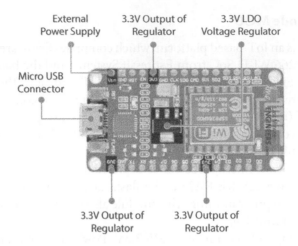

Figure 13.4 Power requirements in Node MCU.

It has a total of 17 GPIO pins that are used to perform all peripheral functions, including ADC channel, UART interface system, PWM output, SPI, I2S interface system, etc., as shown in Figure 13.5.

It has two important buttons, the Reset and FLASH buttons. Reset button is used for the reset purpose of the chip and FLASH button is utilized for upgrading the firmware. It has a LED indicator that is programmable and connected to a D0 pin as shown in Figure 13.6.

It also includes a CP2102 USB-to-UART controller as shown in Figure 13.7, which transforms a USB signal to serial. Through this, the processor communicates with the ESP8266 chip.

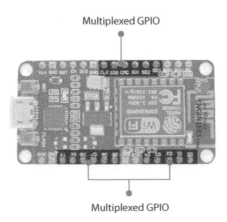

Figure 13.5 Peripherals and I/O.

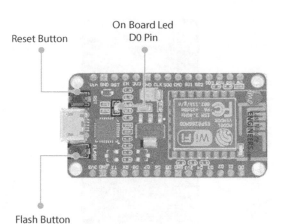

Figure 13.6 On-board switches and LED indicators.

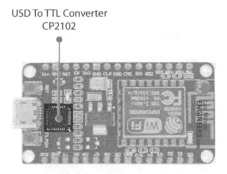

Figure 13.7 CP2102 in Node MCU.

The ESP8266 Node consists of 30 pins to interface with the outside world. Figure 13.8 depicts the pin diagram. The explanation of each pin is discussed in [1].

13.2.2   Heart Rate/Pulse Sensor

Figure 13.9 depicts the pulse sensor. It is used to capture the heart rate. This sensor clips to a fingertip and plugs right in Arduino using a jumper. It is integrated with a tracking or monitoring app that plots the pulse rate in real time.

It has three pins: the VCC, GND, and analog pins. It works within 3.3 to 5V DC voltage range. The heart logo indicates the front side of the sensor,

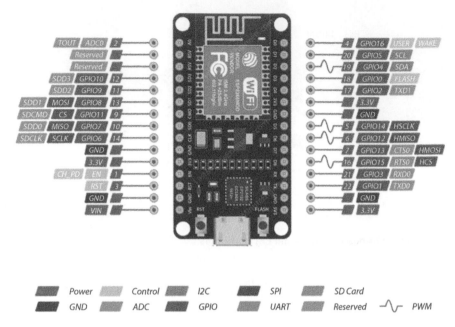

Figure 13.8 Complete pin diagram of the Node MCU.

Figure 13.9 Pulse rate sensor.

where the finger is placed. At the front side, there is a small circular hole, where the reverse-mounted LED acts as an indicator as shown in Figure 13.10.

Below the LED, there is a photo sensor to control the screen brightness in different lighting situations. At the back side, other components are the microchip's MCP6001 Op-Amp, and a number of resistances (R) and capacitors (C). It is also connected to a protection diode to prevent damage. The module is depicted in Figure 13.11.

The working principle of optical heart-rate sensors is very simple. The working of a pulse sensor is depicted in Figure 13.12 and Figure 13.13.

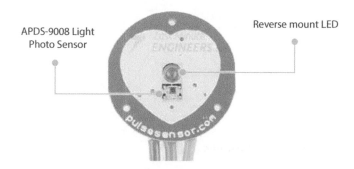

APDS-9008 Light Photo Sensor

Reverse mount LED

Figure 13.10 Hardware diagram of a heart rate sensor.

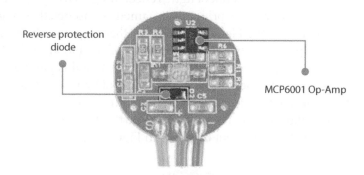

Reverse protection diode

MCP6001 Op-Amp

Figure 13.11 Op-Amp and reverse protection diode.

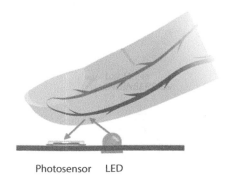

Photosensor   LED

Figure 13.12 Working of a pulse sensor.

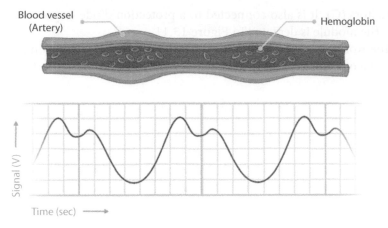

Figure 13.13 Working of a pulse sensor.

A pulse sensor works by flashing a green color light of ~550 nm on the finger and measuring the amount of light-reflected signal using a photosensor. This operation or working principle is named as photoplethysmogram.

The hemoglobin of the blood has features that help absorb the green light. This absorption depends on the redness of the blood. If the blood is redder, then it absorbs more green lights. If the blood is pumped using the finger, for each of the heartbeats, the quantity of light reflected changes and creates a varying waveform. If we continue this process and store the readings of the photosensor, then we get a heartbeat reading.

The diagram with the pin-out is shown in Figure 13.14.

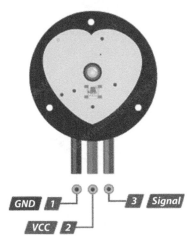

Figure 13.14 Pin diagram of the pulse sensor.

S (Signal): is the signal output.

+ (VCC): is the VCC pin (supply voltage)

- (GND): is the ground pin

13.2.3   Temperature Sensor (LM35)

The LM35 is a temperature sensor as depicted in Figure 13.15. This chip provides a voltage output that is linearly proportional with the temperature at °C. This sensor is satisfactorily precise and works under any environmental conditions. Complete specifications are given in Table 13.1.

It measures the temperature, utilizing solid-state technique. It uses the concept of voltage drop between the base and emitter (forward voltage – V_{be}) of the transistor and decreases as the temperature rises. It amplifies this voltage variation and generatesan analog signal, which is directly proportional with temperature. Temperature vs. I_c collector currentis shown in Figure 13.16.

Figure 13.15 LM35.

Table 13.1 LM35 sensor specifications.

Supply voltage	4V–30V
Current draw	60 μA
Range of temperature	(−55°C) – (+155°C)
Precision	± 0.5°C
Scaling factor	10 mV/°C

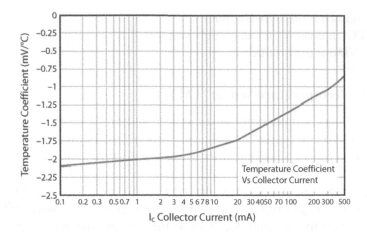

Figure 13.16 Temperature vs. I_c collector current.

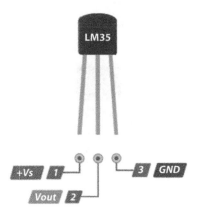

Figure 13.17 Temperature vs. I_c collector current.

Let's take a look at its pin-out as in Figure 13.17.

+Vs: power supply (4V to 30V)

Vout: output (analog voltage)

GND: ground pin

13.3 IoT Platform

IoT refers to a new type of world where almost all devices are connected within a network. These can be used collaboratively to achieve complex tasks. In this system, IoT devices are equipped with different sensors, processors, transceivers, etc. These sensors are actually used to collect data regarding physical parameters and after that, these are stored and processed in an intelligent way in order to provide effective interfaces from it. But the capabilities of the processing techniques of an IoT object is restricted by the availability of resources and face constraints due to limitations of energy, storage space, size, and computational complexity. So, it is a challenge for the researcher to ensure that the perfect data are obtained at the desired level of accuracy. This types of communication among IoT appliances and devices are mainly wireless connections, which are installed at dispersed locations.

13.3.1 ThingSpeak—IoT Platform Used in This Work

IoT is an emerging field of research in which a lot of devices or things are communicated through the Internet. These devices interact with other different things and often send sensor data to cloud storage and the collected data are further reprocessed and analyzed to obtain important characteristics. On Figure 13.18, at the extreme left, smart devices or "things" of IoT are shown and which stay at the edge of this network.

These smart devices are used to collect required data in real time. In the middle part, we have the cloud in which collected data from different sensors or devices are summarized and analyzed in real time and sometimes, other IoT analytics platforms are used to address this purpose. Here, the algorithm development part is associated with this application to analyze the collected data. Data are analyzed in a software environment in

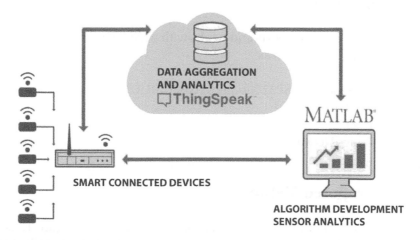

Figure 13.18 ThingSpeak.

the cloud or using a smart device. Then ThingSpeak provides platforms that collect and analyze data. We can send data to ThingSpeak from our devices, create an instant picture of live data, and send necessary notifications. Figure 13.19 shows the working process of ThingSpeak.

How ThingSpeak works:

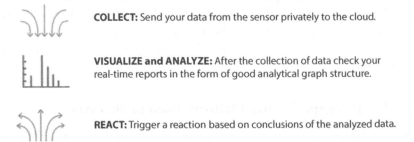

COLLECT: Send your data from the sensor privately to the cloud.

VISUALIZE and ANALYZE: After the collection of data check your real-time reports in the form of good analytical graph structure.

REACT: Trigger a reaction based on conclusions of the analyzed data.

Figure 13.19 Working process of ThingSpeak.

Features of ThingSpeak:

- ✓ ThingSpeak features a collection of data in private channels and shares them with public channels
- ✓ Real-time data collection and processing
- ✓ It supports MATLAB analytics and visualization
- ✓ Supports Arduino, Raspberry Pi, Node MCU, etc.
- ✓ Supports event scheduling and sending alerts

ThingSpeak works with

- ✓ ThingSpeak supports and works with wide range microcontroler boards such as
- ✓ Arduino
- ✓ ESP8266 and ESP32 Modules (Node MCU)
- ✓ Raspberry Pi
- ✓ Senet
- ✓ Things Network, etc.

13.4   Proposed Method

The flow diagram of the presented technique is depicted in Figure 13.20. This IOT-based patient monitoring system integrates Node MCU, ESP8266

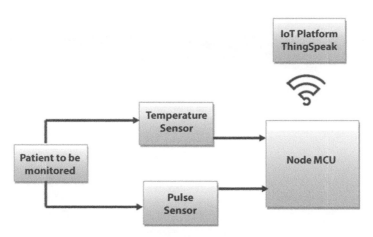

Figure 13.20 Flow diagram of the proposed technique.

chip, and two sensor modules to measure the parameters, body temperature and pulse rate. These sensors are connected with a patient's body, which collect the temperature and pulse rate data and are then directly uploaded or fed into a cloud platform, ThingSpeak, in real time through the ESP-12E (Wi-Fi) module. It can detect a serious abnormality in a patient based on the obtained parameter data.

13.5 Experimental Setup and Result

The programming for Node MCU is done on the Arduino Software (version 1.8.19). The programming IDE is depicted in Figure 13.21.

ThingSpeak Setup
ThingSpeak setup procedures are explained below as stepwise:

Step 1. Channel setup for feeding data, with a unique channel ID as shown in Figure 13.22.
Step 2. Copying the Write API, and configuring it into the Arduino development software (as shown in Figure 13.23).
Step 3. Connecting the hardware components: Online schematic made using circuito.io online circuit design as shown in Figure 13.24.
Step 4. After completing all the hardware connection (Figure 13.25), write down the source code onto the Arduino script.

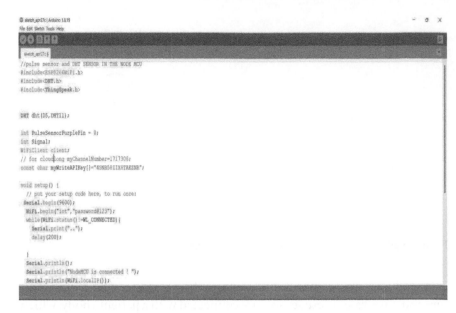

Figure 13.21 Arduino programming IDE.

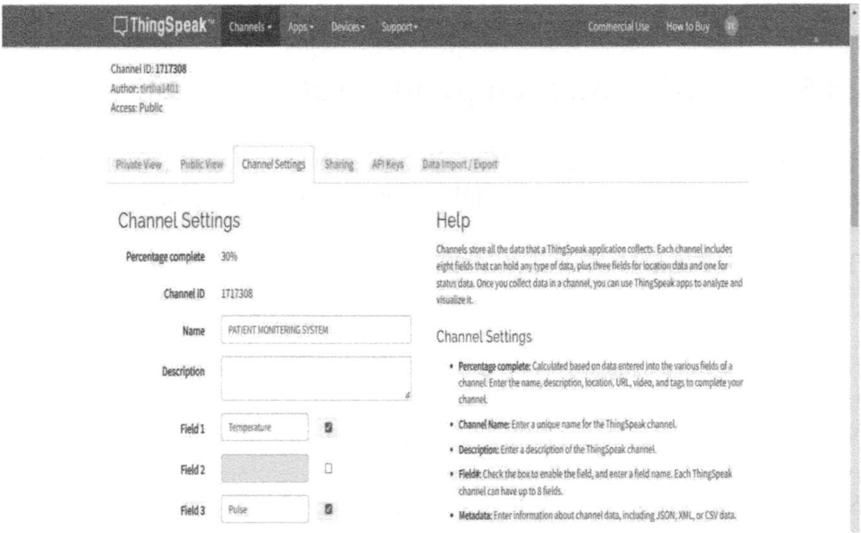

Figure 13.22 Creating channel fields.

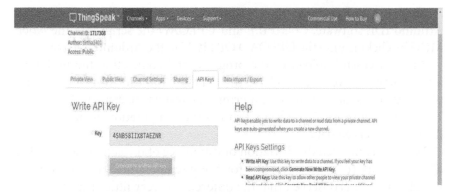

Figure 13.23 Write API key.

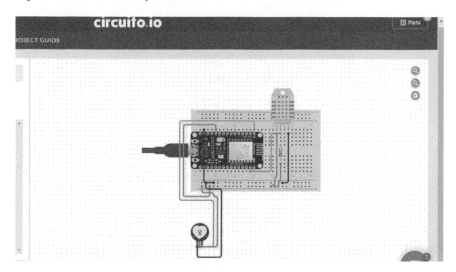

Figure 13.24 Implemented online virtual schematic.

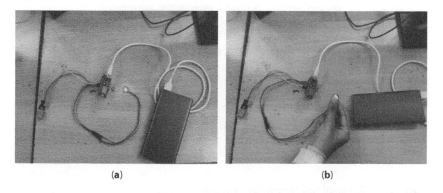

(a)   (b)

Figure 13.25 (a) Hardware connection and (b) checking vitals real time.

Step 5. Connect Node MCU using the COM5/COM6 port with the Arduino IDE software, COMPILE and UPLOAD the script into the Node MCU by clicking onto the UPLOAD OPTION in the Arduino IDE software.

After successful upload of the program and connecting the peripherals correctly, we were able to have the data fed into the ThingSpeak cloud platform. The snapshots of the experimental results are displayed in Figure 13.26 and Figure 13.27. Table 13.2 shows the computation errors of actual data and observed data.

We have computed the deviation or difference of the actual data and the observed data (proposed system) for body temperature (in °F), as given in Table 13.3. It is observed that the difference is very little. This deviation occurred because of slight mis-positioning of the system.

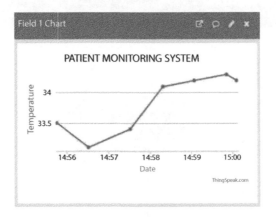

Figure 13.26 Measured real-time data of patient temperature.

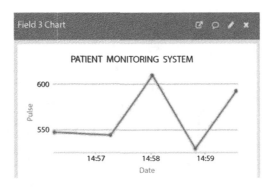

Figure 13.27 Measured real-time data of patient pulse rate.

Table 13.2 Computation of errors of actual data and observed data.

Number of observations	Actual data (°C)	Actual data (°F)	Observed data (°F) from the proposed method	Difference
1	36.33	97.4	97.6	0.2
2	36.77	98.2	98.5	0.3
3	36.88	98.4	98.6	0.2
4	36.61	97.9	98.4	0.5
5	37.16	98.9	99.3	0.4

Table 13.3 Comparison with other techniques.

Reference	Method	Sensors used
[22]	Digital hospital IoT-based hospital management system	ECG and EKG
[23]	Health monitoring system to detect cardiac disorder	ECG
[24]	IoT-enabled health monitoring sensor	Temperature, blood Pressure, and glucose
[25]	Health monitoring system using mobile	ECG
Proposed method	IoT-enabled health tracking or monitoring system	Temperature and pulse

13.6   Conclusion

In this work, we have implemented an IoT-based patient monitoring or tracking system, which reduces the requirement of manpower to observe a patient 24 hours and solve the shortage of nurses and doctors. The proposed technique is capable of measuring a patient's body temperature and pulse rate and then the measured data are sent wirelessly to android apps using an IOT platform. The results can be displayed and exported onto the cloud. This work also minimizes the workload for nurses/doctors in the hospital. Here, we have also measured the deviation or difference between actual data and observed data of the temperature, which shows a very little difference. In our future work, we want to measure other important patient parameters and use more advanced sensors to acquire more accurate data.

The OR method has many constraints and challenges. It may not always yield successful or good results. In our future work, we want to develop an OR-based technique or OR-based patient monitoring system with minimum cost and with high performance or accuracy.

References

1. https://docs.arduino.cc
2. Ufoaroh, S.U., Oranugo, C.O., Uchechukwu, M.E., Heartbeat monitoring and alert system using GSM technology. *Int. J. Eng. Res. Gen. Sci.*, 3, 4, July-August, 2015.
3. Gupta, S., Kashaudhan, S., Pandey, D.C., Gaur, P.P.S., IoT based patient health monitoring system. *Int. Res. J. Eng Technol. (IRJET)*, 04, 03, 1–6, Mar-2017.
4. Senthamilarasi, C., Rani, J.J., Vidhya, B., Aritha, H., A smart patient health monitoring system using IoT. *Int. J. Pure Appl. Math.*, 119, 16, 59–70, 2018.
5. Akhila, V., Vasavi, Y., Nissie, K., Rao, P.V., An IoT based patient health monitoring system using arduino uno. *Int. J. Res. Inf. Technol.*, 1, 1, 1–6, November 2017.
6. Gopal, S.R. and Patan, S.A., Design and analysis of heterogeneous hybrid topology for VLAN configuration. *Int. J. Emerg. Trends Eng. Res.*, 7, 11, 487–491, November, 2019.
7. Karthik, B.N., Parameswari, L.D., Harshini, R., Akshaya, A., Survey on IoT & arduino based patient health monitoring system. *Int. J. Sci. Res. Comput. Sci. Eng. Inf. Technol.*, 3, 1, 1414–1417, 2018, ISSN : 2456-3307.
8. Hamim, M., Paul, S., Hoque, S., II, Rahman, N., Baqee, I.-A., IoT based remote health monitoring system for patients and elderly people, in: *2019 International Conference on Robotics, Electrical and Signal Processing Techniques (ICREST)*, pp. 533–538, Jan. 2019, doi: 10.1109/ ICREST.2019.8644514.
9. Ghosh, A.M., Halder, D., Hossain, S.K.A., Remote health monitoring system through IoT. *2016 5th International Conference on Informatics, Electronics and Vision (ICIEV)*, pp. 921–926, May 2016, doi: 10.1109/ICIEV.2016.7760135.
10. Andrews, L.J.B. and Raja, L., Remote based patient monitoring system using wearable sensors through online and offline mode for android based mobile platforms, in: *2017 International Conference on Infocom Technologies and Unmanned Systems (Trends and FutureDirections) (ICTUS)*, Dec. 2017, pp. 602–606, doi: 10.1109/ICTUS.2017.8286080.
11. Murthy, P.R., *Operations Research*, 2nd ed, pp. 1–21, New Age International Publishers, New Delhi, 2007.

12. Sathe, P.V., *Epidemiology and Management for Health Care for All*, 3rd ed, pp. 167–88, Vora Medical Publications, Maharastra, 2009.
13. Fisher, A.A., Laing, J.E., Stoeckel, J.E., Townsend, J.W., *Handbook for Family Planning Operations Research Design*, 2nd ed, Population Council, New York, 1991.
14. Framework for Operations and Implementation Research in Health, The World Bank Global HIV/AIDS Program, pp. 1–58, 2022. Available from: http://www.who.int/hiv/pub/operational/framework/en/ index.html.
15. Kumar, G., Public health panorama of operational research: A narrative review. *Int. J. Prev. Med.*, 10, 1–6, 2019, DOI: 10.4103/ijpvm.IJPVM_93_16.
16. Zachariah, R., Spielmann, M.P., Chinji, C., Gomani, P., Arendt, V., Hargreaves, N.J. *et al.*, Voluntary counselling HIV testing and adjunctive cotrimoxazole reduces mortality in tuberculosis patients in Thyolo Malawi. *AIDS*, 17, 1053–61, 2003.
17. Sai Babu, B., Satyanarayana, A.V., Venkateshwaralu, G., Ramakrishna, U., Vikram, P., Sahu, S. *et al.*, Initial default among diagnosed sputum positive pulmonary tuberculosis patients in Andhra Pradesh India. *Int. J. Tuberc. Lung Dis.*, 12, 1055–8, 2008.
18. Bedelu, M., Ford, N., Hilderbrand, K., Reuter, H., Implementing antiretroviral therapy in rural communities: The Lusikisiki model of decentralized HIV/AIDS care. *J. Infect. Dis.*, 196 Suppl 3, S464–8, 2007.
19. Tripathy, P., Nair, N., Barnett, S., Mahapatra, R., Borghi, J., Rath, S. *et al.*, Effect of a articipatory intervention with women's groups on birth outcomes and maternal depression in Jharkhand and Orissa, India: A cluster-randomised controlled trial. *Lancet*, 375, 1182–92, 2010.
20. Zachariah, R., Van Engelgem, I., Massaquoi, M., Kocholla, L., Manzi, M., Suleh, A. *et al.*, Payment for antiretroviral drugs is associated with a higher rate of patients lost to follow-up than those offered free-of-charge therapy in Nairobi, Kenya. *Trans. R. Soc. Trop. Med. Hyg.*, 102, 288–93, 2008.
21. Varkey, L.C., Mishra, A., Das, A., Ottolenghi, E., Huntington, D., Adamchak, S. *et al.*, Involving men in maternity care in India, Population Council, New York, 2004.
22. Thangaraj, M., Ponmalar, P.P., Anuradha, S., Internet of things (IOT) enabled smart autonomous hospital management system – A real world health care use case with the technology drivers. *2015 IEEE International Conference on Computational Intelligence and Computing Research.*
23. Bansal, A., Kumar, S., Bajpai, A., Tiwari, V.N., Nayak, M., Venkatesan, S., Narayanan, R., Remote health monitoring system for detecting cardiac disorders. *IET Syst. Biol.*, 9, 6, 309–314, 2015.
24. Mdhaffar, A., Chaari, T., Larbi, K., Jmaiel, M., Freisleben, B., IoT-based health monitoring via LoRaWAN. *IEEE EUROCON*, 2017.
25. Masud, M.M., Serhani, M.A., Navaz, A.N., Resource-aware mobile based health monitoring, pp. 2168–2194, IEEE J-BHI, UAEU Interdisciplinary 2015.

14

Fog Computing and Its Emergence with Reference to Applications and Potentialities in Traditional and Digital Educational Systems: A Scientific Review

P. K. Paul

Department of CIS, and Information Scientist (Offg.), Raiganj University, Raiganj, West Bengal, India

Abstract

Among the emerging technologies within Information Technology, Fog Computing is considered worthy and growing. It is very close with Cloud Computing and is considered as next-level Cloud development. Cisco, the major networking technology giant company is considered as the initial developer of Fog Computing, and later, other gradual development took place in the field of Fog Computing and it continues to rise gradually. Initially, Cisco popularized this technology as Cisco Fog Computing and later, contributions from other organizations and industries led to Fog Computing, in general. As far as general Fog Computing is concerned, IBM is sometimes considered as an important name. OpenFog, which was established in 2015, is also important, along with different founding member institutions, namely, ARM, Cisco, Microsoft Corporation, Dell, Intel, and from the university, the role of Princeton University.

Fog Computing is known to have a decentralized architecture and it also preserves information between sources and also each cloud resource. Fog Computing enhances and speeds up data delivery, and reduces overhead data transfer, and also increases efficiency of the computation systems in a cloud network. It also reduces the need of the process and also holds a large amount of data quantities of superfluous data. This is considered as paradigm shifting of cloud towards healthy and sophisticated virtualization aided by not only cloud but also Internet of Things (IoT). Fog Computing not only helps in traditional education systems but also in

Email: pkpaul.infotech@gmail.com

Chandan Banerjee, Anupam Ghosh, Rajdeep Chakraborty and Ahmed A. Elngar (eds.) Fog Computing for Intelligent Cloud IoT Systems, (331–354) © 2024 Scrivener Publishing LLC

online and digital educational systems. Its benefits include boosting educational institutions' operations and functionalities.

Fog computing supports platforms with agility and modern technologies for better educational management. In real time educational management, Fog computing can also be useful in online content management and student monitoring. Online learning management will be more flexible and sophisticated with potential Fog Computing applications. This chapter highlights the fundamentals of Fog Computing, including features, functions, and emergence. This chapter also highlights the basic role and potentialities of Fog Computing in educational systems and overall management.

Keywords: Fog computing, educational technology, digital education, emerging technology, higher education, Education 4.0

14.1   Background

Fog Computing, which is a decentralized computing and IT infrastructure, is rapidly developing, and it was proposed by and originated from the network giant, Cisco Systems, Inc. (USA). In this kind of system and mechanism, computing resources are basically stored and located in a cloud or in a data center [1, 2, 11]. This is an emerging alternative of Cloud Computing and it has the capability of managing large numbers of devices and computing equipment. Here, uses of edge network also play a crucial role by locating desired devices compared to the establishment of cloud channels for effective utilizations of different IT resources, *viz.* storage, users aggregate, and bandwidth at the access points, *viz.* network routers. Therefore, this mechanism is important in reducing overall bandwidth, and this is because of the limited data transmission from data centers, happening across different cloud channels. In some context, Fog Computing is also known as Fogging and Fog Networking. Ultimately, this is an architecture useful in edge devices, though the concept was first developed and discussed in 2012 by Cisco, but gradually, it has changed drastically in terms of its technologies, means, scope, and periphery [5, 27, 36]. In 2015, the OpenFog Consortium was established by some other IT expert organizations and companies, *viz.*

- Cisco Systems
- Dell Corporation
- Microsoft Corporation
- ARM Holdings
- Princeton University

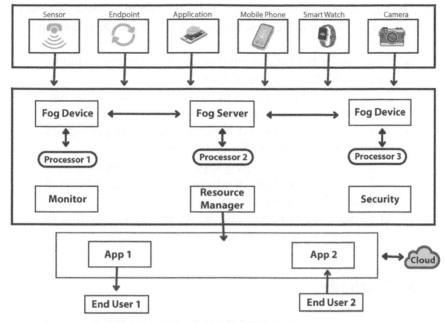

Fog Computing Architecture

Figure 14.1 Basic fog computing architecture.

Fog Computing uses and connects with the Internet of Things (IoT) and in such mechanism, numerous communications each day become possible, and in this context Fog Computing is effective [3, 13, 26]. The network of Fog basically consists of a control plane and a data plane, and different IP-enabled devices such as smartphones, wearable health monitoring devices, and connected vehicles may be well connected and their data shared effectively. A basic architecture of Fog Computing provided by Spiceworks is depicted here in Figure 14.1.

The impact and significance of Fog Computing in different sectors are without a doubt, going to be worthy and relevant, and different bodies, agencies, and institutions are offering their focus on Fog Computing and allied technologies. As far as education, training, and research are concerned, Fog Computing is impactful, and it has potential on various grounds.

14.2 Objectives

The present work entitled 'Fog Computing and Its Emergence with Reference to Applications and Potentialities in Traditional and Digital

Educational Systems: *A Scientific Review*' is a scientific review and overview, with a number of objectives, but are not limited to the following:

- Learn about the fundamental of Fog Computing including its birth, foundation, and history.
- Get ideas about the architecture of Fog Computing and fogging with references to their core activities.
- Know the advantages and benefits of Fog Computing and allied architecture for wider IT infrastructure.
- Learn the basic and emerging applications of Fog Computing and networking systems in education, teaching, and overall educational administration.
- Determine the potential and issues of Fog Computing in general and in the educational context.

14.3   Methods

This chapter entitled 'Fog Computing and Its Emergence with Reference to Applications and Potentialities in Traditional and Digital Educational Systems: *A Scientific Review*' is a basic, theoretical, and conceptual work based on existing work and literature. For this study, different journals and books related to the fields of Computing, Fog Computing, and Cloud Computing were analyzed and reported accordingly. Google Scholar was used with Fog Computing to find more research in this field and to address the goals of this work.

14.4   Fog Computing: Basics and Advantages

Fog Computing is the term used for extended cloud-based services to the edge-based systems. It empowers multiple users, devices, and electronic gadgets to share their resources. Fog-based systems allow data, applications, and other resources to be closer with the systems and users or end users (refer to Figure 14.2) [8, 9, 18]. As far as transportation, agriculture, retail and marketing industries, and governance are concerned, Fog Computing is an important destination to be used to use and maximize. Regarding the Education sector, Fog Computing comes with ample opportunities, *viz.* educational operations and management, platform flexibilities in digital education, and day-to-day office management and administration.

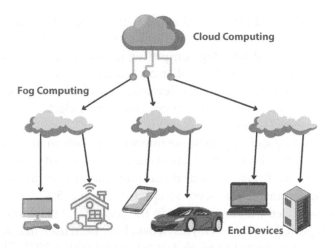

Figure 14.2 Fog computing and in-contrast with end devices.

According to the experts there are eight fog computing architecture pillars and these are

- Security,
- Scalability,
- Openness,
- Autonomy,
- Reliability,
- Agility,
- Hierarchical Organization, and
- Programmability.

Fog Computing has four core types. First is **device-level fog computing**, and this level or layer works with basic networking devices such as sensors, switches, and computer routers, and in certain cases, low-powered systems and hardware [6, 17, 37]. This kind of fog computing layer is useful in gathering data from such electronic devices and later it sends the same to the respective cloud for proper analysis.

Second, **edge-level fog computing** basically works on the server (may have a large number in certain cases) or similar appliances performing on the edge of a network. Such types of electronic devices are used for the processing of data before they move to the cloud. Third, **gateway-level fog computing** is another kind of devices that works as a gateway, and this generally works in-between the edge and the cloud. Such electronic systems are useful in managing traffic and allied network activities. Additionally, it also ensures only relevant data are sent to the cloud with proper functioning. Fourth, **cloud-level fog computing** is another level of system and it works on servers and similar appliances located in cloud-based systems. It is important to note that similar devices are useful in the processing of data before they are sent to the required computer or electronic systems or simply, end users [15, 16].

Fog Computing and its growth are important to note in modern Digital Society, as it deals with IoT applications of the network edge, and as such, it is applicable in diverse areas and communication systems. A study of Domo's ninth annual 'Data Never Sleeps' infographic, 5.17 billion people had been associated with the Internet in the year 2021. Furthermore, it has also been reported that 79 zettabytes of data have been used that year alone and the figure is expected to reach 180 zettabytes within 2025. This number of growing Internet and electronic and IT uses in society rises rapidly, consequently growing IT devices connected with IoT and edge-based systems rapidly. Regardless of the IT sector's verticals, modern organizations are basically spate of data from esteemed consumers. Here IoT drivers and data-intensive customer experience are basically associated with anything related to network devices. In addition to IoT, Cloud-based Systems, and AI and Machine Learning also allow healthy, robust, and dynamic data processing and storage systems. The result of such devices is simply 'data' and it is increasing rapidly in different ways, and therefore, this also enables companies and organizations to stay informed and benefit from intelligent decision-making systems. Cloud-based systems come with several advantages but it is costly to some extent, but helps in data management and requirement. Finally, small storage systems of data, before their move to the cloud, is simply, the 'Fog'. In such systems, usage of devices is done with lower processing capabilities [10, 12, 38]. Fog Computing is useful with the cloud when it is in fulfillment of a long-term goal, is resource intensive, and analytically focused. Note that Edge Computing is a subset of Fog Computing, and it is also involved with sending and sharing the right data to the right destination effectively, using various edge devices such as

- Edge-based routers,
- Edge-based cameras,
- Edge-based switches and embedded servers as well as sensors, and
- Edge-supported controllers.

In Edge-based systems, all the data are basically stored within the system itself and using Fog-based computing, it works in layers between the edge device and with the cloud [20, 22, 42]. Here, servers are connected to each other, and centralized cloud servers and intelligent systems are also associated; therefore, they work together for handling pre-processing data, including short-term storage as well as real-time monitoring grounded on rule-based systems. Therefore, Fog Computing simply reduces the amount of data transformation, and increases efficiency.

14.4.1 Existing Major Works

The present work entitled 'Fog Computing and Its Emergence with Reference to Applications and Potentialities in Traditional and Digital Educational Systems: *A Scientific Review*' is a theoretical work and is review-based; therefore, various literature have been consulted and prepared for this entire work. Some of the major works used here have been reported in this section briefly. Alli and Alam [4], in their work, mentioned that Fog Computing is a decentralized computer infrastructure useful in computation, storage, as well as processing of data. This is connected with Edge Computing and the enhanced version of cloud computing, which offer different advantages in flexible information technology infrastructure. In their work, they studied and reported that Fog Computing reduces data fetching time and saves in educational database space. According to Bagheri and Movahed [7], Education is becoming an emerging industry, and therefore, different opportunities are becoming more available in ICT in Education, but at the same time, there are some obstacles regarding the development of educational norms. Such obstacles, mainly latency reduction and security minimization become solvable using Fog-based models and architecture. Long and Siemens [25] focused on Fog Computing with reference to micro-data facilities, which are required in on-site systems and technologies, and such systems can be adopted by colleges and institutions as per requirements. LMS or Learning Management System is most effective and productive in flexible education systems development, and Fog Computing helps to reach goals in this context and others.

Bittencourt, L. F. *et al.* (2017) [9] examined Fog Computing and found that it offers a distributed infrastructure and it results in low-latency access. It also helps in new resource allocation. Many devices work with Fog Computing and therefore, allow storage at various locations. They have analyzed scheduling problem and also focused on user mobility and as such, also influenced the applications performance. Liu, Y., Fieldsend, J. E., and Min, G. (2017) [23] discussed Fog computing in their work and analyzed how this technology is worthy in distributed computing platforms and also helps in computations. They have also examined its role in reducing latency and the cost of data delivery to the remote cloud.

Naha, R. K. *et al.* (2018) [30] analyzed and reported research trends and also the basic and technical differences of cloud and fog. They also discussed and investigated different proposed Fog Computing architecture and later described the components of these architecture. Further, a taxonomy of such kind of computing was proposed with research works and gaps, with proper resource allocation and scheduling. They also discussed fog-based micro-services. Khan, S., Parkinson, S., and Qin, Y. (2017) [19] also reviewed the literature on Fog Computing for finding common security gaps. They studied and analyzed Edge Computing, and observed that majority of Fog applications are basically motivated by the desire for functionality as well as satisfying the need of end users. They studied the benefits of Fog Computing over existing models and also the impact of possible solutions and to offer security-relevant directions. Raman, A. (2019) [40] studied Fog Computing especially on educational systems and educational administration. The author discussed the increasing trend and other potential of Fog Computing in educational operations compared to other existing models and described how it is a modern and improved technology for the betterment of education, including security aspects.

Hamid (2023) completed a research work that emphasized Fog Computing applications and potentialities on Education and also discussed IoT and Cloud Systems in day-to-day educational activities [26]. Pecori, R. (2018) studied a work on Educational Technology applications with a focus on Fog Computing and Big Data Analytics and proposed different aspects for better virtual learning practices. In this work, aspects of numerous and growing electronic devices were discussed with the view of managing such devices in educational context and digital education platforms [33]. Urokova, S. B. (2020) discussed the benefits and advantages of online education and different technologies applicable in promoting online education. This work also highlights the demerits of online education [51].

14.4.2   Fog Computing Advantages

Fog Computing brings several advantages over traditional Computing and IT-based systems. Some of them are as follows:

Latency Minimization—Fog Computing very smoothly and effectively operates; therefore, it minimizes latency. As it reduces cascading system failure and the shutdown of manufacturing lines, data analysis can be conducted in real time; therefore, this advantage makes it attractive for major organizations to adopt [14, 21]. Furthermore, due to its nature, it becomes faster and less dangerous for users and also minimizes time lost.

Conservation of Network Bandwidth—Fog Computing saves the bandwidth multiple ways and also fulfills most of the critical tasks as it does not require scale that cloud-based storage and processing system requires. Here, connected devices always create a good number of data and eliminate further requirement of transporting data, and thus, automatically eliminates network bandwidth.

Reduced Implementation and Operating Cost—As far as installation, implementation, and operating cost is concerned, Fog Computing can reduce cost drastically compared to other existing technologies and systems. When operating the systems, it also reduces the cost as data are stored locally and thus, reduces network bandwidth.

Enhanced Security and Privacy—Fog Computing also helps in enhancing security in different contexts. As data are stored locally in one's own devices, there is less chance of data loss. Further, it protects IoT data and here, users can monitor and protect their own fog systems and nodes, and thus, it offers secure systems. Moreover, with the use of Fog Computing architecture, the same control panels, policies, and techniques are used, including procedures; therefore, it saves an entire IT environment systematically [24, 28]. As far as maintaining privacy is concerned, Fog Computing also maintains privacy as there is no need to analyze data by any third party through the cloud.

Increased Reliability—The fog architecture also improves reliability as IoT devices are sometimes deployed in many critical conditions like emergencies, in certain cases, data transformation is reduced.

Increased Scalability—As far as scalability is concerned, such architecture also helps in increasing scalability since more and more data and resources are normally added in the edge of the systems or networks [11, 32, 39].

Speed and Business Growth—Fog Computing due to its wider opportunities and features increase business growth. As Fog developers are always engaged in developing newer fog and allied applications, it can be readily deployed. Using Fog Computing models, users and consumers can get their desired services and thus, increase capabilities and processing power.

14.4.3 Fog Computing: Applications

Fog Computing has wider and diverse applications and this trend is growing rapidly throughout the world. Due to the benefit of sophisticated, effective services, it is basically governed by a set of rules and programs. Here, all the elements and components are to be governed by an abstraction layer and this is basically offered by a common interface and works with a common set of protocols for communication. Please refer to Figure 14.3 for its basic advantages and beneficiaries [29, 31, 45].

14.4.3.1 In Smart Homes and Residences

Fog Computing has wide usefulness in smart homes and allied residential systems as such establishments have technology-controlled ventilation. Here, modern and smart lighting is considered as important, including programmable shades. All these systems are collecting data in different environments and along with existing Cloud and IoT-based systems, Fog Computing helps in modern and effective operation [42]. In Nest Learning Thermostat, sprinklers and smart intercom systems data basically communicate with people and here, Fog Computing and networking are useful in creating personalized alarm systems. Different automatic activities can be operated using Fog-based models.

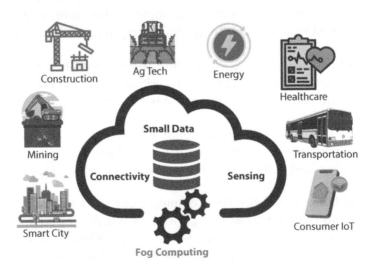

Figure 14.3 Fog computing advantages and its beneficiaries.

14.4.3.2   In Smart Cities and Township Projects

Similar to Smart Homes, in 'smart cities and townships,' Fog Computing and fogging are important and applicable in diverse contexts such as in intelligent, data-driven traffic management systems. Here, different sensors are dedicated to collecting data from general and highly used traffic areas and signals for different activities, *viz.* detecting pedestrians, cyclists, and vehicles [46, 47]. A speedometer is effective in measuring speed and detecting result in collision. Sensors are usable in wireless data collection, including date from traffic signals in different situations and also help in deciding the time frame of the red or green traffic lights.

14.4.3.3   In Monitoring Video Surveillance

As far as Fog Computing applications in video surveillance are concerned, it is useful in collecting continuous stream videos, which are large enough and transferable across network. The data latency problem, including network challenges, can be addressed using Fog Computing-based systems [43, 54]. Fog-based systema and technologies can find and detect anomalies in a crowd pattern. It can also alert authorities in case of any emergency. Here, fog-based models are useful in data collection and storage in their own system without requiring any third-party cloud.

14.4.3.4   In Intelligent Healthcare and Medical Systems

As far as the healthcare and medical sector is concerned, different IT and Computing tools are being used and emerging rapidly. With Fog Computing applications in healthcare, real-time data collection is very important using various medical and electronic devices, including CCTV cameras. In blood glucose monitoring using heart monitoring devices, data are frequently collected and Fog-based models are instantly useful in managing such data locally without any issues in security and privacy. In many countries, health-related regulations exist, such as HIPAA in the United States, and Fog-based systems are effective and important in such cases.

There are other sectors in society where Fog Computing applications are also useful, impactful, and emerging like marketing and retail, oil and gas industries, the military sector and industries, and hospitality and tourism. Where existing systems use Cloud-based models, there too is where Fog Computing is effectively useful.

14.5   Growing Fog Computing Applications Emphasizing Education

Like different sectors discussed before, Fog Computing has a wider impact and potential in different educational spaces such as Educational Management, Teaching–Learning Process, Research and Development, Basic Office Activities, and Student Communication and Management [41, 49]. Education is now becoming an industry and ICT-based education (including Online and Digital Education) is growing, but it has many obstacles such as collecting data real time and technology development paradigm, and in all such cases, Fog-based architecture is useful. Students nowadays, throughout all the phases of education use different technologies and are digitally equipped and connected. In modern days, technology is fruitful in managing educational systems, the changes in chalkboard into the smartboard is a significant example of ICT in Education, and here, a lot of data are basically generated using Cloud and IoT-based systems. Here, applications of Fog Computing can be noted and data can be collected in an instant, ready and real time as Fogging depends on in-house device storage and data location. Today, educators and teachers are assigning home task and assignment using online and digital tools, and here, data can be used effectively using Fog architecture. Today, higher institutions and universities use online and digital office applications and other messaging services and different web solutions. Here, parents and other stakeholders also communicate using ICT models, and here, Fog architecture is useful in data collection, management, and instant analysis. There are certain cases where low latency hampers a model concept of education, including teaching–learning, and the concept of Fog reduces latency and is considered as fruitful and productive. However, note the positive impact of and need for IoT and Cloud Services for real-life data, along with Fog Computing-based systems. Better platform in data collection including communication channel is effectively possible using Fog architecture. Modern education systems collect huge amounts of data of different types such as of students, teachers, staffs, and administration in different areas, therefore fogging in association with other cloud-based models can be fruitful. Matching of different data and required stakeholders are important and the use of IoT is important for such matching supported by Cloud-based systems, and here, Fog Computing is useful in local storage and management [44, 48]. Fog Computing-based infrastructure is required in connecting various fog nodes for better scalability, elasticity, and redundancy; therefore, effective applications in education may be important in promoting on-site and online educational models.

14.6   Impact of Fog Computing in Education

14.6.1   Cases of Fog in Education

The traditional mode of education is and widely practiced everywhere, and these days, such non-digital educational modes are also adopting digital tools and technologies. As a result, different kinds of tools are being used and that collect different kinds of data. The data supplied by esteemed potential educational seekers and current students are needed to manage and use at the same time whenever required. Managing such types and amount of data is effectively possible using Fog-based models. Students are being offered critical information, financial information, and personal information, and as Fog Computing does not use third-party systems, therefore, managing data becomes easy with security and privacy. Here, internal and external data can be managed and data loss, data damage, and different aspects of data manipulation can be minimized effectively and in a sophisticated way, using Fog-based systems. The integration Internet of Things (IOT) along with Cloud Computing, Edge-based Systems (i.e., Edge Computing) requires a higher degree of Fog Computing association for the wider benefit of the following (but not limited to)

- Students,
- Researchers,
- Educational Officers,
- Teachers, and
- Staffs.

As a whole, Fog Computing and Fogging are important in different educational models and services mentioned below (also refer to Figure 14.4).

14.6.1.1   *In Collaborative Teaching–Learning Process*

Fog Computing is helpful in a collaborative teaching–learning process powered by its virtualization, including the educational system [33]. Using Fog Computing, any institute may collaborate with other institutes and data can be stored without any issues of security and privacy. The faculty, resources, and infrastructure can be shared using this type of collaboration.

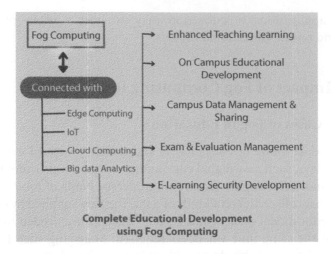

Figure 14.4 Fog computing potential utilization in education and allied areas.

14.6.1.2 In the Promotion of On-Campus Education

As far as on campus education is concerned, Fog Computing is effective in face-to-face education for utilization of existing resources, sharing of library books and documents, need-based online education and meetings, etc., and other effective uses of data whenever required.

14.6.1.3 In Developing and Managing Online Education

The need of online and virtual education systems is increasing rapidly in contemporary scenarios. Today, various certificate, diploma, bachelor, masters, and research degrees are being offered in online mode, and as such, real-time data can be collected and managed effectively.

14.6.1.4 In Continuing Workshop and Training

In educational systems and organizations, key components are workshop and training programs for overall development in many streams such as engineering, computing, health, science, and social work. Today, apart from on-site events, there are many digital events in various emerging technologies such as cloud computing along with IoT, effective in saving money, energy, and also for instant communication powered by Fog models [33, 50].

14.6.1.5   In Promoting Blended and Hybrid Modes of Education

Today, modes of education are changing and modern IT systems such as Cloud computing, IoT along with Fog Computing are useful in developing a new age and modern educational system. The combination of traditional and online modes has developed a new mode, that is, blended mode of education, sometimes also called as hybrid mode of education. In all such educational systems, it is important to use Fog-based models in collecting and managing data.

14.6.1.6   In Uses of Cloud Computing for the Library and for Archival

Applications of modern tools and technologies is very much important in modern educational systems. As far as cloud computing and virtualization technique are concerned, Fog models are effective in numerous activities such as document management including barcoding and RFID activities. Additionally, in a digital library design, development, and management, huge amounts of data are collected and managed, and this is where Fog Systems are worthy and effective.

14.6.1.7   In Developing Examination and Allied Evaluation Processes

As far as examination and evaluation are concerned, today, different ICT tools are widely used for the purpose of examination process, accessing E-answer script using a cloud platform, soft-copy-based or online examination live viva-voce, etc. All these are generally huge amount of data that are later used for analysis and this is where Fog-based models are important and impactful [34, 52].

14.7   Education Industry and Fog: Future Context

Fog Computing is an emerging industry rather than a part of the public service sector. Today, educational programs are offered in different modes such as online education, digital (recorded-non live) mode, and e-learning mode, including blended mode of education. As far as higher educational institutions are concerned, they adopt different technologies such as Cloud Computing, Big Data and Analytics, Internet of Things (IoT), Blockchain Technologies, and Cyber Physical Systems. Due to advent of technologies, and at the same time, the emerging applications of such technologies into education (both on-campus and on-line) in addition to the mentioned technologies, Fog Computing and System plays an important role either individually or jointly in performing different activities. Today, a lot of data generate new age educational models from students and partially from the faculty, staffs, and HR. As far as future potentialities are concerned, Fog Computing significantly helps in microdata facilities for the modern on-site and online education for the complete learning management system (LMS). In this regard, in addition to existing technologies, some other tools such as Oracle or similar databases, Skyward and Procare, are being used [42, 47].

To be more efficient, well-connected systems including inter- and intra-networking Fog Computing can be effective and worthy. By bringing information locally and on-site, latencies are not only reduced but better individual experiences of students and teachers are also observed. Some of universities these days have trained IT personnel for proper and effective remote management systems. According to a market survey agency, Research and Market, the international education technology industry is growing rapidly. It was valued at $193 billion in 2016, whereas the Indian Education Technology market was valued at USD 3.42 billion in 2021 as per agency Global data, and further compounded annual growth rate (CAGR) of more than 30% in the timeline of 2021–2026. Globally, Education Technology is increasing and has reached USD 125.3 billion in 2022 and is expected to grow at 13.2% annually, amounting to USD 232.9 billion within 2027 as per Research and Markets [21, 35, 55]. Colleges and other modern educational institutions are associating with Fog computing for effective services with simplicity and greater impact on user experience. As Fog computing is local computing, therefore, integrity is necessary and the same can be deployed rapidly and quickly. When many universities and Higer Educational Institutions just focused on traditional computing, switching to advanced and fog computing no doubt need of the hour for better Digital education practice, substantially latest technologies like Fog based architecture also dedicated in improving the experience of students as well as educators. According to the Grandview Research, a major Tech market research organization, the market size for Digital Education could be valued at USD 77.23 billion within 2028 and the annual growth rate would be 30.5% during the forecast period. Since Digital Education not only a concept also technology supported by advanced IT and computing therefore such market growth is significant and noticeable. For ultimate technology-enhanced learning (TEL), Fog-based system would be worthy and impactful in many contexts.

In 2020, Coursera had taken the initiative to offer digital education for their worldwide educational partners with professional courses such as train the trainers, and in such context, Fog or any other emerging technologies are worthy for real-life practice. Different Digital Education platforms and companies are going to be impactful if we analyze the role of Fog Computing. Some of the giant organizations in this context are as follows:

- Coursera Inc. (USA) founded by Professors Andrew Ng and Daphne Koller
- edX Inc. (USA) founded by Anant Agarwal
- Pluralsight LLC (USA) created by VSE
- Brain4ce Education Solutions Pvt. Ltd. (India) and founded by Edureka Bangalore
- Udacity, Inc. (USA) founded by Sebastian Thrun, David Stavens, and Mike Sokolsky
- Udemy, Inc. (USA) founded by Eren Bali, Gagan Biyani, and Oktay Caglar
- Miriadax (Spain) *founded by Pedro Aranzadi*
- Jigsaw Academy (India) founded by Gaurav Vohra
- Iversity (Germany) founded by Jonas Liepmann and Hannes Klöpper
- Intellipaat (India) founded by Diwakar Chittora [34, 52].

All such types of organizations are generating huge amounts of data from different circles and operating their Digital Education businesses.

14.8   Fog Computing and Its Role in IOT Security: The Context of Campus

Fog Computing and its impact in the technology spectrum are wide and quite important. Security-related benefits can be observed from Fog Computing and among these, some of the more important ones are as follows:

- As Fog Computing works with IoT and also Cloud-based systems, security-related aspects are important, but since Fog works within their devices, there is less chance in losing security and privacy. Thus, the whole campus benefit.

- Different small devices, in-house devices, and sensor-enable devices are effectively manageable using Fog Computing or a similar architecture; therefore, educational institutions including digital educational giants benefit.
- A large number of devices can be managed effectively using cloud computing-based systems powered by Fog architecture, thus, on a case-to-case basis, security can be effectively managed. Thus, a large campus, if it uses Fog Computing, can benefit greatly [14, 53].
- As Fog Computing is a network and its architecture depends and relies on distributed systems, security can be managed in different network points using sophisticated systems, thus, keeping the whole campus safe.
- Fog Computing allows and offers real-time data (for the connected devices using IoT model) and generated reports; therefore, IT teams can respond to breaches even without closing the main system or units. Thus, campuses can perform their duties effectively.

14.8.1   Issues and Disadvantages of Fog in General and in Educational Systems

Fog Computing comes with ample opportunities and benefits, but still, it has some issues and challenges that can hamper traditional technology systems in the campus and digital systems, in certain cases. Regarding heavy reliance on data transport, a Fog-based system faces problems.

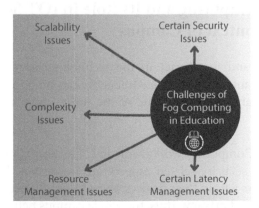

Figure 14.5 Certain fog computing issues in education and allied areas.

Limited resources are an important concern that experts expressed, and it is because of the dependencies of Fog to the edge of the network. Fog Computing is somehow complex in terms of real implementation and management, and it is because of the distributed architecture. Moreover, as Fog Computing is comparatively a new and emerging technology, some of the concerns on limited coverage regarding devices and locations would benefit from evaluation and resolution (see Figure 14.5).

14.9 Concluding Remarks

Internationally, the Digital Education market is growing, and some countries are booming in this area and leading countries in this regard are United States, Germany, Canada, Mexico, France, United Kingdom, Japan, China, India, and Brazil. The global digital education market may grow by 30.5% by 2028 from 2021, and this may reach USD 77.23 billion (within 2028). As far as continents are concerned, North America dominates the entire Education Technology market, with a share of 38.1% for 2020. As far as the growth of digital education market is concerned, digital education technology development, Internet penetration, and increasing microlearning are considered as worthy and impactful. Decentralization and flexibility are the core differences with respect to Fog computing and cloud computing. Though there are many benefits, issues remain with respect to Fog Computing utilizations in the Education sector, including on campus and online or a combination of both. Fog computing security issues may be considered important including aspects of segmentation of bandwidth traffic and additional firewall management in the network. Fog computing maintains some of the features of cloud computing and IoT; therefore, on a case-to-case basis, such features, benefits, and advantages may be reviewed.

References

1. Adel, A., Utilizing technologies of fog computing in educational IoT systems: Privacy, security, and agility perspective. *J. Big Data*, 7, 1, 2020.
2. Alassery, H.A.A.F., Securing fog computing for e-learning system using integration of two encryption algorithms. *J. Cybersecur.*, 3, 149, 2021.
3. Al-Emran, M., Malik, S., II, Al-Kabi, M.N., A survey of internet of things (IoT) in education: Opportunities and challenges, in: *Toward Social Internet of Things (SIoT): Enabling Technologies, Architectures and Applications:*

Emerging Technologies for Connected and Smart Social Objects, pp. 197–209, 2020.

4. Alli, A.A. and Alam, M.M., The fog cloud of things: A survey on concepts, architecture, standards, tools, and applications. *Internet Things*, vol. 9, p. 100177, 2022.

5. Amor, A.B., Abid, M., Meddeb, A., Secure fog-based e-learning scheme. *IEEE Access*, 8, 31920, 2020.

6. Atlam, H.F., Walters, R.J., Wills, G.B., Fog computing and the internet of things: A review. *Big Data Cogn. Comput.*, 2, 10, 2018.

7. Bagheri, M. and Movahed, S.H., The effect of the internet of things (IoT) on education business model, in: *2016 12th International Conference on Signal-Image Technology & Internet-Based Systems (SITIS)*, pp. 435–41, IEEE, 2026.

8. Bao, L. and Yu, P., Evaluation method of online and offline hybrid teaching quality of physical education based on mobile edge computing. *Mobile Netw. Appl.*, 26, 2188, 2021.

9. Bittencourt, L.F., Diaz-Montes, J., Buyya, R., Rana, O.F., Parashar, M., Mobility-aware application scheduling in fog computing. *IEEE Cloud Comput.*, 4, 26, 2017.

10. Cook, C.W. and Sonnenberg, C., Technology and online education: Models for change. *Contemp. Issues Educ. Res. (CIER)*, 7, 171, 171–188, 2014.

11. Decuypere, M., Grimaldi, E., Landri, P., Introduction: Critical studies of digital education platforms. *Crit. Stud. Educ.*, 62, 1, 2021.

12. Dillenbourg, P., The evolution of research on digital education. *Int. J. Artif. Intell. Educ.*, 26, 544, 2016.

13. Emejulu, A. and McGregor, C., Towards a radical digital citizenship in digital education. *Crit. Stud. Educ.*, 60, 131, 2019.

14. Gourlay, L., There is no 'virtual learning': The materiality of digital education. *J. New Approaches Educ. Res.*, 10, 57, 2021.

15. Guevara, J.C., Torres, R.D.S., Da Fonseca, N.L., On the classification of fog computing applications: A machine learning perspective. *J. Netw. Comput. Appl.*, 159, 102596, 2020.

16. Hamid, S.A., Fog computing architecture in higher education institutions. *Eurasian Res. Bull.*, 17, 92, 2023.

17. Hwang, W.Y. and Nurtantyana, R., X-education: Education of all things with AI and edge computing—One case study for EFL learning. *Sustainability*, 14, 12533, 2022.

18. Kassab, M., DeFranco, J., Laplante, P., A systematic literature review on internet of things in education: Benefits and challenges. *J. Comput. Assist Learn*, 36, 115, 2020.

19. Khan, S., Parkinson, S., Qin, Y., Fog computing security: A review of current applications and security solutions. *J. Cloud Comput.*, 6, 1, 2017.

20. Kim, K.J. and Bonk, C.J., The future of online teaching and learning in higher education. *Educause Q.*, *29*, 22, 2006.
21. Kumar, V., Laghari, A.A., Karim, S., Shakir, M., Brohi, A.A., Comparison of fog computing & cloud computing. *Int. J. Math. Sci. Comput.*, *1*, 31, 2019.
22. Laroui, M., Nour, B., Moungla, H., Cherif, M.A., Afifi, H., Guizani, M., Edge and fog computing for IoT: A survey on current research activities & future directions. *Comput. Commun.*, *180*, 210, 2021.
23. Liu, Y., Fieldsend, J.E., Min, G., A framework of fog computing: Architecture, challenges, and optimization. *IEEE Access*, *5*, 25445, 2017.
24. Liu, F., Gong, Q., Zhou, J., Reform of the practice teaching system of entrepreneurship education based on 5G fog computing in colleges and universities. *Sci. Program.*, *2021*, 1, 2021.
25. Long, P. and Siemens, G., Penetrating the fog: Analytics in learning and education. *Ital J. Educ. Technol.*, *22*, 132, 2014.
26. Lu, L. and Zhou, J., Research on mining of applied mathematics educational resources based on edge computing and data stream classification. *Mobile Inf. Syst.*, *2021*, 1, 2021.
27. Mahmud, R., Kotagiri, R., Buyya, R., Fog computing: A taxonomy, survey and future directions, in: *Internet of Everything*, pp. 103–130, Springer, Singapore, 2018.
28. Mathews, S.P. and Gondkar, R.R., Solution integration approach using IoT in education system. *Int. J. Comput. Trends Technol.*, *45*, 1, 45–49, 2017.
29. McGreal, R. and Elliott, M., Technologies of online learning (e-learning), in: *Theory and Practice of Online Learning*, p. 115, 2008.
30. Naha, R.K., Garg, S., Georgakopoulos, D., Jayaraman, P.P., Gao, L., Xiang, Y., Ranjan, R., Fog computing: Survey of trends, architectures, requirements, and research directions. *IEEE Access*, *6*, 47980, 2018.
31. Palvia, S., Aeron, P., Gupta, P., Mahapatra, D., Parida, R., Rosner, R., Sindhi, S., Online education: Worldwide status, challenges, trends, and implications. *J. Glob. Inf. Technol. Manage.*, *21*, 233, 2018.
32. Pan, Y. and Luo, G., Cloud computing, fog computing, and dew computing. *ZTE Commun.*, *15*, 1, 2017.
33. Paul, P.K. and Dangwal, K.L., Digital and institutional repositories in India: With special reference to educational opportunities in this emerging field. *Asian Man (The)-An Int. J.*, *6*, 171, 2012.
34. Paul, P.K., Bhimali, A., Kalishankar, T., Aithal, P.S., Rajesh, R., Digital education and learning: The growing trend in academic and business spaces—An international overview. *Int. J. Recent Res. Sci. Eng. Technol.*, *6*, 11, 2018.
35. Paul, P.K., Digital education: From the discipline to academic opportunities and possible academic innovations—International context and indian strategies, in: *Digital Education for the 21st Century*, pp. 255–281, Apple Academic Press, Florida, USA, 2021.

36. Pecori, R., A virtual learning architecture enhanced by fog computing and big data streams. *Future Internet, 10*, 4, 2018.

37. Peter, N., Fog computing and its real time applications. *Int. J. Emerg. Technol. Adv. Eng, 5*, 266, 2015.

38. Rahman, G. and Chai, C.W., Fog computing, applications, security and challenges, review. *Int. J. Eng. Technol., 7*, 1615, 2018.

39. Raja, R. and Nagasubramani, P.C., Impact of modern technology in education. *J. Appl. Adv. Res., 3*, 33, 2018.

40. Raman, A., Potentials of fog computing in higher education. *Int. J. Emerg. Technol. Learn., 14*, 194–202, 2019.

41. Ross, J., Speculative method in digital education research. *Learn. Media Technol., 42*, 214, 2017.

42. Sabireen, H. and Neelanarayanan, V.J., II, A review on fog computing: Architecture, fog with IoT, algorithms and research challenges. *ICT Express, 7*, 162, 2021.

43. Sarkar, S. and Misra, S., Theoretical modelling of fog computing: A green computing paradigm to support IoT applications. *IET Networks, 5*, 23, 23–29, 2016.

44. Selwyn, N. and Facer, K., The sociology of education and digital technology: Past, present and future. *Oxf. Rev. Educ., 40*, 482, 2014.

45. Sepasgozar, S.M., Digital twin and web-based virtual gaming technologies for online education: A case of construction management and engineering. *Appl. Sci., 10*, 4678, 2022.

46. Suduc, A.M., Bîzoi, M., Gorghiu, G., A survey on IoT in education. *Rev. Rom. Educ. Multidimens., 10*, 25, 103–111, 2018.

47. Sun, H., Wang, X., Wang, X., Application of blockchain technology in online education. *Int. J. Emerg. Technol. Learn., 13*, 252–259, 2018.

48. Sun, W. and Gao, Y., The design of university physical education management framework based on edge computing and data analysis. *Wirel. Commun. Mob. Comput., 1*, 1–8, 2021.

49. Tsarapkina, J.M., Anisimova, A.V., Gadzhimetova, B.D., Kireycheva, A.M., Mironov, A.G., The impact of digital education transformation on technical college teachers. *J. Phys. Conf. Ser., 2001*, 1, 012030, 2021, IOP Publishing.

50. Tursunalievich, A.Z. and Rahmat, A., Challenges in developing a digital educational environment. *Aksara: J. Ilmu. Pendidik. Nonform., 7*, 247, 2021.

51. Urokova, S.B., Advantages and disadvantages of online education. *J. Theor. Appl. Sci., 9*, 34, 2022.

52. Williamson, B., Digital education governance: An introduction. *Eur. Educ. Res. J., 15*, 3, 2016.

53. Williamson, B., Digital education governance: Data visualization, predictive analytics, and 'real-time' policy instruments. *J. Educ. Policy, 31*, 123, 2016.

54. Zhang, C., Design and application of fog computing and internet of things service platform for smart city. *Future Gener. Comput. Syst.*, *112*, 630, 2022.

55. Zolfaghari, B., Srivastava, G., Roy, S., Nemati, H.R., Afghah, F., Koshiba, T., Rai, B.K. *et al.*, Content delivery networks: State of the art, trends, and future roadmap. *ACM Comput. Surv (CSUR)*, 2020, 53, 1, 2020.

Part III
SECURITY IN FOG COMPUTING

Blockchain Security for Fog Computing

Saiyam Varshney* and Gur Mauj Saran Srivastava†

Department of Physics and Computer Science, Dayalbagh Educational Institute,
Agra, India

Abstract

Fog computing (FC) is a modern computing approach that provides latency-aware and highly scalable services to geographically dispersed end-users. Consequently, it significantly reduces the overhead of processing and transmission of large-scale data, which is comparatively more secure than cloud computing (CC), as the information is stored and evaluated on fog nodes since it locates close to these devices. As revealed by the recent literature fog computing is affected by various security and privacy challenges. Blockchain (BC) technology has emerged in recent years as one of the surprising, inventive, and rapidly growing developments in all fields that provide an open platform with an emphasis on data security and privacy. On the other hand, the consensus process in blockchain technology provides a notable assurance of data protection and integrity, which has led to its widespread adoption in a diverse range of applications, benefiting from its inherent features such as security, privacy, distributed trust management, and reliability. Notably, blockchain security for fog computing has recently gained considerable popularity across various domains. This chapter describes blockchain security for fog computing that supports reliable fog services for secure data transactions, trustless, and identity management in a distributed environment.

Keywords: Blockchain technology, Fog computing, Cloud computing, IoT, big data, security issues

**Corresponding author*: saiyamvarshney1@gmail.com
†*Corresponding author*: gurmaujsaran@gmail.com

Chandan Banerjee, Anupam Ghosh, Rajdeep Chakraborty and Ahmed A. Elngar (eds.) Fog Computing for Intelligent Cloud IoT Systems, (357–378) © 2024 Scrivener Publishing LLC

15.1   Introduction

The technological growth of smart IoT devices has triggered cutting-edge applications, and they now play an important and prominent role in connecting many application areas, including smart homes, smart businesses, smart cities, and health care monitoring. According to [1], these connected devices are increasing day by day, from 2020 to 2025 their number will increase from 50 billion to 500 billion. These IoT devices produce massive amounts of heterogeneous data for analysis that need massive storage capacity, computing resources, and network bandwidth. The presence of billions of connected devices will result in a plethora of data that needs to be handled and analyzed efficiently. Then, Cloud computing has emerged as a viable approach to address the difficulty of managing and analyzing large amounts of data while providing end users with essentially unlimited computer resources on a pay-as-you-go basis. The cloud computing paradigm employs centralized cloud server clusters that handle massive data and then give end-user utilities based on their needs [2]. Figure 15.1 shows the main three layers (cloud layer, fog layer, and IoT devices), which can be seen Fog computing structure of network resource, computing, and storage, e.g., "offering support to a well-organized intermediate layer that fully bridges the gap between IoT and cloud computing".

Cloud computing deals with the effective management and analysis of huge data with on-demand capabilities such as data analytics over the Internet, but it does not support real-time data processing for IoT applications. Since centralized data is stored on a server that is geographically away from end users with high response time and transmission latency for real-time applications, data must inevitably be processed near the data sources [3]. Cisco [4] proposed a new processing node termed fog computing, a form of distributed computing that brings cloud services closer

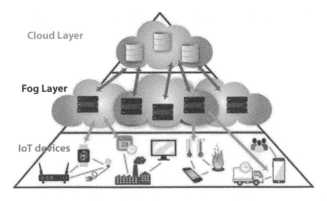

Figure 15.1   Fog computing structure [2].

to 'things' and analyses IoT data. It consists of embedded servers and smart gateways such as smart routers, switches, actuators, and sensors, which can be installed anywhere on a network to provide processing, networking, and storage capabilities to keep cloud services closer to the user [5].

The main benefits of the fog paradigm especially for mission-critical applications such as cloud robotics, control of airways traffic system, and the antilock braking system on vehicles, and others that require real-time data processing to reduce the network latency. These connected applications exploit actuators to provide quick responses in fog environments [6]. Advantages of this paradigm include processing data from heterogeneous devices, real-time and mobility support services, reduction of overall network congestion, cost-effectiveness, and energy usage [7].

On the other hand, the fog paradigm poses several security risks as each device is susceptible to security attacks and is connected to different and heterogeneous fog nodes on the network. For this reason, a hacker can impersonate a device to access user data without permission [8]. Besides, each fog node is more vulnerable to a security attack that requires special protection. Due to fundamental incompatibilities between both paradigms such as the cloud layer being more secure using specialized security techniques as compared to the fog layer, which cannot be applied at the fog layer [8, 9]. According to available literature, user authentication, data privacy, intrusion detection, and access control, are the main security issues in fog computing.

These types of security challenges are in terms of immutable, shared, and distributed communities that require efficient data transactions in the fog environment. Those security challenges can be resolved by using blockchain technology (BT). As a result of the blockchain network's use of hash values and consensus agreements, data transactions are guaranteed to be irreversible, tamper-proof, clear, and quiet [10]. In the field of Information and Communication Technology (ICT), many sectors including banking, IoT, government, education, and others have benefited from the advent of blockchain in distributed networks. Blockchain technology has enabled a distributed and decentralized system that benefits both consumers and service providers with the potential to reduce storage costs by up to 80 percent and enhance security. According to [11], Amazon S3 storage costs $25 per TB/month, while the blockchain costs around $2. For this reason, it may be cheaper to use blockchain to store large amounts of IoT data.

The rest of this chapter is structured as follows: upcoming sections describe preceding works in the field of fog computing as well as its various security issues in terms of user authentication, access control, and data security issues. These security issues can be avoided by adopting blockchain technology. The next section explains the blockchain-based fog computing architecture that leads to data transactions in a shielded manner and concludes the summary.

15.2   State of the Art

In this section, we examine several research articles proposed in the literature to deal with the security concerns raised by the growing fog computing. The majority of these research papers either presented fog security or emphasized the fog security aspect. Here, we compile concepts from several of these research papers to briefly define and describe fog protection.

There are many studies related to fog computing security issues being done. In a study on the uses of blockchain technology to overcome security issues in fog computing [12], the author describes the main differences between cloud and fog computing concerning certain parameters such as architecture, latency, support for mobility, and security. In [8], the author discussed the three-layer architecture of fog computing, including a bottommost layer sensing (end device), middleware (communication layer), and potential security issues with fog servers and remedies for each layer of the architecture.

In [9], the author presents the concepts of fog computing and the obstacles to fog computing adoption from a research perspective. These constraints are classified into two categories – (i) Inherent constraints such as lack of standardized hardware, edge services, management effort for numerous nodes, managing Quality of Services (QoS), and no network transparency, and (ii) external constraints including the need to protect sensitive information from physical threats and legal obligations. In [13], the authors address the benefits of the technology on the connecting path of IoT devices to centralized cloud data centers in a critical analysis of fog-based computing with cloud computing.

Furthermore, many researchers have also discovered that cutting-edge applications face specific challenges including authentication problems, denial of service (DoS) threats, and lack of privacy. According to [14] and [15], the authors discuss the security challenges of overcoming fog computing with IoT integration environments in terms of authentication issues. In [16], the author also described various challenges of security and privacy with existing solutions in fog computing, which can be implemented in fog nodes, data travel between fog nodes, and network security. In [17], the author provides an in-depth analysis of the many security threats affecting mobile edge computing, which is divided into two parts. The first part deals with security threats arising in edge-based computing architectures, including authentication, access control, identity verification methods, intrusion detection, and privacy; While the second section mainly deals with potential threats and flaws.

Based on the available literature, the fog paradigm is susceptible to various types of security attacks. These attacks can be potentially and effectively countered by blockchain technology. In [18] the authors propose a blockchain-based access control system and encryption for the least significant bit, thereby securing data leakage of IoT data. In [19], the authors propose a blockchain-based activity for healthcare services through which the security of various and many different health monitoring devices is provided. Accordingly, it can monitor and verify the smart devices that generate the data. In [20] the authors exploit the advantages of the Hyper Ledger blockchain for data verification and security in the Fog ecosystem for Industrial IoT, thereby avoiding data fraud. Similarly, fog computing-based smart city infrastructure that requires blockchain for data transfer, such as surveillance cameras, traffic systems, alarm systems, and others, as data blocks that contain encrypted data and are, therefore, protected from unauthorized access.

According to [21], the author analyzed personal e-health records with a different approach to storage and sharing and the ability of blockchain to effectively prove the privacy and authentication of data. In [22] the authors innovated private blockchain to enable the efficient and secure use of sensors and remove the dangers associated with remote-affected person control systems. The authors provided real-time patient monitoring and medical remotely and protected archives of all occasions and transactions. In [13] the authors present a blockchain-based model "BlocHIE" that proposes a health system to track most cancer patients and allows contracts to regulate security in hospitals and their homes.

15.3   Security Issues in the Fog Computing Environments

Although fog computing provides significant advantages for time-sensitive applications, the fog paradigm also faces several difficulties, which are covered in the previous section. According to [3], the author discusses security attacks in the fog environments that relate to Trust, Authentication, Access Control, Data Protection, and Privacy, as shown in Figure 15.2. The main causes of these security attacks are discussed in more depth below and include a lack of improper user authentication, inadequate or non-existent access controls, and inadequate data security.

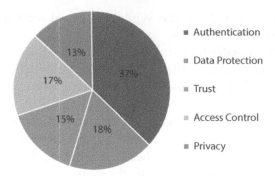

Figure 15.2 Security attack issues in fog computing.

15.3.1 Trust and Authentications in Fog Computing

The distributed and decentralized nature of fog computing presents a significant challenge to data or information security as users can access real-time data that has been processed and analyzed by smart devices on fog nodes. Fog architecture is essential to provide reliable and robust end-user authentication for accessing billions of diverse devices connected to a network. Fog computing is vulnerable to many types of attacks or security issues, including man-in-the-middle attacks, brute-force attacks, physical theft of smart devices, spoofing, and more.

It is clearly observed in Table 15.1 through several proposed techniques, which state their purpose, benefits, and drawbacks based on existing literature to address challenges such as trust and authentication in fog computing.

15.3.2 Data Protection, Privacy, and Access Controls in Fog Computing

Fog computing has proven beneficial for real-time IoT applications such as smart cities, homes, healthcare, and transportation systems that address privacy concerns by transferring sensitive user data from edge devices to the fog layer. On the other hand, the security threats posed by edge devices at the edge of the network can be mitigated with strict access control, data privacy, and security. For example, in healthcare systems, it is essential to create appropriate access privileges for patients, doctors, and other stakeholders to protect confidential medical information from unauthorized access.

It is clearly observed in Table 15.2 through several proposed techniques, which state their purpose, benefits, and drawbacks based on existing

Table 15.1 Trust and authentication techniques in fog computing.

Paper(s)	Purpose	Benefits	Drawbacks
Mookherji *et al.* 2023 [23]	Fog-based semi-centralized architectures are used in e-health applications for device authentication.	A proposed single sign-on authentication protocol ensures that user keys are distinct from centralized authority keys to establish centralized trust.	Not suitable for maintaining data integrity and long-distance communication on the Fog servers.
Nakkar *et al.* 2023 [24]	A group authentication scheme with key agreements in a three-tier structure.	A proposed protocol supports multiple authentications with a key agreement for cloud-edge-IoT.	More concerned with proof of security assets and preventing attacks.
Ramamurthy *et al.* 2023 [25]	Estimate the secure connection between a fog node and a fog client using logistic regression.	A bidirectional trust management method provides reliable and trusted fog communication between requesters and providers.	Not suitable for countering trust-based attacks.

(Continued)

Table 15.1 Trust and authentication techniques in fog computing. (*Continued*)

Paper(s)	Purpose	Benefits	Drawbacks
Dwivedi *et al.* 2022 [26]	Trustworthy schemes for secure storage of data and device authentication in fog computing.	A proposed scheme to enhance data sharing using data contracts and device authentication using smart contracts and IPFS infrastructure in fog computing.	Not applicable in decentralized infrastructure with Trusted Third Party.
Chen *et al.* 2021 [27]	Key exchange and authentication protocol.	An authenticated key exchange protocol protects against an ephemeral secret leak attack.	The proposed approach is not adaptable as its efficacy has only been demonstrated against a small number of attackers.
Guo *et al.* 2021 [28]	Authenticated with key agreement scheme.	An authentication scheme enforces the need for third-party trust in a fog computing environment by using mutual authentication between fog users and fog devices.	This scheme does not support decentralized authentication.

(*Continued*)

Table 15.1 Trust and authentication techniques in fog computing. (*Continued*)

Paper(s)	Purpose	Benefits	Drawbacks
Jia *et al.* 2020 [29]	Anonymity and un-traceability may be accomplished through mutual authentication in MEC.	An identity-based authorization with just a single message exchange to confirm authentication.	This protocol is not concerned with robust security due to regulation changes.
Zhu *et al.* 2019 [30]	Authentication for smart grid communication in a fog environment.	The technique provides an efficient scheme for data aggregation and privacy protection of users' sensitive data.	This technique does not successfully prevent collision attacks.
Wazid *et al.* 2019 [31]	Secure authentication mechanisms using key agreement in fog computing.	Protects users' sensitive data with anonymity and untraceability.	This scheme does not successfully reduce network storage overhead.
Shen *et al.* 2019 [32]	A lightweight authentication scheme using matrix-based key agreement in healthcare environments.	It provides a lightweight authentication method for secure communication between doctors and patients as well as between fog sensors and patients.	The proposed method does not provide security against specific types of attacks, including but not traceable, spoof attacks, and man-in-the-middle.

Table 15.2 Data protection, privacy, and access control techniques in fog computing.

Paper(s)	Purpose	Benefits	Drawbacks
Wang *et al.* 2023 [33]	A privacy-preserving with data aggregation technique offers the potential for dynamic billing and arbitrage in fog-based smart grids.	A proposed PPDB scheme based on a four-tier data aggregation structure, employing fog nodes to receive and aggregate energy usage data encrypted with the ElGamal cryptosystem and decryption based on a trusted third party for arbitration of disputed bill distribution.	The construction of a new scheme that does not support reliable authority and safe channels for a strong plan.

(Continued)

Table 15.2 Data protection, privacy, and access control techniques in fog computing. (*Continued*)

Paper(s)	Purpose	Benefits	Drawbacks
Zeng *et al.* 2023 [34]	A robust and optional privacy data aggregation scheme to enhance the security and privacy of IoT networks augmented by fog computing.	A proposed model based on dual encrypt techniques for smart devices that independently choose an encryption method to upload their data, and the cloud center aggregates it by synchronous homomorphic decryption of the data.	Not considering the optional privacy aspect of the multi-subset or multi-dimensional data aggregation problem.
Zhao *et al.* 2021 [35]	A robust and extensible fine-grained access control mechanism within Fog-enabled applications with a primary focus on preserving user data security and privacy.	A proposed scheme to improve the efficiency of the FOG-enabled e-health system with outsourcing and attribute revocation.	Not concerned with the inclusion of traceability.

(*Continued*)

Table 15.2 Data protection, privacy, and access control techniques in fog computing. (*Continued*)

Paper(s)	Purpose	Benefits	Drawbacks
Zhang *et al.* 2021 [36]	A dynamic and flexible access control framework that meets the specific needs of connected and autonomous vehicles such as ensuring optimal security and adaptability.	A proposed AC4AV access control framework based on three different access control models such as discretionary, identity-based, and attribute-based access control that supports real-time and historical data.	More concerned with reducing latency with various parameters.
Altulyan *et al.* 2020 [37]	Ensuring data lifecycle integrity in smart cities using confidential sharing of sensitive data.	A proposed scheme ensures the data reaches the network node and is unaware of the data content until it reaches the destination.	The technique does not deal with network latency and energy consumption issues.

(*Continued*)

Table 15.2 Data protection, privacy, and access control techniques in fog computing. (*Continued*)

Paper(s)	Purpose	Benefits	Drawbacks
Liu *et al.* 2020 [38]	Ensuring efficient and robust access control in the context of IoT in the sharing economy environment, while maintaining a high level of security.	A proposed protocol incorporates identity-based authentication as a means of preventing shared devices and malicious gateways from accessing systems. Additionally, it especially designed unique protocols for devices that operate concurrently with users.	Not concerned with data collection by IoT providers without revealing users' privacy.
Fan *et al.* 2019 [39]	Multi-authority access control with privacy-preserving leverage attribute-based encryption.	The one-way key agreement feature maintains user confidentiality and anonymity due to the outsourcing of the decryption process.	Data security must be considered while maintaining confidentiality.

literature to address challenges such as access control and data privacy and protection in fog computing.

15.4   Blockchain Technology

As we know and mentioned in [40], Blockchain technology, is a decentralized distributed framework with peer-to-peer communication, which was introduced in 2008 with the bitcoin cryptocurrency [41]. The technology is attracting more attention for its use of involving multi-field infrastructure construction, secure computing for decentralized authority over public or private network systems, and a distributed consensus algorithm to solve traditional database synchronization problems. It has since been used in many areas and the undiscovered potential of blockchain programs and domain names is being investigated. Blockchain technology works as a chain that supports a distributed network in storing information in a decentralized manner, transactional data is identified and stored as a sequence of blocks linked together by hash values.

Blockchain is a decentralized distributed mechanism that allows an openly and fully verifiable digital record of each transaction by a group of unreliable actors which is creating an immutable, transparent, secure, and auditable ledger. The blockchain procedure structure all information into a chain of blocks and consists of a collection of Bitcoin transactions that occur at a given time [42]. As shown in Figure 15.3, the blocks are linked with each other to form a chain that each block refers to the previous block.

15.4.1   Features of Blockchain to Increase the Transparency

A distributed ledger network based on blockchain enables nodes to share a single data document as opposed to maintaining separate copies on

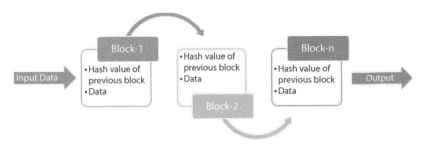

Figure 15.3 Structure of blockchain.

each node. Blockchain works on a consensus protocol that does not update the shared copy of data until each block in the network has agreed. Only one new data block can be added to a series of blocks; if a transaction is to be modified or changed, the entire blockchain of the network must be updated. As a result, compared to traditional record-keeping systems, data in a blockchain is transparent and reliable because all functional nodes in the network can see the same information.

15.4.1.1   Peer-to-Peer (P2P) Networks

Blockchain technology enables multiple nodes to be connected to a computer network without any intermediaries. For example, two or more nodes exchange data directly with each other through a distributed database. It is also referred to as a point-to-point (P2P) network because it involves the exchange of data between two nodes that is confirmed by each node in a blockchain network. As a result, blockchain network participants may share data explicitly and securely within seconds.

15.4.1.2   Decentralized

Blockchain technology is based on decentralized and distributed among participants who do not trust each other, yet each network participant has equal access to records and rights. Therefore, the blockchain network is transparent and secure because each member has a copy of the ledger and the ability to validate transactions.

15.4.1.3   Immutable and Incorruptible

By the nature of both peer-to-peer (P2P) and decentralized, there is no middleman in data sharing, as a copy of the record is available to all participants in the network chain. As a result, the data held in the blockchain is tamper-proof and immutable. Furthermore, since we have secured a block (set of information) using blockchain cryptography or hashing techniques, it is difficult to hack and modify any record because each block has a different hash that is related both to the hash of the preceding block and to itself. When someone tampers with a record in the blockchain, the hash function of the block on the blockchain changes when the record is changed, which disrupts the overall hash function of the chain making it easier to detect or track tampering of records.

Blockchain is primarily used in the financial sector, but because of its ability to guarantee irreversible and transparent transactions and preserve historical information without intermediaries i.e. automatically the threat spread to many extraordinary domains within the blockchain community. Smart contracts are utilized to complete transactions by attempting to solve certain mathematical problems; only then the transactions will be considered to be taken forward. Additionally, the network maintains its consensus. For example, a transaction will only take place if all network nodes agree to it [43].

A blockchain is a collection of distinct block sequences, each block having a structure consisting of a body and a header (see Figure 15.3). The header includes data such as the version of the blockchain, headers from previous blocks in the chain, timestamps, Merkle trees, metadata, and a lot of other information. This version establishes a set of the defined data block. To ensure that facts do not change, it is common to execute a Merkle tree for each transaction [44]. The security of transactions is further enabled by virtual signing or hashing. Additionally, one block is linked to another block using a hash value because each block has a unique hash value. Therefore, the header block is the first durable block in the chain of the blockchain to be persistent. The header is the initial block in the chain that establishes a new block during a transaction request event and stores the data in that block's memory for a specific amount of time [45]. After that, the elements of the transaction are protected within the frame of the block by creating a Merkle tree, which encapsulates the hash function using some cryptographic techniques. As a result, each block has its own distinct and individual hash value, which helps maintain the order of the chain. After the hashing value is generated, the timestamp of the transaction is generated and as a result, eventually, the block is formed [45].

The blockchain architecture is divided into several layers, each providing a unique and dedicated functionality as illustrated in Figure 15.4. This data layer is a part of the foundation layer which is responsible for gathering data from IoT devices (hardware) and connecting it to security. Therefore hashing, Merkle trees, virtual signatures, and cryptographic techniques [43] are implemented at this layer. The responsibility of the network layer is to secure peer-to-peer connections, verification, and communication across distributed nodes. The consensus layer comes next, providing consensus across devices and ensuring the dependability of nodes [46]. As mentioned above, the three levels are known as the essential layers inside the blockchain framework. In evaluation, an optional layer containing essential functionality may be present. The infrastructure also includes smart contracts to facilitate faster transactions with n intermediaries.

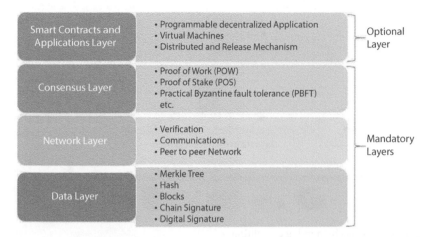

Figure 15.4 Blockchain layered architecture.

15.5 Blockchain Security for Fog Computing Environment

As mentioned earlier, the benefits of blockchain technology (BT) offer a potential paradigm for ensuring the security of critical data traveling in fog environments. As shown in Figure 15.5, each fog node is a prospective node for the blockchain, which uses secret keys to securely transmit and store user authentication and permission information, such as indestructible and immutable, ensuring transparency in transaction data.

The raw data is produced and acquired from a variety of smart IoT devices, including smartphones, security cameras, health monitors, and wearables like blood pressure and pulse monitors, among others. Consequently, to ensure the security and integrity of sensitive User information, such as banking information, health records, etc., User's data and personal details are stored in an encrypted mode using certain cryptographic techniques and virtual signatures. Only authorized users using appropriate authentication methods and cryptographic tools (public and private keys) will be able to access and transfer data over the Fog network.

The blocks of encrypted data are sent across the network and arrive at fog nodes. Miners are responsible for regulating the security of the network in the fog environment, by preserving the security of the shared secret keys. Once a transaction is initiated, miners are in charge of verifying it. The transaction could not have been finalized without his participation. In order to guarantee that the consensus process is followed, miners

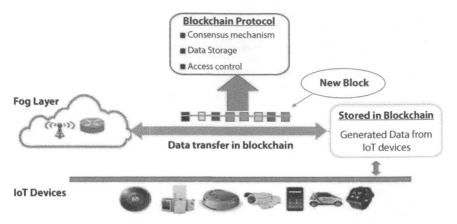

Figure 15.5 Blockchain in fog computing.

must perform additional difficult computations that require the disclosure of transactions.

The major objective of the exercise under discussion is to provide a framework for handling records during data transaction activities and the period of data on the fog layer. Therefore, the proposed methodology helps in transmitting data security and protection, as the data is presided over by fog nodes, which allow access only to authorized users. Furthermore, the data is kept in an encrypted manner, its security cannot be affected even if personal data is breached. Additionally, a distributed model enables keys to be spread among blockchain nodes, reducing or even removing a supervisory authority that, if ineffective, can lead to problems with information privacy. Blockchain technology secures data in transactions by regulating hashing values and employing consensus agreements. Moreover, the security and integrity of clients' sensitive data are protected since blockchain supports data encryption. Adoption of such a design can ensure the security and privacy of personal data in fog environments and provide real-time data to enable quick response in time-sensitive situations.

15.6   Summary and Conclusion

In this chapter, we provide an in-depth analysis of fog computing in the context of various security challenges. Drawing from key security challenges and attributes identified such as insufficient user trust and authentication methods, limitations of access controls, and data protection. For this reason, maintaining data integrity and unauthorized access in a secure manner by adopting blockchain security techniques in the fog environment. Furthermore, based on our analysis, it ensures secure data transmission to the network's billions of Fog nodes, improving the security and isolation of sensitive data.

References

1. Abbasi, B.Z. and Shah, M.A., Fog computing: Security issues, solutions and robust practices, in: *2017 23rd International Conference on Automation and Computing (ICAC)*, Sep. 2017, pp. 1–6, doi: 10.23919/IConAC.2017.8082079.

2. Gomes, E., Costa, F., De Rolt, C., Plentz, P., Dantas, M., A survey from real-time to near real-time applications in fog computing environments. *Telecom*, 2, 4, 489–517, Dec. 2021, doi: 10.3390/telecom2040028.

3. Kaur, J., Agrawal, A., Khan, R.A., Security issues in fog environment: A Systematic literature review. *Int. J. Wirel. Inf. Netw.*, 27, 3, 467–483, Sep. 2020, doi: 10.1007/s10776-020-00491-7.

4. You, W. and Learn, W., Fog computing and the internet of things: extend the cloud to where the things are what you will learn cisco, 2015, [Online]. Available: https://www.cisco.com/c/dam/en_us/solutions/trends/iot/docs/computing-overview.pdf.

5. Kunal, S., Saha, A., Amin, R., An overview of cloud-fog computing: Architectures, applications with security challenges. *Secur. Priv.*, 2, 4, 1–14, 2019, doi: 10.1002/spy2.72.

6. Gupta, H., Vahid Dastjerdi, A., Ghosh, S.K., Buyya, R., iFogSim: A toolkit for modeling and simulation of resource management techniques in the internet of things, edge and fog computing environments. *Software Pract. Exp.*, 47, 9, 1275–1296, Sep. 2017, doi: 10.1002/spe.2509.

7. Bonomi, F., Milito, R., Zhu, J., Addepalli, S., Fog computing and its role in the internet of things, in: *Proceedings of the first edition of the MCC workshop on Mobile cloud computing - MCC '12*, p. 13, 2012, doi: 10.1145/2342509.2342513.

8. Puthal, D., Mohanty, S.P., Bhavake, S.A., Morgan, G., Ranjan, R., Fog Computing Security Challenges and Future Directions [Energy and Security]. *IEEE Consum. Electron. Mag.*, 8, 3, 92–96, 2019, doi: 10.1109/MCE.2019.2893674.

9. Bermbach, D. *et al.*, A research perspective on fog computing, in: *Lecture Notes in Computer Science (including subseries Lecture Notes in Artificial Intelligence and Lecture Notes in Bioinformatics)*, vol. 10797, pp. 198–210, LNCS, Springer International Publishing, Cham, Switzerland, 2018, doi: 10.1007/978-3-319-91764-1_16.

10. Coutinho, E.F., Paulo, D.E., Abreu, A.W., Carla, I.M.B., Towards cloud computing and blockchain integrated applications. *Proc. - 2020 IEEE Int. Conf.*

Softw. Archit. Companion, ICSA-C 2020, pp. 139–142, 2020, doi: 10.1109/ICSA-C50368.2020.00033.

11. Singh, P., Nayyar, A., Kaur, A., Ghosh, U., Blockchain and fog based architecture for internet of everything in smart cities. *Future Internet,* 12, 4, 1–12, 2020, doi: 10.3390/FI12040061.

12. Sunyaev, A., Fog and edge computing, in: *Internet Computing,* pp. 237–264, Springer International Publishing, Cham, Switzerland, 2020, doi: 10.1007/978-3-030-34957-8_8.

13. Mahmud, R., Kotagiri, R., Buyya, R., Fog computing: A taxonomy, survey and future directions, in: *Internet of Things,* issue 9789811058608, pp. 103–130, 2018.

14. Alwakeel, A.M., An overview of fog computing and edge computing security and privacy issues. *Sensors,* 21, 24, 1–20, 2021, doi: 10.3390/ s21248226.

15. Lata, M. and Kumar, V., Security and privacy issues in fog computing environment. *Int. J. Electron. Secur. Digit. Forensics,* 14, 3, 289–307, 2022, doi: 10.1504/IJESDF.2022.122588.

16. Gaba, S., Dahiya, S., Kaushik, K., Security and privacy issues in fog computing, in: *Fog Computing,* pp. 85–96, Chapman and Hall/CRC, Boca Raton, 2022, doi: 10.1201/9781003188230-6.

17. Roman, R., Lopez, J., Mambo, M., Mobile edge computing, fog et al.: A survey and analysis of security threats and challenges. *Futur. Gener. Comput. Syst.,* 78, 680–698, 2018, doi: 10.1016/j.future.2016.11.009.

18. Liu, Y., Zhang, J., Zhan, J., Privacy protection for fog computing and the internet of things data based on blockchain. *Cluster Comput.,* 24, 2, 1331–1345, Jun. 2021, doi: 10.1007/s10586-020-03190-3.

19. Islam, N., Faheem, Y., Din, I.U., Talha, M., Guizani, M., Khalil, M., A blockchain-based fog computing framework for activity recognition as an application to e-healthcare services. *Futur. Gener. Comput. Syst.,* 100, 569–578, 2019, doi: 10.1016/j.future.2019.05.059.

20. Jang, S.-H., Guejong, J., Jeong, J., Sangmin, B., Fog computing architecture based blockchain for industrial IoT, in: *International Conference Computation,* vol. 11538, pp. 593–606, Cham: Springer International Publishing, 2019, doi: 10.1007/978-3-030-22744-9_46.

21. Jiang, S., Cao, J., Wu, H., Yang, Y., Ma, M., He, J., Blochie: A blockchain-based platform for healthcare information exchange. *Proc. - 2018 IEEE Int. Conf. Smart Comput. SMARTCOMP 2018,* pp. 49–56, 2018, doi: 10.1109/ SMARTCOMP.2018.00073.

22. Griggs, K.N., Ossipova, O., Kohlios, C.P., Baccarini, A.N., Howson, E.A., Hayajneh, T., Healthcare blockchain system using smart contracts for secure automated remote patient monitoring. *J. Med. Syst.,* 42, 7, 1–7, 2018, doi: 10.1007/s10916-018-0982-x.

23. Mookherji, S., Odelu, V., Prasath, R., Das, A.K., Park, Y., Fog-based single sign-on authentication protocol for electronic healthcare applications. *IEEE Internet Things J.,* 10, 1–1, 2023, doi: 10.1109/JIOT.2023.3242903.

24. Nakkar, M., Altawy, R., Youssef, A., GASE: A lightweight group authentication scheme with key agreement for edge computing applications. *IEEE Internet Things J.*, 10, 1, 840–854, Jan. 2023, doi: 10.1109/JIOT.2022.3204335.

25. Ramamurthy, P. and Nandagopal, M., Bi-directional trust management system in fog computing using logistic regression. *Indones. J. Electr. Eng. Comput. Sci.*, 29, 2, 808–815, 2023, doi: 10.11591/ijeecs.v29 i2.pp808-815.

26. Dwivedi, S.K., Amin, R., Vollala, S., Smart contract and IPFS-based trustworthy secure data storage and device authentication scheme in fog computing environment. *Peer-to-Peer Netw. Appl.*, 16, 1, 1–21, Sep. 2022, doi: 10.1007/s12083-022-01376-7.

27. Chen, C.M., Huang, Y., Wang, K.H., Kumari, S., Wu, M.E., A secure authenticated and key exchange scheme for fog computing. *Enterp. Inf. Syst.*, 15, 9, 1200–1215, 2021, doi: 10.1080/17517575.2020.1712746.

28. Guo, Y., Zhang, Z., Guo, Y., Fog-centric authenticated key agreement scheme without trusted parties. *IEEE Syst. J.*, 15, 4, 5057–5066, Dec. 2021, doi: 10.1109/JSYST.2020.3022244.

29. Jia, X., He, D., Kumar, N., Choo, K.K.R., A provably secure and efficient identity-based anonymous authentication scheme for mobile edge computing. *IEEE Syst. J.*, 14, 1, 560–571, 2020, doi: 10.1109/JSYST.2019.2896064.

30. Zhu, L. *et al.*, Privacy-preserving authentication and data aggregation for fog-based smart grid. *IEEE Commun. Mag.*, 57, 6, 80–85, 2019, doi: 10.1109/MCOM.2019.1700859.

31. Wazid, M., Das, A.K., Kumar, N., Vasilakos, A.V., Design of secure key management and user authentication scheme for fog computing services. *Futur. Gener. Comput. Syst.*, 91, 475–492, 2019, doi: 10.1016/j.future.2018.09.017.

32. Shen, J., Yang, H., Wang, A., Zhou, T., Wang, C., Lightweight authentication and matrix-based key agreement scheme for healthcare in fog computing. *Peer-to-Peer Netw. Appl.*, 12, 4, 924–933, Jul. 2019, doi: 10.1007/s12083-018-0696-3.

33. Wang, H., Gong, Y., Ding, Y., Tang, S., Wang, Y., Privacy-preserving data aggregation with dynamic billing in fog-based smart grid. *Appl. Sci.*, 13, 2, 748, Jan. 2023, doi: 10.3390/app13020748.

34. Zeng, Z., Liu, Y., Chang, L., A robust and optional privacy data aggregation scheme for fog-enhanced IoT network. *IEEE Syst. J.*, 17, 1, 1110–1120, Mar. 2023, doi: 10.1109/JSYST.2022.3177418.

35. Zhao, J., Zeng, P., Choo, K.K.R., An efficient access control scheme with outsourcing and attribute revocation for fog-enabled e-health. *IEEE Access*, 9, 13789–13799, 2021, doi: 10.1109/ACCESS.2021.3052247.

36. Zhang, Q., Zhong, H., Cui, J., Ren, L., Shi, W., AC4AV: A flexible and dynamic access control framework for connected and autonomous vehicles. *IEEE Internet Things J.*, 8, 3, 1946–1958, Feb. 2021, doi: 10.1109/JIOT.2020.3016961.

37. Altulyan, M., Yao, L., Kanhere, S.S., Wang, X., Huang, C., A unified framework for data integrity protection in people-centric smart cities. *Multimed. Tools Appl.*, 79, 7–8 , 4989–5002, 2020, doi: 10.1007/ s11042-019-7182-7.

38. Liu, Y., Xue, K., He, P., Wei, D.S.L., Guizani, M., An efficient, accountable, and privacy-preserving access control scheme for internet of things in a sharing economy environment. *IEEE Internet Things J.*, 7, 7, 6634–6646, Jul. 2020, doi: 10.1109/JIOT.2020.2975140.

39. Fan, K., Xu, H., Gao, L., Li, H., Yang, Y., Efficient and privacy preserving access control scheme for fog-enabled IoT. *Futur. Gener. Comput. Syst.*, 99, 134–142, 2019, doi: 10.1016/j.future.2019.04.003.

40. Li, L. *et al.*, CreditCoin: A privacy-preserving blockchain-based incentive announcement network for communications of smart vehicles. *IEEE Trans. Intell. Transp. Syst.*, 19, 7, 2204–2220, 2018, doi: 10.1109/ TITS.2017.2777990.

41. Zhang, R., Xue, R., Liu, L., Security and privacy on blockchain. *ACM Comput. Surv.*, 52, 3, 1541–1562, 2019, doi: 10.1145/3316481.

42. Reyna, A., Martín, C., Chen, J., Soler, E., Díaz, M., On blockchain and its integration with IoT. Challenges and opportunities. *Futur. Gener. Comput. Syst.*, 88, 2018, 173–190, 2018, doi: 10.1016/j.future.2018.05.046.

43. Xia, Q., Sifah, E.B., Asamoah, K.O., Gao, J., Du, X., Guizani, M., MeDShare: Trust-less medical data sharing among cloud service providers via blockchain. *IEEE Access*, 5, c, 14757–14767, 2017, doi: 10.1109/ ACCESS.2017.2730843.

44. Mohan, A.P., Mohamed Asfak, R., Gladston, A., Merkle tree and blockchain-based cloud data auditing. *Int. J. Cloud Appl. Comput.*, 10, 3, 54–66, Jul. 2020, doi: 10.4018/ijcac.2020070103.

45. Jiao, Y., Wang, P., Niyato, D., Suankaewmanee, K., Auction mechanisms in cloud/fog computing resource allocation for public blockchain networks. *IEEE Trans. Parallel Distrib. Syst.*, 30, 9, 1975–1989, Sep. 2019, doi: 10.1109/ TPDS.2019.2900238.

46. Jyoti, A. and Chauhan, R.K., A blockchain and smart contract-based data provenance collection and storing in cloud environment. *Wirel. Netw.*, 28, 4, 1541–1562, May 2022, doi: 10.1007/s11276-022-02924-y.

16

Blockchain Security for Fog Computing and Internet of Things

Awais Khan Jumani[1,2*], Waqas Ahmed Siddique[3], Muhammad Farhan Siddiqui[4] and Kanwal[5]

[1]*School of Electronic and Information Engineering, South China University of Technology, Guangzhou, Guangdong, China*
[2]*Department of Computer Science, ILMA University Karachi, Sindh, Pakistan*
[3]*Department of Computer Science, Millennium Institute of Technology & Entrepreneurship (MiTE), Karachi, Karachi City, Sindh, Pakistan*
[4]*Karachi Institute of Economics and Technology (KIET), Karachi, Pakistan*
[5]*Indus University, Karachi, Pakistan*

Abstract

The Blockchain network is used to send and receive data for creating tamper-proof records of shared agreements. This technology ensures that the data is stored securely and cannot be easily modified by anyone. Blockchain is a crucial component of digital data exchange, as it enables the creation of a distributed database that is replicated and shared across a network. It was originally developed for Bitcoin and is designed to maintain an immutable and transparent ledger of transactions by storing information in a series of blocks that are resistant to alteration or damage. Every block in the chain will be linked with the previous block present in the chain with the help of hashes of the preceding block of the chain. Blockchain is about to revolutionize every area of digital commerce. Blockchain is more important than the Internet. When you combine Blockchain and the Internet of Things (IoT), you get two far bigger deals than the Internet that require each other for a variety of reasons. It is normal for this to happen that the Blockchain which is also known as the technology of the ledger in the distributed form will provide its function to help in making the gadgets correspond directly with one another. Freight transportation, component tracking, and compliance log operational maintenance data are some of the areas where we can feel the presence of IoT and Blockchain. Some of the benefits that can take can be, relying on security,

Corresponding author: awaisjumani@yahoo.com

Chandan Banerjee, Anupam Ghosh, Rajdeep Chakraborty and Ahmed A. Elngar (eds.) Fog Computing for Intelligent Cloud IoT Systems, (379–404) © 2024 Scrivener Publishing LLC

getting flexibility while handling the data, etc. This chapter will provide the concept of Blockchain security in fog computing and the IoT. Research and development in this area is still ongoing, and further work is needed to address these challenges and fully realize the potential benefits of combining blockchain and fog computing for security.

Keywords: Blockchain, blockchain application and security, blockchain in health, blockchain framework, Internet of things, fog computing, fog computing security, IoT security

16.1 Introduction

Combining blockchain and fog computing can potentially provide a more secure and efficient solution for various applications such as the IoT, Smart cities, and Industry 4.0. Blockchain can enhance the security of fog computing by providing tamper-proof and decentralized record-keeping, which can be used to ensure the integrity of the data and devices in the fog network. Smart contracts, for example, can be used to automate trust and security-related processes in the fog network, such as device authentication and access control [1]. On the other hand, Fog computing can enhance the scalability and responsiveness of blockchain by bringing computation and storage closer to the edge of the network. This can reduce the latency and network congestion associated with traditional centralized blockchain architectures, which can be a bottleneck for real-time applications. However, there are also challenges that need to be addressed when combining blockchain and fog computing, such as:

- Interoperability: Ensuring that different blockchain networks and fog networks can communicate and share data seamlessly.
- Scalability: Ensuring that the combined system can handle a large number of transactions and devices.
- Privacy and anonymity: Ensuring that the users' data is protected and that their identities are kept private.
- Compliance: Ensuring that the system complies with relevant security regulations and standards.

The rest of the chapter consist on pros and cons of Blockchain, its properties, attacks it may face, and its application in the healthcare industry, as well as the concept of Fog Computing, its security concerns, and optimization. In the last, open research issues in Blockchain and Fog Computing security.

16.1.1   Simply Vital Health

Because of confidentiality and protection concerns, and the additional costs associated with aligning various systems, the healthcare sector has had difficulty sharing data. Simply Vital Health, a company dedicated to improving health data management, utilizes Blockchain technology to enable consumers and healthcare professionals to obtain, exchange, and even transfer their patient records [2]. The platform ensures stable and sound teamwork and collaboration with other service suppliers, as well as the creation of an accounting system that can be relied upon. As everyone can understand, Blockchain is a highly adaptable platform with almost limitless possibilities — these samples are just the tip of the iceberg [3]. If you want to see your organization harness the potential of new innovations, industry seminars are a great approach to educate people on the prevalence of technological innovation and adoption in your business. To learn more, contact us. There is no better approach to expose the minds and attention even for the most resistant stakeholders to the potential benefits of digital technologies such as Cloud computing than to use humor and storytelling [4].

Bitcoin payments are documented on a digital database known as a Blockchain, which is a distributed ledger system. Hacking bitcoins has become more difficult due to the usage of Blockchain infrastructure and the continuous evaluation of the system by users. The most common way for attackers to grab bitcoins is to get access to the digital accounts of bitcoin subscribers. The IoT is almost exactly what it feels like [5]. The IoT is a developing system of billions of gadgets — or things — across the globe that is connected to the internet and to one another via Wi-Fi communication and are increasing in importance. Though its term "IoT" may be new to users, you will be much more acquainted with the term "intelligent homes" or "linked homes," which refer to a linked ecosystem that includes a variety of Internet-connected gadgets that make your life easier [6]. However, IoT devices may be found in places other than the home. From a Wi-Fi pet camera mounted on your bookshelf to a medical gadget placed in your body, such as a pacemaker, they may be anything. The IoT may be regarded as a device as long as it is capable of connecting to the internet and has sensors that send data. Despite the fact that your smartphone can do all functions, it is not an IoT device [7].

16.1.2   Blockchain-Based Frameworks for IoT Security and Privacy

As an alternate answer to the confidentiality and safety issues that have arisen in the IoT, experts have been working on creating Blockchain architecture. Various privacy protection methods for Blockchain-based IoT platforms have been developed and tested. Encryption, anonymization, secret contracts, blending, and variable security are some of the methods that may be used [8]. The authors provide an overview of Blockchain technology and applications for IoT networks, as well as a discussion of how Blockchain methods may be used to solve safety issues in IOT systems [9]. It has been identified as one of the most significant difficulties in the application of Blockchain innovation in the IoT that include the absence of a complete common design, cloud server availability and scalability, vulnerability to tampering, and cost restrictions. LSB (Lightweight Scalable Blockchain) is a new technology introduced that aims to improve the confidentiality and protection of IoT equipment. With the Blockchain-based architecture deployment running on platforms with strong computing capabilities, an overlay network is suggested to accomplish decentralization while maintaining end-to-end security and secrecy from the beginning to the finish [10]. It is suggested that a new Evidence of Block and Trade (PoBT) agreement method be used to overcome the difficulties involved with combining salable IoT systems with Blockchain infrastructure. The goal of the study is to decrease the calculation time required for the verification of transactions and block transactions [11]. The project is also being explored as a ledger delivery method for IoT devices, with the goal of lowering the memory needs of these systems. LSB is proposed for use in the construction of a Blockchain-based architecture built on a redesigned consensus technique, with the goal of reducing the difficulty associated with the Proof of Work (PoW) deployment [12]. As a result, the PoW was substituted with a distributed trusted consensus method developed by the author. The idea improves the privacy and security of IoT systems in a decentralized way. Confidentiality, safety, fault-tolerance, and autonomous action problems are addressed [13].

16.1.3   Permissioned Blockchain in IoT

Using Hyperledger Fabric (HLF) [14], a distributed database platform, organizations may benefit from endorsing worthy infrastructure that is not dependent on a centralized authority while maintaining a high level of adaptability, agility, and secrecy. When it comes to HLF, the consensus process is an open structure. It gives you the ability to change the setup and improve functionality in a diverse manner. A new authentication mechanism for an IoT network that is modeled on the HLF mechanism, the study is primarily concerned with improving the consensus method by including the GA optimization. The goal is to find the optimal configuration using input transactions and success percentages as input variables to the GA technique in order to get the best result [15].

16.1.4   Multi-Layer Security Framework

The suggested network design is intended to offer a secure and trustworthy safety strategy for IoT systems while taking use of the efficiency and characteristics of the communication channels. In an attempt to encapsulate the multi-layer architecture, a smart grouping and machine learning method built on Swarm Intelligence (SI) and Evolutionary Computation (EC) techniques are implemented [16]. Because of Blockchain innovation, this concept proposes an architecture for the lightweight identification and authorization of IoT networked equipment (items and nodes). Using the multi-layer network architecture described here, the completely cellular-enabled IoT network is divided into several tiers. Layer 1 is made up of a variety of groups and IoT nodes. Sink nodes and administrative equipment, such as group heads, are included in the second layer. The BSS of a mobile network is located at the third layer. As a mobile gadget, all of the CHs have phone connections with the 5G BSs and, as a result, have the capacity to communicate with other CHs through the BSs/D2D capabilities. With the proper servers and CPUs, the BSs are capable of implementing the decentralized Blockchain method at Layer 3 of the Blockchain architecture. The entire system model is shown in Figure 16.1. The adoption of Blockchain technology may result in increased overhead and scalability problems. Multi-layer connectivity modeling, as illustrated in Figure 16.1, is suggested for reducing overhead, reducing delays, and increasing responsiveness [17]. It also allows for the creation of affiliated mediums to pick up particular statistics, ensure encrypted connection, and discuss the requirement for network scalability. A wide variety of computing capabilities and energy sources are found in the equipment and terminals at the first layer of the network. In the IoT network, devices that are directly enrolled make use of identification and authorization services provided by local permission software that is managed by the network's cluster heads. This layer consists of CH nodes, authority endpoints, edge-computing endpoints, and portals, among other things. A lightweight consensus is used in the Blockchain ecosystem, so CH nodes may safely interact with one

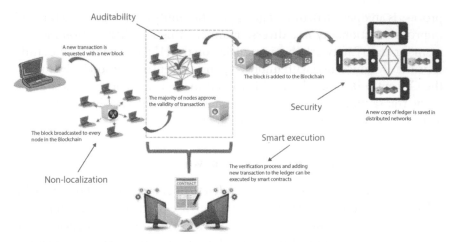

Figure 16.1 Steps in block chain information and transactions [21].

another. This layer contains the implementation of the HLF Blockchain with localized permissions. In mobile networks, the final level is made up of base stations (BSs). Under the HLF Blockchain, this upper level, which is comprised of assets with significant computing capacity, may be organized as a collection of distinct structures [18]. It is possible to implement a robust asymmetric cryptography system at this level of abstraction.

The blockchain system is a decentralized directory of record-keeping or shareable public invoices of all electronic occurrences that have been performed and communicated between Blockchain collaborating officials [19]. Its origins may be traced back to the development of distributed database innovation. Among the many ways in which Blockchain innovation varies mostly from current information platform architectures are the following four important features: non-localization (decentralization), privacy, the integrity of data, and intelligent operation. In Blockchain, an operator is responsible for creating a fresh event that will be included in the Blockchain. This updated activity is published to the system so that it may be verified and audited by other users. Once a deal has been accepted by a large portion of the stations in the network in accordance with the pre-accepted criteria, it is introduced to the channel as a separate frame and becomes part of the Blockchain. For the sake of safety, a copy of the event is stored on many dispersed locations. However, the intelligent agreement, which is a key element of Blockchain software, enables for the execution of legitimate operations without the participation of third parties. One significant distinction among the present architecture of the Internet and Blockchain system is that while the Internet was intended to transfer data (not worth) and duplicates of objects, while Blockchain software was created to transfer duplicates of items (not original information). When using Blockchain, worth is reflected by events that are kept in a public database and protected by giving a checkable, time-stamped log of activities, which allows for safe and highly secure data to be maintained [20]. These activities emerge because of a confirmation procedure that is in accordance with the network's consensus guidelines. Once a fresh item has been validated and uploaded to the Blockchain, numerous duplicates of the document are generated in a decentralized way in order to establish a trustworthy chain between the two records.

16.1.5   Blockchain-Based Supply Chain

A disruptive solution for the architecture, organization, maintenance, and fundamental administration of supply chain processes. Blockchain has the ability to be a game changer. It is anticipated that Blockchain technology would significantly alter supply chains and supply chain administration because to its capacity to provide dependability, tracking, and validity of content as well as intelligent legal agreements in a system where confidence is not required. Specifically, we will look at the product offering of Blockchain system and its application to the products and production supply chain, as well as the architecture of the Blockchain platform as well as potential additional elements for controlling a supply chain in particular part. The specifics of how Blockchain works in the environment of the supply chain still are up for debate and research. While bitcoin and similar economic Blockchain systems may be open to the community, Blockchain-based supply chain systems may need a restricted, confidential, permissioned Blockchain with a restricted number of participants, similar to bitcoin and similar economic Blockchain systems [22]. However, it is possible that the opportunity will remain available for a much more visible collection of connections. The selection of the security factor is among the first considerations to be made. One conventional supply chain is shown in Figure 16.2 as it undergoes transition into a Blockchain-based distribution chain. When it comes to Blockchain-based supply networks, four main elements play a significant role, some of which are not visible in conventional supply chains. Registrars are organizations that give individual identifiers to players in a system. Specifications organizations, which establish standards frameworks, including Fairtrade for responsible supply chains or Blockchain regulations and technical specifications, are also known as criteria bodies. Registrars are those who give certificates to parties in order for them to participate in supply chain networks. The network confidence

Supply Chain

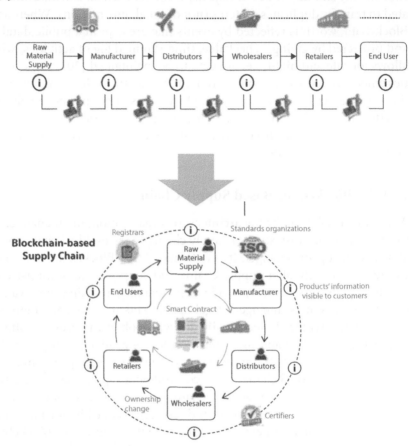

Figure 16.2 Supply chain transformation through blockchain [21].

is maintained through the certification of players, such as producers, merchants, and consumers, who must be verified by a licensed auditors or regulatory agency [23].

Intelligent agreements, which are defined principles that are recorded on the Blockchain, may aid in the definition of network player communication with one another and along with rest of the platform. Information exchange among supply chain players is influenced by intelligent agreements, which also have an impact on ongoing operational improvements. Auditors and regulatory organizations, for example, electronically check the identities of actors and the goods they sell. A digitized portfolio is created for individuals and goods on the system, which contains details such as a summary, a geographical position, certificates, and affiliation with other goods. Each participant in the supply chain has the ability to record essential details about a specific item and its current state into the Blockchain system [24]. When applied to a Blockchain-based supply chain, intelligent agreement administration and workflow standards may be used to control operator accreditation and authorization, as well as which operations they are permitted to view and are required for advancement. Without any kind of consensus mechanism, the players will be unable to alter the standards [25].

In addition to incorporating peer-to-peer systems and employing dispersed consensus algorithms to overcome the conventional dispersed server synchronization problem, Blockchain techniques also include cryptosystems, arithmetic, algorithms, and business theories [26, 27]. Blockchain techniques are being used to build an interconnected multi-field development design. Usually, Blockchain systems are comprised of six fundamental components.

- Decentralized
- Transparent
- Open Source
- Autonomy
- Immutable
- Anonymity

16.1.5.1 Decentralized

Because Blockchain does not depend on a single point, information may be captured, saved, and upgraded on a variety of different platforms.

16.1.5.2 Transparent

The information file maintained by the Blockchain platform is visible to every other cluster, and all of these endpoints have the ability to further modify the information, resulting in a visible and reliable platform.

16.1.5.3 Open Source

Everybody can access the majority of Blockchain systems, records can indeed be checked openly, and anyone may utilize Blockchain technology to build whatever programs they desire.

16.1.5.4   Autonomy

Due to the foundation of consensus, any station on the Blockchain network may securely transmit or modify information; the goal is to place confidence in everyone, from a single individual to the entire network, with no one being able to interfere.

16.1.5.5   Immutable

Any data would be retained in perpetuity and would not be able to be altered until whoever with control over more than 51% of the nodes does so at the exact moment.

16.1.5.6   Secrecy

Due to the fact that Blockchain innovations have addressed the confidence issue among endpoints, information transmission or perhaps even activity may be anonymously; all we need to understand is the individual's Blockchain identity in order to do this [28].

16.2   Pros and Cons of Blockchain

Disintermediation is the removal of a middleman. The fundamental benefit of a Blockchain is whether it allows a dataset to be accessed easily among users eliminating the need for a centralized controller. To implement the restrictions, Blockchain activities get their own evidence of authenticity and permission, as opposed to relying on central program functionality to fulfill the restrictions. In this way, activities may be validated and executed individually since the Blockchain serves as a consensus method to guarantee that all stations are in synchronization with one another. However, why does disintermediation beneficial to us? Because a record, despite the fact that it is made up of merely bits and bytes, is nonetheless a physical object. The information of a dataset kept in the storage and drive of a specific computing device operated by a third party, even though that third party is a trustworthy institution, may be readily corrupted by anybody who has control to that computing device [29]. Figure 16.3, As a result, third-party companies, particularly those in charge of significant datasets, must employ a large number of persons and implement many procedures in order to avoid the information from being manipulated with.

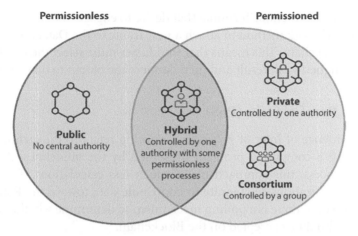

Figure 16.3 Several types of block chain and trust levels [30].

- Users who are authorized have complete authority over their data and financial activities.
- High-quality content: Information stored on the Blockchain is comprehensive, uniform, fast, correct, and publicly accessible. Blockchain does not really have a single source of collapse and is thus more resistant to malicious assaults.
- Process Reliability: Clients may have confidence that activities will be performed precisely as specified by the standard instructions, eliminating the requirement for a trustworthy third entity to oversee the activities.
- Clarity and flexibility are essential: Updates to open Blockchain are visible to all participants and can be tracked, resulting in greater
- Ecosystem simplification: By consolidating all events onto a unified open record, it minimizes the clutter and difficulties associated with maintaining numerous ledgers in different places [31].

16.3   The Properties of Blockchain

16.3.1   Proof of Work (PoW)

The mechanism of the protection is known as the PoW. The method of overcoming a computing barrier presented by the PoW algorithm is referred to as extraction. Terminal that desire to engage in mining employs the Proof-of-Work method to attach a new frame to the Database and add it to the blockchain. This means that the cluster must select the block with both the highest hash result and then connect the blocks to that chain.

16.3.2   Proof of Stake (PoS)

In the Evidence of Interest procedure, minting refers to the technique of completing a computing problem presented by the guidelines. And for mining process, this approach needs much less calculations. The trustworthy organizations collaborate to contribute data toward the PoS algorithm; however, there is a polling mechanism to determine whether or not the batch should be accepted on the Blockchain.

16.3.3   Smart Contracts

The intelligent agreement is a document that is kept upon that Blockchain and can be accessed by anybody. In addition to its own distinct location, the intelligent agreement also contains a collection of execution algorithms and environment parameters. By directing the activity to the intelligent agreement, the client initiates the smarter service agreement. Following that, the consensus algorithm is autonomously and freely executed on each base station of the network in the specified sequence, based on the facts included in the ongoing operation and the information included in the ongoing operation [32]. The construction of the intelligent agreement is shown in Figure 16.4.

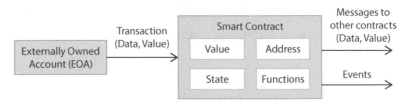

Figure 16.4 The structure of the smart contract [33].

16.4   The Attacks on Blockchain

16.4.1   Attack of 51%

The situation will arise if two miners calculate the hashes of the batch at almost the same moment and both get the identical conclusions. As a consequence, consumers have two distinct networks, both of which are deemed to be correct, and the Blockchain will divide as a response of this.

16.4.2   Double-Spending

The principles of this assault are the same as those of the prior strike; however, the break of the network may be utilized to waste extra cash once more in this instance.

16.4.3   Sybil's Attack

It is conceivable when a single terminal receives multiple elements since the system is unable to genuinely differentiate between the actual computers involved in the transaction. Using Sybil's assault, it is possible to populate the Blockchain with individuals who are beneath Sybil's command. It has the potential to progress to the prior two assaults as well as the capacity to view all actions via the use of unique applications.

16.4.4   DDos's Attack

The strike is comprised of a huge number of responses that are identical in nature. There is security against DDoS threats - the length of a frame may be approximately 1 MB, the length of every template can be approximately to 10000 bytes, up to 20000 identities can be checked, and the highest number of credentials in verification can be up to 20.

16.4.5   Cracking of the Cryptographic

It is conceivable if you employ quantum techniques such as the one known as 'Shora,' that can crack the RSA security. Specifically, the researchers are working on cryptographic methods that are based on hash operations.

16.4.6   Blockchain 1.0 – Digital Currency

Blockchain 1.0 refers to the initial era of Blockchain-based apps that were developed in the earlier 2000s. It relates to the inherent technology channel (i.e. harvesting, hashing, and the community passbook), the overburden method (i.e. payment facilitating apps), and the virtual money (i.e. bitcoin or numerous different electronic vouchers) that serve as a warehouse of worth as well as a source of worth for the guidelines on its own. Bitcoin appears to be one of the few instances in which experience appears to have surpassed the concept. A few of Bitcoin's most significant benefits are as follows:

- When making electronic transactions, Bitcoin provides the option of significantly lower payment costs. Compared to payment and debit cards, Bitcoin enables more privacy. A pseudonymous identity is used, and the method is intended to promote the usage of unique login information for every operation.
- Bitcoin and similar virtual money are protected from inflation due to their distributed existence. When it comes to conventional commodities, the government relies on the banking system to maintain a stable currency production by putting fresh cash into exchange when it is required. While Bitcoin makes use of cryptography to provide comparatively stable cash production, it also allows for the expansion of the money source on a consistent basis.

16.4.7   Blockchain 2.0 – Digital Economy

Despite the fact that the idea of the virtual market was first suggested over two decades back, it is only now that it has been given a suitable technological foundation. It is the broad variety of business and market uses that occur besides basic payouts, exchanges, and operations that are referred to as "Blockchain 2.0." Classical banking mechanisms such as lending and mortgage, sophisticated financial industry tools such as shares, bonds, futures, and swaps, as well as regulatory frameworks such as titles, agreements, as well as other resources and commodities that may be monetized, are examples of such uses. The transaction clearance mechanism and bank card record databases may be suitable situations for the use of blockchain technology. Intelligent settlements are a major new application of blockchain innovations that are becoming more popular. Smarter agreements are essentially computer algorithms that may be programmed to autonomously carry out the provisions of an agreement. The participants engaged in a legal deal may be autonomously paid according to the terms of the deal when a post requirement in a smarter deal involving collaborating businesses is fulfilled, which can be done in a clear way. The companies Visa and DocuSign showed intelligent agreements for renting automobiles in 2015, which eliminated the need to carry out paper lease agreements. Ethereum is the most possibly the best framework for running intelligent contracts, and it is also the most widely used. However, there are certain safety issues that may allow an attacker to influence the implementation of a smart deal in order to earn benefits.

16.4.8   Blockchain 3.0 – Digital Society

Rather than including wealth, cash, trade, currency sector, or even other economic engagement, Blockchain 3.0 applies to a wide variety of operations that do not include cash, the money system, trade, currency sector, or other economical action. Artwork, healthcare, research, identification, government, schooling, public infrastructure, and other forms of civilization and interaction are just a few examples that may be made. It has been suggested that intelligent cities are the most successful software of blockchain software. Smart cities are comprised of horizontally cumulative aspects such as intelligent management, intelligent movement, intelligent living, and the intelligent use of normal resources, as well as intelligent citizens, and an intelligent economy. The IoT is evolving into a new infrastructure for e-business operations. Previous business practices, on the other hand, were not well suited for IoT. Using P2P trading and smart contracts, it is feasible to execute the transfer of intelligent assets and paid content on the IoT. This is facilitated by Blockchain innovation and smart contracts. Using the IoT, it is feasible to effectively implement Blockchain software to enable machine-to-machine (M2M) interrelations and to create an M2M electricity market, where power manufacturers and energy users trade with one another over a Blockchain in the regard of the chemical sector [34].

16.5   Application of Blockchain Technology in Healthcare

Following are some of the applications of blockchain technology in healthcare.

16.5.1   Electronic Health Records

The adoption of Blockchain innovation in medical companies has a number of advantages over other technologies. The most apparent benefit is the ability to manage digital clinical information for patients. Nowadays, client documentation is kept safely in a variety of locations, dispersed across a variety of organizations, hospitals, and insurance organizations, and without complete availability to a centralized individual record. Patients who have their health information recorded in a Blockchain may be allowed to offer their structured information accessible to scientists in return for a predetermined cryptocurrency price. Patients would be able to give accessibility to their digital health information to external organizations at their discretion if they used such client digital health care platforms, which would make inputs counterfeit evidence. Also advantageous is that patients would no longer be required to bring a stack of documents detailing their medical past and testing process findings with them whenever they sought advice from a different healthcare practitioner. Workers of healthcare could readily examine all of a patient's medical information, irrespective of when and where the treatments were provided. Patients might become more active in their very own healthcare if they were able to participate in the administration of their own health information. Using intelligent contracts (self-executing agreements with the aspects of the agreement among involved parties actively published into scripts), which are constructed as a stack of Blockchain, each of these variables have the ability to decrease storage expenses and increase efficiency, possibly even incorporating fully automated insurance billing processes.

16.5.2   Public Health

Medical firms may be able to utilize anonymously and encrypted health evidence in order to improve and accelerate the creation of customized medications. In the future, large volumes of anonymized client records may be used to drive public care policy for whole communities, allowing for more efficient deployment of assets to the areas where they are greatest required now. To add to this, the Centers for Disease Control and Protection, the nation's premier national general health institution, has begun exploring the potential of blockchain technology for the effective sharing of medical data across various institutions. For example, in the event of a disaster or epidemic, very important individual client details must be communicated with a large number of organizations, and speed is critical. Because many of the procedures must now be completed directly, significant time is being wasted needlessly. When used in healthcare, blockchain offers the ability to retain files safe and confidential while also enabling healthcare officials to transfer and exchange information as quickly as feasible.

16.5.3   Education

Another field in which the adoption of blockchain technology may be beneficial is medical schooling. It is possible to utilize this innovation to contain and monitor student accomplishments all through the syllabus, as well as to report skills and knowledge obtained through a variety of different medical configurations and specializations, thus serving as an electronic data system for each attendee, well before they graduate from medical school. Because medical schooling is a lifetime education experience, the information on this electronic registry may keep expanding, preserving every meeting participated, every paper published, and the percentages of effective therapy for every client treated or operation done, among other things. Healthcare professionals may then select whether or not they wanted to disclose this knowledge, and in this manner, verifiable certificates and certificates could be given more quickly and readily, while also being more cost effective and counterfeit evidence [35].

16.6   Fog Computing

A computer infrastructure that is positioned among both the cloud and gadgets that create information is referred to as fog computing or edge computing. Cisco was the first company to develop this kind of processing. However, because of its dynamic nature, the framework enables the placement of assets, such as programs and information, in logical areas, which boosts speed. As a result, the primary objective of this movable architecture is to provide the fundamental analyzing operations to the outermost portions of the network. In addition, information from the IoT equipment is generated at the network's edge, which is known as the periphery [36]. The formation of low-latency communication networks between equipment and analytics destinations is the primary function of fog computing.

16.7   Confidentiality Concerns in Fog Computing

There are various pieces of equipment linked to fog nodes and at multiple portals, which creates safety challenges for fog computing:

16.7.1   Security

Despite the fact that verification appears to be playing a significant part in the process of constructing the preliminary set of links between IoT gadgets and fog nodes in a system, this alone is not satisfactory because there is always the possibility that gadgets will misfire or be vulnerable to suspicious threats [36].

16.7.2   Confidentiality in Fog Computing

Maintaining users' confidentiality is a more difficult task than usual since fog nodes may capture personally identifiable information. As a direct consequence of this, in terms of the identification of end-users in comparison to the distant cloud server that is located in the core channel. In addition, since fog endpoints are dispersed over such huge distances, it is impossible to exercise centralized control [37].

16.7.3   Concerns Regarding Identification and Reliability

Since fog-based operations are provided on a massive volume, identification is among the most significant challenges that have arisen as a result of this technology. Cloud resource suppliers, internet services suppliers, and end-users are all examples of the types of companies that might function as fog service providers. This adaptability makes the fog's overall structure as well as its trust status more complicated. A fog gadget that falsely represents itself as legitimate in order to get end users to join it is known as a "rogue fog node." After a user has connected to it, it is able to simply execute assaults and modify the data that are traveling from and through the client to the cloud [38].

16.8   Cloud Computing Security

- Local information archiving and the evaluation of information that is time-sensitive may be simplified with the use of fog computing.
- Because of this, the amount of information that is transmitted to the cloud and the length it travels are both decreased, which in turn decreases the effect that worries about security and privacy have.

- Fog computing offers a quicker response to problems with privacy and security by reducing latency and reducing the amount of time it takes to take action [39].

16.9 Fog Computing Security Breaches

The quantity of data that is sent to and from the cloud is kept to a minimum by fog computing, which results in a reduction in both the delay that is caused by local processing and the number of safety concerns. When enormous volumes of information are being moved across systems, there is a greater possibility that there may be a security breach. One guideline may be developed for fog computing based on the following standards:

- It lessens the amount of congestion on the network.
- It calls for high adaptability and low latency.
- It is well suited for the duties and inquiries associated with the IoT
- Raw data handling
- Source monitoring
- Resource allocation

For a couple of decades, Cisco has advocated for the use of fog computing as an essential element of an IoT framework that is extensible, reliable, and economically profitable. Through the development of Commercial IoT strategies based on Cisco IOx, incoming information from "things" may be locally screened, processed, and altered on IIoT gateways and exchanges that are positioned at the border of OT networks. As a result of the handling of information at the edge, it is necessary to develop best practices for both privacy and security that may be implemented within a fog computing architecture. In addition to the information that is being communicated by Cisco IOx gadgets, it is critical to ensure the safety of the information and programs that could be running on tens of thousands, hundreds of thousands, or even millions of gadgets that are part of an IIoT network. The term "security" has rarely referred to a single operation, technology, or procedure in isolation. It is a multi-tiered mechanism that, much like when constructing a home, requires strong grounds in order to function properly. Optimal safety requirements for Cisco IOS network operations and IOx computing are included in each and every step of the roll-out process for fog computing [40]. This establishes the basis (as depicted in Figure 16.5).

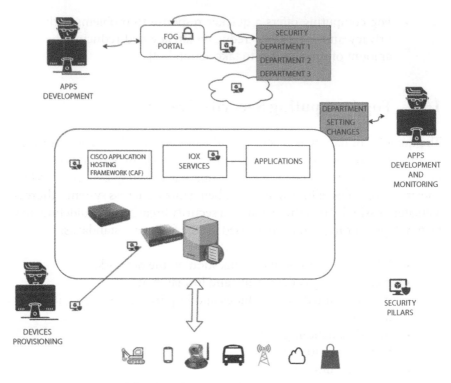

Figure 16.5 Cisco IOx lifecycle and security pillars.

16.10   Optimized Fog Computing

Higher delay is a primary concern in regard to cloud computing. The distribution of content takes more duration on the cloud infrastructure since it is not located geographically close to the information point of origin. Because of this, the effectiveness of latency-sensitive operations and products may suffer as a result. Processing in the fog assists eliminate latency while also expanding the total range of the cloud provider to the information point of origin. Energy over Ethernet is an additional technique that increases the network's versatility for your company (PoE). PoE gives the managers of your network the ability to position powered gadgets in the most advantageous area in order to maximize operational effectiveness, production, and safety. During an ideal situation, you would be able to employ isolated wiring for your exterior locations and industrial-grade powered equipment for a variety of your commercial settings [41].

16.11   Open Research Issues in Blockchain and Fog Computing Security

There are several open research issues in the area of blockchain and fog computing security, including:

- Scalability: Blockchain networks currently have limitations on the number of transactions they can process per second, leading to delays and increased user costs. Researchers are working on solutions such as sharing and off-chain transactions to improve scalability [42].
- Privacy and anonymity: Blockchain networks are designed to be transparent, but this can make it difficult for users to maintain privacy. Research is being done on techniques such as zero-knowledge proofs and ring signatures to improve privacy and anonymity on the blockchain [43].
- Consensus mechanisms: Blockchain networks rely on consensus mechanisms to ensure that all network nodes agree on the Blockchain's state. Researchers are working on alternative consensus mechanisms, such as proof of stake, that are more energy-efficient than proof of work [44].
- Fog computing security: Fog computing is a distributed computing paradigm that brings computing and storage closer to the edge of the network. As fog computing is becoming increasingly popular, researchers are looking into the security implications of this paradigm, such as the privacy and trustworthiness of the devices [45].
- Smart contract security: Smart contracts are self-executing contracts with the terms of the agreement between buyer and seller being directly written into lines of code. Researchers are looking into the security of smart contracts, as errors or vulnerabilities in the code can lead to financial losses [46].
- Interoperability: Blockchain networks are currently siloed, and it can be difficult for them to communicate with each other. Researchers are exploring ways to improve interoperability between different blockchain networks [47].

16.12   Conclusion

The integration of blockchain technology with fog computing and the IoT offers numerous benefits in terms of security, decentralization, and trust.

Blockchain's decentralized and distributed nature provides a secure and tamper-proof way to store and transfer data, making it well-suited for use in IoT and fog computing environments. Additionally, the use of smart contracts and consensus mechanisms in blockchain technology can provide a means for secure communication and decision-making among IoT devices and fog nodes. However, it's important to note that implementing blockchain technology in these environments still presents challenges such as scalability, energy consumption, and interoperability. Therefore, further research and development are needed to fully realize the potential of blockchain in fog computing and IoT.

References

1. Kumar, N.M. and Mallick, P.K., Blockchain technology for security issues and challenges in IoT. *Procedia Comput. Sci.*, 132, 1815–1823, 2018.
2. Sengupta, J., Ruj, S., Bit, S.D., A comprehensive survey on attacks, security issues and blockchain solutions for IoT and IIoT. *J. Network Comput. Appl.*, 149, 102481, 2020.
3. Dasgupta, D., Shrein, J.M., Gupta, K.D., A survey of blockchain from security perspective. *J. Bank. Financial Technol.*, 3, 1, 1–17, 2019.
4. Mohanta, B.K., Jena, D., Ramasubbareddy, S., Daneshmand, M., Gandomi, A.H., Addressing security and privacy issues of IoT using blockchain technology. *IEEE Internet Things J.*, 8, 2, 881–888, 2020.
5. Li, X., Jiang, P., Chen, T., Luo, X., Wen, Q., A survey on the security of blockchain systems. *Future Gener. Comput. Syst.*, 107, 841–853, 2020.
6. Mohanta, B.K., Jena, D., Panda, S.S., Sobhanayak, S., Blockchain technology: A survey on applications and security privacy challenges. *Internet Things*, 8, 100107, 2019.
7. Khan, M.A. and Salah, K., IoT security: Review, blockchain solutions, and open challenges. *Future Gener. Comput. Syst.*, 82, 395–411, 2018.
8. Yu, Y., Li, Y., Tian, J., Liu, J., Blockchain-based solutions to security and privacy issues in the internet of things. *IEEE Wirel. Commun.*, 25, 6, 12–18, 2018.
9. Ferrag, M.A. and Shu, L., The performance evaluation of blockchain-based security and privacy systems for the internet of things: A tutorial. *IEEE Internet Things J.*, 8, 24, 17236–17260, 2021.
10. Qahtan, S., Yatim, K., Zaidan, A.A., Alsattar, H.A., Albahri, O.S., Zaidan, B.B., Mohammed, R.T., Novel multi security and privacy benchmarking framework for blockchain-based IoT healthcare industry 4.0 Systems. *IEEE Trans. Ind. Inf.*, 18, 9, 6415–6423, 2022.
11. Patil, A.S., Tama, B.A., Park, Y., Rhee, K.H., A framework for blockchain based secure smart green house farming, in: *International Conference*

on Ubiquitous Information Technologies and Applications, International Conference on Computer Science and its Applications, Springer, Singapore, pp. 1162–1167, 2018.

12. Uddin, M., Khalique, A., Jumani, A.K., Ullah, S.S., Hussain, S., Next-generation blockchain-enabled virtualized cloud security solutions: Review and open challenges. *Electronics,* 10, 20, 2493, 2021.

13. Jumani, A.K., Laghari, A.A., Khan, A.A., Blockchain and big data: Supportive aid for daily life, in: *Security Issues and Privacy Concerns in Industry 4.0 Applications,* pp. 141–178, 2021.

14. Siddique, W.A., Jumani, A.K., Laghari, A.A., Introduction to internet of things with flavor of blockchain technology, in: *Blockchain,* pp. 51–72, Chapman and Hall/CRC, New York, Taylor Francis, 2022.

15. Brotsis, S., Kolokotronis, N., Limniotis, K., Shiaeles, S., On the security of permissioned blockchain solutions for iot applications, in: *2020 6th IEEE Conference on Network Softwarization (NetSoft),* pp. 465–472, IEEE, 2020, June.

16. Vochescu, A., Culic, I., Radovici, A., Multi-layer security framework for IoT devices, in: *2020 19th RoEduNet Conference: Networking in Education and Research (RoEduNet),* pp. 1–5, IEEE, 2020, December.

17. Bica, I., Chifor, B.C., Arseni, Ş.C., Matei, I., Multi-layer IoT security framework for ambient intelligence environments. *Sensors,* 19, 18, 4038, 2019.

18. Rashid, M.A. and Pajooh, H.H., A security framework for IoT authentication and authorization based on blockchain technology, in: *2019 18th IEEE International Conference on Trust, Security and Privacy in Computing and Communications/13th IEEE International Conference on Big Data Science and Engineering (TrustCom/BigDataSE),* pp. 264–271, IEEE, 2019, August.

19. Topal, O.A., Demir, M.O., Liang, Z., Pusane, A.E., Dartmann, G., Ascheid, G., Kur, G.K., A physical layer security framework for cognitive cyber-physical systems. *IEEE Wirel. Commun.,* 27, 4, 32–39, 2020.

20. Chen, J., Mohamed, M.A., Dampage, U., Rezaei, M., Salmen, S.H., Obaid, S.A., Annuk, A., A multi-layer security scheme for mitigating smart grid vulnerability against faults and cyber-attacks. *Appl. Sci.,* 11, 21, 9972, 2021.

21. Saberi, S., Kouhizadeh, M., Sarkis, J., Shen, L., Blockchain technology and its relationships to sustainable supply chain management. *Int. J. Prod. Res.,* 57, 7, 2117–2135, 2019.

22. Shahid, A., Almogren, A., Javaid, N., Al-Zahrani, F.A., Zuair, M., Alam, M., Blockchain-based agri-food supply chain: A complete solution. *IEEE Access,* 8, 69230–69243, 2020.

23. Köhler, S. and Pizzol, M., Technology assessment of blockchain-based technologies in the food supply chain. *J. Cleaner Prod.,* 269, 122193, 2020.

24. Al-Farsi, S., Rathore, M.M., Bakiras, S., Security of blockchain-based supply chain management systems: challenges and opportunities. *Appl. Sci.,* 11, 12, 5585, 2021.

25. Hussain, M., Javed, W., Hakeem, O., Yousafzai, A., Younas, A., Awan, M.J., Zain, A.M., Blockchain-based IoT devices in supply chain management: A systematic literature review. *Sustainability*, 13, 24, 13646, 2021.

26. Al-Amin, S., Sharkar, S.R., Kaiser, M.S., Biswas, M., Towards a blockchain-based supply chain management for e-agro business system, in: *Proceedings of International Conference on Trends in Computational and Cognitive Engineering*, pp. 329–339, Springer, Singapore, 2021.

27. Shoaib, M., Lim, M.K., Wang, C., An integrated framework to prioritize blockchain-based supply chain success factors. *Ind. Manage. Data Syst.*, 120, 11, 2103–2131, 2020.

28. Bernabe, J.B., Canovas, J.L., Hernandez-Ramos, J.L., Moreno, R.T., Skarmeta, A., Privacy-preserving solutions for blockchain: Review and challenges. *IEEE Access*, 7, 164908–164940, 2019.

29. Quasim, M.T., Khan, M.A., Algarni, F., Alharthy, A., Alshmrani, G.M.M., Blockchain frameworks, in: *Decentralised Internet of Things*, pp. 75–89, Springer, Cham, Springer Nature Switzerland, 2020.

30. Wegrzyn, E.K.E. and Wang, E., Types of blockchain: Public, private, or something in between, Foley&Lardner LLP, Austin, 2021.

31. Zhou, Z., Liu, X., Zhong, F., Shi, J., Improving the reliability of the information disclosure in supply chain based on blockchain technology. *Electron Commer Res. Appl.*, 52, 101121, 2022.

32. Chowdhury, M.J.M., Colman, A., Kabir, M.A., Han, J., Sarda, P., Blockchain versus database: A critical analysis, in: *2018 17th IEEE International Conference on Trust, Security and Privacy in Computing and Communications/12th IEEE International Conference on Big Data Science and Engineering (TrustCom/BigDataSE)*, pp. 1348–1353, IEEE, 2018, August.

33. Mohanta, B.K., Panda, S.S., Jena, D., An overview of smart contract and use cases in blockchain technology, in: *2018 9th International Conference on Computing, Communication and Networking Technologies (ICCCNT)*, pp. 1–4, IEEE, 2018, July.

34. Aggarwal, S. and Kumar, N., Attacks on blockchain, in: *Advances in Computers*, vol. 121, pp. 399–410, Elsevier, 2021.

35. Fekih, R.B. and Lahami, M., Application of blockchain technology in healthcare: A comprehensive study, in: *International Conference on Smart Homes and Health Telematics*, pp. 268–276, Springer, Cham, 2020, June.

36. Laghari, A.A., Jumani, A.K., Laghari, R.A., Review and state of art of fog computing. *Arch. Comput. Methods Eng.*, 28, 5, 3631–3643, 2021.

37. Kumar, V., Laghari, A.A., Karim, S., Shakir, M., Brohi, A.A., Comparison of fog computing & cloud computing. *Int. J. Math. Sci. Comput.*, 1, 31–41, 2019.

38. Pareek, K., Tiwari, P.K., Bhatnagar, V., Fog computing in healthcare: A review. *IOP Conf. Ser.: Mater. Sci. Eng.*, 1099, 1, 012025, 2021, March.

39. Popović, K. and Hocenski, Ž., Cloud computing security issues and challenges, in: *The 33rd International Convention MIPRO*, pp. 344–349, IEEE, 2010, May.

40. Awaisi, K.S., Hussain, S., Ahmed, M., Khan, A.A., Ahmed, G., Leveraging IoT and fog computing in healthcare systems. *IEEE Internet Things Mag.*, 3, 2, 52–56, 2020.

41. Bellendorf, J. and Mann, Z.Á., Classification of optimization problems in fog computing. *Future Gener. Comput. Syst.*, 107, 158–176, 2020.

42. Hashim, F., Shuaib, K., Zaki, N., Sharding for scalable blockchain networks. *SN Comput. Sci.*, 4, 1, 1–17, 2023.

43. Feng, Q., He, D., Zeadally, S., Khan, M.K., Kumar, N., A survey on privacy protection in blockchain system. *J. Network Comput. Appl.*, 126, 45–58, 2019.

44. Lashkari, B. and Musilek, P., A comprehensive review of blockchain consensus mechanisms. *IEEE Access*, 9, 43620–43652, 2021.

45. Alzoubi, Y., II, Osmanaj, V.H., Jaradat, A., Al-Ahmad, A., Fog computing security and privacy for the internet of thing applications: State-of- the-art. *Secur. Privacy*, 4, 2, e145, 2021.

46. Wan, Z., Xia, X., Lo, D., Chen, J., Luo, X., Yang, X., Smart contract security: A practitioners' perspective, in: *2021 IEEE/ACM 43rd International Conference on Software Engineering (ICSE)*, pp. 1410–1422, IEEE, 2021, May.

47. Reegu, F.A., Abas, H., Hakami, Z., Tiwari, S., Akmam, R., Muda, I., Jain, R., Systematic assessment of the interoperability requirements and challenges of secure blockchain-based electronic health records. *Secur. Commun. Netw.*, 2022, 1–12, 2022.

17

Fine-Grained Access Through Attribute-Based Encryption for Fog Computing

Malabika Das

Heramba Chandra College, Kolkata, West Bengal, India

Abstract

Attribute-based encryption is a generalization of public key cryptography based on one-to-many encryptions that allow users to encrypt and decrypt data based on user attributes. It is different from identity-based encryption, in which access control is based on the identities of users such as their email addresses, and usernames. In ABE, each user is associated with a set of attributes. These attributes can be various characteristics such as jobs, organizations, age groups, or any other criteria. In decentralized attribute-based encryption, any party can create a public key and private key for different users which reflect their attributes without any collaboration.

ABE has been widely used to impose fine-grained access control on encrypted data. Fine-grained access control is a method of controlling who can access certain data. It is essential because it sets access parameters for specific data even when data is stored together, which means it specifies the access rights of individual users. It is often used in cloud computing where a large amount of data is stored together and it gives each piece of data its own specified policy for access. For example, one individual may be given access to edit and make changes to a piece of data while another might be given access only to read the data without making any changes.

Fog computing extends the cloud computing paradigm to the edge of the network. The main difference between fog computing and cloud computing is decentralization and flexibility. Fog computing brings computing to the networks' edge by moving storage and computing systems as near as possible to the applications, components, and devices that need thus reducing processing latency and improving efficiencies. Fog computing implementation involves either writing or porting IoT devices at the network edge for fog nodes using fog tools. Those nodes take

---

Email: malabika.mail@gmail.com

Chandan Banerjee, Anupam Ghosh, Rajdeep Chakraborty and Ahmed A. Elngar (eds.) Fog Computing for Intelligent Cloud IoT Systems, (405–424) © 2024 Scrivener Publishing LLC

in the data from the other edge devices and then direct the data into the optimal location for analysis.

Keywords: Attribute-based cryptography, fine-grained access, fog computing, KP-ABE, CP-ABE

17.1   Introduction

Encryption and cryptography have been in various forms for thousands of years since ancient Egypt age. Most probably the formal study of cryptography started around World War II when Polish cryptologist Rejewski tried to break the German military ciphers. That research was continued by Alan Turing and his team and was successful and famously known as breaking the Enigma. Since then, there have been new types of cryptography. In the beginning the encryption process was very simple. The ancient Spartans used a scytale device to send secret messages during battle. This device consists of a leather strap wrapped around a wooden rod. Similar or correct size rod is required to get the message otherwise the message makes no sense. In 60 BC Julius Caesar invent a cipher that shifts characters by three places in the alphabet, i.e., A becomes D, B becomes E etc. simple yet effective encryption methods at that time. In 1553, Charles Wheatstone invents the Playfair cipher, which encrypts pairs of letters instead of single ones, so it is harder to crack. Now what is cryptography and encryption? Cryptography is the science of concealing a message with a proper secret code whereas encryption is the way to encrypt and decrypt data. So, cryptography is all about studying the methods to make a message secure between two parties and encryption is about the process itself. The encryption process encrypts or encodes a piece of information into a cipher which is unreadable without the right decoding key or algorithm. It's like a secret code protecting sensitive data by changing it into something unintelligible. Only those who have the decoding key can decipher the code and get the original message, just like a secret message between friends to keep messages safe from others.

However, the rise of internet usage and cloud computing has changed the perspective of cryptography. In our day-to-day lives, cryptography has become an essential part. For example, we use it for online purchases, bank transfers, sending emails, and so on. Cryptography is used to secure all transmitted information in our IoT-connected world and to authenticate people and devices and devices to other devices. Clearly, the old classical cryptography techniques are no longer appropriate. A vast system of electronic communication, commerce, and intellectual property needs to be secure across the world with the modern cryptographic system. The basic principle of a modern cryptographic system is that we no longer depend on the used algorithm, but rely on the secret keys. The four essential goals of a cryptographic system are:

- Confidentiality: Information can never be accessed by someone who is not authorized to see it.
- Identification and authentication: Before any information is exchanged, identify and then authorize both the sender and the recipient.
- Integrity: Information must not be modified in transit. Any modification must be detectable.
- Non-repudiation: Cannot disclaim transmission of the message. This provides digital legitimacy.

There are mainly two types of cryptographing, one is symmetric cryptography and another one is asymmetric or public-key cryptography.

Symmetric cryptography is the simplest and oldest cryptography and by far the most used, it involves only one secret key to cipher and decipher information. It uses a secret key that can either be a word or a number or a string of random letters. With the secret key, the plaintext is changed into a ciphertext. The sender and the recipient should know the secret key that is used to encrypt and decrypt the messages. Figure 17.1 illustrates symmetric key cryptography where a single key is used fro encryption and decryption. The most widely used symmetric algorithms are AES-128, AES-192 and AES-256.

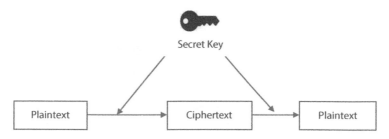

Figure 17.1 Symmetric-key cryptography.

Advantages:

- Since it uses a single key for encryption and decryption, it is faster to execute.
- It uses password authentication as a security purpose to prove the receiver's identity

Disadvantages:

- The chances of sharing encryption keys securely are less; it is difficult and challenging to share keys in symmetric encryption.
- Symmetric is not that scalable, as it's not suitable for various users.

Asymmetric cryptography is a relatively new method that uses two keys to encrypt and decrypt. Secret keys are exchanged over the internet or a large network. It ensures no third party can misuse the key. Now the two keys used in this process, one is public key which made freely available to anyone who might want to send you a message. The second private key is kept a secret so that you can only know. As shown in Figure 17.2, asymmetric cryptography uses a public key for encryption and a private key for decryption.

Advantages:

- Asymmetric encryption has two keys, one public and private, so there's no problem with the distributing keys
- Again, with a pair of keys, it is not difficult to communicate with multiple parties and that's how it is more scalable in large networks

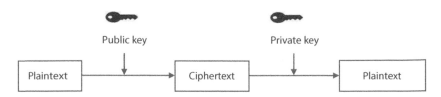

Figure 17.2 Asymmetric-key cryptography.

Disadvantages:

- Asymmetric encryption is slower compared to symmetric encryption
- Asymmetric is not that easy to implement and manage due to its large key sizes.

Later, identity-based encryption was introduced. Identity-based systems allow any party to generate a public key from a known identity value such as an ASCII string. As a result, parties may encrypt messages with no prior distribution of key between individual participants. This is useful in cases where pre-distribution of authenticated keys is inconvenient or infeasible due to technical restraints.

Attribute-based encryption is an extension of identity-based encryption [27].

Here, Section 17.2 discusses about attribute-based encryption, Section 17.3 discussed fine grained access through ABE, Section 17.4 gives ABE model for fine grained access. Section 17.5 describes the application of ABE in fog computing, Section 17.6 gives a comparison between different ABE schemes.

17.2   Attribute-Based Encryption

Attribute-based encryption is a new technique in cryptography. In 1984, Adi Shamir introduced the idea of Identity-based encryption. Seven years later, another cryptographer, Dan Boneh, proposed a practical implementation of IBE using a variant of the computation of Diffie Hellman problem. This proposal relied upon the private key generator (PKG) which is a certain drawback for general use. In 2005, Amit Sahai and Brent Waters [1] approached the idea from another angle. In a paper titled "Fuzzy Identity – based Encryption", they suggested and proved that a secure system was possible using multiple private keys with a single key. In 2018 the European standard body ETSI issued specifications for using ABE to secure access control. In 2020 the scientific organization gave the original Sahai Waters paper "Test of Time" award.

Attribute-based encryption is probably a generalization of identity-based encryption. In ABE data is encrypted and decrypted based on user attributes or properties not on the identities of the users. In ABE, each user and data object are associated with set of attributes [23]. These attributes represent various characteristics or properties of the user or the data such as job title, company name, department, or any other relevant information. Encryption and decryption operation are performed based on matching attributes.

Attribute-based encryption offer several advantages compared to traditional encryption schemes:

1. Fine grained access control: ABE provides a fine-grained access control [44] mechanism that allows data owners to specify access policies based on attributes rather than specific identities. This enables more precise control over who can access the data. So, it gives more flexible and customizable access policies.

2. Data confidentiality: ABE ensures data confidentiality by encrypting the data based on attributes and only users having those specified attributes can access the encrypted data. So, it provides an additional layer of security beyond traditional identity-based encryption.

3. Scalability: ABE is scalable and suitable for large scale systems with large number of users and data objects. It does not require a specific user-to-user or user-to-data mapping.

4. Flexible and dynamic attribute management: ABE enables dynamic attribute management [25], where attributes can be easily added, modified, or revoked without requiring re-encryption of the data. This flexibility allows for efficient access control policy updates and simplifies attribute management in dynamic environments.

5. Secure data sharing: ABE facilitates secure data sharing by encrypting data based on attributes. This enables data owners to share the data with specific user group or individuals with those attributes. It allows for secure collaboration in various scenarios such as cloud storage, decentralize networks, or multi-user environments.

6. Privacy preservation: ABE can preserve privacy by encrypting data based on attributes without revealing the actual attributes to unauthorized partied.

7. Reduce Key management complexity: ABE simplifies key management compared to traditional encryption schemes. Instead of maintaining individual encryption keys for user, ABE employs attribute-based keys.

Figure 17.3 Attribute-based encryption.

ABE algorithm [2] has four steps:

- **Setup:** This is a randomized algorithm that takes no point other than the implicit security parameter. It output the public parameters Pk and a master key Mk.
- **Encryption:** This is a randomized algorithm that takes as input message m, a set of attributes γ, and the public parameters Pk. It outputs the ciphertext E.
- **Key Generation:** It takes as input an access structure A, the master key Mk, and the public parameters Pk. It outputs a decryption key D.
- **Decryption:** It takes as input the ciphertext E that was encrypted under the set S of attributes, the decryption key D for access control structure A, and public parameters Pk. It outputs the message M if $S \in A$.

In Figure 17.3 attribute based encryption is described. The mathematical aspects of ABE ensure the correctness, security and efficiency of the encryption and decryption operations.

17.3   Fine-Grained Access Through ABE

Access control refers to policies and procedures that an organization puts to control which people have access to specific data. Fine-grained access control, a dimension of attribute-based access control [2, 8], gives access rights to a user of the organization based on defined attributes and roles. It allows for fine-grained granularity in defining and enforcing access policies based on specific attributes, actions and resources. Access control should be as simplified and automated as possible. By automating and simplifying the policies and fine-tuning them appropriately, the organization can focus resources on creating business value.

In a fine-grained access control model, access permissions can be specified at a very granular level, going beyond basic permissions like read, write, or execute. It enables administrators or system owners to define access policies based on various factors such as attributes i.e., job title, departments, etc. Fine-grained access control is particularly important in complex systems with multiple users, diverse resources, and varying levels of sensitivity.

As data has become more valuable and a crucial part of any modern business, the ability to implement fine-grained access control has also become incredibly important. Some of the reasons are given below:

- Confidentiality: Fine-grained access control provides with the tools to abide by the relevant regulation and ensure that any personal information is treated with the utmost confidentiality. Only the user who has rights can access it.
- Centralized Data storage: In today's data-driven organizations, data is stored in a centralized data store such as a data warehouse. Fine-grained access control allows you to accomplish this without exposing the internal data to everyone in that organization as a result.
- Precision: Fine-grained access offers flexibility such as if a specific piece of data that requires special treatment, can be implemented quickly without impacting other parts of the data.
- Improved Security: implementing a fine-grained access control scheme gives better chance of reducing security risks. Since the access control is granular and clear, it lowers the risk of data exposure.
- Efficient Authorizations for non-employees: there are certain scenarios where an organization wants to expose special data which are no longer relevant like vendors, customers, partners, etc., in such cases fine-grained access control helps to limit the scope of data shared precisely what it wants to share with third parties.

In today's modern world, more and more work is happening in non-traditional environments, making it difficult to maintain control over data access protocols. Fine-grained access control measures can add extra flexibility to the policies, allowing them to grant and revoke access according to information like time of the day, and location, rather them merely just their profiles.

Attribute-based encryption (ABE) [45] is a one-to-many encryption scheme that makes it unnecessary for data owners to know the number and identity of users in the encryption stage. Data owners only need to define unique access structures for sensitive data based on user attributes. Moreover, ABE combines attributes with ciphertexts and users' private keys so that users can access sensitive data only if the intersection of their attribute set and ciphertext attribute set satisfies the access structure defined in the encryption stage. ABE has become an important tool for meeting the needs of fine-grained access control in cloud storage applications. In the next section, we will give a simple example of how it works.

17.4   ABE Model for Fine-Grained Access

Whereas fine-grained access controls allow users to use or access a particular data, ABE is used for achieving different security objectives. In an ABE model [5, 6, 16], access to encrypted data is granted based on attributes associated with users and data. It uses a particular set of attributes as the public key to encrypt data and the private key is assigned to the users by PKG based on their attributes. So, Attribute-based encryption is well-suited for achieving fine-grained access control.

In a cloud computing environment, we assume that data owners are fully trusted. In ABE scheme one ciphertext can be decrypted by a group of users with attributes which is stated in the policy by the data owner. ABE scheme has an efficient advantage in fine-grained access control [11, 29]. In ABE, ciphertexts are labelled with a set of attributes and a particular key can decrypt a particular ciphertext only if there is a match between the attributes of the ciphertext and the user's key.

For example, in Figure 17.4, in an X-organization, a certain piece of encrypted data can be accessed by employees with different roles or attributes. Here, the attributes are president and Manager.

So, in X-organization, a president and a manager can access data and use it but the staff of that organization cannot access it, or any other president from another organization cannot access it. This type of specificity can help an organization or company avoid inconvenience because their permissions are fully restricted. Apart from being based on roles or identity, variables like time and location can be used to control data access.

In paper [43] authors showed ABE can be deployed in the IIoT to provide fine-grained access control. They also implemented a Java and Kotlin based CP-ABE system with outsourced decryption and presented

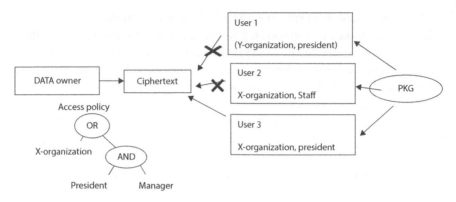

Figure 17.4 Fine-grain data access control.

the performance data. They deployed the implementation in the Siemens MindSphere cloud to achieve fine-grained access control.

Fine-grained access can be achieved in fog computing environments through ABE, which will be discussed in the next section.

17.5   Application of ABE on Fog Computing

Attribute-based encryption can be applied to enhance access control in fog computing. Fog computing is a paradigm that extends cloud computing [13, 30, 33] to the edge of the networks, closer to the data source.

Cloud computing provides a reliable service to store, compute, and process user data. It helps a user to outsource storage and computational power. Cloud computing ensures that user data is shared with the Internet of Things (IoT) devices remain concealed. IoT devices are limited in computational and processing resources, so the data has to be processed on the cloud before it is sent to the IoT devices. This increases the load of the cloud server, which reduces the efficiency of the system. Fog computing is a type of distributed computing that helps to solve this problem. The Fog computing technique adds a new layer between the cloud and the IoT devices [18, 19]. Fog computing uses fog nodes that communicate with the cloud server and IoT devices [32]. The fog nodes [31, 35] are given a set of IoT devices that are in their zones and they have to communicate with these devices on behalf of the cloud server. Fog computing pre-processes the data sent and received from the IoT devices, which helps to reduce the work of cloud servers which improves the efficiency of the system.

Fog computing [39] assists in resolving a number of issues, including the limited computational capacity of IoT devices, lowering server load, and improving network organization. Fog computing inherits security challenges from cloud computing in addition to other benefits [41]. Fog computing faces the same security challenges as cloud computing [17], such as privacy protection and data security. An access control system could be used to protect the data stored in the cloud from any unauthorized access. Additionally vulnerable to assaults, data in transit needs to be protected. Unencrypted cloud storage data is vulnerable to attacks and compromises user privacy. Access control [23] security methods such as user-based, role-based, and attribute-based access control protocols have been developed to address various security challenges. Each has advantages and restrictions of its own. The user-based access control approach is simpler to implement because it simply needs to keep track of a list of authorized users, but it is not appropriate for environments like fog and clouds that have a large number of users. According to what they do inside a system, the role-based method authorizes the user. The authorization of the user for such data is determined by the user's attributes and a specified access policy in an attribute-based access control technique. A user's unique attribute set may include a combination of their identity, current location, joining date, etc. The access policy is represented as a tree, with the leaf nodes serving as characteristics and the inside nodes serving as threshold gates (AND, OR) [7]. Only if the set of attributes fits the access rules would the use be permitted access to the data. The attribute-based method makes it easier to keep data on an unreliable cloud server since only users with the right combination of attributes can decode the data. The two kinds of attribute-based encryption (ABE) are key policy attribute-based encryption (KP-ABE) [42] and cipher-text policy attribute-based encryption (CP-ABE) [15, 22, 28]. In the KP-ABE scheme, the user key is generated using the access policy, but the ciphertext is defined using the attribute set that was generated using the user's attributes. In contrast, CP-ABE uses the access policy to define the ciphertext while the attribute set is used to generate the user key [23, 24]. The ABE method is further divided into centralized and decentralized ABE methods based on architecture. The centralized method generates keys and controls communication by using a Central Authority (CA), such as a Key generation Server or an Access Control Server. Due to its heavy demand, the CA occasionally becomes an issue in the system. The strategy also runs into issues when many organizations with various access policies need to share data. The decentralized ABE scheme deals with the disadvantages of the centralized approach. Decentralized ABE, also known as Multi-Authority Attribute-Based Encryption [4], is more appropriate for fog computing since users can hold many attributes, and data owners can share data using an access structure set over attributes provided by several authorities [7]. Take a medical record [10, 34, 36] as an example. By distributing separate keys by different authorities, the record might be accessed by a hospital doctor as well as a medical researcher. In decentralized ABE, the possibility of single-point failure is eliminated by the lack of a central authority for key creation and distribution. A user who has been given access in the past might not be qualified for future system transactions because user qualities change with time. It is a security issue that has to be resolved if this user is still able to access data after being labelled ineligible. Therefore, the user revocation issue in ABE schemes needs to be resolved. Because of the power and resource limitations of fog computing [40], encryption, and decryption need a lot of processing, which raises the algorithm's cost. The encryption process could be split into online and offline operations to overcome the issue. A proxy server could potentially perform some decryption in order to facilitate the fog nodes' work. However, this process must be completed without compromising data privacy while keeping security in mind. A decentralized computing architecture called fog computing brings cloud computing capabilities out to the network's edge.

In fog computing, instead of depending entirely on centralized cloud servers, storage and networking resources are spread closer to the edge devices, such as sensors and Internet of Things (IoT) devices [9, 33]. The key concept of fog computing is to bring computing resources closer to where data is generated and consumed. This offers several benefits including reduced latency [14], improved performance, enhanced data privacy and bandwidth saving. Here are some key aspects of fog computing:

- Scalability: Fog computing environments can involve a large number of fog nodes and users.
  Scalability is a critical aspect of fog computing, it can accommodate growing number of devices and users and effectively utilize the available computing resources.
- Secure Data sharing: In fog environments ABE enables secure data sharing while maintaining fine-grained access control. Here, fog nodes can act as attribute authorities and ABE allows for data to be encrypted based on attributes.
- Dynamic access control: fog computing environments [35] are characterized by dynamic and distributed computing resources. ABE access policy can be modified or updated without reencrypting the entire dataset.

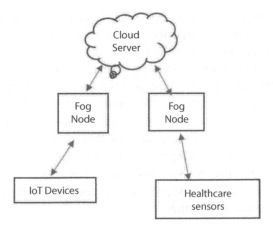

Figure 17.5 ABE in fog computing.

- Fine-grained privacy preservation: fog computing involves processing sensitive data at the edge, closer to where to generated. ABE can be used to enforce fine-grained privacy preservation in fog computing environments.

By applying ABE in fog computing environments, organizations can enhance data security, enforce fine-grained access control and preserve privacy. Figure 17.4 shows fine-grained data access control mechanism and Figure 17.5, a fog subsystem of healthcare is illustrated. With fog computing patient will take possession of their health data locally. Those data will be stored in fog nodes such as smartphones or devices.

17.6   A Comparison of ABE Scheme

There are several variants of ABE schemes each with its own features. Some of the schemes are discussed below

Key Policy ABE (KP-ABE)
It is a modified version of the ABE classical model. An access structure (AS) is used to assign users based on the properties of the data. The user's secret key is defined to mirror the access structure. To limit which cipher texts a user can decrypt, cipher texts are labelled with sets of attributes, and private keys are linked to monotonic access structures [20, 21]. Key policy Attribute Based Encryption (KP-ABE) [3, 42] scheme is designed for one to-many communications.

The algorithm returns the system master secret key MK and the public key PK after receiving the security parameter K as input. Senders of messages encrypt their messages with PK.MK is only known to the authority and is used to create user secret keys. A message M, the public key (PK), and a list of attributes are required as input for the encryption algorithm. The cipher text (CT) is produced. The master secret key MK and an access structure (AS) are the inputs for the key generation algorithm. If and only if T matches, it produces a secret key SK that allows the user to decrypt a message that has been encrypted using a set of attributes. Only if the attribute set satisfies the user's access structure is decryption possible. The KP-ABE scheme can achieve secured access control and more flexibility to control users than ABE scheme.

Disadvantages

The issue with KP-ABE scheme is that the encryptor is unable to select a suitable user to decrypt the encrypted data. A data owner must trust the key issuer, since it can only select descriptive features for the data, making it inappropriate for particular applications.

Ciphertext Policy ABE (CP-ABE)

Sahai's improved version of KP-ABE is known as CP-ABE [3, 28]. Every cipher text in a CP-ABE scheme has an associated access policy on attributes, and every user's private key has an associated set of attributes. A user can only successfully decrypt a cipher text if the set of attributes linked to their private key satisfy the cipher text's access policy. KP-ABE operates in the opposite manner from CP-ABE. The algorithm [37, 38] returns both the system master secret key MK and the public key PK after receiving the security parameter K as input. Senders of messages encrypt their messages with PK. MK is only known to the authority and is used to create user secret keys. The message M, the access structure AS, and the public parameter PK are the inputs that the method needs to encrypt data. The cipher text CT is the result. Key-Generation is an algorithm that accepts a set of user and master key MK properties as input. If and only if T matches, it generates a secret key SK that enables the user to decrypt a message encrypted using T's access tree structure. Data decryption is only possible if the access structure required by the cipher text CT is met. The KP-ABE flaw that the encrypted data cannot select the decryptor is improved. It is capable of supporting access control in a real-world setting. Additionally, the user's private key in this scheme combines a number of different properties, thus the user can only use this combination of features to decrypt data.

Disadvantages

The disadvantages of the majority of CP-ABE schemes still prevent them from meeting the enterprise requirements for access control, which need a high degree of flexibility and effectiveness. There are restrictions with CP-ABE when it comes to controlling user attributes and establishing policies. A user can only use all conceivable permutations of user attributes in a single set issued in their keys to satisfy policies in a CP-ABE scheme since decryption keys only support user attributes that are logically organized as a single set.

Hierarchical Attribute-Based Encryption

Wang *et al.* developed hierarchal attribute-based encryption (HABE) [3]. The components of the HABE model include a root master (RM), which stands in for the third trusted party (TTP), several domain masters (DMs), of which the top-level DMs stand in for numerous enterprise users, and numerous users, which stand in for all of the employees in a company. In order to produce keys, this scheme made advantage of the HIBE scheme's hierarchal key generation feature. Then, the randomized polynomial time approach is presented to define the HABE scheme. The Root Master (RM) outputs system parameters (params) and the root master key MK0 after receiving a suitably large security parameter K as input. The DM algorithm determines whether U is qualified for a, which is handled independently, and also determines whether the RM or the DM creates master keys for the DM's directly under parameters and its master key. If so, it uses params and its master key to create a user identity secret key and a user attribute secret key for U. Otherwise, "NULL" is output. The algorithm generates a cipher text CT after receiving as inputs a file f, a DNF access control policy A, and public keys for all of A's characteristics. If the j-th conjunctive clause is satisfied, decryption is carried out. This plan can meet the requirements for full delegation, scalability, and secured access control. On an office setting, it can share data for users on the cloud. It can also be used to accomplish proxy re-encryption.

Disadvantages

It is unsuitable to execute in real life. The same attribute may be governed by different domain authorities under this system because all attributes in a single conjunctive phrase may be handled by the same domain authority.

Multi-Authority Attribute Based Encryption

Multi-authority attribute-based encryption [3] scheme uses multiple parties to distribute attributes for users. K attribute authorities and one central authority make up a Multi Authority ABE system. Also given a value is each attribute authority, which is dk. a randomized algorithm that must be controlled by a reliable entity (such as a central authority). It takes the security parameter K as an input and produces a system public key and master secret key that will be utilized by the central authority (PKca, SKca), as well as a public key and secret key pair for each of the attribute authorities (PKa, SKa). The authority's secret key, the authority's value dk, a user's GID, and a set of attributes in the authority's domain AkC are all inputs for the attribute key generation process, which produces a secret key for the user. Encryption is done by randomized algorithm run by a sender, it accepts a message, the system public key, and a set of attributes for each authority as inputs and outputs the cipher text. An attribute set

Table 17.1 Comparison table of ABE schemes [3].

	KP-ABE	**CP-ABE**	**HABE**	**MABE**
Component	Data is associated with an access policy	Ciphertext is associated with an access policy	Hierarchical generation of key	Multiple authorities
Efficiency	Average	Average	Better	Scalable
Secured access control	Low	Average	High	Average
Data confidentiality	No	Yes	Yes	Yes
User accountability	No	No	No	Yes
Scalability	No	Yes	No	Yes
User revocation	No	No	Yes	Yes
Limitation	It cannot decide who can encrypt data	Decrypt key only support user attributes that are organized logically	Unsuitable to implement	Each authority attribute set should be disjoint.
Computational overhead	High	Average	More	More

A-encrypted cipher text and attribute set Au's decryption keys are inputs to a user-run decryption algorithm and produces the message M. It accepts any number of corrupted authorities and permits any polynomial number of independent authorities to distribute private keys and monitor attributes. In this model, a receiver is described by a collection of properties rather than a single string.

Drawbacks
Complication in multi-authority scheme required that each authority's attribute set be disjoint. Here, Table 17.1 summarises the comparison between the different schemes.

17.7 Conclusion

Here, we discussed fine grained access control and fog computing through attribute-based encryption. We also discussed about different types of ABE schemes: KP-ABE, CP-ABE, HABE, MABE and their comparisons. We can say, ABE is a cryptographic solution for fine-grained access control. The combination of ABE and fog computing addresses the security and access control in edge computing environments. The practical applicability of ABE in fog computing enables secure and fine-grained access in wide range of fog computing application like, IoT, industrial automation, healthcare sectors, smart cities, edge AI. Further research should focus on improving ABE efficiency with the appropriate selection of attributes and software and hardware optimizations for the cryptographic library.

References

1. Sahai, A. and Waters, B., Fuzzy identity-based encryption. *Lecture Notes in Computer Science,* 3494, 457–473, 2005.
2. Goyal, V., Pandey, O., Sahai, A., Waters, B., Attribute based encryption for fine-grained access control of encrypted data. *Computer and Communications Security (CCS 2006),* 89–98, October 30-November 2006, Doi:10. 1145/1180405.1180418.
3. Lakshmi, R.N., Laavanya, R., Meenakshi, M., Dhas, C.S.G., Analysis of attribute based encryption schemes. *Int. J. Comput. Sci. Eng. Commun.,* 3, 1076–1081 2015, ISSN: 2347-8586.
4. Lewko, A. and Waters, B., Decentralizing attribute-based encryption. *Lecture Notes in Computer Science,* 6632, 568–588, 2011.

5. Qiao, Z., Liang, S., Davis, S., Jiang, H., Survey of attribute based encryption, in: *15th IEEE/ACIS International Conference on Software Engineering, Artificial Intelligence, Networking and Parallel/Distributed Computing (SNDP)*, 1–6, June 30–July 2, 2014.

6. Lewko, A., Okamoto, T., Sahai, A., Takashima, K., Waters, B., Fully secure functional encryption: Attribute-based encryption and (hierarchical) inner product encryption. *Lecture Notes in Computer Science*, 6110, 62–91, 2010.

7. Vohra, K. and Dave, M., Multi-authority attribute based data access control in fog computing, in: *International Conference on Computational Intelligence and Data Science*, 2018.

8. Li, J., Chen, X., Li, J., Jia, C., Ma, J., Lou, W., Fine-grained access control system based on outsourced attribute-based encryption. *ESORICS*, 2013.

9. Bonomi, F., Milito, R., Zhu, J., Addepalli, S., Fog computing and its role in the internet of things, *Proceedings of the first edition of the MCC workshop on Mobile cloud computing*, 13–16, August 2012, DOI: 10.1145/2342509.2342513

10. Alshehri, S. and Almehmadi, T., A secure fog-cloud architecture using attribute based encryption for medical internet of things (MIoT). *Int. J. Adv. Comput. Sci. Appl.*, 12, 924–933, 2021.

11. Liu, X., Wang, H., Zhang, B., Zhang, B., An efficient fine-grained data access control system with a bound service number. *Inf. Sci.*, 584, 536–563, 2022, doi: doi.org/10.1016/j. ins.2021.10.038.

13. Wang, L., von Laszewski, G., Kunze, M., Tao, J., Cloud computing: A perspective study. *New Gener. Comput.*, 28, 137–146, 2008.

14. Yi, S., Hao, Z., Qin, Z., Li, Q., Fog computing: Platform and applications, in: *2015 Third IEEE Workshop on Hot Topics in Web Systems and Technologies (HotWeb)*, 73–78, 07 January, 2016, DOI: 10.1109/HotWeb.2015.22.

15. Ghosh, B., Parimi, P., Rout, R.R., Improved attribute-based encryption scheme fog computing environment for healthcare systems. *ICCCNT*, 2020.

16. Hohenberger, S., Lu, G., Waters, B., Wu, D.J., Registered attribute-based encryption. *Advances in cryptology-EUROCRYPT 2023 LNCS 14006*, 511–542, April 23-27, 2023.

17. Mittal, A., Attribute-based encryption for secure data access in cloud. *Culminating Projects in Information Assurance*, 39, 1–109, 2017.

18. Premkamal, P.K., Kumar, P.S., Pja, A., Attribute-based encryption in cloud computing: A survey, gap analysis, and future directions. *J. Netw. Comput. Appl.*, 108, 37–52, 2018. https://doi.org/10.1016/j.jnca.2018.02.009

19. Kumar, N.S., Lakshmi, R.G.V., Balamurugan, B., Enhanced atribute based encryption for cloud computing. *ICICT*, 2014.

20. Li, J., Yu, Q., Zhang, Y., Shen, J., Key-policy attribute-based encryption against continual auxiliary input leakage. *Inf. Sci.*, 470, 175–188, 2019. https://doi.org/10.1016/j.ins.2018.07.077

21. C-J., W.A.N.G. and Luo, J.-F., A key-policy attribute-based encryption scheme with constant size ciphertext. *ICCIS*, 2012.

22. Ambrosin, M., Anzanpour, A., Conti, M., Dargahi, T., On the feasibility of attribute-based encryption on internet of things devices, vol. 36, pp. 25–35, IEEE Micro, USA, 2016.

23. Muhammad, N. and Zain, J.M., Access control: Ciphertext policy – Attribute based in cloud computing. *ICoCSIM 2019*, doi: 10.1088/1742-6596/1830/1/012019.

24. Rasori, M., Manna, M.L., Perazzo, P., Dini, G., A survey on attribute-based encryption schemes suitable for the internet of things. IEEE, vol. 9, pp. 8269–8290, IEEE Internet of Things Journal, USA, 2022.

25. Meng, F., Cheng, L., Wang, M., Ciphertext-policy attribute- based encryption with hidden sensitive policy from keyword search techniques in smart city. *EURASIP J. Wirel. Commun. Netw.*, 1–22, 03 February, 2021, DOI: 10.1186/s13638-020-01875-2.

27. Jain, M. and Singh, M., Identity based and attribute based cryptography: A survey. *Indian J. Eng. Mater. Sci.*, 2, 5, 88–92, May 2015, ISSN-2348-3733.

28. Yuan, Q., Ma, C., Lin, J., Fine-grained access control for big data based on CP-ABE in cloud computing. *ICYCSEE*, vol. CCIS 503, pp. 344–352, 2015.

29. Yang, K., Jia, X., Ren, K., Attribute-based fine-grained access control with efficient revocation in cloud storage systems. *ASIA CCS*, 2013.

30. Balusamy, B., Ramachandran, S., Priya, N., Achieving fine-grained control and mitigating role explosion by utilizing ABE with RBAC. *International Journal of High Performance Computing and Networking* (volume 10), 109-117, 10, 2017, doi: 10.1504/IJHPCN.2017.083208.

31. Alrawais, A., Alhothaily, A., Hu, C., Xing, X., Cheng, X., An attribute-based encryption scheme to secure fog communications IEEE. vol. 5, pp. 9131–9138, IEEE Access, USA, 2016.

32. Xu, Q., Tan, C., Fan, Z., Zhu, W., Xiao, Y., Cheng, F., Secure data access control for fog computing based on multi- authority attribute-based signcryption with computation outsourcing and attribute revocation. *Sensors*, 18, 5, 1609, 2018.

33. Angulo, C.A.P. and Uribe, C.F., Security and private for internet of things and fog computing, CCC-21-003. *INAOE*, 1–37, August, 2021.

34. Nkenyereye, L., Islam, S.M.R., Hossain, M., Abdullah-Al-Wadud, M., Alamri, A., Fog-based secure framework for personal health records systems. *Computers, Materials and Continua*, 66, 1937–1948, 2020, doi: 10.32604/cmc.2020.013025.

35. Krinah, A., Challal, Y., Omar, M., Nouali, O., Using ABE for medical data protection in fog computing. *ICEIS 2019*, pp. 155–16, ISBN: 978-989-758-372-8.

36. Shaheen, S.A., Application of attribute-based encryption in fog infrastructure for securing health-related data. Capital University of Science and Technology, Islamabad, 2022.

37. Meng, F., Wang, M., Cheng, L., ABDKS: Attribute-based encryption with dynamic keyword search in fog computing. *Front. Comput. Sci.*, 15, 1–18, 2021.

38. Saidi, A., Nouali, O., Amira, A., SHARE-ABE: An efficient and secure data sharing framework based on ciphertext-policy attribute-based encryption and fog computing. *Cluster Comput.*, 25, 167–185, 2021, https://doi.org/10.1007/s10586-021-03382-5.

39. Yao, X., Kong, H., Liu, H., Qiu, T., Ning, H., An attribute credential based public key scheme for fog computing in digital manufacturing, IEEE, USA, April, 2019, Doi: 10.1109/TII.2019.2891079.

40. Zhang, P., Chen, Z., Liub, J.K., Liang, K., Liu, H., An efficient access control scheme with outsourcing capability and attribute update for fog computing. *Future Generation of Computer Systems*, 78, 753–762, 2016. https://doi.org/10.1016/j.future.2016.12.015

41. Babitha M, N. and Siddappa, M., A review on data protection and privacy in fog computing network. *International Research Journal on Advanced Science Hub*, 03, 1–5, 2021, e-ISSN: 2582-4376, Doi: 10.47392/IRJASH.2021.101.

42. Meddah, N. and Toumanari, A., Anonymous attribute based access control in cloud computing. *Int. J. Eng. Res. Technol.*, 4, 04, 753-756, April-2015, ISSN: 2278-0181.

43. Ziegler, D., Sabongui, J., Palfinger, G., Fine-grained access control in industrial internet of things evaluating outsourced attribute-based encryption. *IFIP Adv. Inf Commun. Technol.*, 562, 91–104, 2019.

44. Odugu, N.K. and Rajesh, A., A fine-grained access control survey for the secure big data access. *Turk. J. Comput. Math. Educ.*, 12, 10, 4180–4186, 2021.

45. Shweta, S.G. and Jayashree, A., Attribute-based hybrid encryption policy for encrypting the cloud data. *Int. J. Res. Trends Innov.*, 2, 115–118, 2017, ISSN-2456-3315.

Index

Additive manufacturing, 46
Advanced robotics, 45
Agility, 289
Agility and scalability, 285
AHP and TOPSIS, 37
Analysis layer, 58
Application of blockchain technology
    in healthcare, 387
Application taxonomy, 179
Artificial intelligence, 44
Asymmetric cryptography, 402
Attribute-based encryption, 403
Attributes of fog node, 286
Autonomy, 286

Big data, 97, 114, 292
Big data analytics using fog
    computing, 296
Big data applications, 293
Blockchain security for fog
    computing environment, 367,
    368
Blockchain technology, 364-367
    features of blockchain toincrease
        the transparency, 364
    decentralized, 365
    immutable and incorruptible,
        365
    peer-to-peer (P2P) networks,
        365
Blockchain-based frameworks for IoT
    security and privacy, 376
Bluetooth, 50, 56

Carcinoma, 225, 236
Characteristic of big data, 295
Characteristics of fog computing, 284
CISCO, 3
Cloud computing, 1, 2, 8, 44, 46, 171,
    331, 408
Cloud computing vs. fog computing,
    15
Cloudlet, 31, 33, 37, 38
Clustering algorithm, 155
    association rule mining, 160
    independent component analysis,
        158
    principal component analysis, 157
Combined failed node clusters, 49
Community fog, 292
Community health, 190
Complexity, 295
Computation offloading, 31, 32, 35, 40
Computing associated cloud, 38
Confidentiality in fog computing, 390
Confirmed cases, 129
Cost, 283
Cost-effective, 286
Covid patients, 119
CP-ABE, 409, 412
Cropmetrics, 241
Cyber defense, 46

Data analysis, 73
Data as a Service (DaaS), 288
Data cleaning and transformation,
    124

Data flow and control flow in fog
    architecture, 290
Data offloading, 31
Data privacy, 282
Data visualization, 117-120
Day wise symptom detection, 126
Decision tree, 144
Deep Gaussian mixture model,
    228-237
Deep learning algorithm, 153
Deep neural network, 226, 231
Digital education, 338
DSS, 218

Edge computing, 97, 113, 226, 227, 335
Education, 294
e-healthcare, 190
Electronic medical records (EMR), 61
    CT looks, 61
    heart reports, 61
    ultrasound, 61
    X-rays, 61
Energy and utilities, 294
Explainable AI, 165

Faulty node, 57, 58
FBG, 209
Feature extraction, 76
Fiber optic sensor, 207
File control block, 31
Finance, 294
Fine-grained access, 405
Fog, 235, 236
Fog broker, 284
Fog computing, 1, 7, 8, 10, 13, 15, 17,
    19, 22, 78, 97-110, 171, 281, 330,
    389, 408, 410
    applications, 19
    architecture, 10
    basic modules, 13
    challenges, 22
    characteristics, 7
    future, 24
    types, 12

Fog computing architecture, 289
Fog computing security breaches, 391
Fog computing service model, 287
Fog computing vs IoT, 17
Fog deployment models, 292
Fog engine, 298
Fog layer, 48, 57
Fog node, 13, 187, 283
Fog orchestrator, 284
Fog services, 284
Function as a Service (FaaS), 289

Geographically distributed, 284

Healthcare, 172, 293, 295
Healthcare 4.0, 188
Heterogeneity, 285, 286
Hierarchical ABE, 413
Hierarchical cluster, 286
High-quality data, 289
Hospital details, 128
HVAC, 97
Hybrid fog 292
Hyper-parameter tuning, 78
    Bayesian optimization, 87
    grid search, 87
    random search, 87

iFogSim, 21
IIoT, 49, 50, 203, 226
Improved security, 286
Increased scalability, 286
Indication, 126
Industrial revolution, 44
Industry 3.0, 45
Industry 4.0., 43, 51, 200
Information technology, 330
Infrastructure as a Service (IaaS),
    288
Ingestion layer, 122
Internet of Things (IoT), 97-98, 102,
    104, 110, 114, 241, 242, 251, 271,
    305, 326
Interoperability and federation, 285

IoT, 1, 8, 17, 19, 172
IoT protocols, 57
    AMQP, 57
    CoAP, 57
    IPv4, 57
    IPv6, 57
    MQTT, 57
    XMPP, 57

Jade, 38, 39

k-nearest neighbors (kNN), 60
K-NN model, 152
KP-ABE, 409, 411

Latency, 281
Learning rate, 80
Linear regression, 141
Low latency, 286
Low latency and location awareness, 284

MACS, 37, 39
Magneto-optical, 210
Manageability, 286
Manufacturing, 294
MAUI, 35, 39
Maximum depth, 82
MCC, 31, 32, 35
Medical diagnosis, 177
Medical monitoring, 177
Medical notification, 179
Metaphor, 226, 233-235
Metastasis, 236
Mobility, 285
Model selection, 84
    CatBoost, 90
    decision trees, 87
    LightGBM, 90
    Random forest, 88
    XGBoost, 89
Modeling algorithms, 84
Multi-authority ABE, 409, 413

Naive Bayes algorithm, 150
Network bandwidth, 282
NGO address, 125
Node MCU, 305, 309-312, 318-319, 322
Novel coronavirus disease, 118
N-P-K, 78, 80, 82

Offloading, 31, 32, 33, 34
Open research issues in blockchain and fog computing security, 393
Operational research (OR), 241, 265, 266, 307
Optimized fog computing, 392
Oxygen suppliers, 129

Pandemic, 117-119, 131-133
Pandemic alert system, 119-120
Permissioned blockchain in IoT, 376
Personal location data, 295
Phone2Cloud, 38, 39
Physical and virtualization layer, 58
Physical symptoms, 126
Platform as a Service (PaaS), 288
Post-vaccination effects, 130
Power BI, 117, 119, 121-124, 132
Precision farming, 241, 242-249
Predictive maintenance, 203
Pre-processing, 84
Preprocessing layer, 59
Preventing provider lock-in with DaaS, 289
Private fog, 292
Programmability, 286
Public fog, 292
Public sector, 294

Quality of service, 32

Random forest, 146
Real-time communication, 285
Reduced network congestion, 286
Reinforcement learning, 166

Retail, 294, 295
RFID, 55, 56
RFID sensors, 45

Security, 282
Security and privacy, 97, 105, 108, 114
Security issues in the fog computing
    environments, 355-364
    data protection, privacy, and access
        controls in fog computing, 356
    trust and authentications in fog
        computing, 356
Sensor, 2, 5,6
Simple access, 289
Smart farming, 85, 241-245, 247, 249-
    251, 253, 255, 257, 259, 261, 263,
    265, 267
SMD, 32
Software, 97-98, 105, 108-109
Software as a Service (SaaS), 287
Source of big data, 294
State wise helpline email, 125
State wise helpline number, 125
State wise NGO's name, 125
Support vector machine algorithm,
    149

Symmetric cryptography, 401
Symptom detection, 126

Terminal layer, 57
Testing labs, 127
ThingSpeak, 305, 319
Total doses, 129
Train-test split, 85
Transportation, 294

Vaccinated people information, 131
Vaccination centre, 130
Variability, 295
Variety, 295
Velocity, 295
Veracity, 295
Vibration, 217
Virus transmission, 120
Volume, 295

Web of Things (IoT), 44
What is big data, 293
Wireless access, 285
World Health Organization, 119-120

Zigbee, 50, 56

Printed and bound by CPI Group (UK) Ltd, Croydon, CR0 4YY

27/10/2024

14580177-0003